P9-CRU-585

ROWDY

ARIEL TEAL TOOMBS AND COLT BAIRD TOOMBS

ROWDY

THE RODDY PIPER STORY

WITH CRAIG PYETTE

RANDOM HOUSE CANADA

PUBLISHED BY RANDOM HOUSE CANADA

 Published in 2016 by Random House Canada, a division of Penguin Random House Canada Limited. Distributed in Canada and the United States of America by Penguin Random House Canada Limited, Toronto.

www.penguinrandomhouse.ca

Pages 381-2 constitute a continuation of the copyright page.

LIBRARY AND ARCHIVES CANADA CATALOGUING IN PUBLICATION

Toombs, Ariel Teal, author
Rowdy : the Roddy Piper story / Ariel Teal Toombs, Colt Baird Toombs.

Includes bibliographical references and index.
Issued in print and electronic formats.

ISBN 978-0-345-81622-1
ISBN 978-0-345-81623-8

1. Piper, Roddy, 1954–2015. 2. Wrestlers—Canada—Biography. 3. Motion picture actors and actresses—Canada—Biography. 4. Entertainers—Canada—Biography. I. Toombs, Colt Baird, author II. Title.

GV1196.P5T66 2016 796.812092 C2016-903205-1

Book design by Andrew Roberts

Printed and bound in the United States of America

2 4 6 8 9 7 5 3 1

To Dad
and the Toombs Clan

CONTENTS

INTRODUCTION	**This Isn't Supposed to Happen**	ix
1	**A Very Active Child**	1
2	**Concede or Get Up**	35
3	**The Jesus Years**	65
4	**Thanks for the Blood and Guts, Kid**	103
5	**Don't Call Us, We'll Call You**	135
6	**Flair and the Family Man**	167
7	**A Despicable, Disgraceful Display**	203
8	**All Outta Bubble Gum**	245
9	**Frats**	279
10	**Finish**	323
	Acknowledgements	369
	A Note on Sources	373
	Photo Credits	381
	Index	383

INTRODUCTION

This Isn't Supposed to Happen

It's 1986 and Roddy has seen enough of this guy.

Mr. T, a celebrity drop-in recruited to sell tickets and pay-per-view to the first ever WrestleMania at Madison Square Garden in 1985, had been dining out for months on some choice moments from that groundbreaking show. The day after the biggest main event in the history of professional wrestling, newspapers around the world ran a photo of "Rowdy" Roddy Piper, the most hated villain in wrestling, suspended over T's shoulders in a classic fireman's carry. The audience that night slavered for what followed: the mouthy, cheating bad guy bouncing hard off the mat and receiving his just desserts for all the pain and aggravation he had caused Hulk Hogan, the champion, and Mr. T, Hogan's famous tag-team partner.

Though Mr. T had acted as the mouthpiece himself opposite Sylvester Stallone in *Rocky III*, as a guest wrestler he stuck more to the strong, silent type of role he'd been playing recently on TV's *The A-Team*. His choice was part necessity. Caught in the middle of the expertly improvised bombast of the world's most famous professional wrestling feud, actor Laurence Tureaud was without a script and in danger of leaving audiences cold.

Roddy Piper had been wrestling professionally for over a decade. He'd learned the art of antagonism from masters of the business, and he'd taken knives, cigarette butts, and even the threat of bullets for his trouble. WrestleMania promised to vault him and his peers to fame and fortune, so Roddy pushed his boss, the World Wrestling Federation's Vince McMahon Jr., his peers and everyone involved not to blow this chance. He argued that letting Mr. T pin him for the win would diminish not just his own reputation, but the reps of everyone in the business.

Fans bought tickets because they believed wrestlers were the toughest of the tough (often they really were). If you could just borrow a TV star and let him beat up the seasoned trash-talker who was biting mercilessly at the ankles of the beloved All-American champion, Hulk Hogan, how would wrestlers of lesser fame look? If Roddy lost to T, the smallest guy in the ring, or even to the enormous Hogan himself, there was a lot less reason for the audience to come back.

In the end Roddy didn't lose—not exactly. "Mr. Wonderful" did. Paul Orndorff, Roddy's tag-team partner, was pinned by Hogan, not by T. The crowd got their cathartic victory over the bullies, but it took their favourite wrestler to beat them. The good guys still hadn't gotten Piper, not shoulders-down for a three count, fair and square. Now, a year later, Roddy and T find themselves in New York again, on Long Island this time, at Nassau Veterans Memorial Coliseum in Uniondale. The success of WrestleMania has made pop culture icons of the WWF's top performers, Roddy and Hogan foremost among them. Yet Roddy still has a real chip on his shoulder about the TV star who landed in his world. Roddy respects his peers. He knows intimately the work, stress and pain they have all gone through to survive in their business. Every time Mr. T is mentioned in the same breath as pro wrestlers, that chip grows bigger. McMahon, has a promoter's intuition for guessing which scores the audience will pay to see settled, so he's given T a chance to knock that chip off for good—or for Roddy to put an end to the celebrity's dalliance with professional wrestling.

WrestleMania 2 plays out in three locations around the US, each with its own main event. In New York's finale, Roddy and Mr. T step into the ring—to box. Arriving in a plaid robe in place of his usual kilt, Roddy berates T, reminding the actor he'll be on his own this time. While the two literally but heads, the crowd is so loud it's impossible to say which competitor they're cheering on, but the commentator's assumption holds: Mr. T is the good guy here and everyone hates Roddy.

In a post–WrestleMania grudge match, Mr. T had boxed Roddy's real friend and "bodyguard," "Cowboy" Bob Orton (a wrestling lifer and the son and, later, father of wrestling stars). T was getting the better of him—until Roddy crashed the ring, setting up tonight's fight at WrestleMania 2. T is announced as eleven pounds heavier than he was the year before, and his fuller chest and shoulders seem to bear that out. He also weighs exactly one pound more than Roddy's announced 235. Roddy's boxing background—and his martial arts training—don't get a mention from the commentators. It's T who is portrayed as being at home in a boxing ring. But the fact remains that Roddy is a pro wrestler at a pro wrestling main event. Week after week, he is the reason people watch. Even if convention demands that fans hate him for the role he plays, they're smart enough to know he's the one who gives them what they want.

In the first round, Roddy is aggressive while T plays peek-a-boo, waiting for his opponent to abandon his defenses and then cutting loose on Roddy's midsection. When T's gloves find their mark, low or high, Roddy sells it. His head snaps back and forth. Sometimes his reactions to head shots look comical up close on television, but tonight he's doing it for the guy in the back row who can't even see T's reactions when Roddy returns fire.

They break dirty, they keep fighting after the round is over, Roddy pushes the referee out of the way so he can kick T when he's down—the match is a lot of what you'd expect, and if you're a wrestling fan, it's a lot of what you pay to see.

Round two goes mostly Roddy's way, round three T's, including a roundhouse left that lights a fire under Roddy, even though T misses by a substantial margin. Roddy still falls under the ropes and onto the floor as if he's been hammered but he's embarrassed. A pro at his level would rather take that punch square on the jaw than allow it to look so fake. This moment is the culmination of everything about T's presence that frustrates Roddy. During the next break he throws his stool across the ring and hits T in the leg. T doesn't seem to know what to do about it. Pro wrestling is often about capitalizing on chaos, and T seems lost when the script goes out the window.

But that doesn't matter. It's what happened in the second round that's still on Roddy's mind.

After a flurry of shouts in support of Mr. T, a chant rises from the many thousands in the stands, and on the floor. "Roddy, Roddy . . ."

This isn't supposed to happen. There are always a few nuts and die-hards who cheer for the heel—the bad guy—but for a few moments it sounds like half of Nassau Coliseum has turned on Mr. T. They want wrestling, *pro* wrestling, even with boxing gloves on. T might be cast as the babyface—the hero, in wrestling terms—but he's not their guy. And with these few moments of roaring approval for his opponent, they let T know it.

There was something about Roddy Piper: the villain who did his job so well that fans often liked him more than his babyface opponent. It wasn't unprecedented. Fans had long turned out in droves to community centres and small-town arenas to see the cruel and overconfident men who strutted into the ring, insulted the crowd and humiliated their heroes. But America had entered a new cultural dimension, one where a hero like Hogan was worshipped in part because he was morally uncomplicated and easy to love—who wouldn't want their kids to say their prayers and take their vitamins, like Hogan urged kids to do? Piper, though, was the fly in the ointment. He was fun. He was small, by wrestling standards, so he fought dirty. He went with his gut, even when his gut told him to do things that were very, very bad. Nobody watching WrestleMania 2 paid good money to say their prayers and eat their vitamins. Suddenly a heel is becoming a hero while still acting like a bad guy. The WWF's moral universe just got complicated. And the master of that new universe is giving them a night to remember.

The crowd roars, too, when Roddy is fed up and the match comes to a sudden and undignified end. Frustrated, Roddy body slams Mr. T, drawing the trainers and corner men into the ring, and finally giving the screaming crowd what they really came to see: Rowdy Roddy Piper creating chaos and laying waste to the best-laid plans of his bosses and society.

Yep, that was our dad.

In June 2015, our father took an unusual trip. He used to travel constantly for work. Even years after he'd stopped wrestling he still flew around the continent and overseas for appearances, acting gigs, and most recently a one-man stage show. As much as the travel exhausted him, he grew antsy if he wasn't working. But this trip was different. He didn't fly every leg of the trip in first class; there wasn't a driver waiting at every gate; he didn't stay in a suite in the nicest hotel in town. This time he was researching a book, the story of his life told from the beginning. And he thought the project should start with a trip to Vancouver Island and Alberta, where he would see some family and old friends, and begin the business of rediscovering who he had once been, a very long time ago.

Dad told plenty of stories, and had once published a book of them. But he had left many others untold. Many of those untold stories were about who he was as a person, not as a personality. There's a fine line between the two, of course. But the differences between fact and fiction in Dad's life were hazy, even to him. Roddy Piper shared much more in common with Roderick Toombs than most wrestlers did with the person they were at home. But since interviewers were always asking him for stories about himself, he tidied up complicated truths into uncomplicated and entertaining anecdotes, which he told dozens if not hundreds of times. Looking back over his sixty-one years, the truths behind those stories were hard to untangle. So he flew from LA to Vancouver, got in a car and set out to visit those friends and family, some of whom he hadn't seen in many years. Maybe they could help him remember.

Work intervened and he had to cut the trip short, but he was looking forward to picking up the trail very soon, driving across the country, seeing the old places and people, jogging long-forgotten memories—getting to the truth he wanted his book to tell. He saw the book as both a legacy for his family and a chance to figure out who he was if he wasn't "Rowdy" Roddy Piper anymore. He had dropped the "Rowdy" from his acting and even wrestling credits a decade earlier—it no longer felt right for a father and grandfather who made his living in Hollywood to call himself "Rowdy." He even gave his blessing to star UFC competitor Ronda Rousey to use his nickname. By the time he set about writing his book, he was looking to drop the "Piper" as well.

His attempt to shed his adopted names pointed to a deeper struggle. Retired from wrestling and having parted ways with the WWE (the WWF changed its name in 2002), a major part of his identity was gone. What remained in its absence? The gap he felt inside was more than just an athlete's diminishment by age. Wrestling had given him the means to feed himself as a teenager and then have a family, and it taught him how to protect them. Despite his outward confidence, as he kept turning on that million-dollar smile for fans and business partners, he felt himself drifting. "You can be lost and walk around, I guess," he told one of his sisters during that trip. "I'm lost right now." The lost feeling had always been there, but he had always been able to ignore it. The demands of work and family, and his relentless ambition to try new things had kept it at bay. Looking back, it's no surprise he used to sign his name, "Ever forward, Roddy Piper." To slow down was to let the past catch up with him—he hadn't been ready for that to happen, until that trip.

In his mind, that gap between past and present was leading to distance from his family. Part of that feeling came from the fact that we, as well as our other siblings, Anastasia and Falon, had all grown up and left home. He'd missed much of our childhoods in Portland, Oregon, where our mother grew up, and her mother before her. He had been on the road up to three hundred nights a year. The house was empty now, his job was over, and the job at home was done as well. "You don't know what comes next, what your name is," he said, musing about his future. "I'm lucky and grateful to get the accolades I have, but how'd I get here? What am I doing?"

A sense of home always eluded him: "The kids went to the same school as their grandma. Oregon is home for them. They don't see why Rod's got no home. Home is the place where the hole is filled." To hear your father say the place where he raised you was not his home was a difficult thing. We'd argue with him about it, but you can't tell a person what he feels—not our father, that's for sure.

He was grateful for his success, but his life had been a blur. If he was going to fill that hole where Roddy Piper used to be, he had to figure out who Roderick Toombs was. There was no better place to start than at the beginning. So he took that trip and started compiling many of the stories you'll read in this book. Sadly, though, wrestling and the lifestyle that went with it had taken a terrible toll on his body. Its debts came due before he could finish the book, and he passed away in his sleep early on the morning of July 31, 2015.

Our family has always been private and we've cherished our personal lives outside of our father's spotlight. As kids growing up in the presence of a huge personality like Roddy Piper, we all found that too much time around his fame could make you feel like you didn't have an identity of your own. How many times have we each been introduced as "Roddy Piper's kid"? When you're young, that can leave you feeling like you have no value as an individual.

That feeling changed over time. We both came to appreciate what an exceptional thing our dad's life was. His accomplishments were profound enough that they carried through to all his children. They weren't really ours, of course, but even when he shielded us from the spotlight we shined a little brighter because of him. The older we became, the more of him we saw up close. The more we saw, the more we appreciated just what a mountain he'd climbed to become the man he was.

Our family members have remained private people, except the two of us; we went a little bit our father's way. That's why it's us you're reading now. Ariel headed to Los Angeles in her late teens to pursue an acting and musical career. Roddy worked in LA often and would bunk in at her apartment. As his focus turned to film work, they became roommates for a while. Colt got the athlete genes. He fought as an amateur in mixed martial arts through his early twenties and then trained with Roddy for his more recent pro wrestling career. For many years, Colt had travelled with him to matches and appearances, then worked for him as a bodyguard when he was older.

Between us we met most of our father's friends and colleagues. We sat up late at night with him and heard his stories, learned what interested him when he wasn't thinking about work. But of course we didn't know everything. His youth remained a mystery that he rarely discussed with anyone. We used to joke that the time before he met our mother were his "Jesus Years," after the gap in the Bible's account of the life of Jesus. Not to get carried away with the comparison, but Dad seemed to have gone through the same thing at the same age. Until his late twenties, what was he doing? We knew bits and pieces, but far from all of it.

Our father often felt misunderstood. That was no surprise. He was a generous man who played a villain, a private man who had an enormous public profile, a quiet man who had started riots for a living. He'd had such an unusual life, he was hoping if he shared more of what made him who he was, people would relate to him better. People's misunderstandings really were an issue.

How many times were we and our sisters pulled aside and questioned by teachers at school who had watched our father in some crazy storyline on television and been convinced that he must be an abusive parent. They would grill us, and we would assure them that nothing was further from the truth. Sure, his voice could rattle the rafters when we made him cross, but for the record, he never raised a hand. His own childhood, we discovered, had taught him the terrible price of violence against children; there was no way he was going to pass that down to his own family. "Family first" was another expression he used a lot. He meant it. He forgave many people many things because they'd had to put the interests of their family ahead of their business with Roddy Piper.

That said . . . he and Colt roughhoused constantly when Colt was small. Once he got Roddy in such a good sleeper hold that he couldn't break it without doing something that might genuinely hurt his son—and hurting any of us was not an option. Fortunately, Colt had the good sense to let go. Roddy turned and took a deep breath. He looked his son in the eye and said, "When you turn eighteen, I'm going to light you up, just once."

Years passed. Roughhousing turned to real training. Colt sparred with Roddy often as he learned his way around a ring and an opponent. Then on the morning of his eighteenth birthday Colt came downstairs. He was nervous. Dad was waiting for him. He feinted in Colt's direction, but laughed it off. This went on all day. It was terrifying—funny for the rest of us, but terrifying for Colt. Dad never did make good on that old threat, but you can bet he relished the torture. Welcome to a ribbing, son, wrestling style.

About a year before Roddy died, Colt was working professionally as a fighter and Roddy was still pitching in to help him learn. Colt had trained at the Los Angeles dojo of Roddy's old instructor and friend, "Judo" Gene LeBell. He was twenty-five, fit and very capable in the ring, where he had gone undefeated as an amateur MMA fighter. Roddy was sixty—with all the wear and tear the age implies. They got sparring and decided to go pretty hard.

A son is supposed to challenge his father. From things like eating a bigger plate of dinner to being able to outmuscle him some day, this is just life's natural order. But on the mat, Colt couldn't beat him.

As much as it broke our hearts to lose our father so soon, there's no denying that it was likely a small mercy for him. He never had to endure his own inevitable infirmity. With all the punishment his body had taken, a future in a wheelchair was likely. That would have driven him crazy.

Still, we know that when he died he felt both misunderstood and unknown to himself and to his family, and that he saw this book as a chance for the kind of self-reflection he'd never had time to indulge. That unfinished business weighed on us. But there was one more thing that drove us to pick up where he left off. We missed our father. So we decided to finish the job for him. We would tell the story of our father's life.

Working on this book has given us the chance to get close to him one more time. And close to many other people, too. We have interviewed dozens of his old friends to help round out the story—from his childhood through his introduction to wrestling as he worked his way through the regional territories to the WWF/WWE, then into movies and stepping away from the ring. Through the memories they've generously shared, we can keep our dad's extraordinary life close to us, and pass it down through our family for future generations.

Even when the stories were painful, the experience of compiling them was wonderful. People's willingness to help has gone beyond obligation. Roddy was never a fairweather friend to anyone, and in the end his friends have helped us ride out the turmoil of his passing. We are grateful to them—and we are pretty sure he is, too.

ARIEL TEAL TOOMBS, Los Angeles, CA
COLT BAIRD TOOMBS, Portland, OR
March 2016

1

A Very Active Child

However you remember him, Roddy Piper began life as something a lot more ordinary. And he didn't come from Glasgow.

Roderick George Toombs was born in Saskatoon, Saskatchewan, on April 17, 1954. His parents already had two daughters, Marilyn and Cheryl, and had been hoping for a boy. For their father, a man without a male heir was missing something. If that sounds painfully traditional, it's for good reason. Though both Saskatchewan born, Stanley Baird Toombs and his wife, Eileen Anderson, were fiercely loyal to the stiff Victorian ways of their British roots.

So Roddy was Canadian, not Scottish. In fact, he never gave up his Canadian citizenship. But he did come by his Scottish wrestling gimmick honestly. His grandfather George Toombs brought his bride, Euphemia Baird, to Canada in the earliest years of the twentieth century. When she left behind the

Hebrides in Northwest Scotland, she also left behind the Scottish Gaelic language she'd always spoken. She was a gentle woman who spoke softly to her children and sang quietly as she worked. She and George had two children, Jack and Frances, and then nearly a decade later, two more, Gracie and Stanley, Roddy's father. But Euphemia struggled with English, motherhood and the unforgiving landscape. She grew depressed and was institutionalized in a "rest home," as such places were called, as if a few good sleeps and a little break from responsibility were all she needed to get out of a slump. Stanley was eleven years old when Euphemia returned home from her rest. He quickly got bored of her same porridge, roast beef and bread, so he learned to cook and took over his mother's kitchen. Stanley was fifteen when she was buried. Like many struggling to survive in Canada in the early twentieth century, the family lost touch with its roots, and Euphemia bore the brunt of that dislocation.

Her husband, Roddy's grandfather George Toombs, was a strict Presbyterian, driven by a relentless work ethic, who eventually held a senior position with the Great West Life Assurance Company. His grandchildren were on strict orders for best behaviour when they visited George's rooms at The Bessborough, a distinguished hotel built in Saskatoon by the Canadian National Railway. A butterscotch candy from the stash he kept in a desk drawer hung in the balance.

George is remembered by his grandchildren as a man with little time for weakness, such as his wife's mental illness or pursuits he regarded as dalliances. His eldest son, Jack, was doing well pursuing a career as an artist in New York City. George told him it was time to come home to Saskatoon and take a job with the insurance company, effectively the family business. Jack did.

Then there are the Andersons. The family tree lightens up here, a little, on Roddy's mother's side. Roddy's grandmother, Charlotte Anderson, came from Chehalis, Washington, and grew up around Tacoma. Remembered by family as a generous, saintly character, Charlotte cooked for lumber camps and schools, and was well loved by everyone who knew her.

The Andersons were all remembered as sweet, fun people. But Roddy and his sisters all recalled one exception: their maternal grandfather.

Charlotte was married to Ernie Anderson, who grew up in Washington as well. At age eighteen he set out with his twin sisters and parents, following the promise of cheap land in Saskatchewan. A few years later, he met Charlotte, his future bride, while looking for work in tiny Nordegg, Alberta. She was working as a hotel housekeeper in the nearby town of Rocky Mountain House. They married and had six children—Stan (not to be confused with Roddy's father, Stanley Toombs), Eileen (Roddy's mother), Glen, Barbara, Gordon, each a year apart, and then twelve years later, Bob. In the Depression years, the desperate search for work dragged families across the mountains and prairies of the Canadian west. When Eileen was only eight years old, Ernie snuck himself on a westbound train. He left Biggar (named after a Scottish town near Edinburgh) and joined the hobos. He found a forestry job in Prince George, British Columbia. Once he'd settled, Charlotte packed up the kids and followed, but stopped halfway there, in Rocky Mountain House. Whooping cough was making its way through the children, and she got them off the train to recover with relatives before packing them up again and joining her husband in BC.

Ernie Anderson became a heavy-equipment driver and had set up a logging firm, which kept him in the bush for much of the year. The way Roddy and his sisters tell it, his absence was a mercy for the grandchildren. He made the kids uncomfortable, and had an unhealthy taste for liquor and a knack for hurting feelings with a few well-chosen words.

That lethal tongue found its way down the family tree to Roddy, as did the inclination to drink hard. But the Andersons might have graced him with another familiar quality. When one of his uncles tired of an old boat he'd picked up somewhere, he buried it in his backyard. If the simplest solution to a problem was also jaw-droppingly unconventional, so much the better. From coconuts to fire extinguishers, witty T-shirts to mules with Mexican headgear, Roddy's future admirers would become well acquainted with the family's creative streak.

Roddy's father, Stanley Toombs, grew into a blend of his mother's sensitivity and his father's inflexible ways. He also portended his son's capacity for violence.

"Dad was tough," says Cheryl, "never communicated, no talking. But he loved us dearly. He wasn't heartless." His reticence fit with his stiff Victorian upbringing.

Stanley met Eileen one summer when he was with the military in Prince George. Eileen had just finished high school and found a job as a waitress. The Second World War was raging, and it was common for rail bridges to be guarded closely. Stanley's job included supervising the young guards. "He had bridge guards," Eileen recalled. "So he said to me, one Sunday afternoon, 'Would you like to walk down to the bridge guards?' He wanted to check on them, to see if they needed anything. I said yes. Then the next day he said, 'Would you like to go for another walk today?' 'Yes,' I said. So we knew each other just three months and we got married." Stanley had aspired to university and a career as an architect. He was a clever man, with a penchant for precise thinking, in math and chemistry in particular. His intellect, ambition and willingness to work should have made success easier to achieve. But his early marriage and the responsibilities of family life were stumbling blocks.

The newlyweds settled in Saskatoon, where Stanley continued with the military. Marilyn was born there in 1943, and the endless supply of military work proved finite in a couple of years. While it remained, though, Stanley showed a bit of his son's flair for playful trouble—and luck. "My dad trained the pilots that were going to the front lines," explained Marilyn. "He would [fly] his squadron over the house and make Mother very angry. They'd tip their wings to say hello and then fly back to wherever he was training them. She would say, 'Stop that! You keep waking up the baby.'"

As an adult, bewildered at how he'd survived yet another flirtation with his own doom, Roddy would often lower his head and murmur, "Angels . . ." In 1945, those angels saved his father from history itself. Stanley was ordered to travel with his trainees overseas to the front lines. Training was finished and it was time to join the fight in Europe. On the way there, they were told to turn around and go home. Germany had surrendered.

With the war over, Eileen kept busy as a Red Cross volunteer (at the age of ninety-two, when Roddy last saw her, she was still volunteering with disabled senior citizens, many of them a decade younger than she was). Stanley found work with the CN Police Service, a private police force that kept the trains and other properties of the Canadian National Railway secure—no small responsibility in the remote towns and villages of the Canadian west, some accessible only by rail.

Cheryl was born a few years later. Roderick followed in 1954, when the world had settled down enough to get back to work. It was a complicated time for men like Stanley Toombs. His youngest daughter, Cheryl, reflected, "The men gave their lives for the old ways then came home and everything changed: civil rights, feminism. They had been just getting used to women wearing pants." Beaten up by the war—or at least coached in its rigid ways—men like Stanley pushed back hard when their children pushed tradition's boundaries.

An ambitious man could dream, though. Stanley led his young family across several thousand kilometres of Canadian landscape chasing one career opportunity after another, a difficult life that meant calling no place home.

Roddy's nomadic life didn't begin until he was six, in 1960. Before then, as far as he was concerned, the world at 1802 Victoria Avenue in Saskatoon was idyllic. Cheryl was smitten with her baby brother. Pushing him in his pram too close to the road, she was warned by their Grandmother Anderson to stay in the garden. Cheryl turned the pram on Charlotte and chased her around the flowers and vegetables. Roderick squealed with delight.

Cheryl described the reality of those years in a prairie city succinctly: "There were so many rules, and there were no rules." The Victorian rulebook kept morals in check but did little for the safety of curious children. Between meals, the kids roamed freely and fended for themselves. Their mother taught the children a song to remember their address, a simple jingle that even the most frightened little person would never forget: "We live at 1802 / Victoria Avenue / My phone number's 923-4962." She put them through another drill if they left home and didn't tell her where they were going. She would make them sit and listen to a record of songs meant to teach children to be safe: "Be sure Mommy knows where you go . . ."

Roderick didn't have to go far to find trouble, and for a time he was safer outside the house than in it. "In those days, the snowsuits were very heavy and wool," began Marilyn. "Mother was doing the laundry in a huge old washing machine with a ringer. You would swing the ringer over a bathtub full of water to rinse the clothing. She had to run outside to hang one last item, and she said to [a snowsuit-clad] Rod, '*Do not* go in the bathroom,' which is just asking for it." When Eileen raced back into the house only moments later, Roderick was nowhere to be seen. She ran to the tub and yanked her son out of the rinse water. The snowsuit had absorbed so much water he'd sunk to the bottom and couldn't move. "He was always doing something like that," sighed Marilyn.

Our father never mentioned the tub incident. But Eileen was outside the house another day when her four-year-old son's curiosity got the better of him, and this episode, also involving laundry, he would remember—vividly. Determined to help, Roderick approached the electric wringer washer, which was in the basement. He stuck his hands in the wringer, somehow turned it on, and it pulled his right arm through the rollers right up to the shoulder. What exactly happened next is lost to time. Marilyn figured Rod must have pressed the kill switch. He remembered the machine being plugged into a dangling outlet that he could reach and that he unplugged it. Either way, he showed remarkable presence of mind. Terrified, he yanked out his arm and scraped off a long strip of skin.

He set out for his aunt Barb's house, a few blocks down Victoria Avenue. Once there, he fell into a rocking chair and started rocking, trying to blank out the pain while his aunt tried to figure out what her nephew had done to himself. That day Roderick Toombs began a lifelong acquaintance with hospital emergency departments. He spent two weeks in the hospital with his arm suspended.

Remembering the incident many years later, Roddy's mother asked him if the accident had left any scars.

"No, nothing," he answered, looking down the length of his right arm. "As a matter of fact, some people say it's the most beautiful arm they've ever seen."

Roderick started school in Saskatoon. When Eileen dropped him off at kindergarten, he seemed happy enough. By the time she got home he was waiting at the back door. He had decided that he didn't like school and run home through the back streets to declare himself not interested.

Stanley arrived at Buena Vista Public School one day to deal with his son's unwillingness to stay in class. He looked down at a disconsolate Roderick crying to go home. The boy wrapped his arms around his father's leg and refused to let go, and was dragged along the floor when Stanley tried to walk away. "I think I'll just take the lad home," he told the teachers.

Disappointing your father when you're beginning grade school is one thing. The disappointments would continue, though, and a distance would grow between father and son no matter how hard either tried to hold on.

One of the first athletes Roderick ever met was the neighbourhood milkman. Nobody could remember what sport he was training for, but at the front door every day he ran on the spot while taking payment for his delivery. To maintain his pace, he didn't stop the horse pulling his delivery wagon at each address, and had to race after it to keep up. Roderick and Cheryl would sneak out to the street with carrots to tempt the horse to stop. "You little mites," he'd yell at them. "Get those carrots away from that horse's mouth." Thanks to the running milkman, Roderick thought milk came from horses.

He didn't see many athletes but he saw plenty of animals, and he liked them a lot. Eileen would check his pants pockets routinely before washing them and often come out with a handful of worms. "She kept saying, 'Rod, stop putting the worms in your pocket,'" recalled Marilyn. "'I'm not going to tell you again!' Finally, it took about two weeks of harping on it, it stopped suddenly. She thought, *This is great*. About a month later, we're doing spring cleaning and we had some very expensive rugs lying on the hardwood. She could smell something as she was vacuuming and she lifted up the corner of the carpet and there were hundreds of worms squashed from everybody walking on them. That's where he was putting the worms."

Despite their mother's constant attention and care, Roderick felt an acute absence of affection at home. Cheryl called the family "Victorian and undemonstrative." Looking back, Roddy wondered at his mother's reluctance to give him a simple hug. What felt like indifference from his father caused him agonies, too. "I needed a man to snatch me up and say get your homework done, put me on the right path," he said.

As Roderick got bigger, his father would try to box with him. A little fame in the fight game had entered the family already. An uncle of Stanley's on his father's side, Charles Tupper Toombs, was a boxer and coach. "One Cup Tup" managed the YMCA Soo Boxing Club in Sault Ste. Marie, Ontario, training a number of fighters in the very accomplished little club until he retired in 1959. (Eileen, upon first laying eyes on her baby Roderick, had declared, "He's got shoulders like a boxer!")

When sparring with Roderick, Stanley would hit his son quite soundly, then insist that he not tell Eileen. But if Roddy learned anything in his life, it was that you don't let a solid punch come between people. "That wasn't the source of pain," Roddy said, looking back. "It was the cold absence when he was present."

The CN Rail job was a tough one. Stanley Toombs was valued for many reasons, including his capacity for violence—dealing with it and dealing it out. He rarely discussed work at home, and the tough exterior he cultivated to survive became harder to shed at the end of each day. Visits with his wife's family provided some relief. His brothers-in-law brought out the joker in him, and he'd crack up the kids at the table until they couldn't eat. But such visits were far between. Mostly he sealed himself off from his family and hoped he could keep the turmoil inside.

Then Stanley was offered a promotion. He needed the pay raise. Both he and his wife were working side jobs. Now in her teens, Marilyn watched Roderick and Cheryl after school. Eileen worked as a department store buyer and took hours at a drive-in movie theatre concessions stand. Stanley worked at a gas station every other weekend. They grew and then canned most of their own vegetables in a garden plot. Roddy was assigned a row to weed every day after school. When the offer of more money came, Stanley had little choice but to accept, even though the promotion meant moving to northern Manitoba. And his family had no choice but to follow. "Women and children were still property," said Cheryl, with a sharp mix of irony, resentment and pragmatism. "Dad really did provide. Climbing the ladder was what he was supposed to do." She captures domestic life in the culture that sired Rowdy Roddy Piper with a few quick words: "The psychological well-being of a family meant mom and dad were together and you weren't being beaten; you went to church and you didn't divorce."

Cold comfort in a life that was about to become a lot colder.

No town on the prairies made as deep an impression on Roddy's family as their two years in The Pas. The small Manitoba town sits at the meeting point of two large rivers and the Opaskwayak Cree reserve. In 1960, The Pas had found itself suddenly unpoliced. Stanley hadn't exactly volunteered for the move north to an essentially lawless frontier town—the last place a man could collect unemployment benefits before he disappeared into the nearly ungoverned North. The job required a certain sort of officer, one not worried about being comfortable, and who wouldn't be easily intimidated. The family arrived to a scene out of the Wild West, with trappers drinking on the street and sled dogs staked outside the shops and bars on the main street. "When we arrived the town police could no longer handle the rabble-rousing and they were waiting for the RCMP to come and take over," explained Marilyn. "So there was no other police force there when we arrived. It was quite frightening."

Many kids travelled to school on dogsleds. Stanley would need sled dogs when calls took him away from the only road in and out of town. Native kids from Opaskwayak came to school the same way. They staked their dogs outside and brought the lead dogs to class, where they would sleep beneath their desks. The lead dogs had too much pride to sit outside like pets, and the other dogs wouldn't go far without them.

As cold as Saskatoon could be, The Pas was much colder. "Your tears froze on your face," said Cheryl. "And you didn't worry about a runny nose, it froze on your face, too."

With their mother working, both sisters were taking care of their little brother now, and they sent Roderick to school in mukluks with sanitary napkins in them to keep his feet warm.

In deepest winter The Pas was dark when the kids woke up and nearly dark again when they walked home from school. The snow could be as deep as six-year-old Roderick was tall. He was a cute little kid, but something about him got under people's skin. To keep from being picked on, he stayed away from the roads and well-travelled paths. He didn't much care for the sled dogs either. They were large, brawling animals that could badly hurt a child who didn't know how to handle them.

To keep out of people's way, Roderick walked to and from school along the edge of the forest, a forest that went on and on beyond any distance a boy could imagine—so he imagined the worst.

He'd been warned about what lived in the woods, and that these beasts sometimes roamed its edges, hunting domestic animals and other small creatures. So his mother and sisters taught Roderick to sing aloud as he went.

John Jacob Jingleheimer Schmidt . . .

Every year or two, a child would stumble upon a timber wolf, or a whole pack, before either knew the other was there. Surprising them could be a fatal mistake. If the wolves heard you coming, however, they scuttled back into the trees. And so he sang.

His name is my name, too . . .

Roderick was bullied in The Pas as in every other town in which the family lived from then on. But it was here, in this former trading post, that some of the Toombs kids started learning how to fight back. "They're not that big," Stanley told his kids about the bullies. "Go get them." And, he added, if any were in fact as large as they seemed to his children, "Point them out to me." Surprisingly, the first time a bully was pointed out at the Toombs' home, Stanley was doing the pointing.

One day after school a boy and his father appeared at the door. The boy was nursing a sore nose and a bruised ego. His father had insisted on seeing the Toombs boy who'd beaten up his son, who had, of course, been picking on Roderick.

Stanley promptly presented the aggrieved father with the real culprit: twelve-year-old Cheryl. The father slapped his son out of shame that he'd been bested by a girl. "We were a civilized family," says Cheryl. "We were taught to talk things out. But in that place, fists solved problems."

Cheryl did more for her little brother than punch out neighbourhood bullies. She might have used her hands to nurture his most memorable quality as a wrestler.

A teacher in The Pas who thought Roderick had a nice voice entered him in a singing contest. The song chosen for him was a hymn called "They Didn't Think." He was going to be competing against kids and adults, and the idea of getting up on stage made him nervous. To help, Cheryl held one hand in front of him as he practiced, making movements to go with the song, both to remind him of the words and to give him something to focus on beyond his anxiety.

Once a trap was baited with a dainty piece of cheese;
It tickled so a little mouse it almost made him sneeze.
An old mouse said, "There's danger; be careful where you go."
"Oh, nonsense," said the mousey, "I don't think you know."

When the day of the competition came, Roderick, all of six or seven years old, took to the stage, knees knocking, and opened his mouth to sing. A few rows back in the audience, his sister sat with her hand in the air, guiding him with the mouse movements just like she had in practice.

So he walked in boldly—nobody was in sight;
First he took a nibble, then he took a bite;
Close the trap together snapped as quick as you could wink,
Catching mousey fast there "because he didn't think."

He finished in second place.

Roddy loved telling this story about Cheryl. "A lot of guys in my business, they say the hardest thing to do is cutting promos, getting in front of that camera. I've always been good at it," he said. "I think all these years, I've just been singing into my sister's hand."

Life in The Pas was hard for the kids to get their heads around. When he wasn't getting picked on at school Roderick took his lumps elsewhere.

The family lived on a small highway. One day Marilyn and Cheryl were leaving the house and crossed the road. Roderick got it in his head that he should run across, too, and kiss them goodbye. He didn't look, he just ran. A passing truck hit him and sent him tumbling across the gravel. The driver stopped and got out of the truck, trembling with fear that he'd killed the boy. Establishing another pattern he'd follow throughout his life, Roderick received severe bruising from the collision but otherwise was remarkably uninjured.

As staunch Presbyterians of Scottish extraction, the family had an obvious choice of denomination, the United Church of Canada (the uniquely Canadian church takes its name from bringing together several different protestant streams, in particular Presbyterians). The local congregation got to know Roderick well.

Eileen and Stanley were friendly with a family named Brown. Roderick played with their daughter. "She's always telling him about the ghosts," said Eileen. "Rod come to me, 'Mommy, Mommy, is there ghosts?' I said, 'There's no such thing.'"

His fascination with ghosts made an issue of itself one Sunday morning as the minister was closing his sermon. "He says, of course, 'In the name of the father, the son and the holy ghost.' Rod jumped up on the pew and he said, 'See, Mom! I told you there was a ghost!'"

The church was large, and its pews were long enough that anyone in the middle who tried to get up during the service would bother quite a few neighbours. The family always sat in the middle. On another Sunday, Roderick turned to his mother.

"I have to go to the bathroom, Mom."

"You'll have to wait, Rod. The minister's in the middle of his sermon."

"I have to go to the bathroom, Mom, I have to go now."

Fearing the worst, Eileen led her son down the length of the pew, disturbing everyone along the way, and took him to the washroom. A few minutes later, they returned, disturbing the row again. Her son wasn't finished. "I need a drink of water." "Rod, we were just to the bathroom, you'll have to wait." "Mom, I need a drink of water right now." "Rod, we are not leaving again." "Well, if you don't give me a drink of water, Mom, I'm going to ask God."

His mother turned to him, surprised. "Well, where is He?" she challenged him.

He stood up in the pew and pointed to the minister. "Right there!"

Roderick's misunderstanding concerned the minister enough that he held a special sermon the following week. He brought all the children to the front, so he could explain to the kids that the minister of a church isn't God, and he put Roderick Toombs front and centre.

Stanley was finding The Pas a rough go, but the CN Rail officer was no shrinking violet. If a quarrelsome prisoner was acting up while being marched back to the station, Stanley wouldn't hesitate to handcuff him to a fence post in the cold to settle him down while he took his time and peed behind a tree.

When winter storms blocked the roads, days could pass before they were plowed. The rail line was more likely to be clear and was the easiest way through town. Once Stanley was walking the line with his youngest children when they approached a parked train. He noticed one of the boxcar doors was slightly open. "Take Roderick home, now," he said firmly. Cheryl and Roderick stopped, alarmed at their father's sudden change in demeanour. "Now!" he growled. They turned and ran.

"I'm trying," Rod said as his sister urged him forward. His short legs made it hard to keep pace in the deep snow.

Behind them, Stanley yanked open the door and a man with a knife jumped out. Before the man could strike, Stanley stopped him with a hard punch, cried "home, now!" one more time to his kids, then knocked the man out with a second blow.

When the kids arrived at the house, breathless and scared, their mother asked them what happened. When they told her, she just said, "Oh, Dad was having trouble with a baddie." If Eileen couldn't hide the brutality of her husband's job from her children, she'd at least try to sugarcoat it.

Life's lessons found her young son, regardless, and they hit as hard as his father could.

Roderick got his first dog while living along that highway in The Pas, a small golden Lab puppy he named Tammy. Eileen and Stanley told him repeatedly to keep the front gate shut. Realizing the welfare of his new dog depended on him, Roderick routinely locked the gate behind him on the way to school.

But one day, just a minute after he'd passed through the gate, locking it as usual, he heard a screech behind him as a car braked on the highway. It didn't stop, though, and passed him where he stood on the shoulder of the road. He ran back and found Tammy lying in the dirt.

A neighbour had gone to the house and opened the gate. The dog got out.

From inside the house, Marilyn heard her brother crying at the back door. She found him standing there with the puppy in his arms, bleeding all down him. "It had died," said Marilyn. "My brother was devastated. The smell, the metallic smell of the blood, never, ever left him."

Roderick was confused enough by what had happened that he wanted his father to give the little dog mouth-to-mouth. Stanley buried the animal.

For all the bullying, Roderick made a few friends in The Pas. One was a girl his age who lived with her family across the highway. The two played together often and, given how far north they lived, *often* meant they usually played in ice and snow. One day the girl went through some thin ice in a bog and they both got soaked. The kids trudged back to her home and stripped down in her garage, placing their winter clothes in front of a blazing wood stove. The girl's mother found them undressed and cried "Rape!" She then called the police.

It's hard to imagine anyone accusing a boy of rape when he is barely old enough to spell his name. Imagine how that boy felt when the police arrived, and the officer was his father. Whatever wrath Stanley brought down on his son, half a century later Roddy could only shake his head and shudder when asked about it. He would tell many friends about many beatings he endured for misbehaviours, some as minor as this. One friend we spoke with said he'd told her he was beaten so badly once he'd had to stay home from school for a week. As a little boy, he'd been puzzled by the uproar and trouble. But he recalled clearly the whole town calling him a "pervert."

Before Roderick was old enough to understand love, he felt shame. Like the smell of his dog's blood, it never left him—the shame of the accusation and his terror of his father. By the age of seven, he'd learned the value of silence in the face of suffering. Best keep it to himself.

The town left a painful impression on him, and so did his father's strict adherence to Victorian propriety. He wasn't the only one in the family who suffered its narrow confines.

Marilyn won a local beauty contest—Miss Field Day Princess—and was asked to try her charisma and good looks at the provincial level. She went home excited by the prospect. Stanley's response was devastating, if no surprise.

"Absolutely not. No daughter of mine will be entering that type of contest."

As the oldest child in the family, Marilyn was the sharp end of the spear in the children's effort to penetrate their father's tough exterior. She didn't get very deep. Marilyn was voted prom queen but Stanley wouldn't allow any drinking, and the after-party was to take place at a bar. The prom queen herself was forbidden to attend. "It was just a little strict," she said.

In territory like northern Manitoba in the 1960s, a police officer had his reasons for keeping his kids on a short leash. One of Marilyn's classmates died in a car crash that night. The roads in the area shifted wildly with the freeze and thaw of the seasons. Hard to navigate and pitch black at night, the roads in winter and spring could also be sheer ice. Typical of life in the North, even the most celebratory of nights is tempered by awareness of human fragility. You either learned to deal with the possibility that the next moment could kill you, or you struggled miserably.

A young woman from England joined the staff at the local grade school. She was one who struggled. The teacher insisted the Cree kids leave their sled dogs outside. Unable to sit still and ever thinking beyond the boundaries meant to contain a boy his age, Roderick wasn't going to have an easy time with a disciplinarian like that. She sent him repeatedly to the office for the strap. There were calls to his parents. "She thought she was running a military academy," Cheryl said. "Dad had a word with her." When Stanley found a teacher too strict, it became less of a mystery how a prim young Englishwoman had ended up in a place as rough and remote as The Pas.

But the town remained a puzzle, one the family never really solved. "We were outsiders," said Cheryl, "we didn't know the rules." One of those rules—the unwritten ones—had to do with the Cree kids from Opaskwayak across the river: stick to your own kind. In the stratified world of teenage social life, the rule was taken seriously. The Toombs kids didn't understand that. Marilyn, Cheryl and Roderick talked to the Native kids, hung out with them, and sat in the wrong part of the movie theatre. The beatings and bullying they endured came mostly from white kids who didn't like seeing those lines crossed.

Stanley and Eileen's tireless son tested his parents' patience. Neither the strap at school nor the back of his father's hand at home slowed Roderick down. "There was a surprise every day with you, Rod," his mother teased him during their last visit, early in his last summer. "I love you to death, but . . ."

He smiled at her playful chiding, but lowered his head. The sting of all those childhood reprimands lingered.

Eileen recalled a story that made it clear how her son's tendency to tinker with things frustrated his parents.

Roderick discovered his mother's new electric floor polisher, and whenever she ran it around the house, he sat on it for the ride. One day she found him sitting on the kitchen floor leaning intently over the polisher. The casing around its motor was open. Roderick held a screwdriver in one hand. "He had it in the insides and he was breaking all the—"

"I was fixing it!" Roddy interjected, his head snapping up in protest.

"I said, 'Why on earth would you do something like that?' I don't know. There was never a dull moment, dear."

In 1962, Eileen and Stanley left town for a few days to search for an apartment in Dauphin, several hundred miles south. Another move was in the works. They took Roderick with them. Their nearly grown daughters stayed at home. The girls woke up one morning to the smell of bacon and eggs. Downstairs in the kitchen they found a boy they knew from school. Frightened and angry, they screamed at him to leave.

The intruder tried to talk his way into staying, complaining that the girls weren't being very nice. He'd made them breakfast, after all. "We were able to get him out and lock the door," said Marilyn. "There wasn't a lot to do in The Pas."

Looking back, Marilyn was even more relieved that she and her younger sister were able to chase the boy away. He would later be involved in the infamous 1971 murder of an area Cree woman, Helen Betty Osborne.

When the family left The Pas and its very real dangers they were intact but not unscathed.

The end of winter meant a chance for Stanley to spend some time with the family away from the pressures of work. Thanks to his job the whole family travelled by train for free. Trips "home" were common, back to Saskatoon, where Aunt Barb still lived. "We would go down there in the spring," says Marilyn. "All in our mukluks and heavy coats to get off the train in Saskatoon and everybody's in spring jackets and looked at us like, 'Where are you from?'" It was on one such trip to Saskatoon that Roderick got such a bad stomach ache he had to be rushed off the train.

Roddy remembered crying and hugging himself in a dark room, being poked with needles by doctors and nurses unsure what was causing him so much pain. He woke up and looked around and couldn't find his parents. Eventually the doctors realized it was appendicitis and he had an emergency appendectomy.

Perhaps the terror in his recollection was just a function of being a child at the time. But the memory that remained was of being abandoned while suffering—alone when his body turned on him.

Summer brought long train trips west to join the Anderson grandparents, uncles and aunts who lived near Prince George, in and around a little place called Burns Lake. The train crew brought Roddy to the locomotive. When they neared a turn, they said, "Lean," to help get the train around the bend. He did and they laughed, but the boy had a job to do and took it seriously.

The Andersons were in the lumber business, and most of them possessed a down-to-earth good nature. Their pleasant company peeled the stress away from the policeman and his family—though the remote location was hardly carefree. Prince George is cradled by Rocky Mountain country, and the house sat on the edge of a deep, wooded valley that hid many wild things, beautiful and deadly.

A herd of wild horses lived in the valley. The river nearby was so pristine, people drank from it. Cougars roamed the woods, and Roderick left the outhouse one day only to walk right into the path of a bear. He ran one way and the bear ran the other. After that, Ernie Anderson built a screened-in walkway to the outhouse.

Evenings at the Anderson home were often given over to music. By the dim light of a Coleman lantern, Eileen played the harmonica, sometimes with one end in a drinking glass to give the instrument an extra, haunting quality. Aunt Doris played the accordion and Uncle Glen played the guitar. Somebody always picked up the spoons and everybody sang along. "It was like the Beverly Hillbillies," Roddy remembered with a smile.

"Everybody was happy," said Eileen.

At ninety-two, Eileen could still play the mouth organ with

one end in a glass. Roddy tried and couldn't quite get it. She showed him how. "That sound like a hillbilly?" she said.

Roderick's penchant for mishaps caught up with him in the BC woods. "I remember Uncle Glen one time," said Roddy, "he was my favourite uncle. And they were all lumberjacks. We got out in the bush. And of course I wanted to start the tractor." The boy turned the key but let go when the noisy engine began to turn over. It clicked oddly and fell silent. Roderick's heart sank, figuring he'd ruined the machine. "I thought we were going to be stuck there for months." Glen began groaning that they were in trouble, and made a big show of how serious a problem this was. Roderick was mortified. "He took a wrench . . . and we're off again." There was nothing wrong with the tractor, of course. Glen was just teasing his mechanically disinclined nephew. Just how disinclined became evident when he was about ten.

Someone was taking a family photo outside the house at Burns Lake. Roderick wasn't in the picture. He was in the background, tinkering in the cockpit of a large Caterpillar logging machine. He tinkered too much, and suddenly the Cat rolled into the shot.

"Everybody was screaming," said Eileen. "He came so close to the house."

"I wasn't strong enough to pull the lever to turn the Cat." Roddy smiled sheepishly. "I didn't have that down yet." He thought for a moment, trying to complete the image. "I don't know who took the picture," he said. "Do you remember?"

"No," replied his mother. "I was too busy screaming!"

Not surprisingly, Roderick and his sisters were under strict orders to stay inside at night. Cheryl followed her grandfather outside anyway, curious what he could be up to in the dark and too young to imagine he might simply want a moment alone. She startled him and he wound up to hit her. Realizing who it was, he stormed back into the house and exclaimed to Eileen, "Your children have no fear! What's wrong with them?!"

"There were no dull moments when he was young," said Eileen. During their final visit, the number of times she shook her head with a laugh and called him "an active child" became a running joke between them. Roddy's curiosity, imagination and stubbornness were well established in childhood—so was his suspicious nature.

Once, he was alone at the Anderson's house. Word in the area was that a man had recently escaped from jail in Prince George. "I was on the couch, whittling with a knife. I went up the stairs and when I came down, I couldn't find the knife, and I knew that escaped con had my knife. I got on my bike." A dirt road connected the Anderson grandparents' house to their daughter's. "I started riding my bike and in the middle of it were all these cows. So I went around the trees and the cows started chasing me. I got around them and I got to Aunt Doris's. Cause they needed to go get that man I was positive had my knife."

Eileen picked up the story. "My sister-in-law lived about half a mile from my mother's place. Rod would go over there to play with the kids in the daytime. I looked and he come running as fast as he could, 'Mommy, Mommy, would you come and get that she cow that won't leave me alone!' Any cow in our household was a *she cow.*"

It's a cute story, like many about Roddy's childhood—when others tell them. Eileen remembered the she cows. Roddy remembered the knife.

Summers never last, and fall 1962 landed the family in the small apartment they'd found in Dauphin. Five hundred kilometres east of Saskatoon, Dauphin was mercifully well south of The Pas. A sleepy little town, it did come with some consolations.

The apartment they moved into was right behind an A&W. Roderick often asked his mother to take him for a hamburger. She rarely said no.

"You'd sit there and eat it and you would relish it," Eileen remembered. "And I used to look at you and, 'You think I could have another one?' I couldn't help, if I had money enough, to get you another one to watch you eat it."

Roderick was struggling in school. In some parts of the country, math and spelling were taught during those years by a form of memorization—visual learning—that would be abandoned shortly after he passed through the affected grades. Further, education standards and methods weren't consistent from province to province. These were reason enough to find school difficult. But added to this, Roddy often described himself as suffering from what we would now call ADD—attention deficit disorder—and struggled to focus on things that didn't greatly interest him. Education was bound to prove more than a chore. Although as an adult he loved history and could recite passages from Shakespeare, he claimed to have never read a book in its entirety.

In Dauphin Roderick's parents enrolled him in bagpipe lessons. He was taught the eight holes on the chanter, practicing the simple scales of the military instrument. His teacher struck him on the knuckles when he made a mistake. The elimination of Scots Gaelic culture from the family was about to receive a hard correction, borne on the still-slight shoulders of its youngest son.

After several months in the apartment, Eileen found the family a three-storey Victorian house with a wraparound porch and a weeping willow in the yard. It was the perfect family home, and they soon moved in. She and the kids wanted to stay in it permanently. Dauphin was small and quiet, an ideal place for the kids to grow up. But after close to two years, the CN Rail Police had other ideas.

Cheryl came home from school to find her mother pulling clothes out of the drawers. "What are you doing?" Cheryl asked. "Packing," Eileen replied.

"What else is new," Cheryl groaned

Roderick was on the move again.

On the northwest shore of Lake Superior, a very long way from anywhere—except Duluth, Minnesota, which most Americans would consider a very long way from anywhere—sat the twin towns of Port Arthur, where the family moved to next, and Fort William. Today, they are a single city known as Thunder Bay, and it's still about as isolated a city as any near the Canada–US border.

Being the new kids in the neighbourhood, Roderick and his sister were once again tested, beat up, or somehow made to prove themselves. Marilyn had moved on to nursing school in Fort William, so she was out of the mix, and Cheryl was in high school—more likely now to be teased than outright beat up. Roderick, however, was only ten, and still a target.

Marilyn remembered: "I think he was only in grade four at that time. This guy was always after him, but Rod was quick, even at that age. The kid kept saying, 'I'm going to get you after school. I'm going to beat you up again,' and Rod said to him, 'Oh, hey man, you must be talking about my twin brother, that's the guy you're after!' It worked once and then he was back in the doghouse."

One particular bully on Roderick's case was nicknamed Jinx. Both boys had a paper route and they'd collect their papers at the same place every day. Jinx would go after Roderick every chance he got. The tables turned only briefly. Jinx was a catcher and during one baseball game Rod took him out hard when running in to home plate. The insult would be avenged, however, and Jinx spent recess chasing him all over the school, kicking him in the behind every time he got close.

Cheryl got a job as an usherette in the local movie theatre. She could get her brother in to see movies for free, spoiling him with gratis popcorn and candy. He took full advantage. When *The Sound of Music* was held over, he watched it five Saturday afternoons in a row. The wartime musical—a staple on any list of wholesome entertainment—mesmerized him.

Even the movie theatre wasn't safe harbour, though. Unattended boys in dark rooms presented easy targets for sexual predators. One approached him and he fled the theatre. Bullies of every sort found Roderick. It's no wonder he learned to move so fast.

At home, the doghouse was soon Rod's exclusive space. He was getting older, and his mishaps more serious—and there were no other kids left to occupy it. After high school Cheryl left for Toronto. Being much closer to home, Marilyn still visited every other weekend. One Friday, she saw how her brother's behaviour was outgrowing their parents' ability to contain it.

Eileen picked up Marilyn in Fort William for the weekend. When they pulled into the driveway, Eileen thought something was wrong. The other family car—a dilapidated Oldsmobile that betrayed just how frugal Stanley really was—seemed to be not exactly as she'd left it. She couldn't put her finger on what was bothering her, though, and they went inside.

When Marilyn and Eileen entered the house, the phone rang. It was a friend of the family. "Eileen, were you out with the Oldsmobile today?" asked the friend.

"No."

"Well, I thought I saw it driving and I couldn't see anybody driving it."

Eileen was certain now that something was wrong. She went outside again and this time noticed a little chip out of the cement front-door step.

She went back inside, found her son, and asked, "Rod, did you move the car today?"

"Uh . . . I just backed it out and put it back in the right place for you, 'cause you said the snow drifts were too deep."

Marilyn laughed to remember the episode. "The little beggar had taken the car, had driven down onto one of the busiest streets of Port Arthur and got it all the way back, up a huge hill and into the driveway, and quietly put the keys away," she said. He'd bumped the step when he pulled up to the house, but figured no one would notice. "Nothin' to it!"

Roderick continued his bagpipe lessons. "Every Friday I had to go to band practice," he said. "So all the other guys are playing baseball. Who would ever figure it would be my career? Make a living playing the bagpipes . . ." The baseball diamond nearby taunted him. Normal kids started their weekends there. He didn't. Though he did sleep in the dugout a few times, when his father scared him too much to stay at home.

Roddy never told his mother or his sister that he drove that old car to the ballpark and spun it in circles with the gas pedal floored—"doing doughnuts," as Canadians like to call the stunt—around and around the ball diamond.

When in 2015 he confessed to Cheryl about that day, he wondered aloud, "Why'd I steal that car?" as if through the fog of his accumulated years he couldn't put together the building anger in his juvenile heart and the absence of any way to vent those feelings. It was hard to make friends when you moved every two years, and now there was no one left at home he could share his anxieties with. He was a sensitive kid raised to be tough, and the opposing natures were souring in one another's company.

"You were too bright, too curious, needed an outlet. The car was just another way to find out how something worked," Cheryl answered him. The memory is another case of our father's life looking cute from the outside while feeling like something entirely different to him. "I don't think you were bad. It was a rigid home. You had no room to explore your intelligence."

Roddy looked at his sister. He looked away. He seemed unconvinced.

Young Roderick did find a friend in Port Arthur, and he never forgot his name: Bobby Hansen. Rod fell through the ice again, and this time in considerably deeper water. Lake Superior rarely freezes over. As the name suggests, it's a massive body of fresh water, so broad that the sun sets half an hour earlier on its eastern shore than its west. The shoreline waters do freeze, however, and Roderick and Bobby found themselves on the ice one day. Roddy shrugged off what should have worried him: the ice was too thin. If Bobby hadn't been there to grab his hand and pull him out, you wouldn't be reading this story.

The pattern had been set with the move from Saskatoon—uproot, relocate, get beat up, get in trouble, make a friend, move on. It intensified in Port Arthur. Eileen was working as a buyer for the Zellers chain of department stores. Stanley was as elusive as ever, either working or distant from his son when around. Roderick came home from school every day to an empty house.

When anxious, he developed a habit of sitting on the edge of his bed or a chair and rocking back and forth. He rocked on one couch so much he broke it. With his sisters gone, the house was silent, overpoweringly empty. He sat at the foot of their beds and rocked the hours away. Wishing more than anything that he could have gone with them, he wondered what joy life could hold in their absence.

Hiding at the baseball diamond at night, driving the old car: these were small misdemeanors next to what was to come. It was time to move again.

At age twelve, Rod found himself living in the newly developed suburb of Don Mills, on the edge of English-speaking Canada's largest city. Toronto in 1967 was only hinting at the multicultural place it has since become. Its killjoy focus on work echoed every quality that Stanley Toombs felt made a man worthy of the title Head of the Household. No place could have made him more aware of the growing distance between himself and his boy. Roddy's enchantment with mischief continued, and so did the bagpiping. "I was a good bagpiper," remembered Roddy. He recalled a Highland Games in Toronto where he played for an audience. "I was so young. At the end of the games we had a ceilidh. The guys'd be in there drinking. There was no place for me, but I loved meat pies. So, I'm lurking and I can't go in the [beer] tent and I see this box of meat pies. There must have been twelve of them. It was like a bonanza. I stowed the meat pies. I went to run, but I didn't see the rope holding up the tent. I tripped and those meat pies—all over the dance floor. Well, the punishment was for the rest of that season. When the dancers are competing, the drummers they all need a piper. I had to play all damn day for them. Can't help getting better at it."

Caber Feidh was the name of one pipe band Rod joined in Toronto. He was just turning thirteen, but many of the band were grown men. Stanley left him in their hands during long rehearsals and trips to competitions out of town. "Lotta pipe bands," Roddy said, voice trailing off. Talking about them seemed to draw him away to unhappy memories.

He and his parents had settled in an apartment. The unit was in one of several close buildings, each about twenty storeys tall. "It was so many fuckin' people." Just talking about those years made Roddy edgy. "It got ugly in Toronto, because I would leave," he said. Some nights he took off and didn't come home for days on end.

The meat-pie story might be funny fifty years later, but it was another embarrassing episode for Stanley. Discipline wasn't working, but that didn't stop him from trying, the only way he knew how.

Fortunately, there was some respite for Roderick—from the new city and the troubles beckoning him, and from the increasing tension between him and his father. Come summer, they all went back to Burns Lake for a few more weeks among the Andersons. In the bush, where Stanley could let down his guard, father and son's natures found temporary common ground.

The Andersons had an old gas-powered washing machine. It ran on a kick-start Briggs & Stratton two-stroke engine. When the washing machine broke, Roderick tried to make a go-kart out of the motor. When Stanley's vacation was over and it was time to return east to Toronto, he had the motor shipped from BC to the apartment in Don Mills. Roderick and Stanley worked on it on their apartment balcony, making them popular with the neighbours, no doubt.

"You guys started it and the odour from it was just horrible," said Eileen.

"That'd be the same balcony where I had to play my bagpipes every Sunday," said Roddy. His practice regimen was strictly enforced, but as he improved he started enjoying the instrument.

He also played them in parks, sometimes busking. Eileen remembered, "We would go out, we'd jump in the car and take it out to the park. Rod would stand there playing 'The Lone Piper' or something on the bagpipes. He had an audience every time. It was lovely."

"The kids at school didn't think it was quite so lovely."

"I love the bagpipes," Eileen said.

If there's any mystery why Roddy stayed so committed to his gimmick throughout his life—aside from the fact it worked so well—the answer might be as simple as this. He wanted to make his mother happy.

Roddy learned another skill in Toronto that shaped his professional wrestling career. "I started boxing in Lansdowne. I don't know how I found it. It was so far away. I'd sleep in that subway station at Lansdowne 'cause they shut down at a certain time."

The Lansdowne Boxing Club was a focal point of the Toronto fight scene. How Roderick found his way to the cramped little gym is a mystery. Stanley had tried to teach him to box, and his uncle Tupper was a renowned boxing coach. It's possible Rod showed up at Lansdowne at his father's urging, another attempt at instilling some discipline in his wayward son that went very wrong. "It was a really rough gym," Roddy recalled. He thrived at the sport, eventually competing in a Golden Gloves competition, a sort of gold standard—if you didn't get that from the name—for amateur fighters. But where Stanley might have wanted to instill discipline, he cultivated his son's independence instead.

Don Mills is northeast of the city core and Lansdowne Road well west of downtown. By bus and subway, it's nearly twenty kilometres. At age thirteen, Roderick would have travelled alone on public transit for a couple hours each way. It's no wonder he woke up hidden in some nook of the Lansdowne subway station, either ready to box before heading back to Don Mills for school or too late to catch the last train home. Don Mills was a mid-century commuters' paradise, filled with ranch-style bungalows on wide lots. Lansdowne was one of the most crime-ridden streets in the city.

Roderick missed the last train home a lot. He was missing a lot of school, too. In junior high, a vice principal made the boys strip naked for swim class. Roderick refused and pulled a switchblade to make sure his position on the matter was understood.

Around thirteen or fourteen, little Roderick, favoured target of bullies across half the width of Canada, grew tall. He was suddenly tall enough that movie theatres wouldn't let him in for children's prices. To get the kids' deal, Stanley had to go with him and insist.

Marilyn came back to live with the family when she started a job in Toronto. (Cheryl had since moved on.) Then she got married and was quickly gone again. "Rod wouldn't leave me at my wedding. He kept following me to the car because he didn't want me to leave. So I said, 'Rod, I'm getting in the car now. I have to go.' 'I don't want you to go!' He felt abandoned by us a bit."

Straying ever more from his parents, he started sleeping over at the home of a senior member of the pipe band. "I stayed there, wouldn't come home," he remembered. "Then I started drinking, and got really drunk one night on homemade wine. My dad finally said just fuckin' let him be your father." For all the grief he was causing his father's sense of pride and propriety, he was reaching out to his mother in some small measure by continuing with the band. It was a decision Roddy would regret. "It was almost like a fuckin' Charlie Manson commune or something," he said of the way the band was run. Junior members were often targeted for abuse. *The Toronto Star* ran a photo that Rod remembered well, in which he appears marching with the band in a parade. The photo doesn't reveal much beyond the well-rehearsed unity and singular purpose of a well-drilled band that would finish fifth in international competition—a result he frequently cited later in life. But he marched in pain that day. He'd been made to wear boots two sizes too small as punishment for not going along with some demeaning bit of hazing or another. He came home after an overnight trip with the band and dumped clothes stained with blood in the laundry basket. No questions were asked. No suggestion was offered that he quit.

Fathers. Teachers. Leaders of any stripe. It was enough to convince a teenager well on his disillusioned way that authority exists only as a means to exploit you. If you don't possess it, you suffer its will.

And then the ultimate authority in his life was gone. His parents moved away, and this time Roderick—now well into his teens and tall enough to intimidate on the street when he needed to—didn't join them for the trip.

"I guess they left," he said of his parents. He wondered, too, how he eventually caught up to them. "I cannot recall how. I was never on an airplane. Must have been on a train. Got into Winnipeg."

2

Concede or Get Up

Our dad met his first real friend the way you'd expect. "My buddies brought Rod over to my house, and they knocked on my back door. They said, 'Hey, Cam, you're pretty tough and this guy's pretty tough, why don't you guys have a fight?' I go, 'Okay.'"

Over six feet tall, Cam Connor was still, at sixty-one, an imposing presence. The years had been kinder to him than to Roddy. When they saw each other for the last time in 2015, it had been over forty years since they'd first met in Winnipeg. Roddy brightened considerably in Cam's company.

The steadfast trust between them hadn't come easily, but it had come quickly. "We walked inside, my friends stayed out. Just the two of us went in the garage and closed the door. Then we went at it," Cam recalled.

Cam lives in Edmonton now, where he works in sales for a camp and catering company servicing the Alberta oil industry.

It's not his first career. In 1979, he scored a double-overtime playoff-series winning goal for the National Hockey League's Montreal Canadiens on their way to a Stanley Cup championship, eliminating their arch-rival, the Toronto Maple Leafs. Later, he played for the Wayne Gretzky–led Edmonton Oilers and the New York Rangers as well. And given the company he kept as a teenager, the part that won't surprise you is that he spent a significant proportion of his NHL career in the penalty box, a consequence of being big, fierce and willing to fight for his teammates.

Cam continued the story: "Every time he threw, it was so fast, and I'd barely get my head out of the way and a fist would come flying. He was throwing hooks at me."

After about thirty seconds of trading punches, Cam realized the new kid wasn't going to kick or tackle him. He wanted to fight standing up. "I knew this guy was trained. I could tell when he moved his head just a little bit, he knew what he was doing." Most teenagers in a fight would jump out of the way to avoid a punch. Roddy—the name Roderick was becoming a relic of family life—avoided Cam's fists with subtle shifts of weight, an elegance that required genuine skill. "He just dodged the punches, minimal effort, and that's when I said to myself, 'Uh-oh, I'm gonna have to knock him out if I'm going to beat him.'"

Cam went all in. He threw a roundhouse right, hoping to turn the tide of the fight. It had worked in hockey fights, and he'd ended his share of street fights the same way. He missed. The force of the punch tore a muscle in his arm. "That's when he started hitting me. I couldn't use the arm anymore 'cause my triceps was gone." Roddy grunted with every punch. "He hit me a few times, then, honest to God, I had a motorcycle parked there, whoop, I went over the motorcycle. Just like in the movies."

If Roddy had come around that motorcycle and tried to finish it, Cam would have been just one more guy in one more fight.

But he didn't. Both kids would soon be professional fighters, and already they grasped the most basic of codes between opponents. Rod stood back and gave Cam a chance to concede or get up. "The fight was over," said Cam. "I go, 'What's your name again? I think I'm gonna be your friend.'"

Having followed his parents to Winnipeg, Rod moved in with them. But he quickly fell into the old pattern, calling his parents' place home while sleeping many nights wherever else he could find.

He enrolled in high school. For a tough guy, he had an unexpected impact on his new best friend, who was an unrepentant jock with a nose for trouble. "Rod always talked to the nerdy guys. He changed my outlook with people different than me. He'd see good people inside." Roddy quickly became popular with classmates. He didn't strut through the halls, hassling smaller students or picking fights to prove himself. He would strike up a conversation with anyone.

Cam recalled them walking down Portage Avenue, one of Winnipeg's main streets, and passing an older man begging for change. Being teenagers, neither kid had much money. Roddy had $30 to his name. "Rod turned around and put twenty dollars in the old guy's tin, never mentioned it after."

If parents often notice the worst in their teenage kids, peers sometimes see their friends at their best. But that doesn't mean Roddy left Toronto and became a saint.

He had a favourite trick when trying to avoid school. If the classroom was empty before class began, he would jam a toothpick into the lock and break it off. When the teacher arrived and tried to unlock the door, the key would push the toothpick in farther. By the time the janitor was called and got it open, the period was half over and class got cancelled. Talking it over one day, several teachers realized they weren't the only ones who had found a scrunched piece of wood in the lock. So they compared which students they had in common. "Turned out to be Rod, me and the smartest guy in the school," said Cam. "They always thought it was me. I never squealed."

Though Rod kept up with school and joined a local pipe band, his relationship with his father continued to sour. The streets in the notoriously cold city were equally inhospitable. As generous as he could be with people who posed no threat to him, a kid looking to survive on those streets had to be mean and a little ruthless. Roddy was fast learning to be both.

Looking back, he couldn't remember exactly when he robbed a Shell station. But he remembered getting caught. Scared, he asked the police if there was any way he could avoid getting a criminal record. The cops knew him a little. They might also have known his father, still with the CN police, as every new promotion sent him a little higher up the force's hierarchy. Maybe they decided to help a troubled kid whose life was going wrong. Maybe they just used him. Whatever their intent, their proposal nearly got him killed.

The cops told him that a student at Windsor Park High School was selling drugs. At the cops' request, Roddy arranged to meet him at a popular restaurant where drug deals were common. It just so happened that our father and Cam had already developed an interesting working relationship with that establishment. "We used to be bouncers in a restaurant, if you could believe that," says Cam. "It was where the gang members hung out. It was called the Burger Bar. It was pretty rowdy in there." The tough clientele didn't deter the two friends from keeping the peace, even if they weren't getting paid to do it. Their compensation was more immediately satisfying: cheeseburgers and milkshakes.

Roddy kept the peace with diplomacy more often than force. "He'd be calm with people, not confrontational," said Cam. "Not looking for a fight, not bull against bull. He'd just go, 'Ah, buddy, you could probably kick our ass, but the boss doesn't need any trouble in here.'"

The police's scheme to catch the drug pusher went sideways when he showed up at the Burger Bar. He was a very popular high-school student and Roddy tried to keep him out of trouble. "When I saw it was him—and I liked him—I tipped him off," recalled Roddy. "I said get out of here. Well, that tipped everybody off to me."

The police hauled their target out of the restaurant and left Roddy behind. Their oversight wasn't lost on Cam, who ran outside and told the cops they were hanging Roddy out to dry if they didn't appear to arrest him, too. It would be obvious to anyone watching that Roddy was in on the sting. The cops went back in, grabbed Roddy and took him to a car. It was too little, too late.

The pusher was a good customer to a group of Winnipeg gangsters, and not the calibre of gangsters who hung out at the Burger Bar. These were serious men who weren't going to allow the loss of business to go unpunished. Roddy was back at school right away (in case people hadn't already figured out he'd cooperated with police), and the gang went to work on him.

As he approached his locker one day, a trickle of red was leaking from inside and pooling on the hall floor. He opened the locker to find his books soaked in blood and a pig's head staring out at him. Small dead things sometimes found their way into the lockers and desks of prairie kids, to make a point or just to get a rise out of a squeamish schoolmate. A whole pig's head was a statement of a different order. Roddy was in trouble. "All of a sudden," he said, "everybody fuckin' turned."

If the severed head wasn't signal enough that the drug bust would be avenged, he happened on another sign, one meant for more than just him. "On the drug dealer's court date, I went into the bathroom. I closed the stall door and carved into it was a coffin with a little cross in it, and 'Jan 23 Toombsday,' 'cause that was gonna be the day." It was a warning to anyone who disagreed, and a rallying call to others who wanted to avenge the student's arrest.

Toombsday arrived officially after school when a couple of bikers caught up with Roddy in an open field near his parents' house. "I was good with my hands, I was good. But they were much older than me. They got me, rolled me a little bit. But I could tighten up. A little bit of pain, but they couldn't get my teeth, my nose. I got balled up. They had a bike chain made into a belt." The kicks and punches and lashes weren't intended to kill him, exactly, just to kill any ambitions he might have harboured of challenging for their drug turf. "Things got pretty fuckin' testy there."

So many years later, you wouldn't expect anyone to get the facts perfectly straight about an emotionally charged episode like Roddy's Toombsday story. It says a lot about our father that, until he and Cam sorted out during their last visit exactly how it all went down, Roddy remembered events a little differently: "I went into the marijuana selling business," he said. "Other people were taking my turf over. So I went right to the cops." In Roddy's mind—which often understood everything bad that happened to him or those around him by way of his own guilt—he had made a very calculated decision: he would use the cops to burn a rival pot dealer. "I made up a story about how my sister had OD'd or died or whatever, and I set these guys up. I set up a buy and I told the cops, 'Yes, it's business, get them off my turf.'"

He did remember trying to warn the drug-dealing student to get out of the restaurant. But in his memory, he obscured that small act of grace with the belief that he had caused the whole mess. And to whatever degree the sloppy bust was not his fault, he believed the police were to blame. For decades he remained certain that after his criminal ambition had led him to co-operate, the police abandoned him: "Cops came in, saying I was a stooge. I denied it, but they sent people to get me."

When anyone had leverage over him, the one thing—and only thing—he trusted them to do with it was betray him.

With his departure from Toronto, Roddy left boxing behind. He played a few sports at school, but wrestling soon became his athletic focus. He quickly climbed the ranks of the local high school competitions but got frustrated when a wrestler from Louis Riel, the French school across town, proved impossible to beat. Losing to this kid drove him to distraction until he finally won the Manitoba 167-pound amateur wrestling championship. The amount of time he spent on the streets was giving him ample opportunity to practice fighting away from the mat and outside the rules as well.

Winnipeg had one of the country's largest French-speaking populations outside Quebec. The passing of Canada's Official Languages Act in 1969—which meant that government services in the whole country had to be offered in English and French—had put the multilingual city on edge, especially the English-speaking teenagers at Roddy's school, Windsor Park, and their rivals at Louis Riel. "A lot, a lot of street fights," remembered Roddy. French and English kids got along individually, but in sports or in large groups, small differences became big excuses to fight. "There were constant rumbles," said Roddy. I'm a WASP,

I wasn't allowed to date a French or a Catholic girl." Of course, he found a girlfriend who was French *and* Catholic—or at least had a French last name.

Roddy's amateur wrestling coach was a priest named O'Malley. Having some concern for the souls of all his young charges, O'Malley worried especially about the troubled ways of his star wrestler. Roddy remembered his coach sitting him down so he could consider an idea that might appeal to him.

"Father O'Malley says, 'You know, Roderick, this is what's going to happen to you. You're going to go out some night, you're going to be cold. You're gonna rob a 7-Eleven, they're going to catch you, they're going to put you in jail, they're going to rape you, then they're going to kill you.'"

You sure about this? wondered Roddy. Maybe his coach was just trying to scare him—and maybe Father O'Malley's warning became more colourful over the years with each time Roddy told the story—but the priest probably wasn't that far off the mark.

Rod's involvement in petty crime wasn't letting up. Being an effectively homeless teenager targeted by gangsters and on the outs with police was keeping him desperate. He was hanging his hat in whatever place would have him, trying to stay warm and safe. "There was some lady with an enclosed front porch on her house and there was a bed in there and a little toilet and electric burner. I don't know what I had to pay for it. Well, I do know. Don't know in money, but I had to . . . I kinda slept where I could." Roddy also hustled billiards. To get enough money to get in a game, he worked with a group of thieves who would take him to new car lots at night. "They'd have someone sneak in and take all the lug nuts off the tires and jack up the front. The tires came off. I could do two tires, one with each hand. Roll them out, around the corner, and into a U-Haul truck with a ramp. Twenty-five bucks. Boom. So I had money to go play pool and make what I could make."

Until that point, Roddy had been a hungry kid who broke the law so he could eat. But where do you draw the line between petty crime and the real thing? "I think that I was real close to becoming a career criminal. I didn't steal just to steal . . . yeah, I did."

One friend would follow him into variety stores. Roddy would go to the cashier and pretend he couldn't talk while trying to communicate interest in something. While the clerk was distracted, his friend would loot the back of the store. Rod wasn't always so strategic, impulsively grabbing the cherry lights off the top of police cars, for instance. But the constant misadventure was becomingly increasingly dangerous—to him and others.

He found himself outside a house one night with a BB gun. He didn't remember exactly why he shot out a window, but was pretty sure somebody had paid him to do it. The idea was just to intimidate whoever was inside, but the window shattered and glass landed near the woman who lived there. Her husband ran outside and came after Roddy in a car, with a few teenagers also giving chase. "I just ran. It was dark, running in this field and there's telephone poles." In the darkness and his haste, Roddy didn't see a guideline for one pole. "Bam, I hit the fuckin' wire. Motherfucker."

The other teenagers caught him and roughed him up. The man caught up and put some more fear into him, but for some reason he took pity on Roddy. "You're going to pay back every penny it takes to replace the window," the man said.

For all his thieving and fighting, Roddy wouldn't back down on a promise—though trying to make things right didn't necessarily make them better. He stole from church collections and showed up to the man's home with a bag of coins to pay his debt.

The man looked at the bag, imagining where the loose change had come from, and shook his head. "I never want to see you again," he said. And he didn't.

Cam got up to his share of trouble with Roddy. Still, some happier memories endure.

Cam was already a serious hockey player, with great potential to pursue the game at the highest levels. He wanted to join the Winnipeg Junior Jets, but in order to complete a necessary course in time he had to attend a particular high school. He and Rod went to the school to see if they could talk the principal into accepting Cam's transfer.

Roddy told Cam to wait outside while he went to the office. Cam waited a few minutes and Roddy emerged with a big smile. Perplexed, Cam asked him what had happened. Roddy had told the principal that his friend, who was too shy himself to come in and ask to transfer, had cancer and was only going to live for another six months. "You start Monday!"

Winnipeg was getting much too hot for the troubled teenager. At one point Roddy took off. He headed east, alone. "Toronto, I don't know why. I think I just ended up there. I stayed in youth hostels."

Hostels were cheap, and he made some money busking with his bagpipes on street corners. But cheap isn't free. "I robbed a dry cleaners, and I took off and went to Cheryl's."

Cheryl was living in New Brunswick and had recently had a baby daughter named Samantha. Roddy missed his sister. They hadn't seen much of each other during the two years after she left Port Arthur. He hadn't met his niece. It was a chance to get far away from all the trouble he'd endured—and caused.

Along the way, he lost his high school ID while hitchhiking. The driver who'd picked him up reported the missing ID, and Roddy's parents figured out where he'd gone. He stayed in New Brunswick with his sister only briefly and was soon in Winnipeg again. "I got back, and then it was a little rough there. I lost fear of reprisals."

During their visit in 2015, Cheryl asked, "Weren't you ever afraid of jail or criminality?" She'd left home by the time Roddy had seriously fallen out with his father and started getting into real trouble. Even decades later, hearing about some of the trouble into which he'd gotten himself as a kid, she was astonished. "No," he replied. "I don't have that fear in me." He added one of his patented contradictions to help her grasp his state of mind: "You're scared of so much that you fear nothing. You become comfortable with danger." He ended the story of the trip to New Brunswick with a hint of why he'd run in the first place. "I got in a lot of trouble with the law. I had to go to court. My father was pretty humiliated."

Roddy knew his father was disappointed in him, but to hear it out loud—that moment scarred him as deeply as the death of his dog or the woman in The Pas calling him a rapist. "I don't know what I did wrong with this boy," Stanley had said.

Ultimately, it wasn't fear of reprisal that straightened him out. It was a particularly successful rip-off that made him realize he'd crossed a line. His shame over victimizing the innocent—or the undeserving, at least—proved to be his saving grace. "There was a bar in Winnipeg. I could slip in and out of wherever I wanted to. Everyone kinda knew me." The bar would be the opening scene of an act Roddy called "the last illegal thing I ever did." He would do plenty outside the law, but nothing targeting the innocent. "I'm not very proud of this," he said, "but I did it.

"There was a guy, he was being a real asshole. I saw him open up his wallet. He had a ton of cash in it." Roddy didn't say what else the man was doing to raise people's ire, but flashing a wad of bills was never a good idea in Winnipeg's grittier bars. "I backed off and watched him. When it was time for him to go home, I followed." The man left the bar on foot and Roddy kept pace at a distance. "He decides to head to his back door. Well, it was dark back there and it was perfect timing. I was really, really fast. I've never seen anybody faster. I snatched him. This guy let out a sound like he knew he was going to die. It was chilling. I got his wallet and I was gone, but that sound bothered me. It bothered me a lot."

Roddy's empty stomach was bothering him, too, so he got in a taxi. "I went and bought a steak. I was hungry." That night the man's terrified cry kept playing over in his mind and wouldn't let him sleep. "So the next night, I went back to his house and I snuck in through the back door, and with the exception of the cab money and the steak money, I put his wallet back."

Merv Unger had arrived in Winnipeg from BC in 1971. He was an editor at the *Winnipeg Tribune*. He also helped local promoter Al Tomko run Manitoba for the Minneapolis wrestling promoter, Verne Gagne. The territory run by Gagne's American Wrestling Association stretched from Las Vegas to Chicago, and included Manitoba and parts of western Ontario. Winnipeg was Gagne's top location north of the border.

Unger remembered a skinny teenager walking into Al Tomko's gym. Father O'Malley's young amateur champion had come looking to train with the pros. "He showed up at the gym and wanted to become a wrestler. He was all of a hundred and thirty-five pounds."

Roddy was soon spending his nights sleeping on the wrestling mats in Tomko's gym. The gym was a regular training spot for professional wrestlers, and Roddy was eager to learn from them. They didn't exactly ease him into his education.

To pay some sort of rent to the gym, Tomko asked Roddy to do some chores. One was to maintain the dumbbells, the fixed kind that are a single piece of iron. "My job was to weigh them, paint the weight on the side." It wasn't much to ask a kid squatting in your gym to help tidy up the gear. Roddy had a mischievous side, though, and he didn't fit comfortably into any sort of structured environment. "I don't know what it is. I've had something in me since I was born. I thought it would be pretty funny. I took the eighty-five-pound dumbbells and painted sixty-five pounds on them. I adjusted all the dumbbells. Then the professional wrestlers came into town, from Verne Gagne's camp." While touring, Gagne's wrestlers trained in Tomko's gym, along with the ones who lived in Winnipeg. When they hit the weights that day, many of them found their strength lacking. "I laughed quite hard, until they put it together—it didn't take a genius."

One of the wrestlers in Tomko's gym that day was George Gordienko. "They were calling him Boy Wonder. He's what we call a real-deal shooter." Meaning that if the wrestling were totally real, he'd be one of the last guys standing. "He was kicked out of America for being a communist. "He went to Italy and met a woman who had horses. There was this one horse that was cantankerous, nobody could ride it. George actually got into the stall, very slowly. He got his arms around the horse, and just by slow pressure he choked the horse down. The lady fell in love with him and that's who he married. Gives you an idea of the power of this guy. I don't know much about horses, but a guy who can choke a horse out, he can choke me out."

In the middle of stories about fighting, Roddy would sometimes pause, worried he was coming off like a boastful thug. "Please, none of this was a guy trying to enhance his reputation, none of this was trying to be a tough guy. I was just wild. I was wild. I wasn't trying to build a reputation. Those terms didn't mean much, especially when you get beat up by George Gordienko." That day in Tomko's gym, he got seriously beat up by George Gordienko.

Gordienko, who died in 2002, began his career as a weightlifter, found himself a tag-team partner in Stu Hart (father of Bret "Hitman" Hart and the late Owen Hart) and competed through the 1950s in Hart's Stampede Wrestling organization in Calgary. In the early 1970s, he had nearly a hundred pounds on Roddy. And he knew how to use every single one of them to punish a man. "George was one of the guys who noticed I was being a smart aleck," said Roddy, "and he took me on those mats for forty-five minutes. I broke my foot. He suplexed me off the mat, onto the concrete. It was the first thing he did. He did it belly to belly, and as he did it, he threw me, and I ended up off of the mat so my foot hit the concrete, but with one hand still holding my wrist, and he very slowly dragged me back onto the mat. *Beat up*, let's qualify the term. Most guys don't really know what it is to get beat up. There's a hold called the Sugar Hold. After you get good at it you can almost do it with one hand. And what would happen is, they put their arm behind your head and between your arms, then lay on you, and of course the force . . . the blood has to go someplace, so some of the blood goes down toward your belly button and some of the blood goes toward your head. Comes out your eyes, your nose, your mouth, your ears. They'd hook you in that hold, then, like George was saying to me on the mats that day, I'm going to let you breath for ten, nine, eight, seven . . . two, one. I'm not going to let you breathe for thirty, twenty-nine . . . You'd pass out. Sometimes when he let you breathe, you could just come back. After forty-five minutes, you'd defecate yourself. That's called being beat up. Broke another couple bones."

A beating by an accomplished shooter like George Gordienko—administered while the other wrestlers looked on—would send most teenagers running. Roddy stayed. "As much as they beat me up, they kinda went, you know, the kid's got balls." Tomko and other wrestlers and coaches, like Unger, Tony Condello and Fred Pelloquin, began to train him.

Even when Roddy and Cam were trying to have fun, trouble found them.

In the prairies, a "social" was a party thrown for an engaged couple to help raise money for the wedding and give them a small financial push to get started in life. Bands played and of course there was lots of liquor to help separate guests from their paycheques. Young women and men flocked to these parties. The mix of booze, unattached young women and testosterone led inevitably to one thing.

"I fought five weekends in a row at these things," said Cam. "I remember one guy I fought, his name was Buckles. I fought him the year before, too, at a social. He was a tough dude. But I cleaned his clock."

A lost fight wasn't forgotten. Even with Roddy riding shotgun for his best pal, Buckles wasn't ready to leave well enough alone.

Roddy and Cam attended a social at a church one weekend. There was a weightlifter who used to try to intimidate Cam in the hallways at school. It never worked. Cam was on the dance floor with Sherilyn, his girlfriend, when the guy approached.

Some guys were giving the kid working the door a hard time and the weightlifter figured Cam, who never backed down, would be a good person to ask for help. When there was trouble, Cam and Roddy weren't far behind. "So there's a fight going on. There's a big guy on top of a little guy. I said, 'We gotta stop this, Rod, cause this guy's had enough. If I was on the bottom I'd like someone to break it up.'" Cam leaned in to the clearly beaten man on the ground and asked if he'd had enough. "He says, 'Yeah, I've lost.' And I said, 'Okay, let him up.' The guy on top says, 'No fuckin' way.'"

Cam pulled the man off anyway, ending the fight. But the guy on top wasn't alone, and his friend didn't like Cam breaking up their fun. The friend was Buckles. "Buckles comes in, pushes me and goes, 'Who the fuck do you think you are, buddy?' Now, when you street fight enough, you know—I'm going to have to fight this guy." Still Cam began talking to Buckles, making conciliatory overtures to calm him. They were at a wedding party in a church basement, after all. Buckles didn't care and kept advancing, "and I just drill him right in the mouth, as hard as I could."

Buckles was bloodied but unmoved. "He just stood there and said, 'I'm gonna fuckin' kill you.'"

Cam had given Buckles his best shot. Aside from a split lip, Buckles was ready to fight. "I go, 'Well, you know . . . and I hoofed him right in the balls as hard as I could.'"

Still standing, Buckles warmed to his theme: "You're dead," he growled.

Cam shot a worried look at Roddy. "I hit him hard as I could, I kicked him square in the balls. Rod's standing there and I'm saying to myself, *Rod, fuckin' hit him!*" But Roddy wasn't planning to intervene; he would never want Cam stepping in before he needed him. Roddy respected the rules of engagement enough to let his friend fight his own battles. Fortunately for Cam, his two hard shots finally took their toll. Before he could come after Cam, Buckles groaned and finally collapsed. "I'd be the one scrapping, Rod would just be the cool guy all the time," Cam said.

All these fights were won by paying a price in the gym. Cam was committed to conditioning in order to excel at hockey, even though he didn't yet have a pro career in mind. And Roddy, his ambition ignited by the opportunity wrestling was offering him, was taking their workouts a step further. "Back in high school, we were the old school," Cam recalled. "When you'd think you were done, we'd do another set. Every time, Roddy would push me to my limit. And I was game. But he would have me working so damn hard—and he would work just as hard—that as soon as I'd finish I'd have to go off to the side and puke. He would say, 'Do you want to be average or do you want to be better than average?' Well, I wanted to be better. I never wanted to be average and that was the same for Rod. It was a mental toughness, that's what it gave us. We just knew that this was the right thing to do for the future."

There were other escapes from Winnipeg. Not all were getaways. As a hockey player, Cam had summers free and the two friends hit the road. "You don't want to hitchhike for three or four days with someone," Cam said with a groan, "who says, 'I wanna learn how to play the mouth organ on this trip.'"

Roddy had the Anderson family's knack for music. And he sometimes learned a new instrument the hard way—maybe hardest for those who had to listen to him practice.

At eighteen, he and Cam hitchhiked from Winnipeg to Toronto, a couple of young men throwing their fortunes to the currents of summer one last time before their lives and careers got too serious. Rod practiced harmonica the whole way. "On the side of the road—he was brutal."

There's one route between Winnipeg and Toronto—the TransCanada Highway. On the first half of the journey there are very few places to stop. On the north-east shore of Lake Superior, clear across the lake from Port Arthur and right around the half-way mark from Winnipeg, is a tiny mining town called Wawa that developed a large reputation in hitchiking's heyday. "*Reader's Digest* said that was the worst spot to ever be caught hitchhiking," said Connor. "That's where we were stuck."

Roddy and Cam decided to take four-hour shifts standing at a fork in the road. With a hand-drawn sign reading "Toronto" and a thumb stuck out, Cam tried in vain to solicit the generosity of passing drivers. At the fork in front of them, the TransCanada veered to the west over the lake and a side road led north into town. Thousands of hitchhikers had been stuck on that same narrow strip of gravel and grass. They weren't much welcome in town, and picking up a couple of unshowered, brawny eighteen-year-olds would have appealed to very few passing drivers. The friends were in for a long wait. "I did my four hours and I'm looking forward to lying in the ditch, relaxing. I go, 'Okay, Rod, your turn.' He walks across the street to the gas station to talk to a driver at the pumps. I remember the guy's name. Tom Luck. And I see Rod talking to the guy, and he goes, 'C'mon!' I go, 'What? I want to lay down for four hours.' He'd talked the guy into giving us a ride. Rod could talk a bird out of a tree. Tom was heading to Montreal, so he took us to Toronto. Rod sat in the middle and I sat on the outside. Rod fell asleep."

Roddy nodded off, which wouldn't be a big deal except that Cam knew what he was like when anyone tried to wake him up. "When I'd go to his house to call on him, his mother would say,

'Rod's in his room, go wake him up.' I'd go up in his bedroom, he'd be sleeping and I'd shake his shoulder, 'Get up!' And fuck he'd start swinging, Holy . . . I'd barely get out of the way. Every time, he'd just start swinging. So then I started shaking his feet." With Rod dozing and beginning to lean toward Tom Luck, the seating arrangements in the pickup were becoming uncomfortable. "I told Tom Luck, 'This guy here?' He goes, 'Yeah?' I go, 'Toughest guy I ever fuckin' met. When he sleeps, I try to wake him up, he starts swinging, right away.'" Tom Luck decided to let Roddy sleep, and Cam soon fell asleep against the passenger-side window. When he woke up an hour or two later, Roddy was still unconscious, with one arm draped over the driver's head. "Tom was still driving, with a very worried look on his face. I go, 'Why don't you move?' He goes, 'Oh no!' I laughed my ass off. Tom Luck. He was a good guy. We'd still be in Wawa today without him."

Winnipeg to Wawa was a good twelve hours. Toronto was nearly that far again. When Tom Luck let Cam and Roddy out of his truck—to his considerable relief—they headed for its liveliest and grittiest commercial street. Home to record stores, strip clubs, head shops, massage parlours and more than a few unmarked doors, Yonge Street was an urban mecca for those who weren't easily spooked. "This speaker came on that said, 'We're going out of business, we're selling lighters for five cents and cameras for this much and watches and come on in here.' So we go in," Cam recounted.

They mingled with other curious bargain seekers inside. Shelving behind a long counter held all sorts of trinkets and goods. Once the store was full of people, a few men locked the doors and pulled down the blinds. They got behind the counter and announced to the crowd that they're going out of business and selling everything off cheap. "So, first the guy holds up a camera and says, 'Who'll give me forty bucks for this camera?'" Roddy and Cam look at each other, puzzled. Why would they pay forty dollars for a camera that looks like it's probably worth forty dollars? That's no bargain. "Then one guy in the front row goes, 'Well, I need a camera, I'll give you forty bucks.' So they say, 'Put it on the counter.' The guy puts his forty bucks on the counter and the guy puts the camera on top of the forty." The salesman moved on to another product, then stops. "He goes, 'You know what, buddy, you're the only guy who wanted this, here, here's your forty back and here's the camera.'"

The salesman went through the same routine a few more times with other items. Each time Roddy and Cam wondered why other people were getting excited about paying what they were sure was a regular price. And why, each time someone put their money on the counter, the salesman gave their cash back. "And then he comes up with watches. He said, 'Who'll give me twenty bucks for this, they're worth a hundred.' And we go, 'Oh, it does look pretty good.'" The pair thought about it. "There must have been fifty twenty-dollar bills on the bar, and he put a watch on each one. Then he goes, 'Anybody else want in?' But he'd run out of watches and he says to the other guy, 'We got some more watches for the next crowd, bring 'em out here and we'll get rid of them all."

The helper grabbed another box of watches and they started placing them on more twenties placed all down the length of the counter. Everyone in the store had seen this same pattern repeated over and over, and they were pretty sure they were going to get their money back. "And then he said, 'Now who'll give us twenty bucks for this empty bag?' So Rod and I, we dig into our pockets, and the guy says, 'I'm gonna fill that up with way more than twenty bucks' worth.'"

He didn't. The bags Cam and Roddy were left with were filled with worthless trinkets. "When it was all over he just took everybody's money, put it in his pocket and he left. Rod and I started laughing. We just got conned." The first people to put their money down had been in on the scam.

They walked to the police station and complained. The police didn't care. The deceit played people for suckers, but it wasn't against the law. Chagrined and broke, Roddy and Cam decided they'd get their money back themselves.

The shop closed at eight o'clock. Roddy and Cam waited in the lane behind it for the guys who'd run the scam. Eventually they emerged and locked up the shop. But they weren't alone. Two big men with a military bearing appeared as well. "Rod and I said, 'We don't care, we're gonna go over and confront these guys.'"

They approached the four men and Cam immediately lit into the scam artists. "You fuckin' took our money!"

As usual, Roddy took the opposite approach. "Rod, he's the civil guy, and he's talking polite to these guys. The guy said, 'You know what, you guys gave me the money, you thought you could get something for nothing, like everybody else in there. I did it legitimately. I've been in prison for five years and I sat there for five years thinking how I could perfect this. And you guys, you were suckers.' The guy said to Rod, 'Well, I like you and you guys said you were hitchhikers and you don't have any money left, so here, I'll give you twenty bucks.' He gives Rod twenty. 'But you! You get fuckin' nothin'!' So, another lesson learned from Rod."

Cam learned yet another lesson from Roddy on that trip, one about perseverance.

"By the time we come back from Toronto, he could play the mouth organ!"

A trained boxer and now training with pro wrestlers, packing on muscle with determination: Roddy's course seemed set. But all the turmoil in which he'd grown up still made for some unsettling moments, outbursts that belied his usually diplomatic ways. Too many years of not knowing where he was sleeping at night, too many beatings at the hands of the mentors and authorities in his life—the anger, frustration and pain could boil over. "In high school there was a skinny guy and he was on the basketball team," Cam began. "He was sitting at a bar with his fiancée, the bar Rod bounced at."

The drinking age in Manitoba had recently been lowered to eighteen. At a rough bar called the Windsorian, Rod got a chance to try his diplomatic ways with an older clientele than he and Cam had managed at the Burger Bar—and get paid for it, too.

Cam joined him there one night when Roddy was off duty. The basketball player, who wasn't very tough, needed to call on Rod's services anyway. "This guy came up to us and said, 'Rod, I might need you guys to help me out.' Rod said, 'Why?' He goes, 'See those guys over there?' 'Yeah?' 'They come over and told me I gotta let my fiancée dance with them and she doesn't wanna dance with them and I don't want her to, or else they're gonna just grab her by the hair and beat me up.' Rod says, 'Ah, don't worry about it.' So Rod walked over as polite as always and he said to these two, 'Guys, don't embarrass this guy. This is his fiancée, you know, he can't have you dancing with his girl and she doesn't want to dance with you. So just give him a break and I apologize if he's done something to offend you.' And that's it. He sat down. One of the guys walks over to where Rod's sitting and taps him on the shoulder. Rod looks over and the guy just fuckin' drills Rod right in the face. Knocks him off his chair."

The fight was on. Roddy beat him in the bar and then he and the other bouncers threw him into the parking lot. The troublemaker hadn't had enough.

"'You want to go again?' he asked. "Rod says, 'All right, you just committed professional suicide.'" Suicide by professional was more like it. "By now Rod's wrestling, and of course he can box, and he kicked the shit out of this guy."

Roddy and Cam got into more fights than either could count. It would be naïve to think there weren't some ugly moments. This turned out to be one of them. "When it was over, Rod says, 'You broke my watch.' Rod went over to the guy and gave him a couple more shots and then reached in the guy's pocket and took out whatever amount of money he needed to fix it. One of my friends said, 'Rod, you're gonna kill this guy.' Rod just backhanded my buddy right in the mouth. So my buddy goes, 'Fuck, go ahead then.'"

Cam knew the sickly high a fight could give a young man. "Once you start fighting it's hard to stop." He wasn't so troubled by the memory, though. Underestimating his friend on account of his initially diplomatic approach was a mistake he relished seeing bullies make. "Reach for a rabbit, grab a bear. I always love seeing those punks that pick on people that they think they can beat up. Well, you did that with Rod, just like that guy, he didn't know what he was getting."

In June 1973, Roddy began wrestling with the pros in front of an audience. In his earliest matches, he fought his teachers and some of the locals, men like Condello and Tomko, John Campbell,

Jason Myer. "We were in southern Manitoba, very early times," remembered Merv Unger. Roddy was wrestling against Dave Muir, who was managed by Unger. "I jumped off the top rope. I had a big cane at the time, and aimed it at Roddy. He ducked out of the way and I nailed my own guy."

With Muir levelled and his manager apoplectic over KO'ing his own wrestler, Roddy had what may have been his first victory. Unger chuckled, remembering the night. "That's all that makes up the game."

Roddy learned the game in Winnipeg and places within a day's drive like Brandon, Manitoba—home base for Condello's promotion, West Four Matchmakers, with local TV and seating in the arena for two thousand fans. Unger hosted the television broadcast from Brandon. "That's where Rod got his first microphone experience, which of course was the highlight of his whole career, how he could talk. He was a natural right off the bat." Unger gave the kid pointers on how to come across well, but he drew the line at any notion that he was responsible for Rod's success on camera. "I would never say I trained him. Either the guy's a natural or he isn't."

Unger would also take Roddy aside and discuss the matches coming up in Brandon. The beginner practiced his promos over and over, refining his verbal assaults on upcoming opponents until he was convinced viewers would be engaged. "Being in front of a microphone is just feeling comfortable and then being able to reach out to the people so they listen to you. Right off the bat, Rod could do it."

Roddy held to one piece of advice throughout his career. Viewers would never catch him threatening opponents with acts of violence he would never really commit: *I'll rip your throat out*, for instance. He was much more inclined to belittle his opponents, which angered their fans. That in turn drove the fans to the match to see the mouthy upstart get the beating he was due. "Wrestling is psychology," Unger said. "You've got to psychologically reach the people in your audience. That's what he was good at doing. Whether he was the young guy getting beaten up by Al Tomko, or if he was winning matches he would go in a different direction. It's inborn. It's not something you teach."

The young Roddy wrestled as far east as Dryden, Ontario, and across the border to Minneapolis, Minnesota, where he was beaten by a young American from Memphis, Tennessee. About five years older than the kid from Winnipeg, Ric Flair was barely more famous than the young jobber he pinned for the win.

Some of the matches gave Roddy a view of where wrestling could take him. Others made it clear that he had a long road ahead. Still, it beat trading punches with drunks at the Windsorian, which he could finally give up. Money was still tight, but wrestling was the only chance at a livelihood the world was holding out to him, and he'd gladly go hungry to pursue it. "Rod was always a happy kid," Cam said. "Gonna pay whatever price he's gotta pay to be successful in the wrestling world. He fought in the shittiest places."

One of those places was a logging camp in northern Manitoba. "Al Tomko kinda liked me," said Roddy. "Used to bring me perogies when I was hungry. So he hires a twin-engine plane and brings two midgets, two ladies and four guys. The midgets went, the ladies went, then the four guys, they had single matches. Then the four guys tagged up and had another match. That was the card.

"Well, the plane takes off. We're looking down and it's just pure forest. All of a sudden one of the midgets taps me on the shoulder and points to the left engine. I see oil coming out of it. 'Excuse me, Mr. Pilot, there's oil coming out of the left engine.' I swear to you, the pilot says, 'Yeah, she leaks a bit.'

"It was a pontoon plane. And it came down in a lumberjack camp. We got off the plane and there was no ring. There was a dining hall. They pushed all the chairs away and put a mat in the middle of it. And we wrestled. Tough crowd! Baby Jesus . . . We didn't do much hitting the ropes! However, we did what we could. As we're coming back to the plane, the pilot is filling the left engine with oil. But by the grace of God, we pontooned into wherever we had pontooned out of. We get in the van, all of us, and Al Tomko pulls into a park and that's where we slept that night. The girls got the van and I found a picnic bench.

"There was a PortaPotty and some bears." He rolled his eyes at the unending chaos. "I knocked over a PortaPotty."

Fortunately the wrestlers didn't often have to fight on the floor. Merv Unger described their ring truck, a cleverly devised trailer they towed to the smaller locations within driving distance. "One of the rings was actually the floor of the trailer. When we got into town the sides flopped down and we put on the ring posts and put on the mats and the canvas and the ropes and away you go." The portable ring was a cozy sixteen-by-sixteen feet, four feet short of today's standard. "I remember things weren't going too well," Unger said. Someone was helping Rod pay for a room at the Marlborough Hotel across the street from Tomko's gym, but the small-town fights weren't bringing in much money. "One night at the gym we had a gathering of all the guys. Did they want to continue? Rod stood in the middle of the ring and said, 'I don't care about you guys, but I'm gonna be a professional wrestler.' I figured, of all the guys there, [he had] about the least chance. Well at that weight, he was skinny. But he worked hard at it."

Roddy worked into the new year of 1974 and soon found himself facing another wrestling legend. Unfortunately, this one was in his prime. "We'd go in on Friday nights," said Unger, of the cross-border haul from Winnipeg, "to do the studio TV show in

Minneapolis on Saturday afternoon. He'd wrestle on TV along with two or three other Winnipeg boys."

Rod made the trip south with a few of Tomko's wrestlers for a Minneapolis TV broadcast on Saturday, February 23. He wouldn't be fighting any Winnipeg boy. Superstar Billy Graham was a giant for his time. At a hefty six foot four, Graham fighting a nineteen-year-old Rod would have looked—as Jesse Ventura described it—"like a father beating his son." Graham was a champion bodybuilder, and weighed well over 300 pounds at his peak. "It was brutal," recalled Roddy. "And then he had the nerve to say to me—he was trying to make me feel good—'Listen, I was a little short of time or I would have given you more.'"

Roddy made the trip to Minneapolis a few times while working for Tomko. "He got badly beaten by Mad Dog Vachon," said Unger, "and Pat Patterson, Nick Bockwinkel. . . . Those were three-hundred pounders and here's this guy. He was a bit of a rag doll at that point."

After filming the weekly matches on Saturday night, the wrestlers packed up Sunday morning and drove the five-hundred-plus miles home. "And then," said Roddy, "I just kept on going." The trips continued—south, east, west, north—as did the lopsided defeats.

If you've heard the story of Roddy Piper's first match, you might be wondering at this point if we missed something. He often said he fought his first match at age fifteen. He has called his fight with Superstar Billy Graham his second professional match, but it took place two months before the one he called his first. He was nineteen when he faced Graham.

Wrestlers in that era needed a story. With no Internet to provide constant correction, they devised more or less elaborate histories, and Roddy's fed nicely into his undersized, angry, picked-on persona. The chip on his shoulder made sense, the way he told it. But his story had other benefits. It erased all the trouble he got into in his late teens. If he had been on the road and in the gym from the age of fifteen, his teenage years of criminality couldn't have happened.

The idea of turning pro at fifteen is also impressive. It suits the Brawler, the guy with no past who lives for the fight, the giant-killer—all the tropes Roddy played for the camera in the years to come.

To call our father's made-up history a lie, though, is missing the point. He was selling a character—it was how wrestlers of his time made a living. Since wrestlers were so recognizable when out in public, they couldn't break with those stories when they were away from the arena. Kayfabe—the wrestlers' code that demands fictions about their characters and feuds never be exposed—kept the drama feeling real. Kayfabe kept a crowd's disbelief willingly suspended when a move in the ring or a recovery from a beating didn't look entirely true. It kept the vitriol at full volume, the seats full and the popcorn selling.

That's not to say that Roddy's origin story was all a fabrication. It might well have evolved over the years, blending true elements—living on the streets, coming fifth in a world bagpipe competition—in ways that got him through whatever reporter's question, promo or work he was facing. He owed his fans and his business convincing entertainment, not autobiography. Over the decades, fact and fiction fused, and he forgot the lines between them. Add a few undiagnosed concussions to the mix and chronic pain from a litany of injuries, and whenever he was asked for a story, he found it easier to just tell the story he'd been telling for almost forty years.

Merv Unger believed that even Rod's adopting the name Piper wasn't as he'd told it. "Pro wrestling was really big in Winnipeg in the 1950s," said Unger, "when they had the Madison Boxing and Wrestling Club. One of the top boxers in Manitoba was Dave Piper. That's where the name came from. That's the one Rod adopted."

That might be true. But we grew up with another story. A better story. And it signalled the beginning of the end for Roddy Toombs' tumultuous years in the city that gave birth to Rowdy Roddy Piper.

3

The Jesus Years

Merv Unger and Al Tomko ran into trouble with a Winnipeg card just a few days after Rod's twentieth birthday. "Somebody from Verne Gagne's promotion, maybe it was Buddy Wolff, somebody couldn't show up, got sick, missed the plane, whatever it was," said Roddy, "and Verne needed a substitute. Merv said, 'Hey,' 'cause I was in the gym . . ."

It was a big American Wrestling Association card at the Winnipeg Arena on a Thursday night. Verne Gagne's AWA was the big time. Roddy's previous television appearances were in a Brandon studio and the other fights had been small gigs in smaller towns. Suddenly Tomko was asking him to fight in front of nine thousand people. And he was going to get paid $25, which was a lot more than he'd been getting to fight in Brandon or the likes of Grand Forks, North Dakota.

He thought he needed to make an entrance, but he hadn't seen much in the way of big-time pro wrestling. Left to his own devices, he went to the one extracurricular element in his life that he'd held on to, much to his mother's relief. And he went large. "I went to my pipe band. I said, I don't know what to do and they said, 'We'll play you in.' So I had four bagpipers in full regalia, bass drummer, fully decked out, kilt, big furry hat—there's a big hole in that hat, where they keep a pint of Scotch—and two snare drummers, and then me."

Cam added a twist to Dad's first professional entrance. "Rod had no money, so we picked dandelions and he put them in a basket"—stolen from the Marlborough Hotel— "and as he's walking to the ring he's throwing dandelions at everybody." Rod had wanted roses, but they were more than he could afford. He was wearing plaid trunks and high-topped green boots.

Roddy remembered himself being a little bigger for his big-time debut than Unger does, but the extra pounds wouldn't have made a difference. "I'm a hundred and sixty-seven pounds. And the guy that I wrestled was Larry 'The Axe' Hennig. Three-hundred-and-twenty pounds of Nordic Viking." Wrestling fans from later years will recognize the name Hennig. The Axe was the father of "Mr. Perfect" Curt Hennig. "The concept of upstaging someone, I didn't understand that concept. Didn't take me long to learn it. Larry 'The Axe' Hennig was in the ring and I come down with these bagpipers. Holy cow. Lightning bolts came outta Larry's ass, and the fire in his eyes. The announcer didn't know who I was. I was a substitute. Nor did he give a damn. So, as I'm coming down, the announcer's looking, and he's gotta announce something. He sees the bagpipes and he goes, 'Ladies and gentlemen, from Glasgow, Scotland'—he's hummin' it—and he looks over at me, he knows my first name's Roddy, he sees the bagpipes, and he goes, 'Roddy the Piper!' That's how I got the name. The 'the' just got dropped."

Hennig's displeasure showed as soon as the bell rang. He crossed the ring and hit Rod hard. Rod began falling backwards through the ropes and was headed for the floor when Hennig grabbed him by the hair. He yanked Rod back into the ring and delivered his infamous finishing move, "the Axe."

"Larry just came over and creamed me. Busted open my eye, broke my nose. It lasted ten seconds. And that's with a one-two-three count. Seven. Took a second to get over to me, I'm sure. Or two. Now we're down to five seconds I lasted."

Afterwards, Rod sat in a dressing room, holding his bleeding and broken nose. The pipe band was long gone. Disappointed in himself, he was probably already reducing in memory what records show to have been a two-minute match to the moment-long massacre since enshrined in his own personal legend.

Roddy was excited to be owed $25, but wondered if he'd really need to go through another beating from the likes of Larry Hennig to make that much again. "I'm in the dressing room and my nose is broke and the blood is getting in my eyes," said Roddy. The promoter walked into the dressing room in penny loafers. He remembered the shoes because he couldn't bring himself to look the promoter in the eye. "I think he's going to dupe me out of my twenty-five bucks." The promoter was Al Tomko. And he paid up. "Kid, you did great! How'd you like to go to Kansas City?" "Will he be there?" asked Rod, meaning Hennig. "Don't worry," said Tomko, "we won't overmatch you again."

The problem wasn't being overmatched. He'd wrestled Superstar Billy Graham. The problem was that for all he'd learned about being in the ring, Roddy didn't know how he fit in outside it. That was a dilemma. He wanted to be accepted by the established wrestlers, but he didn't want to accept the place they had in mind for a kid whose trunks still stank like the high school gym.

The only other wrestler left in the dressing room was sitting to Roddy's left. Bald headed with a thick black beard and his lower front teeth missing, he wasn't as tall as Roddy, but he was a lot scarier. Black hair covered every inch of him save the top of his head. Carrying a good fifty pounds more than Roddy, he thoroughly intimidated the quiet kid bleeding in the corner. "Dog," said Tomko on his way out, "Kid needs a ride."

Roddy remembered the man Tomko asked for the ride as "one of the toughest street fighters—ever." A seventh-place wrestler at the London Olympic Games in 1948, Maurice Vachon won gold for Canada in the 1950 British Empire Games (they became the Commonwealth Games in 1954). For all the dignity that the pomp and ceremony of international sport should have lent the man looking him over in the bottom of the Winnipeg Arena, Roddy was much more aware that the guy's nickname was Mad Dog.

Tomko was gone. "Cocksucker?" Mad Dog said, in a thick French-Canadian accent.

Rod froze. He stayed silent on the bench, eyes forward. Did Vachon mean him? "Stupid cocksucker?"

There wasn't anyone else in the room. "Cocksucker, we get in the car or not?"

The ribs—the teasing and hazing of the new kid—had begun. "Mad Dog is a helluva guy," remembered Roddy. "He became one of my dads." Having such a poor relationship with his own father, he showed his affection for the wrestlers who taught him how to be a man by calling them his dads. "I fell in love with those guys. They'd teach me. Like they'd tell me to get naked and they'd put me in the trunk of the car. I'm not sure what I'm supposed to learn there, but that's what they did. The jack's sticking in my kidneys. . . .These sons of bitches go eighty miles an hour over every bump, hill and valley, any deer they could hit!"

The ribbing was relentless and it got a lot less comfortable before it got better. It was meant to prove something good about the new recruit or else weed him out. And it gave the old hands someone to take out their frustrations on.

As for sticking him naked in the trunk, the joke was that another wrestler would open the lid unsuspecting, and there would be the new kid, not so ready to impress.

Tomko sometimes smuggled Roddy across the border himself. Roddy didn't have proper ID, so he feigned sleep in the back seat while Tomko griped to the border guards that his lazy son wouldn't wake up. The guard would sympathize and wave them through. The fact that the promoter himself drove Roddy the 504 miles to Minneapolis says a lot about the value he saw in his young wrestler's future.

Other times, Roddy caught rides with whoever would take him. "I lived, breathed and ate as the lowest on the rung," Roddy said. "One story, I'm being driven from Winnipeg to St. Paul, Minnesota. We had to be there on Saturday morning, so we would leave at six o'clock Friday night and drive all night. It's cold, it's like thirty below. I had a baloney sandwich and a bottle of 7 Up. The two guys driving, one was Dave Muir and the other was Bobby Jones. They turned the heat off. I was really getting cold in the back seat. I was a really quiet guy. I said, 'Sir, could you just turn some heat up?' They started getting mad at me, saying, 'We're sweating up here.' It got cold to the point where all of a sudden my bottle of 7 Up [froze and] exploded in their car."

Much of this driving across the broad stretches of Manitoba and the northern states was taking place during an oil crisis. In the US, gas rationing came into effect. If your license plate ended in an odd number you could buy gas on only odd-numbered dates of the month. If it ended in an even number, you could buy it the next even number. This was a problem for wrestlers driving big cars full of heavy men for six or seven hours a day. Roddy was fast, and his young legs came in useful under the circumstances. "I remember having what they called a six-foot credit card. Six feet of water hose. As they're going, every farmhouse had on stilts a big tank of gas for their tractors. They called it 'pink gas.' It had a pink stain in it because farmers got it cheap. You got in trouble if you were caught with it in your car. But that wasn't *my* trouble. They'd give me the gas cans and they'd drive down the road a bit and I'd go suck some gas with the garden hose. Every farm had a German shepherd. I'd be running back with cans of gas, whipping the hose back behind me. I didn't speak any German, and this German shepherd didn't look like he liked me much, trying to bite my ass. I don't know how many times I did that. This was a daily occurrence for a while."

Wrestlers indeed made good teachers, but what exactly they were teaching was questionable. Big men coached in the art of hurting people, all in on a carefully guarded secret, often baiting thousands of frothing fans at a time, wrestlers didn't make much money and were used to getting nickel-and-dimed by promoters. The education suited the environment.

On another trip, Roddy got a ride with a wrestler known as Ivan the Terrible. Juan Kachmanian broke into the business twenty years earlier, and he seemed to have done all right for himself. He dressed well and drove a Cadillac. Roddy got in the back seat. No complaints about the heat this time. Just the radio. "He turns on the radio, AM radio, and it starts talking about aluminum siding—put it on the side of your house, your house will never get wet again! For a hundred and fifty miles this guy talks about aluminum siding."

After an interminable drive listening to this, Ivan pulls up to a roadside diner. "He stops the car and just leaves me." Roddy had $25 in his pocket—Canadian. He didn't expect the diner would accept it. But hunger was gnawing a hole in his stomach and he eventually followed Ivan inside. "By the time I make my way into the diner, he's at the counter. He's eating a salad, soup. I come in and . . ." Ivan didn't like the idea of the rookie sitting near him in public, and suggested in not so many words that he sit a little farther down the counter. A waitress—a real Polly "Flo" Holliday type—soon approached. Roddy ordered a glass of water. "I don't know what happened to this guy, but all of a sudden he looks over and says, 'Oh, little boy. You hungry?'" He speaks loud enough for the whole restaurant to hear, and then orders me steak and everything else he's having. "All of a sudden here comes salad and soup and steak . . . I'm eating like a king. He's eating like a king and he's talking to me like I'd known him all my life."

When that food was finished, he ordered lemon pie, so Roddy did too. Ivan's demeanour suddenly turned. He started yelling something about fighting in the war and Roddy disrespecting a veteran. Bewildered, Roddy watched as Ivan's face reddened and his mouth began to foam and he grabbed at his chest.

Sure Ivan was having a heart attack, Rod asked a waiter to call an ambulance. Ivan muttered, "No, you stupid shit, get me to the car." Somehow Roddy muscled the 285-pound man out of the restaurant and into the passenger seat. Panicking, he shut the door on Ivan's ankle, which caused him to erupt in more shouting. Roddy didn't have a license, but he got behind the wheel and took off down the highway.

The emergency ended as quickly as it began. Ivan stopped his choking. He flipped down the sun visor and wiped his mouth clean. He tidied himself in the mirror. He also spit out the remains of an Alka-Seltzer.

Roddy kept driving. The stunt to get a free meal was like something he would have done. After these painful years of wandering, could it be that in the carnival-like world of pro wrestling he'd finally found a home?

Promoters knew enough to inject fresh blood into their cards. Verne Gagne would swap wrestlers with the promoters of other territories so the new faces and angles—storylines, in wrestling terminology—would keep his audiences intrigued. By late 1974, Roddy had several dozen pro matches under his belt, piping his own way down to the ring each time. Gagne started sending him farther afield to places like Waterloo, Iowa, and Kansas City, Kansas, and to St. Louis, where he was curiously billed as Ronnie Piper. In all likelihood it was an oversight on a promoter's part. If a preliminary's name was spelled wrong, a promoter was hardly going to replace his posters for the sake of correcting it.

"They put me in a van with six other wrestlers, including two ladies—they were all as hairy as Larry—and snuck me over the border. I became expendable. I didn't have a social security number. I didn't have a name. Nothing. I was very handy for a gypsy organization like professional wrestling at that time. And they hated me, the wrestlers. It wasn't like I had my first match and then became a star the next day and I'm throwing around Andre the Giant."

It was in St. Louis that he first traded blows with a wrestler nearly thirty years his senior whom WWF fans came to know as a sidekick of Vince McMahon, the Oxford-accented and properly English Lord Alfred Hayes. Hayes would become a friend and mentor to Roddy, but there were dues to be paid first. These dues weren't pretty, but Hayes and the other wrestlers thought they were at least good for a laugh.

Thinking he was alone in a dressing room, Roddy was changing after a match when a toilet stall burst open. Sitting on the can with a handful of himself was Ken Ramey. When you make a living blowing into bagpipes, a gesture like this could be taken the wrong way. And if it was a joke, what's the point if there's no audience? There was no one else around. For a kid off the streets, being molested is an ever-present threat avoided only by constantly, ferociously watching your back.

Roddy didn't think the jerk-off humour was very funny. He was a long way from home, and home itself was hardly home. "I got nowhere to go," he remembered thinking. The jokes were only getting started.

Another day, another dressing room, Hayes came running buck naked and swinging his penis like a club, charging Rod as he was getting out of the shower. Hayes took it a step further one night in Kansas City. Roddy was having a rare talk with NWA president Bob Geigel. Listening intently to Geigel—"Yes sir, Mr. Geigel"—Roddy leaned over a massage table on the back of his hands to better hear what Geigel had to say to him. "And while I'm listening, I don't know, something's wrong."

Something dropped into one hand, but Rod, like any eager young professional talking to a boss, wanted to show Geigel he had his full attention and ignored whatever someone had handed him. Geigel appeared distracted, and Roddy finally looked down. The thing in his hand was Hayes' penis, sitting in his palm like a rolled-up diploma bestowed on a college graduate. "I turned around. My face was red, and there was nobody in the place I could beat up."

He didn't know it yet, but he was graduating—in pro wrestling's peculiar way—from the fraternity's school of hard knocks. Or at least he was being accepted to study with the graduate class.

For the moment, though, Roddy was fed up. He started waiting in the car for his matches. He went looking for the gym at every arena so he could shower somewhere other than the dressing room. He went so far as to carry his wrestling bag to the ring and leave it there for the show, then collect it at the end—anything to avoid older, naked men. He didn't always find a gym. He started to stink. The other wrestlers had no idea how hard their ribbing was impacting the skinny kid from Canada.

Finally Geigel told him to relax, they were ribbing him because they liked him. The hazing was their own way, albeit a sexually deviant way, of accepting him. And soon things changed. The pros started teaching him all he could absorb about wrestling and life on the road. And the fresh-faced young athlete was also proving useful. Women hesitated to approach the beat-up–looking giants at the end of the bar, but if they were as nice as the good-looking blond kid chatting them up and suggesting they go meet these fine champion wrestlers, maybe the women could be convinced to go say hello.

It was during one of these Midwestern swings that Roddy learned to be cautious of a much graver threat to his professional well-being than the pseudo-sexual hijinks of his co-stars.

For whatever reason, in the bowels of an arena in the Midwest, a promoter began screaming at one of the older wrestlers, a black fighter weighing over three hundred pounds. The promoter—or the "P" as Roddy was learning to call them—was a much smaller, pot-bellied white man. "You stupid fucking nigger," he berated the wrestler. Wide-eyed, Roddy awaited the P's comeuppance, which he presumed would be immediate and bloody. It never came.

The wrestler, a man Roddy respected and liked—another of his "dads"—accepted the verbal barrage with slumped shoulders and a hanging head. Rod looked on, angry but silent—if the wrestler wasn't standing up for himself, he wouldn't want a kid barely half his size opening his big mouth in his defense. Roddy's anger soon dissipated. This was just depressing. He'd guarded himself against domination by others on the street as studiously as he'd avoided sexual exploitation. Letting someone get the better of you without a fight was just a recipe for further suffering. Something was going on, he realized, but he couldn't understand what it was.

What sank in finally was that the wrestler had a family. Getting thrown out of a job just to preserve his dignity in an encounter witnessed by no one but his peers—most of whom had been through a version of this themselves, if minus the racism—meant going home to his family empty-handed. Wrestling was his job. He needed the money. Suffering the P's bullshit sucked, but the hulking wrestler put his family first.

Lesson learned.

Roddy was growing in confidence and style as he travelled with Gagne's wrestlers through Minnesota and central Canada, and getting swapped in and out of the Midwest promotions. He was learning the tricks of the trade, too. The most enduring was a simple manoeuvre familiar to anyone who ever watched him wrestle, because he learned it at the beginning and never stopped using it. It proved particularly useful at the age when his body was no longer up to his own punishing high-energy style. "In the Winnipeg Arena there's two guys, shooters, one guy's name was Horst Hoffman, from Germany, and Billy Robinson," he explained. Shooters routinely hurt less experienced wrestlers in the ring for their own pleasure as much as the crowd's entertainment. "The guys are pretty fucking handy. They get in that ring and if you don't know how to defend yourself, you could be in a world of fucking trouble. They're bad guys and they enjoyed doing it."

Hoffman and Robinson and a few others had hooked up with some young women the night before. Too young for Larry Hennig's liking. The Axe was a family guy. Sitting across from them in the dressing room, he got quickly fed up with hearing about their exploits. According to legend—Roddy claimed Al Tomko told him this story and that it happened only months before Roddy started wrestling pro—Hennig told them to shut up about the girls. Hoffman didn't appreciate the advice. "They start having words. Horst Hoffman starts walking slowly toward Larry. The words are getting less and a little quieter, and Larry stands up and pokes Horst Hoffman right in his eyes. It's over and they just sat down."

In a wrestling repertoire that included endless punches, kicks and basically strangling his opponents until they passed out on the mat, Roddy's eyeball poke was comically quick and subtle. The move was usually over before the audience even knew it had happened. He still cracked up to think of its origins. "Everybody thinks it's the three stooges! HH is a big shooter," he laughed, making the trademark two-finger jab to show how little it had taken Hennig to subdue the braggart.

He was learning, and bit by bit he was also putting on the muscle he'd need to put all that learning to good use. In January 1975, Rod got his first taste of life in a distant territory. "When

Rod wanted to go someplace in the bigger time, Verne Gagne got him booked into one of the other territories," said Merv Unger. "Once you start going from one territory to the next, you build up a reputation and that's how Rod did it."

Gagne sent him to Dallas, Texas, where Fritz Von Erich and his family ran Big Time Wrestling out of the Sportatorium. Von Erich was born Jack Adkisson. He'd left Texas in 1957 for Edmonton, Alberta, hoping to land a job in the Canadian Football League. He didn't make the CFL, but he did run into Stu Hart, who taught him to wrestle and helped him conceive his Nazi villain character, Fritz von Erich. His sons adopted the surname when they followed him into the family business.

The Dallas accommodations that Von Erich afforded the twenty-year-old from Canada left very little to be desired. "I stayed in the Alamo Plaza Hotel," said Roddy. "I'm the only guy ever to get kicked out. Nobody gets kicked out of the Alamo Plaza. They don't even clean the rugs, they just put another one on top of it . . ."

It was while wrestling in Texas that Roddy first met Kerry, the Von Erich brother with whom he would bond most closely. "The boys were in school," Roddy said. "We would hang around and drink together." Kerry was the fourth son in the Von Erich family, and still a high school track and field star at the time Roddy was working Texas for Fritz and the family's booker, Red Bastien. Kerry Von Erich kept a surprising secret in later years after joining his father's wrestling promotion. He had lost his right foot after a motorcycle accident and went so far as to shower with his boots on to hide his prosthesis from the other wrestlers and staff. Getting to know Roddy so young developed a trust that lasted the rest of Kerry's short life. "I loved him so much. An incredible athlete. Because I'd known him—he had heeled a room with me, meaning one guy gets a room and two guys split it—he didn't mind taking his leg off with me."

Years after Roddy's first trip to Texas, he and Kerry were rooming together at the Miami Marriott—or Merry-rot, as they joked—after Kerry had joined the WWF in the '80s. Using an old wrestler's trick, they'd extended the security latch on their room door so it would stay ajar. That way they wouldn't need to get out of bed when room service arrived. It wasn't room service that saved them that night, thanks to the open door. "I don't know really what we were thinking. There was allegedly a joint around . . ." The pair climbed out their window and onto a ledge barely wider than their feet were long. "I remember having to push back, 'cause the wind was really strong up there." Then the wind slammed the window shut, locking them outside.

The pair weren't particularly phased by their predicament. "We really didn't mind. We were just talking for a long time."

Looking out over the Miami skyline at night, they had a lot to talk about. Two of the six Von Erich brothers had committed suicide. Roddy might have been shy, but he never had trouble talking privately with a friend. He knew enough about the darkness in men's souls to relate to the turmoil that haunted the Von Erich boys. Kerry took his own life in 1993, but for that night he'd found a good listener in Roddy. Fortunately, their high-risk conversation was interrupted by friends. "Big Boss Man and Curt Hennig came by for a beer and pulled us in." Roddy told this story in 2014. "Out of all those guys, I'm the only one alive." Wrestling drew rough men. It encouraged them to live hard and it put them under great pressure to perform or be replaced. Even the toughest could crack.

Like everyone else, Texans would come to know Roddy in a big way a decade after his first trip to the state, but to those who were watching he endeared himself during that first trip. One Friday night at the Fonde Recreation Center in Houston, it was time to stand for the national anthem. The record skipped.

A local newspaper described it in comically overheated terms: "a raucous sound that blared out of the City of Houston owned p.a. system did not resemble a demonstration of respect for our nation." (As Merv Unger did in Winnipeg, promoters and their staff often wrote the local wrestling dispatch, which explained the entertaining language.)

Seeing a hall full of patriotic Texans standing with hands over hearts and looking none too pleased about the anthem, Houston promoter Paul Boesch sensed an opportunity. Boesch called Roddy up to the ring, pipes in hand. In a stroke of luck that suggests more to do with wrestling angles than wrestling's angels, Roddy just happened to have been practicing "The Star-Spangled Banner."

In the audience that night, and every Friday night in Houston, were two brothers who were fanatical wrestling fans, Tom and Bruce Prichard. They saw every match Roddy fought in Houston, usually at the Coliseum, except nights like this when concerts bumped wrestling to the Fonde Center. "Everybody stood up and clapped for him. Roddy couldn't have been more than twenty, twenty-one years old. He played it very well. I do remember that," said Tom. As a heavily decorated veteran of the Second World War, Boesch was greatly esteemed locally, and the idea of a Scottish kid saving the night by playing the national anthem on his bagpipes was irresistable to Boesch's audience. "Paul being a war hero, of course very patriotic and very ingrained in the community—it was great."

In an added bit of good fortune, Roddy won his match against Don Serrano that evening, which didn't hurt his future value as a draw with the Houston audiences.

He wrestled throughout Texas until mid-April. He acquired three things of great personal value. One was his white 1973 Chevy Vega. The second was a piece of insight that he held near to his heart for the rest of his career. In the Houston dressing room, Johnny Valentine, a legendary wrestler and father of future star Greg "The Hammer" Valentine, grabbed Roddy when he accidentally got in his way and pushed the young guy against a wall. "I can't convince you wrestling's for real," Valentine said, "but I can sure as hell convince you I'm for real." Roddy would use that same line in countless interviews.

The third thing he found in Texas was someone to watch his back and keep him company at night, a pit bull he named Kayfabe. The dog had a problem with seeing its own reflection and Rod had to throw a sheet over the mirror in his room at the Alamo. The dog also had a problem with the hotel owner's poodle, which he beat up one day. This is why, in what had to be a first for the run-down Alamo, the owner kicked the boy and his dog out. Likely this is also why Roddy took to sleeping in the car, a habit he'd find very useful in the weeks to come, because his modest but successful run in Texas was done.

Winnipeg was still home, though Rod was weaning himself from his roots. When he got back in April, he stayed at the Marlborough Hotel. But Kayfabe wasn't exactly housetrained and soon got them tossed out of a second horrible hotel, this time for shitting in the halls. The dog hadn't spoiled Rod's good name at the Windsorian, though. This was good, because they needed some place to park the car while they were living in it.

Cam Connor explained: "Rod would take his Vega, park it at the edge of the parking lot, roll the back window down, take his dog food and pour it all on the floor of the car and leave a big tray of water. And that dog lived in the car." The pit bull jumped through the open window to come and go as it pleased until Rod returned from the road. Nobody touched the Vega. It was just as well, because it's tough to find someone willing to dog-sit a pit bull belonging to a homeless wrestler, even his best friend. "I had a dog," says Cam. "He woulda eaten it."

Or so you'd think.

When Rod drove to Cam's home one day, Pepper, Cam's cocker spaniel, was outside when the Vega pulled up. Kayfabe leaped out and made a beeline for her. Roddy couldn't act quickly enough to get between the dogs. Pepper started barking and, for whatever reason, the incoming pit bull turned tail and jumped back in the Vega. Cam didn't get many chances to upstage his buddy, but he was proud of his dog.

Rod had brought one more thing home to Winnipeg. A recommendation.

In Dallas, the Von Erichs' booker, Red Bastien, was a small, quick wrestler himself, who had grappled with the likes of Verne Gagne in the fifties. Bastien knew a few things about talent: as a trainer, he would later help groom both the Ultimate Warrior and Sting. Bastien had been impressed with the quiet, lanky kid in plaid trunks, who lit up like a pro in front of the camera. An almost entirely losing record over Roddy's final month in Texas suggests he was also willing to play his role and pay his dues in order to earn a shot.

Bastien had called a friend in Los Angeles, Leo Garibaldi, who was booking the legendary Olympic Auditorium. Garibaldi had an eye out for new talent. Texans had liked the kid, win or lose. With his beaming smile and blond hair, Rod struck Bastien as an ideal babyface for California. Garibaldi agreed. He'd give Piper a try if he stopped in Los Angeles for a few days on his way to San Francisco, where Bastien figured Rod could season for a while in Roy Shire's Northern California promotion. That would give them all a clearer sense of the young wrestler's talent. There was no need to rush. In those days, main event–calibre wrestlers were usually in their late thirties or early forties. Younger men weren't trusted with that burden.

Winnipeg had been a tough place to come of age, and Rod was done with it. It was time to get out. California was waiting. If he was ever going to be a star, where better to make it happen? He was a long way from great, but he had been good enough to get in, and he was committed. One commitment cost another.

For all his wandering, Roddy's girlfriend was still in the picture. She'd found an apartment her boyfriend could afford, now that he was earning some legitimate money. On the streets of Winnipeg, Rod had come face-to-face with the worst direction his life could take, and now the only things between him and a huge opportunity were hard work and endless miles of highway. He could handle the pain and he could handle the miles. He couldn't handle the idea of settling down. He had seen enough of domestic life to know the heart he would break by leaving would be broken worse if he stayed.

As spring turned to summer, he packed up the Vega with a head full of California.

"He left Winnipeg and didn't take anybody's phone number with him," Cam said. Guilt nagged him, but it didn't stop him. "He went out and accomplished what he wanted in life."

California would have to wait for the new year, though. First, Roddy was headed back to the Maritimes. This time he wasn't there to stay out of trouble. He wanted trouble, and he wanted to get paid for it, too.

On Sunday, July 13, 1975, "Rod Piper" debuted against Rick Hamilton at the North Sydney Community Forum in Nova Scotia.

In the Maritimes, a young guy who entered the ring in a kilt and playing bagpipes was bound to go over well with audiences—Latin for "New Scotland," Nova Scotia comes by its name honestly.

One local paper reported his debut: "Rod Piper, a newcomer from Scotland, electrified the fans with his speed and wrestling ability, taking the measure of seasoned Rick Hamilton at the seven minute mark. Piper caught Hamilton in an airplane whirl and finished him off with a body press. Both wrestlers showed a lot of class but Piper was the darling of the fans."

Roddy was in yet another new place, but with familiar company. Bulldog Bob Brown had fought him in St. Louis (Unger speculated that he might have been the person who saw Rod in Winnipeg and suggested he be brought down to Kansas City). Brown and another familiar face, Lord Alfred Hayes, appeared on almost all the same Maritime cards as Rod. Community centres in New Glasgow or Fredericton were a step down from the Midwestern cities where he had cut his teeth, and they were certainly small-time after places like Dallas and Houston. But the kid suddenly had a chance to be a bigger fish in a small pond, especially a pond with an ingrained crush on anything Scottish. He was learning, honing all he'd been taught since he'd come into the business only a couple years before. And despite their rocky introduction to each other, Roddy had a mentor in Hayes. "I loved him," Roddy told *Kayfabe Commentaries* in 2014. "He never swore. He taught me the piano. He taught me where to put the fork. He taught me about England and Scotland, and he would correct my grammar. We would talk about Shakespeare . . . In this dysfunctional family, he taught me honour, he taught me class." It would take years for that relationship to develop, but for now what they were developing beat getting chased naked around the dressing rooms of the Midwest.

Best of all, in the Maritimes the drives were shorter than trucking back and forth from Winnipeg to Minneapolis. Roddy made some of those drives with the boss, Emile Duprée. "Emile Duprée, when I wrestled for him, would buy twenty-four bottles of Schooner that we would all chip in on. As Emile would finish his third beer, he would take the beer caps that he had kept in his top pocket, count them, then take what was left of his six so nobody else would get them. In case you didn't get it folks, he was the promoter."

As much as Roddy was learning at the sides of more experienced wrestlers, he was always smart enough to learn the most valuable things by just watching and listening. "The best time I saw with Emile was one night, driving with Don Leo Jonathan and Emile, and Emile said, 'I don't know, Don, it was a helluva house, but I think I deserve some of the credit too.' Don Leo said back to him, 'Emile, you can have all the credit. Just give me the money.' That was about the hundred and fourth wrestling lesson I learned that day."

At six foot six, Don Leo Jonathan was a giant for his time. He was a little smaller when he first broke into show business. "Don Leo Jonathan was one of the Little Rascals," recalled Roddy. Jonathan actually had a small role in *Our Gang*. He was a Little Rascal like Cam Connor was "captain" of the Montreal Canadiens (as Roddy often mistakenly described him)—it never hurt your professional reputation to be a friend of Roddy Piper. Jonathan continued with film and television but, according to Rod, was kicked off a movie set by John Wayne because Jonathan overshadowed him.

Also critical to the success of the Maritime circuit, as promoters and wrestlers, was a family named Cormier. Its most famous son went by the ring name Leo Burke or Tommy Martin when touring the States (French-Canadian names didn't help a wrestler connect with fans in the likes of Missouri or Texas). His brothers fought as "The Beast" and Rudy Kay. "Leo Burke was a real fine man, from a fine family," said Roddy, "and his brother The Beast took me under his wing." In Halifax, Rod wrestled "Mad Dog" Michel Martel, who would die after a match in Puerto Rico in 1978, a year before Rod befriended his younger and much more famous brother, Rick. Rod was too young and too full of steam to notice a trend yet, but the number of friends in the business who were dying young would become hard to ignore.

Roddy also wrestled the great Lou Thesz in the little studio of Halifax TV. When the bell sounded, he made the mistake of antagonizing one of the most devastating wrestlers of his time.

"Come on, ya old bastard," he said.

Lou Thesz took offense, as you'd expect, but surprised his young opponent with how he expressed it.

"Referee, you tell him to watch his language," he said.

The match didn't last long, but Roddy did manage to cover Thesz for a one count. As a result he remembered the match with some pride, but ended the story with a note of humility.

"I'm a fast man," said Roddy. "I'm a fast cat. I covered Lou Thesz, he kicks out. And I winged up to my feet, and there he is standing looking at me. Okay . . . It was just downhill from there. I was so happy when the three taps on the mat came. I'm still alive. It's quite an honour."

Come November, International Wrestling—the promotion in the Maritimes before Emile Duprée founded Grand Prix Wrestling in 1977—shut down for winter. Snowfall through New Brunswick and Nova Scotia is notoriously heavy, rendering the highways too unreliable for a travelling roadshow working back-to-back dates. The other wrestlers packed up and headed west, where Stu Hart's Stampede Wrestling ran through the other half of the year.

Roddy was finally headed west, but not to Alberta. He got in his Vega, ears ringing with the crowds' approval, and aimed for the place he was sure would finally make him famous.

"Who the hell are you?"

Roddy answered that Red Bastien had sent him, from Texas.

The booker at the Olympic Auditorium in Los Angeles wasn't exactly sitting on his hands waiting for Roddy Piper—straight outta New Brunswick. Garibaldi looked at him skeptically.

Stereotypes sometimes originate from a kernel of truth. If anyone in Los Angeles were to imagine a young Canadian showing up to wrestle, he'd look a whole lot like Roddy that day: a grinning guy in jeans and a plaid shirt with a sheathed buck knife strapped to his belt, pulling up in a well-worn Chevy with a big dog hanging its head out the window. "The locker room is down there," Garibaldi said.

Photos of wrestling and boxing greats decorated one wall along the way. Roddy thought out loud that he'd like to see himself on that wall. Garibaldi asked if he had a photo he could put up. Roddy balked. He'd earned every step he'd taken so far; he'd earn his way onto the wall, too. One day. "We used to say the mat in LA was poured in 1807," he remembered. "The Olympic Auditorium at one time was like the Madison Square Garden of the West Coast. There may have been a time when it rivalled the Garden. Back in the late fifties, sixties, that's when it carried Gorgeous George and every fight you ever wanted to see. All the ladies would have mink fur coats on, all the guys would be dressed in suits. It was a big deal."

A hulking stone block, the Olympic Auditorium opened in 1925 in anticipation of the 1932 Los Angeles Olympic Games.

It was the largest indoor venue in the country. By the time Roddy showed up, the polish was still very much on its Romanesque relief columns and wreath above the main entrance, on S. Grand Avenue. It hosted concerts and other entertainments, but it was the fights that kept "the O" so vital to Los Angeles social life. "TV would shoot every Wednesday and the house show was every Friday. I still remember the phone number: *RI. 9-5171, Get your tickets now.*" Those tickets were a whopping five dollars. A dollar fifty for kids. The Olympic not only had televised wrestling, it had a continent-wide audience for its Spanish-language broadcast, and a metropolis-sized audience clamouring for Friday-night tickets. Roddy had worked in some big cities, but LA was on a scale beyond his imagining. He hoped his success might follow suit. "When I got to the O, that was the first time that someone gave me a break, to try to be a main eventer."

That break took a while.

Garibaldi was the booker, but the Olympic's wrestling and boxing business was run by a boss unlike any Roddy had ever met. Aileen Eaton was perfectly suited to the epicentre of the showbiz world. Born and raised in Vancouver, the five-foot-two redhead had married LA boxing promoter Cal Eaton and soon gotten involved in the family business. He died in 1966 and Aileen took the reins of the biggest fight promotion west of the Mississippi. If a diminutive woman from Canada wrangling the biggest names in boxing and wrestling in the 1960s and '70s surprises you, consider her mind for the business.

In 1962 "The Redhead" pinned a button on the lapel of a little-known Olympic gold medalist before a press stunt to announce his first pro boxing match at the Olympic. It read "I Am the Greatest." The boxer was too modest to accept it but she, realizing the press attention he was about to receive, wouldn't take no for an answer. He finally took her advice, and before long Cassius Clay would adopt the slogan on Eaton's little button as his tagline. Eaton knew what she was doing. About twenty years earlier, she'd helped create Gorgeous George, wrestler George Wagner's flamboyant remake into one of the industry's most memorable and successful personalities. You didn't work for Aileen Eaton and not learn how to sell. And if you wanted to sell in Los Angeles, you worked for Aileen Eaton.

Eaton had two sons with her first husband, the late Hollywood surgeon Dr. Maurice LeBell. One of them, Mike LeBell, worked for his mother as a wrestling promoter. Her other son was a little more hands-on. Gene LeBell was a judo and wrestling champion, and when he wasn't fighting, announcing or training wrestlers in his dojo, he worked as a Hollywood stunt man. Both men would have an impact on Roddy; one he would call a dear friend for the rest of his life.

Roddy got started on the third Friday in January, fighting Tony Rocco and taking part in a Battle Royal that included Bob Orton Sr. He was making a habit of getting beaten up by his contemporaries' fathers, which punctuates just how early in life Roddy started his pro career. "Piper was supposed to work a longer period for us after doing [Roy] Shire up in San Francisco," Garibaldi told an interviewer before his death in 2012. "But after I got a load of Piper in January of '76 as a face against Tony Rocco, trying to play his bagpipes but having a difficult time, I asked him and Shire to allow me to put Piper on the following Tuesday card in San Diego as a face. He got over like gangbusters."

As much as he'd started to get around the continent and make a name for himself, Roddy was still raw. They decided to keep him in LA and were ready to invest in him. He could perform and rile up a crowd, but fighting some of these men was taking a toll. Win or lose, Roddy was still a lanky twenty-two-year-old getting pummelled—sometimes in a very real way—by much stronger fighters. Investments need to be insured. It was time someone taught Roddy how to defend himself like the pros did—when the audience was watching, and when they weren't.

"During this time," Roddy remembered, "I ran into a fella named 'Judo' Gene LeBell. Gene LeBell was the toughest man in the world, and not according to him. He trained Bruce Lee, Chuck Norris, I can't tell you how many. He started to teach me how to defend myself, in a professional manner, in a big-time way." By this, Roddy didn't mean playing nice until someone gave him a hard time. "You're not really defending—you're offending and breaking bones."

At the age of eighty-three, Gene LeBell spent only two hours a week in the Hayastan dojo he operates with long-time business partner Gokor Chivichyan. He met with Ariel during those two hours, and, to the aggravation of everyone at the dojo keen for a moment of his time, he gave her an hour and forty minutes. He didn't think twice about the time. "He started off as a preliminary here," recalled LeBell, meaning in Los Angeles. Roddy would fight in the early matches and help flesh out a card anchored by much bigger names—Lou Thesz, the Guerreros, the Sheik—much as he'd done everywhere else he'd fought. "Lou Thesz or Karl Gotch or somebody told him come on down and work with Gene, 'cause he's mentally sick and he'd like that," LeBell joked. But like most of LeBell's jokes, this one has some truth to it. "My belief is, you'll never be good, really good, unless you're a sadistic bastard." In the seventies, LeBell ran a dojo around the corner from Paramount Studios in Hollywood. Roddy was drawn to it like an eager freshman to an Ivy League library: all the knowledge he ever wanted to possess could be found within its walls. "He was a very good boxer," said LeBell, or "Uncle Gene" as Roddy (and eventually we) called him. "And he was a very good wrestler. But he wanted to sharpen his tools. He used to work out with me to learn finishing holds, legitimate shooting holds and really wrestle. To take care of yourself, because your initial investment in wrestling is your body."

Roddy needed to be able to shut down an overly aggressive opponent and make opponents respect him in the ring if his body was going to hold up for a long career. "He was good, but a couple of wrestlers . . ." LeBell explained that there are always a few guys who will take over a match and dominate their opponent just to look good (even forty years later LeBell wouldn't name names). Roddy wasn't sure how to handle them. "I says, 'Beat the shit out of them.'" Even if the match was supposed to be won by the opponent, "Let them up and let them know you can wrestle better than they can. It's happened to me a couple of times. I was told by one of my teachers, if a guy starts to take over the match, hurt him. I worked Roddy the same way." LeBell credits Karl Gotch with the training LeBell in turn passed on to Roddy. Tricks like digging your fingertips under the pecs of a larger opponent. It's an excruciating move that all but immobilizes him. You back him into a corner or up against the ropes and remind him gently that you'll kill him if he doesn't take it down a notch. By the time he was in his forties, LeBell was wrestling only on occasion. He and Roddy fought just a few times, once most memorably in San Bernardino. Roddy had put in some serious time at the buffet table before the match, still thinking like a hungry street kid who wouldn't let an extra calorie escape. Especially turkey and blueberry pie. The preliminary matches ended earlier than he had anticipated and Roddy got into the ring on a full stomach. LeBell cringed and yet smiled as he told the story: "We're wrestling and I'm bouncing on him and everything, and just having a good time. And all of a sudden he stands up and, right in my face, grabs me and throws up this blueberry pie all over me." LeBell could hardly breathe. He bolted for the dressing rooms and straight into the shower. The referee counted him out and Roddy had something to boast about: 'I beat Gene!' And he did. Bastard. Now that I think about it. If he was here I'd body slam him."

Don't let either man's ribbing fool you. Roddy earned his judo teacher's respect in the way that mattered most. "He beat the shit out of all the guys." Not at first. It took some time in the dojo, but Roddy quickly caught up and surpassed what LeBell figures were about 90 percent of his other students. All the different forms of judo LeBell taught were really, in the sensei's estimation, just a "wrestling whizzer" with a different name. "But it isn't beating them up or losing or winning. It's what you know. And he knew . . . I call it 'the dark side of the moon.' What the referee didn't see didn't happen."

Roddy quickly made an impact on the crowds in Los Angeles. Still new, he was used in the ring mostly to help prop up some of the local regulars, who needed the energetic new kid to inject interest into their matches. The promoters worked him as hard as they could. He fought early in the card, refereed another match, fought in another in a mask. He brought to a favorite opponent's mind an old Mexican expression—like a horse's underwear—meaning he was up and down constantly.

In March 1976 he won the NWA Americas title from one of the most popular wrestlers in California, Chavo Guerrero. He took the red felt backing off the belt and replaced it with plaid. It was just one more way to needle Guerrero's fans. "Roddy, he was sharp, man," recalls Guerrero. "He could do a promo about anything, anytime, anywhere. He could change his voice, his pitches. He would ad lib a lot. He was the greatest promo man I ever heard, and I mean that."

Chavo was a commentator during the LA broadcasts, so his opinion was an informed one. And not just on how to talk. Chavo's father, Gory, was patriarch to a clan of great Mexican-American wrestlers, and he himself had debuted back in the 1930s. As Gory's oldest son, Chavo began wrestling in LA only a few months before Roddy arrived. His younger brothers Mando and Hector saw plenty of Roddy in the Olympic Auditorium ring as well. (A final brother joined the family many years later, Eddie, who would claim the WWE heavyweight title in 2004. Chavo's son, Chavo Jr., would also join the family business.) "I'm a wrestler," says Chavo. "Roddy was a brawler. He would never stop, he was like a machine. Always moving. He wouldn't really mess around with the people too much, he would just worry about the guy in the ring. He was just happy being there, having a job, having his dog and having money to eat, and staying on the beach in Santa Monica. We were having a great time. He was doing what he was told. He never complained. He was always quiet in the dressing room."

Garibaldi often brought in Mexican wrestlers, who were popular with the largely Hispanic audience in LA. That was fine in the ring, but promos were a problem. "No offense to Mexicans—I'm Mexican—but they didn't know any English," Chavo said. "So they'd put Roddy in to interview for them. That's how he got a lot of his experience. They would throw all these different characters at him, and he'd make them shine with his talking."

In those early days as champion, Roddy attended a press conference at the Olympic for a most unusual fight. Sitting in the front row, he listened to Muhammad Ali threaten a Japanese wrestling champion named Antonio Inoki. In what was billed as an exhibition match between boxer and wrestler, the two were scheduled to fight in Japan in June 1976. During the press conference, an actor and karate specialist named Joe Lewis pinned Ali twice, exhibiting the threat a martial artist posed to a boxer, even one as dominant as Ali. The champ's entourage didn't like seeing him handled that way and nearly ran Lewis out of the ring. Ali intervened to keep Lewis out of trouble. Next, Ali pointed at Roddy—whose head was roughly shaved from losing a recent haircut match—and dared the young wrestler to get in the ring with him. Roddy was wearing a snug green corduroy suit, hardly his usual attire in the Olympic Auditorium, but when Muhammad Ali tells a fighter of any sort to get in the ring, it's tough to refuse.

Gene LeBell was at the press conference because he was slated to referee the Japanese card. As Roddy made his way to the ring LeBell caught his eye with a look of disbelief. Roddy shrugged, climbed in and locked up with the boxing champion like he would with any wrestler. Ali had barely been able to call off his handlers after Lewis had put him down. He was about to make them even angrier.

Too close for anyone else to hear, Ali told Roddy to hip toss him. Roddy obliged, landing the boxing champ flat on his back. Ali's handlers went nuts, and Roddy got out of the ring.

Only Roddy could have heard Ali say that to him. He was grateful for the little boost to his notoriety. He had a belt, but he wasn't yet the main eventer he hoped to become.

In that first year, Roddy made a few friends who would be dear to him until their early deaths. Two of them would fight him dozens of times, starting in Los Angeles.

One night, Roddy found himself looking across the ring at a man much more than twice his size. Andre the Giant was one of few wrestlers whose nickname was no exaggeration. Over seven feet tall and weighing in excess of five hundred pounds, by just his stature alone, he eliminated the idea that Roddy—or just about anyone—might beat him. Comically, after being thrown out of the ring yet one more time, Roddy threw up his hands in disgust and headed off the Olympic floor toward the dressing rooms. Security escorted him back to the ring moments later to continue his Sisyphean chore. As usual, he failed to beat the Giant, but he made an impression on the towering Frenchman that would pay enormous dividends in the future.

He met another lifelong friend and enemy in Adrian Adonis. As a tag team, they were nicknamed (if not actually billed) as the Twenty-Twos, for their shared age. Adonis was still going by his real name, Keith Franke. He was working a leather-clad biker gimmick, which worked well when he was young and trim (fans of the early WrestleMania years were familiar with him as a much heavier man, usually appearing in a mockery of drag as "Adorable" Adrian Adonis).

In April 1977, another title traded hands between Roddy and Chavo Guererro, the NWA (Mexico) World Lightweight title. The Twenty-Twos would claim the NWA tag-team title from Mando Guerrero and Tom Jones in July, then pass it back a week later.

Roddy was in the winners' circle. The LA stage was big and bright. But was it bright enough to ensure he'd never slip back into obscurity?

Gory Guerrero had endured his own hard path to wrestling legend. He had once been shot at in the ring. The shooter missed him and killed a woman in the front row. He'd been stabbed so many times, he once told his grandson, Chavo Jr., that a knife wound didn't hurt as much as he'd think. Listening to this, Chavo Jr. was seven years old.

Roddy carried his buck knife, but it wasn't his only knife. He was still only two years removed from the streets of Winnipeg. The instincts formed in his teens sometimes moved his hand toward the hilt of one of those knives, this time on a weekend run with Chavo through Texas.

"Roddy hated to be poked in the ass," Chavo said, and laughed. The kilt he wore in the ring drew all sorts of harsh ribbing, even from Chavo, who could get away with a little more teasing than most. "So on that tour, man, I wanted to get even with him for a bunch of shit. I guess I was just trying to fuck with him. That's just me, I fuck with everybody. So I started fucking with his ass."

Roddy grew miserable with the teasing. "Stop it, stop it!"

"We drive to Corpus Christi, we're having a great time. We get to the hotel. We go to the beach for a while. We have our wrestling trunks on, I say, 'Oh, you look so good,' and grab him in the ass." Back at the hotel, the ribbing continued. Roddy came out of the shower and pulled on his pants. "I kinda just slap him on the cheek. He always had the knife attached to his pants."

Before either knew what had happened, Chavo had a shallow slice down the length of his thigh from Roddy's pocket knife. Chavo, however, was never in too much shock to rib his buddy. He went for the emotional jugular. "I'm going, 'Amigo! You stabbed me! You stabbed me!' And of course, me, man, I make it like . . ." Chavo moaned like he'd been stabbed in the gut.

"Oh amigo, I'm sorry! I didn't want to do it!" cried Roddy.

"Man, how could you do that? You're a murderer!" replied Chavo. "I milked that so much. He apologized and kept apologizing, and I said, 'Yeah, right, you did it on purpose. You were waiting your turn, man.'"

By the time they got to the arena that night in Corpus Christi, Chavo had all but forgotten the incident. A cat could have scratched him more seriously than the cut on his leg. So he was surprised to see Roddy throw away the knife when they returned to their hotel.

"What'd you do that for?" asked Chavo.

"Amigo, you know, I felt bad."

"You didn't have to do that, I was just fucking with you."

"I know, but I just . . ."

"Anyway," reflected Chavo when we spoke, "that was Roddy."

In September 1976, Gory Guerrero invited Roddy to Juarez, Mexico, to wrestle with Chavo. The twenty-two year old from Saskatoon had incited brawls and riots, but he really had no idea what to expect from wrestling in a Mexican bullring. Knowing wouldn't have stopped him.

Juarez took the first shot, though, laying Roddy up in the afternoon with a rotten stomach. "The beautiful Mrs. Guerrero made a special chicken noodle soup for me," he said, ever reverent. Whatever was in that soup, it worked wonders. Roddy was at the bullring that night, ready to brawl. He knew who he'd be wrestling, but who he'd be brawling with remained to be seen.

"The place is packed. I had a new style of trunks, they were pure white with little bagpipes on the side. Which really looked like little cockroaches. They come down to just above my knee." Decked out for his first fight in Mexico, Roddy wasn't feeling particularly welcome in the dressing room. Chavo was a friend and understood Roddy. If anything, in Los Angeles Roddy's antagonism in the ring—which often involved antagonizing Mexicans—was helping grow Chavo's own celebrity. But here in the heart of Mexico, the other wrestlers weren't as inclined to forgive a young punk badmouthing their country.

Surrounding the bullring were hard benches. The audience could rent small pillows to sit on. Roddy and Chavo were wrestling in the main event. "Everything's going hunky dory," recalled Roddy. "Come intermission, here comes the torrential flood. God decides to make it rain. The people go for shelter. The rain stops and I'm on."

Soaked with rain, the pillows weigh several pounds. And who would want to sit on wet pillows anyway? "I get in the ring and I start wrestling Chavo. A pillow, upside the head. Hit me like Earnie Shavers." One soaking pillow gives way to another. "Another one. Pom! Finally it's so bad, I need to get out of there." The pillows are coming down like rain. From such close range, many are finding their mark. And what security exists is interested in making sure the audience has paid to get in, not in protecting wrestlers from Los Angeles. Realizing his friend is getting hurt, Chavo tries to dissuade the audience the only way he can. "Chavo was trying to help me by beating me up." Maybe if the crowd saw Roddy taking lumps from their hero, they'd lay off. If the match were to swing the other way, the crowd would rush the ring. So Chavo grabbed Roddy and wrestled him close, hoping the fans wouldn't want to hammer him with wet pillows too. It didn't much help. In a harbinger of the career to come, the fans seemed to hate Roddy more than they loved Chavo.

Chavo explained that the pillows are a habit at the end of the bullring matches: "Any bullring really, the bad guys or the good guys, whether you win or lose, whether the heel wins or the baby loses—especially if they don't like you—they start throwing. It was windy and dusty and a little sprinkle so it made it even nastier. I told him, 'Get out of the ring, buddy.'"

Getting beaten up by Chavo Guerrero was fun if you were a strapping young professional wrestler who included the Mexican-American great as your close friend. Getting beaten up by Chavo and hammered by wet pillows while recovering from a rotten stomach was too much. "He started messing with the people," Chavo said. "I said, 'Get out of the ring, man.' He said, 'I ain't getting out, brother, I'm getting it on!' I said, 'Get out of the ring. Here they come, man. Boom! He was buried in pillows.'"

Chavo warned him of something else as well. In the tunnel to the bullring, the wrestlers were vulnerable to a hostile crowd as they came and went. Chavo warned him to look the crowd in the eye when he wanted to exit, then run for it. Roddy didn't. He sauntered, proudly, slowly, and continued to get pelted, including by a bag of shit.

Once they were safely out of sight of the audience, Roddy turned to Chavo.

"Amigo! Why didn't you tell me?!"

"I told you to get out, dude."

"Why didn't you tell me they were going to throw pillows?"

"I don't know what the people are going to do!"

There were no showers, so Chavo led Roddy to a bathing station for the bulls. "He was steaming hot!" recalled Chavo. "What do you want to do, you want to stay like that," Chavo said to him, "or you wanna take all that shit off?" After Roddy cooled down, he allowed himself to laugh it off, too. "Yeah, he was pissed. Not at me, he was just pissed that he got caught in a situation."

Roddy had fought his way out of some tense situations with fans looking to make it real. He wasn't impressed that he so nearly allowed himself to fall into a situation he might not have gotten out of. Violence was becoming strangely ordinary, and he needed to make sure he never found himself on the wrong end of it. Still, he was young enough to take away more of the thrill than the terror.

"We had a great time," he recalled. "It was dangerous, but . . . holy cow. I lived."

LA drew a large weekend house, but the rest of the week was filled with smaller gigs. One was up north near San Francisco against an opponent Roddy hadn't heard of before.

The San Francisco promoter, Roy Shire, invited Roddy up and he accepted. Shire, after all, was supposed to have been his boss when he drove out from New Brunswick, and Roddy often popped up the coast from LA for a match or two.

Roddy had fought all kinds by now. This fellow, "Victor Bear," couldn't be any worse than he'd seen so far.

Roddy was wrong. He wasn't fighting Victor Bear. He was fighting a de-clawed bear named Victor. As Roddy sat slack-jawed in the locker room before the match, the animal reared up and made short work of a bottle of Wild Turkey. It dropped the empty bottle, which shattered on the floor, and the trainer handed it a bottle of Coke, which it drained and smashed just like it had the bourbon.

The bear's owner and trainer, Tuffy Truesdell, laid down the ground rules for Roddy. "Now, Victor's fang teeth have been taken out for your protection, but his back teeth are about an inch and a half long, so don't get your fingers back there or he'll bite them off. Don't pull Victor's fur or punch him in the stomach, because if you do he'll slap you upside the head and break your neck."

Roddy was looking at Victor, still wondering how he was going to survive this, forget about putting on a good match.

"Obviously he doesn't know I'm the light heavyweight champion of the world," Roddy quipped. He went to the weigh-in, not comforted by the knowledge shared by Truesdell. The trainer was finished dispensing helpful advice and moved on to clear directions.

"Now, Victor don't like standing on his hind legs unless he's been drinking. So when the bell rings I'm gonna jab him in the bum with this stick and that oughta bring him up. You get under him."

Victor weighed roughly twice as much as Superstar Billy Graham and about 150 pounds more than Andre the Giant in the mid-'70s (Andre never stopped growing—and Victor's proportions fluctuated as well, depending which wrestler is recounting his long minutes in the ring with him). His size aside, the bear presented a unique set of problems to a slender young wrestler. First, Victor had just guzzled the largest mixed drink in the history of professional sports. Second, it would be difficult to communicate during the match with a bear. He'd have had better luck pacifying German shepherds while stealing farmers' gasoline in northern Minnesota. Third, and most important, this was feeling like a very bad idea, and a very good way to have his spine snapped in front of an audience.

Rod was deliberating whether to actually fight Victor when wrestler Jay York walked up behind him, slapped him on the bum a few times and said, "Go get him, kid," with a big laugh.

Roddy took a deep breath and got in the ring. Good to his word, Truesdell jabbed the bear with a stick and Rod locked up with him, as wrestlers do. Unfortunately, a bear has no shoulders to hold on to. Bears being natural wrestlers, Victor got behind Roddy and he hit the mat. The bear went straight for his trunks. Forgetting Truesdell's instructions, Roddy kicked, punched, and tried everything he could do to get the bear off him—"I'm snout-pullin', fur-punchin'." His trunks went down and the bear put its substantial snout where nature had not intended. The crowd was shrieking at the sight of the bagpiping wrestler getting mauled.

This was not Victor's first time in the ring. Truesdell had been touring him all over the US and Canada, wrestling professionals and wannabes both. Neither tended to fare very well against the bear. In 1970, at halftime of an NBA game between the Chicago Bulls and Golden State Warriors, Bulls general manager Pat Williams tried his hand at wrestling Victor. It was a short bout. At the end of each match, Victor's handler quickly rewarded the bear with another bottle of Coke. But a soft drink wasn't about to distract him from the buffet he had on the mat in Fresno. When Roddy's posterior lost its appeal, Victor, like any bear raiding a bee's nest, put his very long tongue to work, going deeper, seeking more. Roddy started screaming for his life.

Truesdell had to tranquilize Victor (more than a bottle of Wild Turkey already had), but it took a few minutes to kick in. Roddy managed to get up, but Victor kept taking him down. Knowing a bear's ring strategies is a very different thing from defending yourself against them. Eventually Victor passed out. Not one to stand on ceremony, Roddy hustled out of the ring while trying to get his trunks up where they belonged. He tripped on his way through the ropes, landing face-first on the concrete with his trunks still low enough to give the crowd its money's worth.

Victor wrestled thousands of people over the years, but he never did to anyone else what he did to Roddy. The reason for that, it turned out, was simple. Before slapping his young pal on the backside prior to the match, Jay York had smeared honey all over his hand. Victor had been the object of some good old-fashioned bear baiting. Gene LeBell had been training Roddy to defend himself against liberties in the ring, but even the toughest man in the world couldn't have prepared him for what he suffered that night in Fresno.

Fortunately for Roddy, his days wrestling bears and being treated like a disposable part of anyone's promotion were nearly over. He was about to be asked to try a few new things. One would do great things for his career. The other was a first step in leaving it.

4

Thanks for the Blood and Guts, Kid

Gene LeBell had taken a liking to Roddy. He spent every free moment he could in LeBell's dojo, working on wrestling technique, toughening up. LeBell wasn't gentle, but neither was Roddy. LeBell knew what he was doing on the mats, and a mischievous sense of humour made him hard not to like.

One Sunday, Roddy called him and asked if they could spend some time wrestling at the dojo. LeBell turned him down. Sundays had a much more important purpose. He told Roddy to join him and Chavo Guerrero in indulging his true passion. "Being Gene's friend," said Roddy, "I had to ride motorcycles." Since LeBell paid most of his bills working as a stunt man, riding motorbikes was a crucial skill, and one he'd make any excuse to practice. He sold old bikes to Roddy and Chavo. "You can't be a good wrestler until you can ride motorcycles," LeBell says. "You get your hands and legs in coordination."

They loaded up their dirt bikes and headed for the hills outside LA.

Roddy hesitated to cross a small river on his bike. A more experienced rider, Chavo urged him to ride through. Roddy was still hesitating. With a shake of the head and a twist of the throttle, Chavo decided to show him how it was done. He was immediately up to his neck in water. Roddy laughed so hard, he wasn't able to help his friend pull the bike back onto dry land. LeBell directed them to the bottom of a notoriously steep hill. LeBell dared Roddy to try his luck. By this point in their relationship, if Uncle Gene asked Roddy to do something, he did it. Of all the things about wrestling Roddy was learning from Gene, he didn't yet understand how completely Uncle Gene had mastered the wrestlers' art of "the swerve," the practical joke. "He damned near killed himself," said LeBell.

The way Chavo tells it, Roddy tried again and again to climb that hill. The other two were at the top, watching. "No! I'm not giving up," shouted Roddy. "Nobody's going to beat me, especially not Guerrero!"

"I was chanting for him," says Chavo. "Roddy, Roddy, Roddy . . ."

Chavo and Gene were also sweltering in the sun in their riding gear, and they urged him to get it over with, one way or the other. Roddy hit the gas, crossed a little creek at the bottom of the hill and hit the rise. He made it to the top, but kept going over the crest of the hill and out of sight—until he was caught in a fence strung to protect people from falling off the steep backside of the hill. "I was so scared," said Roddy. "The hill was so tall. I started going backwards off the motorcycle but I hung on and crashed into a bunch of barbed wire." Laying in the dirt tangled in the fence, Roddy looked down—several hundred feet down. In the valley far below lay a rusting old motorcycle. Presumably, crashed by someone who had made the same mistake before the barbed wire went up. "I remember it very clearly—the spokes and a wheel and a cow's head, the white skull."

When Gene found him, he stared at him, amazed. "You goof," said LeBell. "What did you do that for?"

"You told me to, Uncle Gene."

Chavo laughed as he remembered Roddy emerging from the backside of the hill, his gear shredded. "He had all these scratches where he fell on the barbed wire and where he was bleeding. But he couldna been prouder. That was the moment of the day. We would compete for the moment of the day, and that was the moment of the day, brother."

The lessons weren't all for Roddy. As LeBell learned that day, the more something scared his new student, the more likely he was to try it.

Roddy's parents had worked multiple jobs all through his childhood, and now he needed some extra income himself to get out of the Flamingo, the motel he was living in. It was a dump, and a dangerous one at that. Working in the movies, Uncle Gene knew how a wrestler with a fresh face and screen-friendly physique could make a few bucks on the side.

LeBell was running the stunts on a film called *The One and Only*, a story about a struggling actor who boosts his career by wrestling. To get noticed, he takes on a series of outrageous ring personas. The lead was played by Henry Winkler, who was enjoying huge television success at the time as the Fonz in the sitcom *Happy Days*. LeBell got Roddy work in a scene in which Winkler's character was working a sort of Hitler gimmick with a spiked German war helmet. Roddy's character was a GI named Leatherneck Joe Grady, a crowd favourite—though for some reason the filmmakers left Roddy's usual plaid trunks on him. They were shooting in the ring at the Olympic Auditorium.

"What am I supposed to do?" Roddy asked LeBell.

Gene went into the ring and approached Winkler. Roddy followed. The actor didn't know what he was supposed to do either. LeBell had worked with both men before. He couldn't resist the swerve. "We're looking at each other," said Roddy, "and Gene LeBell says, 'Come here, come here,' to Henry Winkler. He gets pretty close. Gene just starts slapping me in the head."

LeBell was saying, "See this kid?" Bop, bop. "This kid here? You can't hurt this kid." Bop bop.

Roddy went to his corner. He knew he was supposed to take a bump in the fight—fall down hard, that is. There was a camera positioned low along the edge of the canvas to catch him hitting the mat.

Winkler wasn't sure what LeBell was suggesting. "You have a German helmet. You take it off and you hit him with it."

"Well, how hard should I hit him?"

LeBell knew Winkler was a nice guy but figured he was a method actor, so LeBell laid it on thick about hitting Roddy over the head with the helmet. "You got it?"

"I got it," said Winkler.

Roddy watched quietly. He knew LeBell couldn't resist a prank, but this was Roddy's first day on a new job. He assumed people in the movie business knew what they were doing. "I didn't say nuthin.'"

The director called action. "The bell rings, Henry's in his corner, I'm in mine. Boy, he took Uncle Gene serious. He took that helmet off and just plowed me. I wanted to get up and just beat him like a baby seal."

The director called cut. Roddy got up. Holding his head, he approached LeBell. "He knocked the shit outta me! What did you tell him?"

"You know, just miss him or something."

Even with his head ringing, Roddy thought that was unlikely.

On his way out of the ring, Roddy passed the director, Carl Reiner. "You got another Robert Redford here," Reiner said to LeBell.

"Okay, sure," Roddy scoffed.

"Do you want to do some movies?" Reiner asked Roddy.

The experience really hadn't inspired Roddy to say yes.

In the film, the Roddy and Winkler characters travel by train from town to town, repeating the match. The filmmakers liked Roddy's twitching collapse into the mat so much that they show it over and over, interspersed with shots of the train whistling through the night. If you watch the movie, you'll see Roddy hitting the canvas again and again and again. "That was my big movie debut," he said ruefully. "I never went to see it. To this day I don't think I've seen it. I think Uncle Gene showed me where I took the bump for this guy. For four or five years I'd been fighting every night trying to get this wrestling thing done. I didn't have much interest in movies. I think Uncle Gene was the one who got me my SAG card—Screen Actors Guild. But I had never in my life thought of being in front of a camera or doing an interview—I just never considered them. Now I'm accidentally in a movie. But it wasn't a big enough part for me to think about my part or my character. I was a wrestler getting the shit kicked out of me! I'd been preparing for that for five years. I didn't need much coaching."

Chavo Guerrero made his film debut in *The One and Only* as well, playing wrestler Indian Joe—"I was the only one that beat the Fonz!"—thanks to Uncle Gene. Guerrero did a few more movies, but stayed focussed on wrestling, though his brother Mando did start a career as a stuntman, also thanks to LeBell. Roddy took the job for all it seemed to be, a payday. He didn't think he'd be back in front of a movie camera again. "I didn't know who Carl Reiner was. I wish I'd taken his offer."

In August, Roddy beat Chavo for the NWA (Los Angeles) Americas title. But he had yet to develop into the kind of indispensible draw he could be and he knew it. So did Mike LeBell and Leo Garibaldi. Still, a hard working kid with an unusual gimmick, great mic work and a bottomless desire to succeed was worth investing in. For about a week. Roddy lost the belt back to Chavo on August 18. Roddy's loss was a safe bet on the promoter's part. The re-match was a loser-leaves-town match. Just to make sure he knew his immediate future lay elsewhere, Roddy lost another loser-leaves-town match the next night in Bakersfield. The California audiences had been given notice. Roddy Piper wouldn't be seen for a while.

The LeBells' promotion in Los Angeles, like most wrestling circuits around the US, Mexico and Canada, had agreements to swap talent with other promotions in other territories. The LeBells were connected to a fledgling wrestler-run promotion called New Japan Pro-Wrestling. It was time Roddy stretched his legs again, though LeBell and Garibaldi weren't giving up on him. This was just a loan to a very distant place.

To make sure Roddy didn't get lost in translation, he was contracted for a six-week tour of Japan in the company of a couple of very big Texans, one of whom, Stan Hansen, would enjoy their tour so much he'd spend much of his career there.

On August 26, still in a daze from jetlag and culture shock, Roddy debuted in Kiryu, Japan, as a tag-team partner to towering Blackjack Mulligan. They lost to Riki Choshu and their new boss, Antonio Inoki, the wrestler who'd fought Muhammad Ali.

A heavyweight champion himself, Inoki was a square-jawed six-foot-three. Though born in Japan, he'd lived and trained in Brazil as a teenager before returning to wrestle in the dominant Japanese promotion, All Japan Pro Wrestling, run by the six-foot-ten Giant Baba. Inoki broke away in 1972 to form the rival business, New Japan.

Hansen would eventually fight with both promotions. "Both companies were run by strong, great, individual wrestlers that were really good," Hansen said. The style of wrestling was less gimmicky than in North America, with less focus on angles and more on shoot, or legitimate, fighting. Inoki in particular liked "strong style," influenced by American pro wrestling but with much more forceful contact. "It's punishing. The Japanese were tough," Hansen said. "They chopped hard, they hit hard and they did everything hard. It was twice as physical as the United States. I mean, it was tough. From getting in and out of the ring to everything. It could be brutal."

Roddy had bulked up since arriving in LA, and had trained enough with Gene LeBell that "brutal" was happily within his wheelhouse. "I think he enjoyed it," said Hansen. "The competition between the people in the ring was . . . I'd say the closest thing to real there is. You might know where you're going to start and where you're going to finish, but what you did in between was really up to whoever was aggressive enough to lead the match. That's where the real competition came in. Roddy fit into that really well."

That's high praise from a man who stood three inches taller than Roddy. Mulligan was almost a half-foot taller than Hansen, and both men weighed over three hundred pounds. If Hansen found Japanese wrestlers that tough, it's a testament to Roddy's aggression and evolving skill that his next tag-team partner in Japan thought he thrived against the local talent.

Roddy recalled the ultra-physical nature of wrestling in Inoki's promotion in similar terms. "When you got in the ring, you just beat them with everything you had. You just beat the dog out of them. I was partner of a guy named Stan Hansen on his very first tour. He's blind as a bat. He had a lariat, which was just a big piece of leather. But when Stan took his glasses off, he couldn't see nothing, half the time he was hitting me. But he'd make the Japanese wrestlers run and he'd beat them."

Japanese audiences weren't sure what to make of a supposed Scotsman piping his way into the ring every night. He fought in gymnasiums and community centres that held at best three or four thousand people. The wailing pipes would have echoed brutally off the high ceilings and stone walls. Japanese audiences weren't inclined to make much noise of their own, like crowds did back home. "In those days, they didn't cheer or boo or nothing. They just were polite, would sit there and watch the matches." And they took their wrestling very seriously, which was all the more reason to disdain the strange and villainous foreigners, or *gaijin*.

"You were definitely the villain," Hansen said, "because you were wrestling mainly the Japanese. Over time, there's a few guys that went long enough that people ended up enjoying them . . . but we were the heels."

The tour was packed tight with matches in different cities, night after night. Through six weeks, it got to be a grind. And it was hard on the visiting wrestlers, socially. They didn't speak the language, they weren't in one place, or even one city, long enough to make connections, and a phone call home, if you could get a clear line, cost several dollars a minute. Fortunately for Roddy, he had the Texans to keep him company. "Roddy and I, we enjoyed going to the movies," Hansen said. Most places they'd wrestle had a movie theatre, and many of them showed American movies with Japanese subtitles. The wrestlers needed something to kill time, because they showed up in each new town around noon but didn't need to report for their matches until about five o'clock. They stayed in business hotels with small rooms and nothing on television that they could understand except sports. Roddy had a habit at the movies to help him feel at home. "I can remember one of his favourite things was he'd buy these Goobers. I think they're chocolate covered peanuts. And he'd get popcorn. The popcorn was never hot. He'd pour these Goobers into the popcorn and say, Ah, this is my favourite way."

They also killed a little time in *yakiniku* restaurants, eating Korean-style barbeque. Steak and most meat was very expensive, so the promoters took the visiting wrestlers out for *yakiniku* once a week. The Westerners, accustomed to a lot more protein in their diets, would feast.

But Goobers and occasional big meals weren't enough to keep Roddy's tumultuous mind entertained, so he, Hansen and Mulligan entertained themselves. Since people already regarded them warily as big, nasty *gaijin*, the threesome decided to have some fun with it. Doing laundry was expensive in Japan, which made an excuse for a contest to see who could go the longest without changing his clothes. These were not small men, and they fought every night for a living. "It started out as a rib," Hansen said, "but after two, three days, we're going, eww man, this is getting a little old. But we all hung in there for about five or six days, maybe longer. But eventually Mulligan and I said forget it." Roddy won. "He was always joking around. He enjoyed life. It was a new experience."

Public baths were a particularly new part of that experience. The warm indoor pools drew all variety of people at the end of the day to unwind among their neighbours and peers. To many Japanese, "skinship" was considered part of proper socialization. To a prairie kid in his early twenties, especially one socialized in a rapid-fire series of very questionable circumstances, the sober-minded benefit of group nudity was a tough sell. "Public baths," remembered Hansen, "it's really a nice thing. But for somebody new that'd never been to one, it was always a little . . . they were thinking, *Wow what is this?* Because a pat down or a massage in the States meant something completely different from an actual muscle massage at a bath house."

Roddy went for a massage. A few minutes later, Hansen heard loud moaning coming from the room where the massage tables were. The moans escalated into yelling and screaming—obviously Roddy. Bathers were getting upset and the masseuse came running out of the room, furious. Hansen laughs, "It wasn't any kind of a sexual deal"—though it was meant to sound like one—"it was just him being crazy."

Through Roddy's time wrestling in LA for Aileen Eaton and Mike LeBell, he lived in the same low-rise, low-rent motel whose back alley hosted its fair share of beatings and murders. The last time most people saw the Flamingo West Motel was in the Wesley Snipes/Woody Harrelson/Rosie Perez movie *White Men*

Can't Jump. It was torn down in the early '90s. But when Roddy returned from six weeks overseas, settling back in at the Flamingo felt like coming home.

"I had a special suite they built for me. They put a built-in cigarette lighter in the wall and bars on the windows. It was wild." Wild enough that Roddy got in the habit of carrying a .357 magnum. Jay York taught him how to load the gun so he wouldn't shoot anyone by accident.

"It's a revolver so there's room for six cartridges," explained Roddy. "It's a pin hammer, and if you drop it, the pin hits the cartridge and there's a good chance of it going off. So I always left the first chamber empty. The next chamber was a .357 blank. The rest of them were the real deal. If you had people coming at you, you could let a round off with no one getting hurt. One time I come home from the gym, and of all people the maids were looking at it and they fired it. Nobody was hurt. God bless Jay York."

Jay "The Alaskan" York—he of the honey on his hands—was a six-foot-five bearded mountain of a wrestler, about sixteen years older than Roddy. He and Roddy became fast friends. "He used to have a twelve-foot bullwhip around his neck. He took cigarettes out of my mouth with that bullwhip. Never once got my skin."

York found himself in the middle of some very unlikely trouble, thanks to a local serial killer. "On a telephone post, just down the street from the Flamingo, was one of the saddest posters I ever saw," said Roddy. "A photo of a little gal, it was written in blood, or to look like blood. 'Help me. Have you seen me?' The Hillside Strangler had got her."

The Hillside Strangler was a nickname given by the police and press to whoever had abducted a string of girls and women who turned up raped, tortured and strangled to death in the hills above

LA. The Strangler's fourth victim, an actress named Jane King, had been killed just days before, on Thursday, November 10.

Jay's brother Ned York, an actor who'd appeared on *Bonanza* and a few other shows, hung around with Jay and Roddy from time to time. He and Jay showed up Sunday night at the Flamingo. "Ned came over and they had an ounce of this smokable stuff. It was called angel dust." Ned had recently worked with Jane King. He talked about her a lot that evening and was in a bad state over her murder. Finally he went home, taking his remaining portion of the drugs with him. "Ned finally picks up the phone, calls the police and says, 'I'm the Hillside Strangler.'"

Wearing just an undershirt and boxers, he went into his backyard. For reasons having almost everything to do with angel dust, he got to playing with a ball. The ball went over the fence and when he tried to retrieve it, the neighbour's dog tore into his left hand. "He had that hand bandaged up and when the police came he was just sitting on the curb. The police started questioning him, and he knew things about this girl who had just been snatched." No doubt York would have had trouble articulating why exactly he knew so much about Jane King. The fresh blood on his hands played into the police's urgent need to make an arrest. That same night two young girls had been killed by what appeared to be the Strangler. The police were desperate to bring in a suspect. Ned York, a big mess of a man, high as a kite and covered in blood, had just fallen into their laps. They arrested him.

Then his brother showed up at the police station.

Roddy woke up late the next afternoon. "I saw it on TV: Jay York going in with a buck knife on his hip to go bail out his innocent brother. When Ned finally started to come down he goes, 'What am I doing here?' It had made the AP. The police were positive. But it wasn't the Hillside Strangler. It was Ned York. I wasn't sure what they gave him a ticket for, trespassing? I'm not sure."

Life in LA was proving a little more colourful than in Roddy's previous stops. Sometimes that meant he kept out of trouble, sometimes it didn't. But he was also meeting varieties of people he'd never met before. One of those people surprised him more than most, and taught him another lesson about how fragile his limited fame really was.

Roddy was back in his little dressing space at the far end of the hall in the basement of the Olympic Auditorium, which he usually shared with guys like Crusher Verdu and Red Shoes Dugan. He'd been gone only a few months, but he couldn't just walk back into the O after dropping all those loser-leaves-town matches against the Guerreros in August. So, come November, he appeared in a red-and-white mask and a white shirt with long red sleeves that read "CANADA" across the back over a red maple leaf as the Canadian (sometimes the Masked Canadian). In a promo for one of those masked matches, where he said little more than "si, maestro"—yes, teacher—the voice was distinctly his, even if the language clearly wasn't. He flexed and strutted like a Mexican wrestler while an actual Mexican wrestler, Black Gordman, the Canadian's erstwhile manager, ranted into Gene LeBell's microphone in Spanish about what his champion would do to the likes of Hector Guerrero or Pat Patterson. In another promo Patterson can barely stop himself from calling out Roddy beneath the mask.

"When you wear a mask, facial's gone," recalled Roddy. With his facial expressions hidden from the audience, he had to learn to use body language to pick up the slack. "You gotta learn a whole different way to get over and a whole different way to sell."

Roddy did learn, and became adept enough at it that he was made champion again, winning the NWA Americas (Los Angeles) title from Chavo Guerrero almost as soon as he returned to the ring.

The ruse continued through February 1978. The Canadian lost the belt to Mando Guerrero (no lightweight in the T-shirt game himself, Mando appeared in a shirt declaring himself "Illegal"). Roddy quickly won it back again, then finally forfeited it to Hector before dropping another loser-leaves-town re-match decision to Hector in San Diego. Then it was back to Japan. Oddly, he appeared throughout March in Japan still masked as the Canadian. The reason is anyone's guess, but this time he was wrestling with All Japan, the promotion run by the towering Giant Baba.

On Roddy's next return to LA, things were going okay, but he wasn't satisfied. His days as a jobber were well behind him. He was a good heel, ratcheting up the crowd's fury and drawing heat on himself to great effect. But he still feared those jobber days could return if he stopped trying so hard. He spent long hours at UCLA, studying reel-to-reel tape of old matches, anything to improve his technique and broaden his strategies. Fortunately, Roddy wasn't the only one who had confidence in his own future popularity—or in his case, popularity's entertaining opposite. "So Leo [Garibaldi] come up and looked at me. I got bagpipes, I'm playing my way down to the ring. He comes up to me and says, 'Kid, I'm gonna give you a break.' All right, he got my attention. He said, 'You see that guy over there?' I looked at him, and the guy I looked at was called Java Ruuk."

Java Ruuk was a New York City–born wrestler named Johnny Rodriguez. Also sometimes known as Johnny Rodz, in mock Arab headdress that looked like someone stole the curtains at the Days Inn, he'd screw up his eyes to seem unhinged in front of the camera. In the ring, the mania seemed less of a put on.

Though well under six feet tall, he had a good twenty or thirty pounds still on Roddy. He was notoriously vicious, scratching and clawing and generally making life as miserable as possible for his opponents. He also didn't say much. "He went *OO-OO-OO-OO* and he just beat the shit out of people," said Roddy.

Garibaldi said, "I want you to go into the ring with that guy. Don't lay a hand on him." Then he walked away. Roddy wasn't pleased, but he was in no position to complain. "This is Wednesday, on TV. I'd had so many people jerk me around, it was just another day. So I went in there, played my little bagpipes down, got in there and this guy came and just whupped the dog out of me for as long as he wanted to." Ruuk's boots had curly toes, like those made infamous years later by the Iron Sheik. At one point he came off the ropes, caught his curly toe on the rope and stumbled, planting an accidental knee in Roddy's ribs. "He pinned me and I left the ring. Well, he left the ring and I slithered out. Of course for me, it was just another shot."

Popular at the time was an ad campaign for Tareyton cigarettes. Billboards showed a cowboy with a black eye, magazines showed sisters with matching black eyes, and the ads all said, "I'd rather fight than switch." Also popular at the time were T-shirts with custom messages in iron-on felt lettering. Garibaldi put the two together and found a way to put Roddy to work, capitalizing on his strongest asset. "A week later, it's TV again, and I see the booker again, Leo Garibaldi. He gave me a T-shirt, and he said, 'Put it on.' The T-shirt said, 'I'd Rather Switch than Fight.' And he made me Java Ruuk's manager. All of a sudden, I was a young, young bad guy and could say anything I want. And that changed the world." Garibaldi was known as a very creative booker, sometimes wildly off the mark but sometimes bang on. He wanted to put Roddy over, and he finally figured out how to do it.

When it came time for Roddy and Ruuk to cut one of their first promos together, Roddy did all the talking. He levelled threats against Chavo Guerrero. Still boyish-looking at age twenty-four, Roddy's mic work was well-developed: the breathless rant, hands and head in constant motion, mimicking an Hispanic accent (which Texas-born Chavo barely possessed), and constant repetition of the opponent's full name—"No disqualification for the Americas title, Chavo Guerrero. I just was talking to the man, Chavo Guerrero, the man is complaining, the man is crying, Chavo Guerrero . . ."—and reminding Guerrero (or the fans, more accurately) that the only time Guerrero and Ruuk fought previously, Guerrero had his hand raised (Roddy won't say "won") when Ruuk was disqualified, but he was nonetheless soundly beaten by Ruuk.

Tellingly, aside from a few wordless hoots, Ruuk stayed silent. Not only was there no space to get a word in, he couldn't possibly have made the promo more entertaining than Roddy was already doing. He was belittling his wrestler's opponent and flattering Ruuk's strength and brutality. By contrast, Guerrero, after he chased Ruuk and Roddy out of the shot and began his own promo for the upcoming title match, seemed to be chasing to keep up with the pace of language that had just been gushing from his antagonist's mouth. It wasn't any shortcoming of Guerrero's that was exposed. He was simply up against a man who was fast becoming one of the best talkers their business had ever seen. Nobody knew that yet—but Garibaldi had a hunch, and he ran with it.

With the go-ahead from the booker, Rod began to assert himself as an antagonist in the ring. One night when he and Java Ruuk stormed onto the mat for a tag team match, Roddy decided he'd slow things down a little. He was the manager, after all. He took control.

As Ruuk was pacing the ring—*"OO-OO-OO-OO"*—Roddy asked announcer Jimmy Lennon to request that the audience stand for the Scottish national anthem. He blew up his bagpipes and waited for the crowd to be quiet. Lennon made the request and after several minutes the raucous crowd calmed down. Roddy started to play "Isle of Skye" while Lennon held the ring microphone next to the bagpipes. To everyone's surprise, the music was lovely, and the crowd perhaps suddenly appreciated Roddy a little more. The cooling of hostilities was brief.

Even the most tone deaf of wrestling fans must have noticed some notes being held for an unpleasantly long time, turning a fine composition into a racket. The crowd lost it. Cigarette butts and drink cups rained down. Then Roddy corrected the song and people grew quiet again. Then he screwed it up again and they got angry again. He teased the crowd back and forth until they could barely stay in their seats. When wrestlers talked about "heat," this was it. Few wrestlers could turn up the heat like Roddy was learning to do. The Roddy Piper school of ring psychology was open for class.

Roddy's presence in the spotlight became a constant. Fight the first match, referee another, manage someone in a third, then wrestle the final: Was this success? Maybe, but some nights it sure didn't feel like wrestling. Mike LeBell handed him a plastic gold watch and sent him into the ring to act like he was hypnotizing wrestler Keith Franke. "I'm going, 'You are getting sleepy,'"—he laughed—"'you will wrestle for free.'"

The gag was embarrassing. The company backstage that day made it worse. "Who's behind camera watching? Harley Race, the world champion. Andre the Giant."

The next week at the Olympic someone from the office chased

Roddy down in the halls. "Hey, Piper, LeBell wants you."

"I didn't do nothing!"

"Get up now."

Roddy found a line of fans in the hall outside the balcony. "There's about twenty people, Hispanic people that have problems, and they want to be hypnotized. They want help. There's a table that's teeter-tottering, and one of those red glass candles with the fishnet stocking around it, lit. I say, 'What?!'"

Word got around and fans—sometimes hundreds—began lining up at the Olympic to get Roddy to hypnotize their troubles away. It ended when a middle-aged man began weeping in the candlelight because his wife had cancer and his kids were having troubles. Realizing the gimmick had gone far enough, Roddy stopped the charade then and there. Fans were pleading in all sincerity for his help. Kayfabe extended deep into the lives of wrestlers, but it had just over-extended its reach. LeBell wasn't happy with Roddy, but he had other ideas. "He said, 'What if we got you to swing into the ring from the balcony? We'll get Batista,'—who was the janitor—'to rig it up.'"

Roddy could see that rope ending up around his neck. There was another, more immediate problem with the idea. Anybody flying laterally as fast as a rope secured in the rafters would carry him would have to let go long before he was over the ring in order to land in it. If he didn't, he'd fly over the ropes and miss the ring. As for letting go before he hit the ring . . . anyway you look at it this was a promoter letting his imagination get the better of his judgement. It seems entertaining in this instance, because it didn't happen. "I think what killed it was this," said Roddy, *"What if he goes out the other side and hurts somebody and we get sued?"*

Refusing LeBell was a brave move, given that Roddy's career was finally starting to gain serious traction, and that LeBell and

Garibaldi controlled the stage where it was happening. Roddy was taking the lumps and whipping up the outrage of the fans, but those two allowed him out there every night to do it. There was a balance to be struck between promoters and wrestlers, and if the promoter held up his end Roddy swore he'd hold up his. With LeBell and Garibaldi, that was good enough.

The hypnotizing gag also signalled Roddy's growing distaste for the wresting term "marks." He thought it belittled fans who bought wholeheartedly into the fictions of the business. A fan who bought a ticket to see him wrestle had placed a level of trust in him, and he had learned not to betray that trust. Besides, you could piss off the most domineering promoter, but if the fans are buying tickets to see you, no promoter could afford to get rid of you. But you had to find a way to sell those tickets.

Roddy had yet another match coming up against Chavo Guerrero in Los Angeles. "We wrestled so many times," Chavo said. "What are you going to say that's going to bring the people to buy a ticket to see you guys again?"

Roddy was mulling over that question. Audience interest sold tickets. Tickets sales put a wrestler at the top. With a fresh handle on getting into the audience's heads, Roddy moved to see how far he could push the boundaries and do his part to fill seats. "They allowed me to get creative," he said.

During commercial break while filming Wednesday's television, the big backstage doors opened and Roddy appeared with a donkey. "What the fuck's going on?" Chavo said to himself.

Roddy knew the largely Hispanic crowds at the auditorium would always cheer for Chavo. He and Chavo had a heel/babyface dynamic they couldn't reverse if they tried. He'd have to up the ante if he wanted to get the audience's attention. Enter the donkey.

"Tijuana zebras" are a tradition that began in the 1930s when Mexican burro cart owners attracted tourists to take pictures with their animals. Pale-haired donkeys didn't show up well in black-and-white photography, so the owners painted stripes on the animals. It struck Roddy as a good place to start his next bit of ring psychology. "So Roddy comes out and he holds the donkey and he puts a little hat on him," Chavo said. "And he says to the donkey, 'Now, Mrs. Guerrero, let me tell you about your kids.'"

Roddy remembered the promo with fondness and a touch of sheepishness. "I did this interview on a donkey painted like a zebra. I had a sombrero on and a stick with a carrot on it." He started complaining about lazy, uneducated Mexicans and threw language around that would be considered scandalous today.

It wasn't the use of stereotypes that got under Chavo's skin, it was the invoking of his mother. To top it off, Roddy was wearing a T-shirt that read, "Conquistador of the Guerreros."

"And I'm hot, brother, I am fuming," remembered Chavo. "And I'm right across the hall and I'm ready to jump this guy, man. You know, he's insulting my mom!" All the wrestlers tolerated a lot of ribbing in promos, and sometimes it hit pretty low, but this was a blow Chavo had not seen coming. "Fuck it! He's calling that donkey Mrs. Guerrero! So, man, they got me hot, and of course he was hilarious in his promos. Then it was my turn. I defended my mother and I was actually really, really hot. I rushed him right after the promo. He said, 'No! Amigo, amigo!' I said, 'Nah, just joking, brother. But that was good, that was good.' We'd come up with some crazy shit. That was all Roddy, man. He had a knack. He was just entertaining."

If Roddy's heel act seems like a politically incorrect horror show in retrospect, at the time he just seemed like a jerk—a jerk Hispanic wrestling fans paid good money to hate. Of course, this was a time when kids watched Speedy Gonzales rescue his drunken Mexican compatriots as their Saturday-morning cartoon fare. (In the ring against Chavo Roddy wore another T-shirt reading "White Is Right" across the back.) "The president of the network, he was going to shut us down," said Roddy. Mike LeBell was afraid Roddy with his donkey interview might have just gotten them thrown off Hispanic television, a contract that saw Wednesday's Olympic wrestling broadcast across the United States and Mexico, wherever there were enough Hispanic viewers. "So during the first interview [after the donkey] I said, 'Ladies and gentlemen, I apologize, I'm very sorry. I'm going to learn how to play the Mexican national anthem on the *gaita*,' the bagpipes in Spanish."

Wednesday's television matches often served to set up Friday's matches at the auditorium. They sold out that Friday, with Roddy's promise to play the anthem. He entered the ring and asked Jimmy Lennon to have the people rise for the Mexican national anthem. People rose and stood hand over heart. Lennon brought the microphone down to the chanter. "I blew up my bagpipes and I started to play—'La Cucaracha.' Here come the chairs that were bolted down!" Riots weren't expected every night, but they happened often enough that they were no surprise when they occurred. "Amigo, you're on your own!" said Chavo from across the ring. "The night never got started. Holy cow, one of the best riots," Roddy recalled. "It was a hell of a house," he added, as ever with his mind on business. "It got over."

Chavo marvels that Roddy had pulled this off with nobody knowing he was going to do it. "Nobody knew about this," he said. "He starts playing 'La Cucaracha.' I'm going, 'What!? If I'm hot and I know him, can you imagine the people at home?' Mexicans, they don't wear the flag on their ass. The flag is sacred. Much less saying it's the national anthem and playing 'La Cucaracha'! Oh, my brother, that was serious heat." Chavo laughed. "These were things that only Piper could come up with. Nobody told him to do that, he just did it. That was Piper."

The stunt worked. Nearly too well. Roddy was trapped in the ring as the crowd erupted, and he had to kick charging fans off the apron as they lowered their heads to climb through the ropes. Wrestlers called the practice "punting." Despite the police's attempts to keep rioting fans at bay, by the end of the night, he'd been stabbed, punched, scratched. "And that's when Vince McMahon Sr. got wind of this kid in LA," Chavo recalled.

Far away in New York, McMahon took his time. Southern California had been a moribund territory before the Piper-Guerrero feud. But he kept listening to the noise building on the West Coast.

Roddy had stirred up a hornet's nest to put himself over with the LA crowds. Getting stung was inevitable.

"One of the fan favourites was, they'd get lit cigarettes and they'd flick them on your back. 'Cause you're sweating, they'd stick. But if you dare acknowledge it you'd get twenty of them. So you just let them burn off."

Cigarette burns were a lesser concern. Another technique for getting at the heel they loved to hate sprung from the most innocuous of sources. "They used to put a knife in the popcorn. Coming down the aisle, it's a tough fuckin' crowd. As you'd come by they'd catch you."

The knives would disappear into the popcorn boxes as quickly as they emerged. If Roddy was quick enough to identify the culprit, the fan who'd slashed him would slip in between others and disappear. Leo Garibaldi approached Mike LeBell about moving the seats away from where the wrestlers entered the floor. "Mike says, 'Why?' 'Cause that's where they're stabbing Roddy. And Mike says, 'That's why they buy those seats.'"

Soldiers, cops, politicians: people in high-risk jobs often go through life wondering if somewhere there is a bullet waiting with their name on it. One night in Los Angeles, Roddy stopped wondering.

Coming down the aisle at the Olympic, he was getting booed and the drink cups were flying. Both were signs of an engaged audience, and reason enough to give the night his best effort. Strangely, he noticed Jimmy Lennon stepping down from the ring. Roddy didn't pay the announcer much mind. He was more concerned with the crowd and getting himself into the ring without being cut or struck by flying objects.

From his vantage point in the ring, Lennon had noticed a man forcing himself to the front of the crowd, in anticipation of Roddy's appearance. Lennon, in his sixties, placed himself between the man and the oblivious wrestler. The man was carrying a .45 handgun. He began yelling, "Move! Move!" at Lennon, who started looking around like he was confused. "Jimmy Lennon saw what was going on and he pretended he didn't know and gave the cops just enough time. They got a high sign and they got undercover cops and they got the guy."

Roddy was still unaware that someone had been trying to shoot him. Lennon, a staunch believer that the show must go on, climbed back through the ropes and announced the match.

In the dressing room after, a cop approached Roddy and asked him to follow him to the office. Roddy still didn't know anything out of the ordinary had taken place. "I go up to the office and there was a .45 and a bullet. The guy had carved my name in it: P. I. P. E. R."

Stoking antagonism is a dangerous way to make a living. Wrestlers had a lot of steam to blow off, and they tended to play hard.

When Mando Guerrero was getting married, some of his wrestling buddies decided to throw him a bachelor party. Mike LeBell footed the bill and invited all the wrestlers and police who regularly worked the arena. The Olympic Auditorium ring was a second home to all of them. With tequila flowing, Mando's brothers coaxed him onto the ring apron. With promises of a bachelor's proper send-off into the fidelities of marriage, they used one officer's handcuffs to tie Mando to the second rope and sat him down to await his parting gift from bachelorhood. "It was about one o'clock in the morning," remembered Roddy. "Here I come down, with just my kilt on. I come up to Mando. They'd put a bag over his head." Mando felt the fabric of the kilt and realized it wasn't the dancer they hired standing over him, it was Roddy. "Sasquatch couldn't have beat him. Everything was moving, everything was punching." Roddy got as close as his legs before a dancer hired for the evening took over the show.

Roddy had endeared himself to Southern California's first family of wrestling—occasionally despite himself. He was remarkably professional in the ring, and the more he and Chavo fought, the more in sync they became. But it was in one of his first ring encounters with the Guerrero clan that he'd set himself up in the audiences' minds as the family's number-one enemy. Looking back after a few years in LA, it surprised him that the family didn't feel the same way as the fans.

There was a clock at the Olympic that counted down backwards. Televised matches were on a tight schedule, so the wrestlers would watch it closely, knowing exactly how long each match was supposed to last. On this night, as Roddy and Chavo were getting close to their finish, Roddy lined up Chavo against the corner post. He rushed Chavo, Chavo moved and Roddy slammed into the post. On the floor behind the post was Gory Guerrero, Chavo's father, who was appearing that night as his son's manager. Looking to wrap up the match with a bang, Roddy reached down past the post and slapped Gory across the head. In a slight miscue, the slap broke the older man's eardrum. "That brings my dad up and the referee goes to put my dad down and Roddy knocks me out and one, two, three," said Chavo. The match finished on time, and by slapping the esteemed Mexican-American wrestler in front of the Olympic's Hispanic audience, Roddy lit a fire beneath the feud he and Chavo had been brewing. "I felt horrible," said Roddy, about the injury. "You didn't fool with Mr. Guerrero. But, you know, it worked."

"He was so sorry," says Chavo. "He apologized and apologized. My dad said, Don't worry about it. I love it. That's the only way to do it." Even the senior Guerrero wasn't above a good rib, and the young Canadian was easy to shame. "I can't hear but that's all right," Gory said. "You did me a favour—I don't have to hear my grandchildren for the rest of my life."

Chavo kept it going. "Roddy, he was all red. Later on I'm ribbing him: 'You did that to my dad on purpose, you son of a bitch.' He still would fall for it."

Gory Guerrero became a mentor to his sons' friend and arch-enemy. "In wrestling, timing is of the essence. Roddy would know when to throw a punch," Chavo said. "He would know when to pull the hair. We would correct him. My dad loved Roddy, too. My dad would tell him, 'Come here, why did you pull the hair *in front* of the referee?'—yessir, no sir. 'Let me tell you why. If you do it in front of the referee, he's watching you. If you do it with the referee not watching you, then you get the heat.' I was learning also myself. Roddy would always listen to him."

The slap set up a future six-man tag-team match designed to let the Guerrero clan settle the score. "All of a sudden there's a whole bunch of people come to see me get my butt kicked," recalled Roddy. "It was a six-man tag. There's Hector, Chavo and

Mando in one corner. There's me, Crusher Verdu and I think it was The Hangman, in the other corner." LeBell billed the card as Guerrero Night, and unbeknownst to the wrestlers, he'd flown the whole Guerrero family in from El Paso to Los Angeles, including their mother, father, two sisters and their little brother, Eddie. "Not only do I have to wrestle one Guerrero," Roddy said to Chavo. "Now there's two, now there's three, now there's four, now there's a little one looking in ringside with mean eyes. There's no hope for me!"

"You're doomed, baby, you're doomed!" Chavo laughed.

Mrs. Guerrero entered the ring with colourful handmade vests and presented them to her sons. In case her sons needed to be reminded, the family's name was at stake. "They put them on, they're sobbing, there's tears coming," said Roddy. "I'm looking like, boys, we're gonna die. I spent fifteen minutes in the air. I was going to give them my frequent flier number." Roddy had come to love Mrs. Guerrero; she'd been kind to him. Her appearance, rallying her sons against him, even as "a work," had made it very clear where his night was going.

Works in the ring didn't change the fact that wrestlers of any stripe could relate to no one else in the world like they could to each other. One weekend, Mando, Chavo and Roddy escaped to the California countryside for a day off. Accompanying them was a man to whom their business owed much, and to whom Roddy in particular owed his entry into Los Angeles, Red Bastien. "Needles, California," said Roddy, "it's got this beautiful river, and high rocks." The foursome had made a date to go waterskiing with Chavo's jet boat, a water-skiers' dream with an enormous Ford Cobra engine. They'd spent the night before at the local Red Dog Saloon, where Bastien cautioned the Guerreros that he couldn't swim. In the morning, as they were making their way down the dock, he was anxious about getting into the boat. The brothers urged him on. They all had life vests. He could just enjoy the ride and leave the waterskiing to them. He got onboard and they were soon racing down the pristine river. "So, I'm water-skiing, Mando's water-skiing. It's Chavo's turn to water-ski. Mando's driving, just like Mando drives!" As Mando ratcheted up the speed, Chavo realized he was going too fast. Mando sped up more and Chavo let go, sinking low in the water. Holding his water-skis, he began drifting slowly away in the current. Instead of circling around to pick him up, Mando turned the wheel hard. It was a small boat. There were only a few seats so Bastien was sitting on the bow, without a lifejacket. The hard turn sent him tumbling into the water. "Now, I'm the only man on earth who saw the rest," said Roddy, barely able to contain himself. Bastien went under the surface of the river and didn't come up. His hat was floating where he'd gone down. Chavo, drifting still, was desperately trying to get someone's attention. Mando was having a good time with Roddy and hadn't seemed to realize Bastien was in the water. Once Mando noticed, he panicked and fell trying to get over the side, scraping his knees bloody in the process. He dove in. Chavo abandoned his skis and tried swimming against the current to reach Bastien, too.

Roddy laughed at the memory. "Red Bastien comes up, spits water out of his mouth and puts his hat on. He'd been in the navy."

Through a heavy steel door and down a dimly lit flight of stairs with paint peeling off the walls and pipes dripping overhead, night after night Roddy headed for the Olympic Auditorium locker rooms. Every night after his match, an old black man shuffled into the showers with a bar of soap and washcloth to scrub him down. Roddy knew him as Tiger Nelson. "Oh,

Horse-cock, you could have heard that heat in Tokyo," Tiger said as he washed Roddy's back. He said the same to all the wrestlers. It was a clever line, as heat—or the crowd's outrage—was a positive result for any wrestler, no matter who won or lost. Tiger didn't watch the matches.

Roddy liked Tiger and would tip him each week. Finally he asked the old man why he called him Horse-cock. "Well, sir, everybody likes to be called Horse-cock, and that way I don't have to remember anybody's name."

One night Roddy found Tiger outside the arena, upset that he'd missed the last bus back to Watts, where he lived. Roddy offered to give him a ride. Tiger was reluctant. "Not many white folks live where I do, sir," he said. Roddy insisted, and Tiger didn't have another option. Besides, he'd never ridden in a Cadillac and Roddy had just bought one.

They drove to Watts and Tiger invited him in to his tiny house for a drink of Ripple, a cheap flavoured wine (Red Foxx on the show *Sanford and Son* joked that he mixed it with ginger ale to make "Champipple"). A poor, elderly black man living in Watts drinking Ripple was easy to imagine. What Roddy stumbled on next was not.

As he scanned a scrapbook full of photos he noticed a picture of two men in black ties, tails and stovepipe hats. One looked like Bob Hope. "That *is* Mr. Hope, sir."

The other was Tiger. He'd owned a nightclub and Hope used to perform there. "When I wore that, people used to give me respect."

Roddy then came across a photo of a woman, Tiger's wife, Rosie. Tiger didn't know what had become of her. "They think that she may have just wandered into the wrong neighbourhood."

Tiger wasn't making sense, thought Roddy. He'd owned a nightclub that could hire Bob Hope, but was so poor his wife could just disappear off the face of the earth. Roddy turned another page and found the answer.

An overhead photo of a boxing ring showed two men in the middle of a match, one of whom Roddy recognized as the great Jack Johnson. When Roddy asked him who Johnson was fighting, Tiger replied, "Why, Mr. Piper, he's fighting me."

Holding on to the great Jack Johnson for fifteen rounds—and Tiger said holding on was all he really did—meant nobody else wanted to fight him. The fight that should have made Tiger famous ended his career. With it went his nightclub and whatever wealth he'd put together from his fame as a fighter.

Throughout telling his story, Tiger had been coughing and holding his side. When he was finished talking, he bent over and let loose a terrible coughing jag. He asked Roddy if he'd mind his laying down for a bit. Of course, said Roddy, and added that he should get going anyway.

It was the last time they saw each other. Tiger Nelson died soon afterward, a forgotten man. Roddy was one of four people at his funeral.

It might have been easy for Roddy to dismiss that hard lesson about fame. Tiger Nelson was an uneducated black man who'd come up in an unforgiving time for black fighters. Johnson himself had been railroaded by trumped-up scandal. Any excuse to shut down a black contender was jumped at.

Nelson was nothing like Roddy. And Roddy had fought his way out of the streets of a rough northern town and into the spotlight of the third biggest city in America. Still, the example nagged at him. No matter how high you climbed, it only took one slip to send you back to wherever you came from.

During his three-and-a-half years in Los Angeles, Roddy made many friends whom he'd wrestle in the years to come. But this was Hollywood. Filled with celebrities and aspirants to fame. Meeting show business people was part of the fun. One Hollywood hopeful used to hang around the Olympic's rear entrance and do his Elvis impersonation for the police who guarded it. This got him in to see the matches for free, which says a little about how security worked at the Olympic.

After the matches, the impersonator, named Andy, sought out Roddy and told him how funny he found him. At the end of one match, Roddy was standing, bloodied, over a few other wrestlers he'd just beat up, giving them hell on the microphone. The thoroughly enraged crowd started to get out of their chairs and push through security toward the stage. A riot was inevitable. Seeing the crowd advance, Roddy said into the microphone, "Is there no justice?" Andy thought this was the funniest thing he'd ever heard.

Roddy couldn't figure out Andy's sense of humour, but the skinny comic entertained him and they got along, so they'd go together to comedy clubs. Andy took the stage at the Improv and, just as strangely, used Roddy's interview and promo lines to do stand up. It made no sense to the crowd either, and they booed him off the stage.

Andy did just about everything differently, even hiring a yellow school bus after his shows to take people out for dessert. He introduced Roddy to the star of a show he was working on, Dick Van Dyke. "So this is the genius you've been talking about?" said Van Dyke.

Roddy never figured out why Andy thought he was so funny or professional wrestling so fascinating. There was a transgressiveness to the spectacle that triggered something in the young comedian.

That purposeful discomfort, that hysteria-inducing obliteration of social norms spilling over into the audience: it left wrestling fans genuinely changed, even if some nights that meant a full-fledged riot stopped the show—or more accurately, became the show. Nobody could turn that transgressive spark into a show-stopping inferno like Roddy, who was now on top in Los Angeles. But Roddy realized that even the hottest fires eventually burn themselves out. All the Mexicans in California couldn't stay mad at him forever.

Roddy told Andy one evening that he was leaving LA. He'd done all he could in Los Angeles, so he had accepted an offer to wrestle elsewhere. To stay any longer would risk all the value he'd built into his name.

With eyes glistening, Andy looked at him, deeply sad, and said, "I'll make you proud of me, Roddy."

With that, Roddy said goodbye. He and Andy Kaufman never saw each other again.

Roddy said his farewells to Mike LeBell and Leo Garibaldi as well. They had given him his first chance to be a main-eventer and he'd pushed the opportunity as far as it would carry him. They had cleaned up at the box office and Roddy had built a reputation and skill set that could take him almost anywhere.

They weren't keen to see him go. By this time, Chavo was doing much of the booking in LA and had been in the office to hear LeBell phoning around the country, trying to determine who was poaching his prize heel. Realizing that Chavo and Roddy were close, he tried to squeeze Chavo to tell. "I never said a word," Chavo said, though he knew full well it was Don Owen in Portland, Oregon.

It was hard not to like Roddy. The other wrestlers admired him, too, and stepped up when they worked against him. And his authenticity lent him an uncommon charisma with fans. He seemed to be exactly who he said he was. In the Southern states, who would recognize the difference between the flatness of a Canadian prairie accent and a Scottish brogue? Beyond the small matter of his origins, his gimmick was hardly a gimmick.

He'd learned a lot in LA. His mic work was second to none, he was the consummate heel and able to handle the heat, and he had developed a style in the ring like something out of a back alley, with a level of reckless energy fans rarely witnessed at such a high professional level. Gene LeBell had given him tools a wrestler just couldn't get in Winnipeg. And Winnipeg had left him with enough simmering aggression to drive his performance for a lifetime. With Gene's training, that aggression bought him space and respect in the ring. Leo Garibaldi had taught him, as well, about selling all that pent-up hostility. The fear was gone, the spirit was willing and the body was finally strong enough to carry him in the only direction an ambitious young man wanted to go. "Thanks for the blood and guts, kid," said Garibaldi on Roddy's way out. The booker went back to work without so much as a handshake.

Roddy threw his bag over his shoulder and headed for the door. As he walked down the hall he'd first traversed barely out of his teens, he passed a photo on the wall of a young blond wrestler in plaid trunks, ready to take on all comers.

5

Don't Call Us, We'll Call You

Roddy stood with his hand out, waiting for more money. Elton Owen laid a few more small bills in Roddy's palm and looked him in the eye. Roddy's hand stayed put. Owen placed a few more bills down and glared at the new recruit. Roddy remained stone-faced. He'd gotten the memo on Elton, Portland promoter Don Owen's brother. Don't smile when he's paying you or he'll stop paying you.

Sometimes, when doling out the night's take, Elton laid down a ten, took it back and replaced it with a five. "You've got a good attitude, son," he'd say, and give the wrestler another five "for beer money." Then he'd lean in, "But don't tell the boys."

"The boys" told each other all they needed to know.

Short-changing the grateful wasn't Elton Owen's only trick. He liked to tell his wrestlers to shoot for the first few minutes of their match—in other words, no showmanship, just compete. After a minute of going at it, if someone hadn't been pinned for a one-count, the referee would tap both men on the shoulder and they'd proceed to lock up like pros. At the end of the night, if the shoot hadn't been decisive, Elton asked the dressing room who they thought had got the upper hand. He gave the consensus winner $25 and the loser $15.

The Pacific Northwest was a more traditional territory than Los Angeles. While young men like Roddy and Chavo Guerrero had ruled Southern California, older men were on top in Portland. The veterans here, guys on short contracts or wrestlers who lived there, were quite capable of handling Elton Owen. Before the matches, the wrestlers flipped a coin to see who would dominate the shoot. When Owen paid out at the end of the night, the "winner" handed the "loser" the extra five dollars to make it an even split.

The ranting, cigar-chomping Owen rubbed the wrestlers the wrong way. Some nights they'd lock him out of the dressing room. It was best for Owen when they did. One night between matches in Salem, Oregon, he began ranting about the night's card being too anemic for his liking. "You guys couldn't draw flies to shit," he growled. He put his cigar down on a massage table so he could really light into the boys.

Roddy's new tag-team partner, Killer Brooks, grabbed that cigar while Owen was distracted with his tirade, dipped the unlit end into the back of his trunks and gave it a good, deep tour of the area. When Owen was done yelling, the promoter found his cigar where he'd left it. He picked it up and headed for the door. "All right, you guys, get out there and I want you to work, work, work!"

Roddy sat on the bench, tears leaking out of his eyes, he was trying so hard not to laugh. Owen noticed him and asked what was the matter. Roddy shook his head, nothing. Owen cussed at the room a little more and shoved the cigar in his mouth.

He opened the door to leave and then stopped. He spun around and the whole room held its breath. "And another thing," he snarled. "It smells like shit in here!"

Fortunately for the wrestlers, Elton Owen wasn't the Owen in charge. Elton watched over the southern towns like Salem, Eugene and Roseberg, but his brother, Don, ran the territory out of Portland. Roddy found him one of the more fair promoters he had worked for. Don Owen brought in talent and trusted them to work their dynamics out for themselves. Roddy's arrival upset the dynamic at work in the territory, but since Owen trusted them to handle it, the wrestlers worked it out.

Buddy Rose was Owen's top heel and Portland's main draw. But Brooks and Roddy had both made their names as heels. They were tag-team partners as well. That was too many bad guys and not enough babyfaces: there was nobody for the fans to love. Fortunately, Roddy and Brooks were both charismatic and unpredictable. Even when fans hated them, they came in droves to see what they would do next.

Buddy Rose had a tag-team partner, too, in Ed Wiskoski. The four wrestlers decided Rose and Wiskoski would do heel duty while Roddy and Brooks would operate in a less clearly defined space. They wouldn't lead the crowd to consider them necessarily heels or faces. Not just anyone could pull that off. Roddy had the vicious tongue of a classic heel, but the crowds warmed to him anyway. It was part of his appeal: he didn't tell the crowd how to think of him, no matter who he was fighting.

During his first month in Portland, Roddy went on a tear, winning almost all of his matches. Don Owen was setting him up for a good long run. He even reunited Roddy and Hector Guerrero for matches in Portland and Eugene, and threw Roddy into a tag-team match against his friend Red Bastien. But it was in the new year that Roddy's running start in Portland really picked up speed.

Portland wrestling fans remember something that Roddy Piper fans in the rest of the world might not know. His feud with Buddy Rose was quite possibly his best. Roddy was that much more experienced in the ring and on the mic than he'd been in LA, and in Rose he had a creative heel he could play off as the audience's mood allowed. And Portland brought few of the big-time pressures that so narrowly defined where Roddy could direct his later, most famous feud with Hulk Hogan.

Bleached blond and on the corpulent side of fit, Buddy Rose was a spectacular professional wrestler. Animated on the mic and creative in the ring, he had a ten-year run in Portland. Away from the ring, he had his appetites and tended not to disguise them from his peers. "I've got a little blood in the old man!" he'd shout when feeling amorous. The walls of the motel where most of the wrestlers stayed were thin, so he kept his van stocked with clean towels for the purpose of relieving the old man's tensions in private.

He routinely taped his favourite soap operas and sitcoms, and stayed up until dawn watching them in the company of his two dachshunds. One day he called Roddy and said, "It's Pebbles's birthday," and invited Roddy to join the festivities. Roddy went to Rose's room, wondering who Pebbles was. "He's got a hat on the dog, a cape on the dog." When the dogs died, Rose had them stuffed to keep him company a little longer.

Though barely heavier than Roddy's two-thirty when they worked together in Portland, by the time he retired in 2005 his taste for fast food and doughnuts had him tipping the scales at a hundred pounds heavier and suffering from diabetes. He spent his more considerable earnings from his later WWF run on a propane-powered Cadillac with a satellite dish on the roof so he could watch television in the car. It was a typical spend for a man who never had a bank account and kept his money in a brown paper bag.

The Piper-Rose feud began at the end of March 1979 with a promo for an absurd upcoming eight-man tag-team match. The four heels—Piper, Rose, Brooks and Wiskoski—were scheduled to take on Adrian Adonis (the re-named Keith Franke), Hector Guerrero, Ron Starr and George Wells. In the Crow's Nest—a platform above the Portland television studio that placed the wrestlers slightly above and thrillingly close to the audience—the heels gathered around a wheelbarrow full of championship belts, crowing about the damage they would soon do to their opponents and how they'd all become richer working together than against one another.

Brooks and Wiskoski mostly stood in the background and grinned, rapt with the sight of two top talkers trying to get a feel for who would take the lead during the anarchic interview. In retrospect, it's clear that Roddy and Rose could never coexist on the same side, because neither could thrive at what he did best—talking—while allowing a partner to take the lead. Both were creative, both were energetic, and both men were impossible to stop watching.

The ensuing match concluded with a debacle of proportions as grand as its eight-man roster. Wiskoski accidentally elbowed his pinned teammate Brooks in the head, ending any chance of victory for the unsteady alliance of bad guys. Roddy, usually tag-team partner to Brooks, immediately sensed conspiracy and accused Rose and Wiskoski of sabotage. They brawled, and Roddy eventually chased them out of the ring and away from the prostrate Brooks.

The feud was on, and it drove fans into a frenzy for as long as Roddy stayed in Portland. Fans were treated to his ever-expanding arsenal of one-liners, one of which he'd utter infamously on national television several years later: "You don't throw rocks at a guy who's got a machine gun!"

Rose's confirmation as top heel in Portland hardly made Roddy a babyface by default. Another feud, and a very peculiar one, kept a dangerous edge in his relationship with the audience. Roddy found himself nose-to-nose with former NWA women's tag-team champion Vicki Williams (who'd wrestled on a card in Brandon with Roddy in 1974). Two years younger than Roddy and nearly a foot shorter, she confronted him during an in-ring interview wearing what looked like a modest one-piece bathing suit with ferns on it. Costumes anywhere in wrestling in 1979 were modest affairs, but Williams' uninspired garb looked like an office assistant had scooped it from a JC Penny bargain bin ten minutes before airtime. Her attempts to get a word in edgewise with Roddy were brief. "You come down here and burn your bra, thinking you're getting in there with men and wrestling with men?!" he shouted.

She shoved him and shouted back over the buzzing crowd, "I'm a woman, and a little boy is what you are!"

After a brief pause to let her insult sink in, Roddy lost it, infuriated by her choice of words. "Little boy?!" He picked her up by the hair and howled, "Listen to me, woman, I'll tell you what I am. Little boy? This is why men wrestle and women don't!" With that, he steered her across the ring and tossed her into the corner.

It's easy to watch the old clip and understand why, years later, teachers who'd watched this younger Roddy Piper on Portland television presumed he was an abusive husband and father.

The rage he channels as he holds Williams with her feet off the ground (if you look closely, she's actually holding herself up by gripping his arms) feels unchecked, too fluidly pouring out of him to be a put-on. His voice is different than usual—raspier and crueller than the usual squeaks and high-pitched spikes in tone that were part of his charm when he got worked up for the camera. For a few seconds, he sounded like he's ripping his vocal cords with every word.

The bra-burning reference cleverly made the ruse all the more believable. Middle America, wrestling's audience, felt as superior to feminism's challenge to the status quo as they did to LA's Mexicans—the kind of superiority that isn't as certain of itself as it likes to think. America had turmoil in its gut, and Roddy instinctively tapped into it and played it out in a way that sold tickets. Many tickets.

On her short-lived talk show only a few years later, the comedienne Joan Rivers would call Roddy "camp." She was right. From his outsized verbal assaults on the interview cameras, to his inexplicable Scottish trappings without any trace of an accent to match, to the cardboard cut-out of a set that was Piper's Pit, and even in the brawling style in which he wrestled, like the most memorable of his WWF peers—Macho Man, Hulk Hogan, the Iron Sheik—Roddy's persona was total camp. But that was a few years away. There's no trace of camp in the promo with Vicki Williams.

Defying anyone who tried to tell him what he could make of himself had been the ongoing struggle of his entire life to date—*I'll tell you what I am!* And he was still young enough to remember the little boy Williams invoked, gripped in the hands of the raging alpha male of his youth. As much as Roddy was attacking his father's estimation of him—what he was and what he was worth—the beatings and the bitter disappointment lived on inside him. Roddy wasn't channelling his rage in that promo, he was channelling his nightmares.

When Roddy finally showed Williams "why men wrestle and women don't," he tossed her as gently into the corner of the ring as he could without looking fake. Whatever old aches he drew on to inflict and imitate pain, Roddy was in charge of Roddy, and he wouldn't hurt anyone who didn't deserve it—his opponents excepted, of course.

That would serve him well in a few years, when that turn toward camp would begin in New York after he'd dealt with another woman in the ring—with many more people watching.

In the meantime, there would be other trips to New York, and they'd start with one that was much less successful.

"I was selling out the Cow Palace," began Roddy. It was a curious place to begin the story of his New York debut, given that he was working in Portland at the time. But Roy Shire, the San Francisco promoter, had long benefitted from Roddy living within a day's drive of the Bay Area. First, he'd stolen a few days from Roddy when he was in LA, then he brought him down for quick tours from Oregon. After a big weekend, Shire and other promoters around the country got on the phones to boast about gate receipts and guys who'd drawn the crowds. Roddy's name had been coming up for a while. Mike LeBell in LA had good things to say, too, and Roddy was still making the occasional run from Oregon to Southern California. In New York, Vince McMahon Sr. had been listening, and now he wanted to see the supposed Scotsman for himself.

"The very first time I was invited to Madison Square Garden," remembered Roddy, "I was still in Portland and living with

Killer Brooks from Waxahachie, Texas; hair everyplace except the top of his head, little cigar. We made a great tag team. I bought a better jacket. I wanted to look better for New York."

Roddy had Brooks give him a ride to the Portland airport. But Roddy froze when they got to the drop-off. "I said, 'Leave.' He says, 'What?' I went home. I lied to them. I told them that there happened to be some kind of a storm some place, and I lied to them. Because I was scared. I was scared that MSG was always known as a big man's territory . . . I'm just this little guy. I knew in my heart . . . I could feel it that I just wasn't good enough, I just wasn't there yet."

The excuse worked too well. McMahon invited Roddy to try his luck with the weather again. Three weeks later he was on a plane to New York City. "I come to MSG in a limousine . . . Captain Lou Albano comes out." Albano greeted him with a bear hug and a characteristic bit of noise and slapping and pinching of his rosy cheeks. Roddy was overwhelmed by the reception.

The Spanish-language broadcasts of lucha libre wrestling from the Olympic Auditorium reached New York, where they found a large Puerto Rican audience in particular. To Roddy's surprise, the New York wrestlers knew very well who had just landed on their turf—and why he'd been invited. "Freddie Blassie come with a cane, hitting me on my shins, 'Ah, ya pencil-neck geek, we don't want you here, we been watching ya, dumb kid' . . . that's wrestler love."

Roddy was scheduled for the third match that night. In the dressing room he was tuning up his bagpipes. Satisfied they were good to go, he set them down and went into the hall for a few hundred pre-match push-ups, trying to make himself look as big as possible before getting in the ring. He'd been working out hard in preparation to fight in New York, where men like Andre the Giant and Superstar Billy Graham were pushing the business to an unprecedented level of interest. "I said to the announcer, 'Tell them to stand for the Scottish national anthem.'" When the announcer responded with bewilderment, Roddy insisted. He might have been intimidated by the lights and size of everything—and everyone—in New York, but he wasn't going to back down. The announcer did as he was asked. "I got this great plan, I'm gonna play them like Jack Benny used to play the violin." This was the same routine he'd used in LA when tag-teaming with Java Ruuk. He'd begin with something nice, then just as the crowd started to buy into his shtick, he'd start stretching out the worst notes, until he'd annoyed the crowd into an angry fit.

The crowd took a few minutes to settle, and when it did Roddy blew up his pipes and began to play. Nothing came out. He tried again. Same result. After a very uncomfortable few moments of this, he tossed the pipes aside and raced at his opponent, a jobber named Juan Rivera who went by the name Steve King. The only angry person in the arena was Roddy. It didn't matter that he won the match, he'd blown the opportunity—if not his pipes. "I fell on my face."

The message was delivered from Vince McMahon Sr. to Roddy, as he sat humiliated in the dressing room, avoiding the other wrestlers. "Don't call us, we'll call you."

On the plane back to Portland, he examined his bagpipes. An enormous wad of toilet paper was stuffed into the chanter, courtesy, he'd later discover, of Freddie Blassie.

He'd let his guard down when he was met with the placating smiles and teasing welcomes of the New York wrestlers. Maybe he'd believed a little too much of his own press. Maybe he'd taken the camaraderie of the wrestlers on the West Coast for granted. Either way, Blassie's rib about them not wanting him there was no joke. The old guard felt threatened by all the new talent forcing its way into New York, and they weren't about to roll over and let some kid in a skirt take their jobs.

Not yet.

Very few restaurants in Portland served prime rib 24/7. Most Saturday nights after the Portland Sports Arena emptied Roddy and a few other wrestlers would drive down Sunset Highway to Jo-Jo's, where they could order a substantial plate of beef at any hour. The late-night meals were no problem for the restaurant. The wrestlers were. The table was always loud, sometimes with a few young women hanging on for a free meal, and it was obvious that they had all been drinking, or getting into something a little harder in order to keep them going late into the night. The older waitresses didn't want anything to do with them, so wrestler duty fell to the youngest woman on staff, a nineteen year old named Kitty.

Kitty was a country girl with deep roots in the Portland area. She regularly worked the graveyard shift at Jo-Jo's. Every morning after work, she drove to high ground so she could watch the sun rise over the hills to the east. She found the best view on Skyline Blvd, and it just happened to be in a graveyard. To this day she laughs at the thought of this quirky routine, spending dawns in a graveyard at the time when she met her future husband, a man named Toombs.

Kitty took one look at the new regulars and figured they were some sort of team. They were big, muscular and obviously popular. The leaner young blond one wore a huge ring in the shape of a man's torso, its arms holding a flaming torch. Looking at it, she wondered if he was a boxer. Little by little, she got to know them, and the blond one got to wishing he knew her better. Kitty recalled, "After about a month, Roddy took me aside and he said, 'Hey, I can't help but notice you're really sweet, and I was wondering if maybe you'd want to go out with me.'" Female wait staff tended to get propositioned from time to time, and Kitty laughed off Roddy's request for a date. She could tell he was a little older than she was and didn't take him very seriously. Besides, given his and his friends' raucous behaviour, she needed more than a pleasant request as an incentive for her to go out with this guy.

Roddy was quite serious, though. As she walked away from the table one night, he leaned over to Killer Brooks and said, "That's the kind of gal a guy could marry."

After a few more weeks of dismissing Roddy's interest, Kitty found herself face to face not with Roddy, but Brooks. "Killer Brooks, who always came into the restaurant with these tire chains around his neck, was just a gnarly looking guy," she said. Brooks was a little shorter than Roddy, but heavier and wore his straggly black hair long so it flowed into his wild black beard. Wrestling fans knew that the hair on the rest of him pretty much followed suit. "He pulls me aside and he says, 'Hey, come on, you got to go out with him. He's my tag-team partner and I'm getting killed out there because all he's thinking about is you. Would you please go out with him?'"

"Fine," Kitty relented. "I'll take his number and I'll call him."

A few days later, she phoned and they agreed to get together.

Roddy didn't know how to plan a date. All he ever did was drive, fight and party along the way. Come Sundays, exhausted by the cycle of wrestling, recording promos, driving, drinking hard and popping pills to pry himself out of bed for the next day, he really did need a rest. Meeting anybody other than the guys in the ring and the odd hanger-on was all but impossible. But Roddy always pushed himself when it counted. He kept the planning simple, and as usually happened when he went with his instincts, he got it right.

He met up with Kitty behind an elementary school on a Sunday evening, where they sat on the swing set and talked the night away. They hit it off immediately. Roddy was no country boy, but he knew a few things about growing up with small-town values. Sure, he was packing a 9mm handgun under his jacket and had smoked a joint on the way there to settle his nerves, but Kitty didn't know that and didn't see trouble in the big grinning guy swinging beside her. The trappings of a wrestler's lifestyle didn't taint her view of Roddy then—and they never really would.

They dated off and on for a few months, both too busy to make a regular thing of their relationship. They grabbed time when and where they could. And when Kitty mentioned to her family who she was spending that time with, Roddy's notoriety finally caught up with their budding romance. Her grandfather was one of the many thousands of Pacific Northwesterners who had been riding the roller coaster that was the Piper-Rose feud, and he thought he knew a few things about the big-mouthed heel in the kilt. At her mention of dating Roddy, he was beside himself. "Roddy Piper!" he cried. "No, you can't go out with him. He's a much older man and he's very bad. He's evil. He's a wrestler!"

He'd been watching Roddy wrestle on television for so long that he figured he must be at least ten or fifteen years older than Kitty. And all those Saturday nights of Roddy's playing the heel left little doubt about the deficiencies in his character. Fortunately, her parents were a little more open-minded, figuring she was smart enough to know if a guy was bad news. Besides, she wasn't a girl who could be told who she could see and who she couldn't.

One morning Kitty walked out of Jo-Jo's and found a photograph of Roddy on her car windshield. Scribbled across his promotional shot were the words, I *love* you. "That's the first time he had said that to me," says Kitty. "But that was also when he left for Hawaii."

Buddy Rose had taken a shine to his new rival. In 1975 in Texas, Rose had met another wrestler with whom he'd become fast friends, a French Canadian named Rick Martel. Martel was a rare specimen in those days, with the chiselled physique of a bodybuilder in the years when wrestlers' appeal came from how dangerous they looked, not how well-suited they were to the cover of a magazine. Martel's square jaw and radiant smile didn't hurt his popularity. He wrestled in New Zealand but took the summer of 1979 to work in Honolulu, where he did double duty as the booker for promoters Steve Rickard and Peter Maivia (grandfather of future WWE superstar and actor Dwayne "The Rock" Johnson). Martel brought Rose to Hawaii, and Rose brought word of a guy Martel should consider bringing to Hawaii too.

"He told me about this young guy, Roddy Piper," Martel said. "'You should bring him in, he'd be great.' We were all young guys, I was twenty-three. I said, 'Yeah, sure.' I brought him in."

Roddy arrived and got straight to work. "Man, the first night I saw Roddy in the ring, the interviews and all that, I said, 'Ah man, that guy's great.' The way I saw the talent, I recognized how great he was.

"Then we got to spend a little time together and man, we clicked right away. It was an instant bond that was created between him and I. That was fun. Professionally and outside, we really got along great."

Roddy spent time with another new friend in Hawaii. He called Kitty one day, out of the blue, and asked her to join him in Honolulu. A visit to Hawaii meant taking a month off from Jo-Jo's, but Roddy was going to fly her out and put her up, so she said yes.

Meanwhile, Roddy and Rick Martel picked up a few new wrestling tricks, one from a wrestler Roddy had gotten to know during his time in the Maritimes, the Cormier brother known as The Beast. "We used to do the interviews every Wednesday morning in the studio," Martel said. They were doing the interviews for an upcoming event at the Blaisdell Center arena in Honolulu. Martel was promoting his cage match against The Beast. "We had the heels on one side, the babyfaces on the other side. I was beside Roddy. We saw this guy, The Beast, come in with a beer bottle in his hand." Puzzled, they figured Cormier was going to chug the beer to make a point about how little he was worried about wrestling Rick. "We saw him do the interviews, and then BOOM!" Cormier drove the full bottle of beer against his forehead, where it exploded into a shower of suds and shattered glass. "We were both like, '*Wow.*' The blood's going, the brew, we're just, 'Man, that's great!'"

Only a madman would shatter a bottle over his own head. Except they both knew The Beast was quite sane. When Martel had started his pro career in the Maritimes as a seventeen year old, two summers before Roddy, The Beast had shown him the ropes just as he'd do for Roddy. "These guys were really strict: respectful, you had to be respectful," said Martel of the Cormier family. "They showed us the right way to do things. How to behave and all that." If the Beast could bottle himself, it couldn't be as bad as it looked. They'd file that trick away for another day. In the meantime, they were enjoying themselves, but Roddy was encountering a crowd reaction familiar from California.

"I went as the Great Haole," said Roddy. *Haole* was a Hawaiian term for white people. Being a haole wasn't necessarily a bad thing, unless you boasted about it. Enter the heel, Roddy Piper. "One of the things that they used to do in Hawaii, those Samoans,

I'd be fighting for my life, literally, with Peter Maivia, Chief Peter Maivia, great man. They'd break the antennas off of cars, and then when you'd come down the aisle they'd bring them out and whip you with them." Car antennas telescoped into a very small piece of metal and were easy to hide. "Really?!" he said, remembering the stinging slashes across the arms. "How much money am I getting for this?"

Kitty spent much of July and August enjoying Hawaii with him before heading home, but quit the graveyard shift at Jo-Jo's shortly after she returned. She found a new job, one suited to her interest in animals, working with show horses at Maxon's Stables several hours east near Walla Walla, Washington. As much as she loved Roddy, they were a long way from settling down and making something serious of their relationship.

By October, Roddy was back in Portland. But that brief summer in Hawaii led to a number of connections. Martel had left Hawaii as well and returned to New Zealand. He wasn't there for long before Luke Williams of the Sheepherders called him and asked if he'd like to come to Portland.

The Sheepherders were a tag team from New Zealand who'd wrestled with Roddy in Hawaii. "Saved us from that island of Oahu," remembered Williams with a laugh. After returning to Oregon, Roddy had called them to say they needed another tag team in the territory. They were interested so he'd hooked them up with Don Owen. Now they were passing the favour on to Martel.

Despite the invitation to join Williams and Miller in the Pacific Northwest, Martel wasn't very keen on the idea. Portland seemed isolated and wasn't a big promotion. "Then he told me Roddy was there," said Martel. "I said, 'Ah man, here I come!'"

Roddy watched with his hands in cuffs. A few feet away, Rick Martel was taken down, kicked, punched and stomped. Roddy didn't mind. He loved these crazy Kiwis. So did Martel.

The Sheepherders had first come to America in 1965, brought into the NWA by Steve Rickard, who booked them in Hawaii and sent them to Don Owen in Portland at Roddy's request.

Shaggy haired, bearded and missing a few front teeth, Butch Miller and Luke Williams tromped around the ring with a certainty to their backwoods Kiwi shtick that fast made them crowd favourites wherever they wrestled, and over the course of three decades together, they wrestled pretty near everywhere. Loud, heavily accented and comically brutish, they were the perfect foil to the youthful charm and camera-friendliness of Piper and Martel. "They're one of the greatest tag teams ever, in history," said Roddy. And as men, he knew few he'd consider so solid.

In Salem, Oregon, they'd handcuffed the vanquished Roddy to the corner post and were taking turns beating up Martel in the middle of the ring. The night was going well. Then someone, maybe a fan who'd taken the scene a little too much to heart, ran to the back office and told Elton Owen what was happening. "He comes back to the ring," Williams said, "he fines us. And by now Butch is pissed off."

The Portland tag teams were coming through Salem every week, and the post-bell beating being delivered by the Sheepherders was intended to build up some heat with the audience that would carry the feud over to next week. Not seeming to get the fundamentals of his own business, Owen and his $5000 fine threw cold water on everything the wrestlers were getting warmed up. "Butch goes and grabs the belts and he tells me to grab him from behind. So I grab Elton from behind. Butch comes and whacks him over the head with the belts." Elton goes down in a heap, his toupee skewed sideways and his glasses on the floor. The temperature ringside was back up to where the crowd wanted it, but at the expense of the promoter's pride.

After the matches, the wrestlers sat in the dressing room, too nervous to go into Elton's office to collect their pay. Nobody wanted to be first. "In the end, Butch went in there and he said, 'Elton, what a hell of a job you did. But next time Luke'll tell you to duck and I'll hit Luke with it and you'll get out of the way and fine us then.' And Elton said to Butch, 'One hell of an idea.' And he gave him extra money for a good attitude."

Elton Owen really didn't seem to get that wrestlers were *trying* to rile up the crowds. One night in Salem, Roddy was marching around the ring, playing his bagpipes. The crowd was booing, throwing things, calling him names. He played louder. He played worse. Suddenly Elton appeared in the ring. "I can't play them," he shouts into the microphone, "you can't play them. Give it up! Give the guy a break!" The crowd relented and a few people applauded. Roddy looked on in wonder. Elton Owen really didn't understand.

Not surprisingly, the houses in Salem and Eugene fell a little short of the constant sell-outs in Portland. The promoter had something to do with it. He was a drinker, which didn't help. "He's the only guy I know to shoot himself in the Niagara Falls," laughed Williams. For reasons that Owen has long since taken to the grave, Elton called testicles Niagara Falls. "He's coming out and he's got the money," explained Roddy, "and he's drunk and he thinks he has to protect things." Owen didn't just have the night's take to dole out to the wrestlers, he had a gun. Drunk, he wasn't handling it very expertly. Juggling the bills and the handgun, he lost his grip and grabbed the thing he cared the most about. Bad decision. "And he shoots himself in the testicles. They brought him to the hospital and the doctor asked him, 'Did you try to commit suicide?' [and he says] 'By shooting myself in the balls?!'"

Yet another night found Roddy and Rick Martel in the ring with the Sheepherders. "We got some heat up," said Williams. "Real heat. Fans are throwing drinks into the ring."

As long as there had been professional wrestling, people had thrown plastic drink cups at heels and lacklustre performers. If you couldn't negotiate a puddle of Orange Crush on the mat, arguably you should be doing something else for a living. So it was all the more confounding for the four men in the ring when Owen's wife climbed into the ring while the match was on, carrying a mop and pail. A wrestler couldn't be faced with a more confusing circumstance in the middle of a match. The wrestlers steered themselves to one corner and put a hold on each other to slow things down while she finished mopping up the puddle of soda.

In Roseberg, the wrestlers had to wash up after their matches with the leftover hot dog water from the concessions (there were no showers). The spartan facilities set a tone. The wrestlers would try to piss off Owen by lining up and clicking their heels like Nazi officers while he played a grand piano on the auditorium stage after the shows. The ribs, screw-ups and hijinks were relentless. "This is just about nine months of the Bushwackers, Roddy Piper, Rick Martel, Killer Brooks, Buddy Rose," remembered Roddy. "Every night, something!"

Roddy and Williams laughed at memories of the shortcomings of life with Elton Owen, but in the end Portland was the seat of a small circuit and its rough edges weren't to every wrestler's taste. Many great wrestlers passed through the territory in those years. Andre the Giant and Jesse Ventura joined Roddy and Martel in a six-man tag-team match, while Buddy Rose or another local joined the Sheepherders to fill out the opposition. Chavo Guerrero came up the coast for a week, thrilled to be reunited with his good friend from Los Angeles. Chavo's run didn't last long. As a wrestling territory, Portland was a far cry from California—but more importantly so was its money. "Why are you leaving?" Roddy asked Chavo, distraught to see his friend packing up after only a week. "Making a hundred dollars a night?" replied Guerrero. "That was okay when we started, but no."

Another wrestler from LA settled in Portland for a little longer. Adrian Adonis and Roddy weren't Twenty-Twos any more, but they still knew how to have fun.

Elton had just secured a new high school gym to use as a venue in one of his southern Oregon towns. "I don't want anything damaged here," he said, having called his wrestlers to order in the middle of the gymnasium floor. "I've just got the building."

As the promoter was speaking, Adonis got down on his hands and knees behind him. He started barking and biting Owen on the ankles. Owen shook his leg and kicked his heels back, but didn't look down so as not to lose eye contact with the group. "Elton's trying to be serious," laughed Roddy. Adonis was gripping the hem of Owen's pants in his teeth. "He literally thinks it's a dog. 'Get off me!'"

Looking back, Williams and Roddy weren't surprised that Elton Owen didn't catch on to the fact his leg was being chewed on by a 250-pound man. "We had full houses. It was full except for Elton's towns." says Williams. "He didn't even know who the champions were."

Roddy and Martel were cooling their heels at the Bomber Motel over a few drinks.

The Bomber was a wooden, one-storey roadside motel with a totem pole out front. Like the Alamo and the Flamingo before it, the Bomber had a reputation. But more famous than the motel was the gas station attached to it. The owner was a WWII veteran, and he'd bought a B-52 bomber after the war and had it mounted above his pumps. Word was he'd taxied it down the roads outside Portland to his property before having a crane lift it into position.

"Hey," Martel asked Roddy, "What do you think about that thing The Beast did, you know with the beer? Why don't we try it, see if we can do it."

"Yeah, let's go try it," said Roddy.

"So we went to the parking lot, you know, we're both hanging on to the garbage can. Okay? You ready? One, two three, GO!" They drove beer bottles into their foreheads, just like they had seen The Beast do in Hawaii.

With foam and blood running off their hair they froze for a second to take stock. Much to their surprise, they were all right—keeping in mind that for professional wrestlers in the 1970s, a little blood and dizziness were a small price to pay to pull off a spectacle as rare as this. Of course, audiences would speculate whether the bottle had been cracked beforehand or somehow fixed. It wasn't. The only trick was to use a full, capped bottle of beer and commit to the hit. Backing off at the last second would result in a concussion and a badly sliced scalp.

Roddy pulled the stunt on television twice, at least. One was a pre-Christmas promo for a 1979 steel-cage match against Buddy Rose. In his own promo, Rose smashed ripe tomatoes into a ring post to inspire red, gushing nightmares in his opponent. In the Crow's Nest, Roddy responded with a different tack. Wearing a Santa hat, he threw money at the audience to shame them into giving to needy kids at Christmas, then bottled himself in reply to Rose. Wrestlers Matt Borne and King Parsons held a towel behind him to protect the audience and television crew from flying glass.

"Showdown, you bet," he concluded, "and I ain't even saddled my ponies yet!" The promo is one of the first times he refers to himself as *Rowdy* Roddy Piper (a few ads from LA advertised him with the nickname, but he hadn't used it consistently).

Throughout 1980, Rick and Roddy wrestled the Sheepherders over a dozen times, swapping back and forth the NWA Pacific Northwest Tag-Team title and the NWA Canadian Tag title (Vancouver was a frequent stop on the PNW circuit). "I'm the first man ever to get licked by the Bushwhackers," Roddy used to boast. Supplementing their crazed bushmen gimmick, Miller used to take a long, ugly lick of his opponents when he had them at his mercy. Crowds thought he was insane, which was the whole point. (For his part, Williams claimed he would put his hand on the back of an opponent's head and lick his hand. Miller, however, lapped at opponents like a "puppy dog.")

Before one of those matches, Roddy bottled himself again, this time ringside with Rick Martel looking on. He fumbled his lines a little after breaking the beer over his head. Bottling hurt, and he'd nearly knocked himself senseless.

Something about the stunt suited Roddy's wrestling persona. And it sold tickets, which was tied directly to his own well-being. But that ring persona wasn't much removed from the real Roddy Toombs. It never was. The turmoil of his youth might have found an outlet in wrestling, or it might have found a lifestyle rough enough, exhausting enough and unrelenting enough to bury that anger good and deep. Times like this, it leaked through, flavouring the show he put on with notes of self-destruction. The crowd loved it. Watching Roddy nearly knock himself out (Martel would do it, too, in Montreal), fans found it easy to believe that anything was possible when these two took to the ring—and that everything was truly and painfully real.

In the early months of 1980, Martel and Roddy got an apartment together. "We spent about close to five months as roommates. What a time. When you live with somebody, you spend twenty-four hours together, you get to know someone."

That proximity gave Martel some insight into his friend's professionalism. At twenty-five, Roddy was entering his prime, for an athlete. But for a professional wrestler he was ahead of the curve, main eventing now in Portland as he'd done in LA, much younger than promoters usually allowed.

Saturday afternoons were given over to preparing for the night's card at the Portland Sports Arena. "We would take our showers and then he would go into his room and get ready for his interviews. He would put on his favourite music. Leadbelly, the blues singer."

Martel would rib Roddy for his eclectic taste. Roddy gave it right back to him about not appreciating real music. "He'd put that Leadbelly on and think about his interviews. I used to be so entertained by the way he would do things, his interviews and stuff, he was great."

Roddy held himself to a high standard, and he knew that such standards were inseparable from his conduct around the arena when he wasn't in the spotlight. "He was a stand-up guy. He didn't take no bullshit from anybody. He didn't take any stuff from the promoters or the boys. I admired that. Some guys in this business, some guys are bullies. They try to take advantage of the weaker guys. Roddy didn't. He would defend them and say, 'Quit this shit.'"

It was one thing to be a stand-up guy in a professional environment, even one as wild as pro wrestling in the late '70s and early '80s. It was another to maintain that quality of character when there were no safety nets.

Wrestlers often found themselves in uncomfortable spots in public. Simultaneously the objects of public fascination and scorn, they could be enjoying a quiet beer together one minute, and a moment later be fighting for their lives. Coming home from an out-of-town card with Chris Colt—who spent much of late 1979 and early 1980 wrestling with Rick and Roddy—they walked into one of those moments. "We get back in Portland," Martel recalled. "Before we go back to our hotel we say, 'Let's go for beers.'" They drove around and saw a bar they hadn't tried before. There were a few Harleys outside and they could hear a band playing. They went in. There were more bikers inside than bikes outside. "It looked like a rough place. So we just sat at our table and had a few drinks. But Chris Colt was . . . if he'd had a few beers and some Jack Daniels, he'd get loud." Colt was a loose cannon, even by wrestling's standards. A rare out-of-the-closet gay man who was working an Alice Cooper look at the time, he reputedly took his name "Colt" from the title of his favourite gay porn magazine. Excessive drinking and drug use made him unpredictable and fascinatingly transgressive (he once freaked out from a drug-induced hallucination during a steel-cage match in Phoenix, thinking giant spiders were entering through the bars; he climbed out in a panic, entered the crowd swinging wildly and started a massive riot). "He got up to go to the restroom and then a couple bikers got in front of him. We could see it was a bad situation. Chris Colt insulted the guy—'Hey, fuck, get outta my fuckin' way.' It was not the place to do it."

The rest of the bikers in the bar smelled blood. They stood up and gathered around. Roddy and Rick could see where this was headed, so they went to stand with Colt. The atmosphere was incredibly tense. The wrestlers were tough men, but they were hopelessly outnumbered by guys who certainly weren't push-overs themselves.

One biker, who seemed to be the boss, reached out and grabbed Colt's whiskey and spit in it. "Chris went, 'You . . .' right away Roddy took that drink and drank it."

For a moment, nobody knew what to do. Depending on whose account of the story you believe (or prefer), Roddy then slammed the empty glass down in front of the biker and said, "Your turn."

The bikers just looked at the wrestlers and the wrestlers waited to see what their futures held. And then the bikers started laughing. "You guys are all right!" Everybody stood down and the bikers spent the rest of the night buying Roddy, Rick and Chris Colt drinks. "Wow, what a move. What a gutsy move. He defused a situation that could have been a very bad situation. He was that kinda guy," said Martel. "He was just that kinda guy."

Rick Martel had arrived in Portland without a car. That bugged him because he had a brand-new Pontiac Firebird Trans Am collecting dust in Hawaii. He had it shipped to Portland, and in April 1980 he and Roddy were finally able to pick it up. Martel might have wished he'd waited a little longer.

On May 18, Mount St. Helens in Washington state erupted. Hours before, the two wrestlers had gotten into the car on a beautiful, bright spring day in Portland and hit the road.

As they sped along the highway toward Tacoma, Washington, the sky grew dark and a grey powder filled the air, like a blizzard of charcoal dust. They heard a large boom. Cresting a hill, they came upon an eighteen-wheeler that had jackknifed trying to stop suddenly in the deepening murk. "We went right beneath that eighteen-wheeler, right up to the windshield,"

Martel remembered. "We were stuck. There were cars in beside us. The doors wouldn't open."

Knowing more cars and trucks would come over that same hill and crash into the pile-up from behind, Roddy tried kicking out his passenger-side window. Martel was in shock, and couldn't believe his friend was kicking his precious Trans Am. "Ah no, my car. Don't do that, Roddy!"

The Firebird had a sunroof. As reality set in, Martel opened it so they could get out of the car and out of the way of any more oncoming vehicles. As the pile-up ended, they helped a number of people out of cars bent as badly as the Firebird. They dealt with the police who were taking stock of injured people and ruined vehicles. Then, with nothing more to do but do their jobs, they grabbed their wrestling bags and pulled out a towel. Once traffic was re-routed around the crash, they wrapped one half of the towel over each of their faces to filter the ash and stuck out their thumbs. "An eighteen-wheeler stopped and he brought us to the building in Tacoma. We made it to the show but we were late."

By the end of that day, volcanic ash had reached 80,000 feet above Washington state, and had spread across several other states and parts of Canada. Fifty people were dead. One of the greatest natural disasters in the history of the United States had slowed the pair down, but it couldn't keep them from arriving like the true professionals they were.

Hair filled with ash, faces and clothes caked with dust, Roddy and Martel walked into the arena, where they were greeted by the booker, Dutch Savage. Martel laughed when he recalled the welcome: "He says, 'You guys are fuckin' late!'"

Roddy and Rick spent most of Martel's short time in Portland as tag-team partners. "Like a hockey team, they change on the fly," enthused one commentator as they ran circles around the Sheepherders. Roddy's high-octane mic work fuelled fans' interest, but Martel had appeal outside the ring, too. One interview gag had Roddy reading his own fan mail out loud. As the letter ended, he'd read the fan's postscript, a request that he help her get a date with Rick. Roddy would storm off camera to give his partner a piece of his mind. "Great teammate," recalled Martel. "All he thought about was business. Give the people one hundred percent. Never mind about how you look or who got the best whatever . . . He was there strictly to make people enjoy their evening and make sure that they got their money's worth."

If that meant Roddy had to take a fall, Roddy took a fall.

One of the biggest was unintended. Every second Monday, Roddy drove with his partner north into British Columbia, usually to wrestle at the PNE Garden Auditorium in Vancouver. As he and Rick Martel crossed the border this time, Roddy's head was still ringing from bottling himself in the recent promo. The cage match against the Sheepherders had a lot of heat going and both men were excited. When they appeared on the floor to join the Sheepherders in the ring, Roddy's excitement took over. "The cage was high, thirty feet high," recalled Roddy, maybe embellishing by a few feet. "The adrenaline's pumping. I saw that cage and I took off running. Like Spiderman crawling up the cage."

Martel followed his lead. As Roddy threw one leg over the top his fear of heights caught up to him. Further dousing his head full of steam, the cage—really just some sections of chain-linked fence tied together with rope—wasn't as solid as he'd expected. "Looking down and there's the two Sheepherders, staring at me. One foot over and it starts swaying." It shook and he fell, right onto the apron. Seeing his tag-team partner flat on his back with his kilt over the wrong half of him, Martel climbed back down and walked into the cage through the door. "We covered our faces up and burst out laughing," Williams said. Roddy was less amused. Much less. He jumped up, trying to look like he'd meant to do it, and joined his partner in the ring.

By summer's end, though, it was Martel who went down. He lost a loser-leaves-town match and moved on from Portland. He left Oregon a happier man for the friendship that had helped sustain him during the past year. "When I met Roddy in '79, I had just lost my brother the year before," Martel said. "Of course it was a big, great void in life. Roddy kind of filled that. I'm not saying he took my brother's place, but I felt such a bond with him that it made me feel better about what was going on. When my brother died, I was on the road and kinda felt by myself. Then I met Roddy and we got to spend time together. He really helped me go through that period."

Roddy would have other tag-team partners in his career, but in Portland it was the guy on the other side of the ring that made his tenure memorable.

Buddy Rose continued to draw crowds when facing Roddy. Their rivalry sold out Portland week after week, and attracted media and fan attention like wrestling rarely had before. Pro wrestling was capturing a rapidly growing piece of the public's imagination. As in Roddy's feud with Chavo Guerrero in LA, Roddy and Rose needed to keep coming up with fresh reasons for the two of them to beat each other up.

Buddy Rose loved his yellow Lincoln Mark IV. It could cruise for hours doing over a hundred miles an hour, valuable for a travelling wrestler. So he and Roddy scheduled a cage match to see if Roddy could win it away from him. The car was put on display in the arena and forty minutes after the steel door slammed shut, Roddy emerged the winner. He accepted the keys triumphantly to the car that became known as the Yellow Canary. That he was seen driving the car around town (many fans assumed the car match was a gag) only furthered interest. If wrestling was fake, he wouldn't really have taken away Buddy's car, would he?

Ring psychology was an ever-improving art in Roddy's hands. Rose's too. They worked the crowd just as effectively when Roddy's time in Portland was coming to an end. He'd been invited to Charlotte, North Carolina, by the booker there, George Scott. And Roddy was sensing something he always had a good take on: it was time to go. He had grown close to the wrestlers in Portland, and as cheap as Elton Owen could be, Roddy maintained a lifelong affection for Don Owen, considering him one of the most honourable promoters in the country.

But it's best to go out while you're still on top, and Roddy had been on top in Portland for long enough. Not so long, however, that he and Buddy couldn't push their rivalry up one more notch before they parted company.

Nobody held loser-leaves-town matches to usher mid-card wrestlers out of state. It was the guys on top who needed a reason to leave. As far as the public was concerned, the reason couldn't be business—which it usually was, in fact—because fans didn't care or even know about their favourite wrestlers' contracts. They cheered lustily because the wrestlers fought lustily and paid their dues with blood and agony. If their hero was leaving them, it had better be for one reason: Someone beat the lust out of him so badly that the only thing left for him to do was hang his head, pack his bags and go someplace where they wouldn't hear from him again for a very long time.

One Wednesday in the middle of September 1980, Roddy stepped out of the ring on Portland television with Buddy Rose's NWA Pacific Northwest Championship belt in his hands. Roddy was playing the babyface at the time, and fans were ecstatic. Rose, of course, wanted his belt back, and that Saturday night at a sold-out Sports Arena, they fought for a full hour to decide the belt's fate. Tickets had sold out in record time, and the two wrestlers, knowing it was Roddy's farewell to Portland, figured they'd work the fans' excitement for all they could.

After forty-five minutes of more or less even fighting, they collided and both hit the mat. The ref began his ten count. If nobody got up, the match would be ruled a draw and nothing would be decided. Seven, eight . . . nobody moved. The fans were livid, watching every limb of the two men in the ring for the slightest twitch, any little movement to suggest he was going to return to consciousness and stand up in time to be declared champion. Neither man moved. The bell rang.

Fans in Portland weren't as volatile as in LA. Riots weren't the norm here. But these people had paid money for closure, and a double count-out was not what they'd paid to see. Fortunately, the men in the ring were far too smart to leave their fans disappointed.

The ref called for buckets of cold water, which were dumped over the wrestlers' heads. With all the shock, dismay and alarm they could muster, Roddy and Rose snapped to and got to their feet, wondering aloud what had happened. The crowd roared and the ref declared the match would go on.

For the next ten minutes, Roddy dominated. He bit Rose, he pinned him repeatedly within a hair of a three count, and he knocked him around the Sports Arena ring with every trick he knew. With the outcome no longer in doubt, he took to the top turnbuckle and jumped knee-first toward Rose's head.

Rose moved.

With a freshly injured leg, Roddy was suddenly vulnerable. Rose kicked, squeezed and bent that knee in every possible direction. Roddy, screaming and ready to concede, was saved by the bell. The match had a one-hour limit, and that hour ended with Roddy only a breath away from giving in.

They would have to try again to determine a winner, and this time there would be no doubt, because the loser would be obligated by the terms of the match to leave town.

Monday, it was south to Salem for the two to lock up in a six-man tag match, Roddy with Mike Popovich and Jonathan Boyd, Rose partnered with Rip Oliver and Fidel Cortez. They fought to another draw, expanding the impact of their impasse across the state, but then hinted at its pending conclusion the next night in Eugene, where Rose and his team won. Wednesday they were back in Portland for television, and their carefully crafted stalemate came to an end. Buddy Rose pummelled Roddy, the belt was his again, and so was the Pacific Northwest.

Roddy hadn't forgotten about the girl in his life. She just wasn't in his life very often. Away in Washington, learning her trade with horses, Kitty had things to do. Smitten as they were, both had the pragmatic good sense at their young ages to take care of business first. The time for sweeping romantic gestures and serious commitments had not yet arrived.

It had been almost five years since Roddy had packed his little white Vega in the Maritimes and driven to California. He packed what he cared about in a much bigger car this time, turned the Yellow Canary east and pointed himself toward North Carolina, where he'd face a similar challenge to sharing a territory with Buddy Rose.

There was a white-haired wild man in Charlotte who'd been making as much noise on the east coast as Roddy had on the west. They'd tangled once before, when Roddy was still a teenager. He'd be a little better prepared this time.

6

Flair and the Family Man

Ric Flair was no Buddy Rose. During Roddy's early months in Charlotte, North Carolina, where he arrived in late 1980 to work for Mid-Atlantic Wrestling, he and Flair were learning to share the spotlight, much as Roddy had done with Rose in Portland. But there was a lot more spotlight to share when the "Nature Boy" was in the ring.

Like Roddy, Flair was tall for the era in which they learned their craft, but hardly a giant like the men beginning to star up the coast in New York. What Flair lacked in size he made up for in showmanship. A pro on the mic who could whip crowds into a frenzy with his platinum blond hair and flashy wardrobe (and taunts to his opponents of, "To be the man, you got to *beat* the man!"), Flair dominated promoter Jimmy Crockett's Mid-Atlantic Wrestling. He forfeited his US title belt in January 1981 to Roddy, establishing Piper as a top draw in the territory. But those titles changed hands frequently, and Flair's popularity wasn't much jeopardized by the arrival of Roddy Piper.

Wrestler Ole Anderson was booking in Richmond, Virginia, part of Crockett's territory. Gruff and impatient with his talent, Anderson had a reputation of his own. And he had established it quickly with a Texas-born teenaged wrestler named Len Denton.

"Ole Anderson to me was an asshole," said Denton. "But I guess he probably had to be to deal with guys like us."

Denton had been wrestling only a couple of years when Roddy arrived in Charlotte, and he was still trying to get his head around the curious business of professional wrestling.

"I was one of the POOMs—'plus one other match,'" explained Denton. Just as Roddy had spent countless hours in the backs of cars with more experienced wrestlers, learning how to live on the road and manipulate the crowds and his opponents, all crucial aspects of the trade, Denton was assigned to drive Flair around so he had a chance to do the same.

"I got a lucky break. Flair lost his license, so they got me to drive Flair for a year. I just really picked his brain," said Denton. "Roddy was the top guy, like Flair. Every time I saw Roddy, I'd ask him a million and one questions. He was always fine with whatever he could help you with."

If Roddy and Flair were happy to impart wisdom to Len Denton—who would eventually hold several belts of his own as "The Grappler"—Ole Anderson was the kind of hard-ass promoter who didn't hesitate to impart his own wisdom to the senior guys.

Whether Anderson was an asshole probably depended who you were. But there was no denying that sometimes the brusque Minnesotan was right.

A main event between Roddy and Flair had filled the arena in Richmond. Denton was watching closely, learning what he could.

Over the past few weeks, Roddy had been watching Flair and his rival Ricky "The Dragon" Steamboat, a high-flying, high-velocity wrestler from New York. Roddy wanted in on the fun.

"They would go and do all these high spots," said Denton, "then Roddy would go out and try to top them. They'd try to top each other." High spots were the aerial manoeuvres that took wrestlers high above the mat, and usually led to them crashing down on top of one another—or worse, missing and slamming into the mat. It was risky, and it could be painful. But the crowd always popped. So on this night in Richmond, wrestling Flair, Roddy spent more time than usual sailing off the top turnbuckle.

After a match that had repeatedly lifted the crowd out of its seats, Ole Anderson was waiting backstage for Roddy.

"I watched this happen," Denton remembered. "Ole goes, 'Piper, what are you doing out there?' Roddy'd had a hell of a match. I'm like, 'What's he talking about? He stole the show, right?'"

Anderson wasn't soliciting opinions from Denton, and he kept the heat on his new main eventer, making sure he got the point.

"He goes, 'You're working like Flair and Steamboat. You a high-spot guy? You're *Rowdy* Roddy Piper. The guy that flies all over like a trapeze artist? It don't even match your damn name! You go out there and kick ass. When you learn how to do that the right way, you're gonna get heat.'"

Chavo Guerrero had said it about Roddy in Los Angeles. He was a "brawler." A rough, uncontainable back-lot scrapper, with moves that had more to do with lateral speed than aerial technique. He sold a match by working an opponent into vulnerable positions where he could apply his sleeper hold, a move he'd based on the blood chokes taught to him by Gene LeBell.

"He was dead on," said Denton, "And Roddy turned it around." Promoters and bookers, even one whose talent had nicknamed him Pig Face, sometimes knew more about what worked than the wrestlers wanted to admit.

The Sheepherders had come to Mid-Atlantic a month ahead of Roddy. By the time he'd caught up to them, his hard-partying ways were picking up steam. His disdain for authority remained healthy, too. Roddy's bad attitude may have held one little soft spot for Don Owen, but Anderson was hardening everything around it, despite the booker's good advice.

One morning, long after midnight, Luke Williams and Butch Miller were coming back to Charlotte with Roddy in the Yellow Canary when police pulled them over. In a mysterious legal manoeuvre, the officer decided that consequences for whatever misdemeanour he'd detected needed to be doled out right then.

"They took us to a courthouse," says Williams. "The judge came out in his bathrobe and slippers." After levying the fine against Roddy, he sent the three of them home. They didn't make it that far before picking up where they'd left off.

As they walked away from the courthouse, they passed a large window. It was the judge's office, and he was at his desk doing what they presumed was the paperwork related to Roddy's fine. "We stood there," says Williams, "looked at him and pissed on the side of the courthouse."

Every Tuesday, from 9 a.m. to 3 p.m., the Mid-Atlantic wrestlers gathered in Charlotte for up to 90 two-minute-and-fifty-four second TV interviews to promote upcoming matches. When they left the studio, police were usually waiting on the highway.

Roddy and the others had to be in Raleigh for the evening's matches, 150 miles away, and were under enough pressure to get there on time that they'd be easy pickings racing down the interstate.

Roddy would look around that studio where they were shooting promos and marvel at the collection of talent. By the time he'd been in Charlotte a year, gathered around him were Bob Orton Jr., Dusty Rhodes, Dick Slater, Ricky Steamboat, Ric Flair, Bob Backlund, Swede Hanson, Jay Youngblood, Greg Valentine, Jack and Jerry Brisco, Sgt. Slaughter and, he remembered most painfully, Wahoo McDaniel.

"Damn that Indian!" he said about Wahoo, and laughed. McDaniel was a Native American who'd dabbled in pro wrestling during summers while starring as a linebacker in the NFL. Once he became a full-time wrestler, he worked an Indian chief gimmick and developed a reputation for his thundering hard chops. Aggravating these powerful blows was the athletic tape he wore on the second knuckle of his fingers. "Every time he'd chop you," Roddy said, "he'd be ripping the flesh off you."

"I used to see Roddy come back after," said Len Denton, "and I'd go, 'Oh my god, Roddy, you okay?' His chest would be lit up. I know it hurt 'cause I got some from Wahoo, too."

Chops were hard strikes across the ribs, executed in a classic karate-chop position. They had few fans among the wrestlers themselves. Chops stung, especially if delivered by a man as strong as McDaniel. And they never decided a match. No audience believed a legitimate contender lost a bout because of a chop across the ribs. But the impact on a broad chest sounds spectacular, and the blows leave a mark, both of which help legitimize the action in the crowd's eyes.

Roddy would get back up and dare McDaniel to try it again. "Come on, lay it here, Indian, come on!"

"I'd chop him back with everything I had. I had the rotator cuff that was torn at the time. So I learned how to bring the hand straight down. He'd have big welts and he wouldn't even say ouch. He wouldn't even put me over, that damn big Indian chief." He smiled. "I loved him to death. He wouldn't back off."

Roddy's resilience worked its magic on the crowd. As Ole Anderson had insisted, he became fully the brawler he really was—the tough-as-nails street fighter who was too vicious to lose. Whether he was working heel or babyface, the crowd respected him.

"That's where Roddy started working, psychological wise," said Denton. "That fit his name, his gimmick. Now he stood out from everybody else."

In July 1982, Roddy took the Mid-Atlantic title from another great talent, Jack Brisco. Brisco was a renowned pro wrestler, and though his skill never translated into the type of mainstream celebrity enjoyed by his Mid-Atlantic peers like Roddy and Ric Flair, his reputation as a performer in the ring was sterling. (So was his knowledge of the business. Only a few years earlier, he and his brother Jerry, who also wrestled Roddy a handful of times in Mid-Atlantic, discovered a hulking young talent named Terry Bollea, though it would be a few years yet before he entered Roddy's story.)

After a match that had gone largely Brisco's way, Roddy took a wild swing at Brisco's jaw and something exploded across the ring. Roddy covered Brisco and got the three count. He rolled out of the ring and collapsed in exhaustion against a wall, where the host confronted him about that exploding something. The camera zoomed in to show several coins and pieces of torn paper wrapper scattered across the mat. He'd clearly decked Brisco with a roll of quarters. "People threw those in there," said Roddy between deep breaths. "I don't know where they came from . . ."

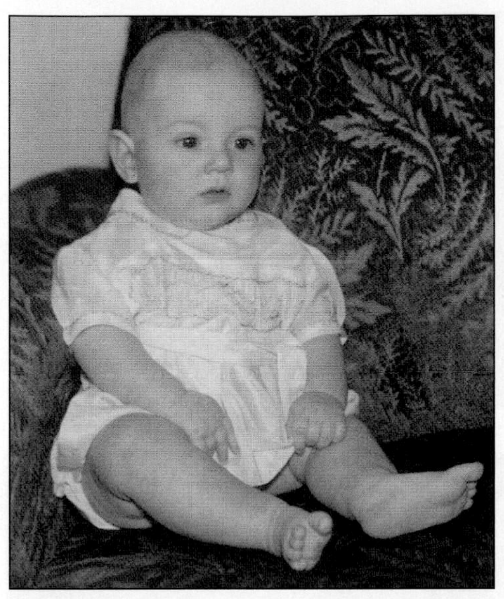

Roderick George Toombs, Saskatoon, 1954.

The wedding of Eileen Anderson and Stanley Toombs.

The Toombs family.

Roderick and Tammy.

Roddy's first Toronto pipe band (tallest boy in back row, second from left).

Visiting the Andersons in BC.

Ready for baseball season in Port Arthur.

Father and son.

WINNIPEG FREE PRESS, THURSDAY, MARCH 11, 1971

Wrestling Finals Twice As Big As Last Year's

of John Taylor and Wilf Berry of Sisler.

Daniel Mac and River East claimed two individual titles each. Randy Stevens of Daniel Mac won the lightest class — the 98 pound division — while schoolmate Bill Whitehead won the 123-pound division.

Champions from River East were Robert Paul, in the 107-pound division, and Ed Loewen in the 175-pound division.

Of the 12 divisions, only one rural competitor figured in the top three. Lawrence Hoeppner of MacGregor won the unlimited division, ahead of runners-up Moe Agnaier of Louis Riel and P. Metzquer of Garden City.

The meet's outstanding wrestlers were Stevens, Pauk, Larry Glenesk of Vincent Massey (115-pound champion), Kochenash, Kelly Gorzen of Louis Riel (155-pound champion) and Loewen.

Other champions were Robert Thirsk of John Taylor (130-pound division), Ron Toombs of Windsor Park (165-pound [cut off] sion) and Guy Plett of S[cut off] (185-pound division).

All told, 76 wrestlers ent[cut off] — more than double last y[cut off] turnout.

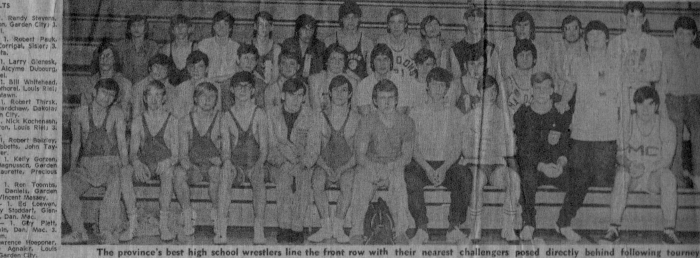

RESULTS

98 lb. Division — 1. Randy Stevens, Dan. Mac; 2. M. Nepon, Garden City; 3. Mike Aquin, Louis Riel.

107 lb. Division — 1. Robert Pauk, River East; 2. Rod Corrigal, Sisler; 3. Doug Webawski, Dakota.

115 lb. Division — 1. Larry Glenesk, Vincent Massey; 2. Alcyme Dubourg, Rick Dunlop, Louis Riel.

123 lb. Division — 1. Bill Whitehead, Dan. Mac; 2. J. B. Bothorel, Louis Riel; 3. Stan Phillipon, Glenlawn.

130 lb. Division — 1. Robert Thirsk, John Taylor; Gary Hardchaw, Dakota; 3. G. Petrycky, Garden City.

137 lb. Division — 1. Nick Kochenash, Dakota; 2. Rolly Perron, Louis Riel; 3. C. Rodin, Garden City.

145 lb. Division — 1. Robert Balzley, Glenlawn; 2. Ron Tibbetts, John Taylor; 3. Wilf Berry, Sisler.

155 lb. Division — 1. Kelly Gorzen, Louis Riel; 2. Guy Magnusson, Garden city, 3. Germain Laurette, Precious Blood.

165 lb. Division — 1. Ron Toombs, Windsor Park; 2. J. Daniels, Garden City; 3. Jim Corbett, Vincent Massey.

175 lb. Division — 1. Ed Loewen, River East; 2. Terry Stoddart, Glenlawn; 3. Scott Dawson, Dan. Mac.

185 lb. Division — 1. Guy Plett, Sisler; 2. Murray Bain, Dan. Mac. 3. Peter Becker, Glenlawn.

Unlimited — 1. Lawrence Hoeppner, MacGregor; 2. Moe Agnaier, Louis Riel; 3. P. Metzquer, Garden City.

The province's best high school wrestlers line the front row with their nearest challengers posed directly behind following tourney

165-pound champ, "Ron" Toombs (front row, fifth from right, in jeans).

Jay "The Alaskan" York in Los Angeles.

"Killer" Brooks in Portland.

PRO WRESTLING

The Hair Match of the Century

Goes until one man is the winner.

Roddy Piper Vs Playboy Buddy Rose

A cage will be put around the ring so nobody can get in or get out of the ring.

Loser must have his hair shaved off in the middle of the ring.

Tues., April 15

8:30 PM

Expo Center Arena

(Marine Drive near Vancouver)

TAG MATCH

Sheepherders vs Ricky Martell & Dutch Savage

Jesse Barr vs Chris Colt

Ivan Volkoff vs Crusher Stasiak

Plus Other Bouts

Hair match with "Playboy" Buddy Rose.

Filming an unusual promo in Georgia.

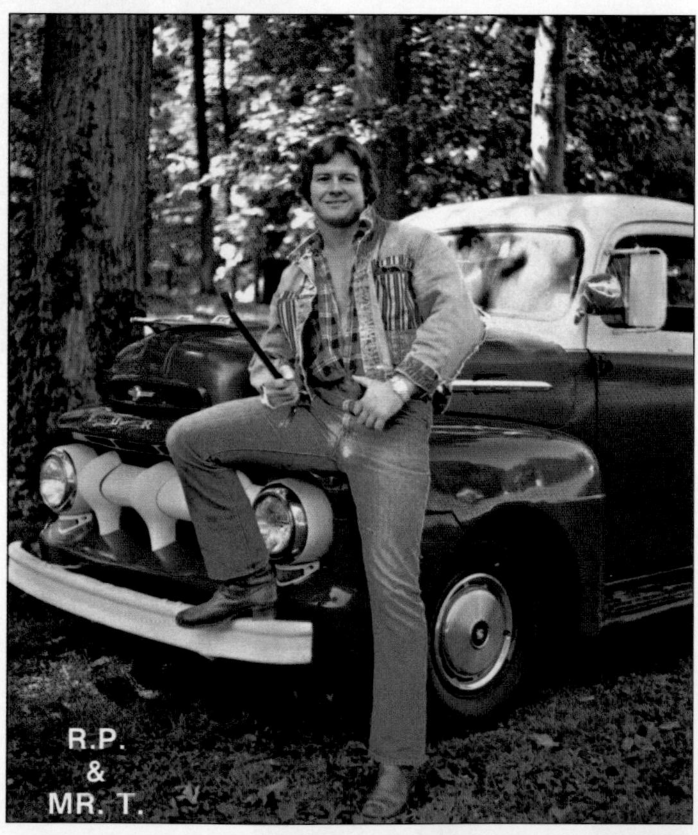

Before the other Mr. T came Tire Iron.

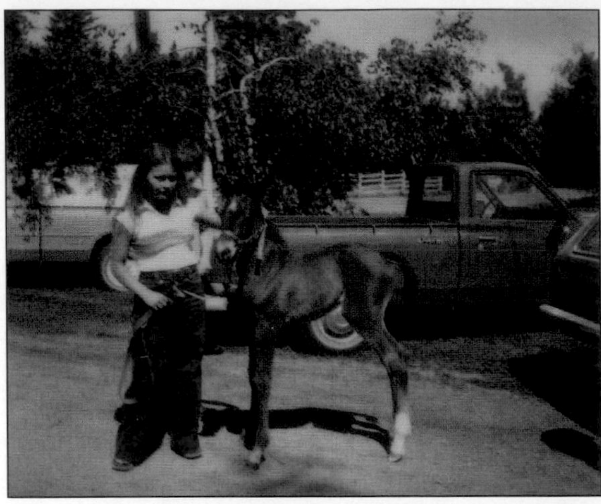

‹ *Nineteen-year-old Kitty Dittrich.*

Best man and booster Red Bastien. ›

‹ *Roddy, Kitty with families, married in 1982.*

Visiting Cam and Sherilyn Connor. ›

‹ *Anastasia arrives.*

One last trip to Japan. ›

‹ *New Year's Eve 1983 with Ricky "The Dragon" Steamboat.*

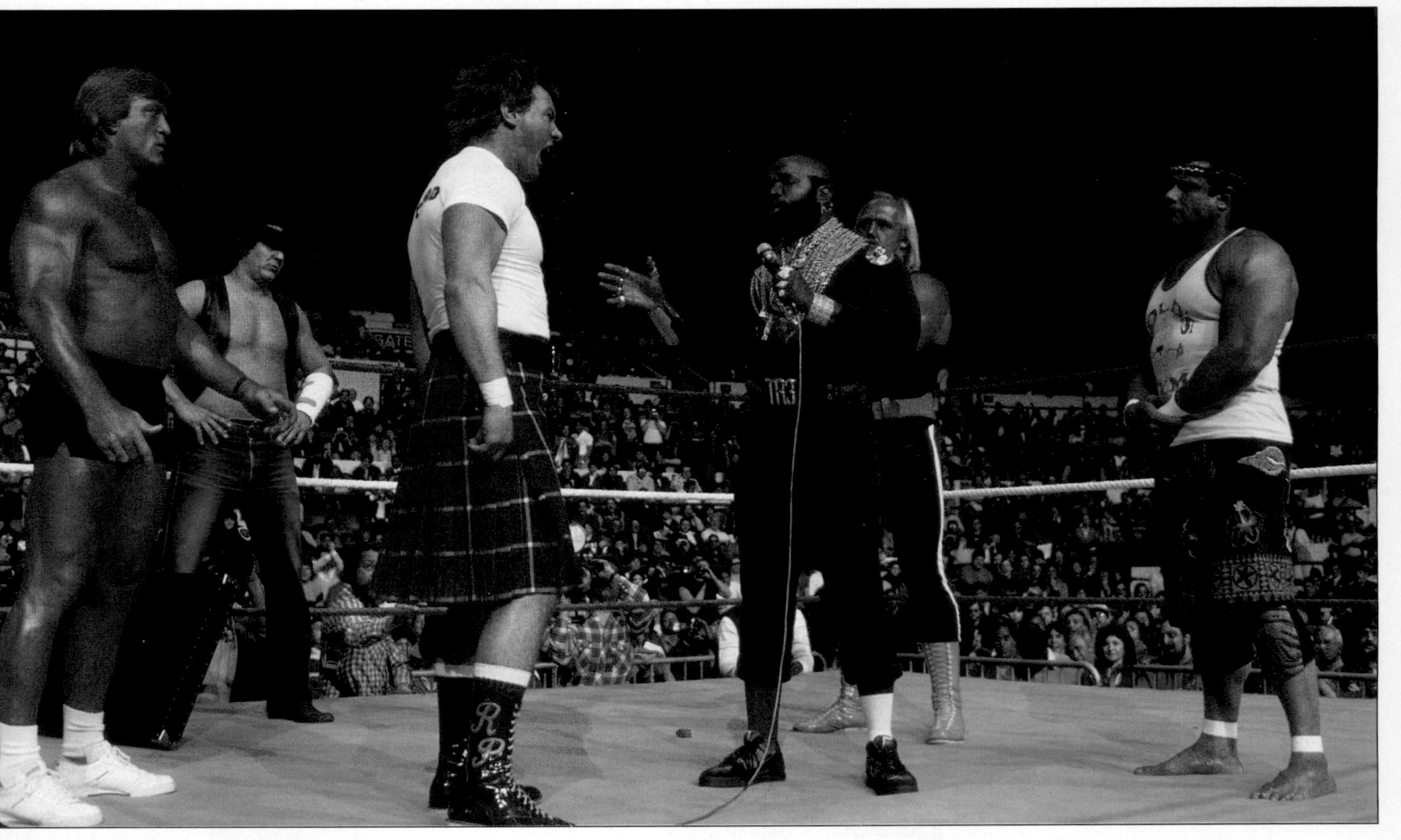

Setting the stage for WrestleMania, with Paul "Mr. Wonderful" Orndorff, "Cowboy" Bob Orton, Mr. T, Hulk Hogan and Jimmy "Superfly" Snuka.

Anastasia and Ariel at the set of They Live.

Boarding the Love Boat.

Roddy and Kitty, 1986.

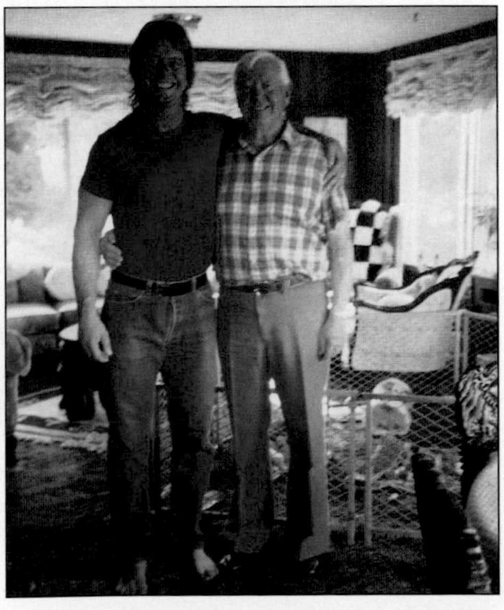

Roddy and Stanley Toombs, 1990.

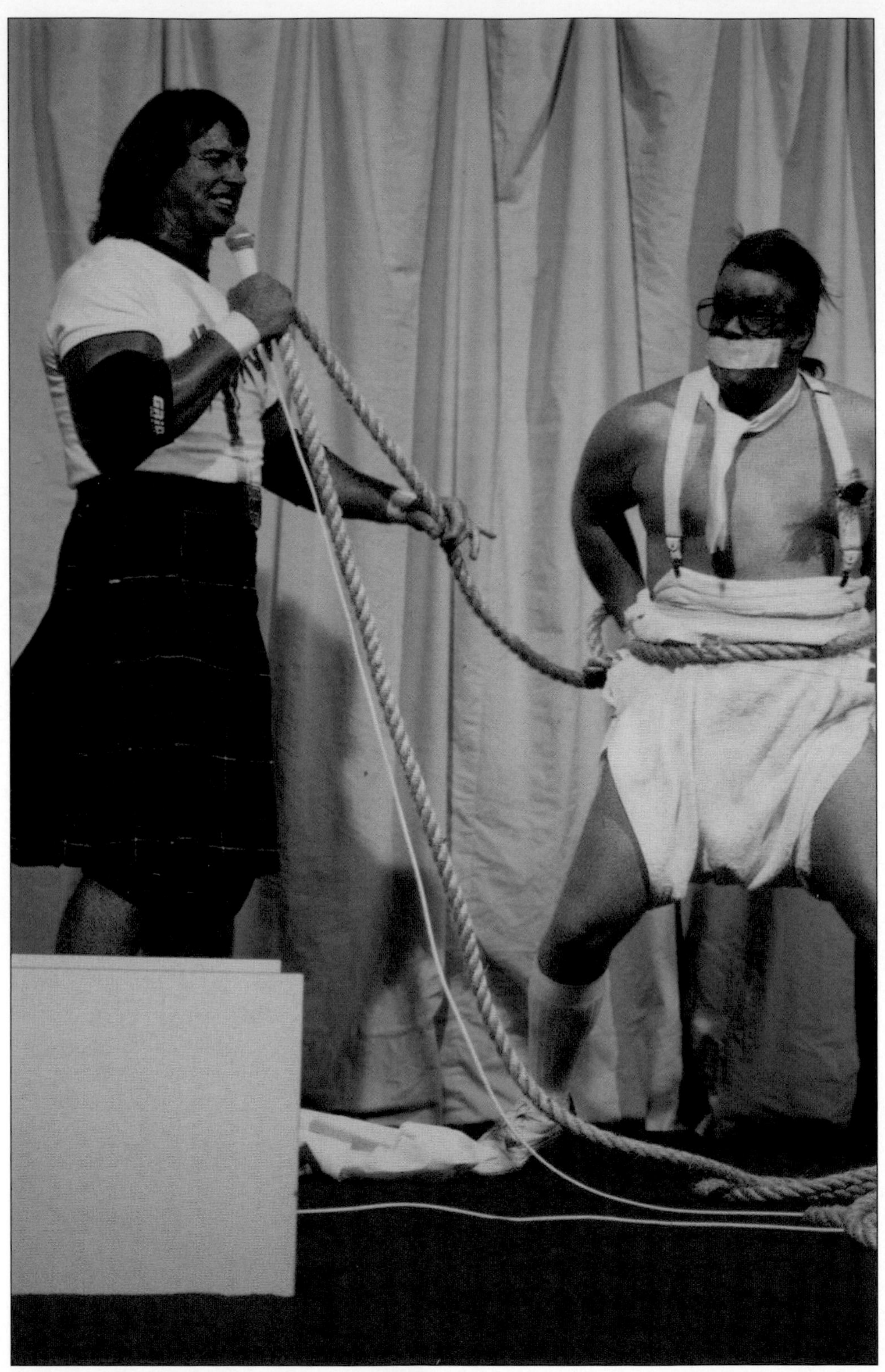

Bruce Prichard as Brother Love.

The Toombs clan gets a taste of the outdoors.

The actor is ready for work.

Making music again, with Alan Snoddy in Niagara Falls.

The last word with TMZ.

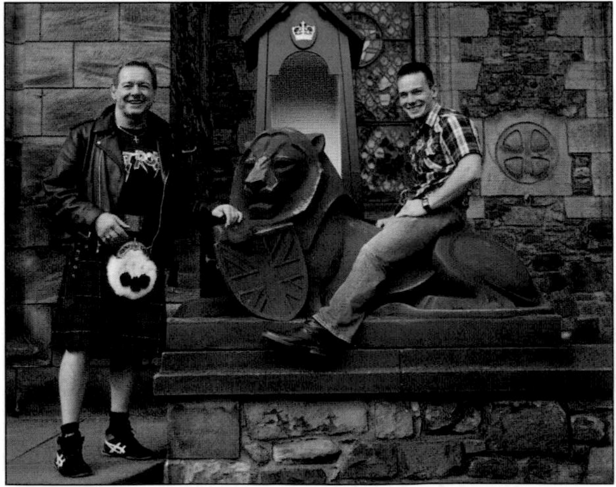

Father and son getting back to their roots outside Edinburgh Castle.

The reference Roddy made to his torn rotator cuff reveals a simple fact of life for wrestlers in that era—maybe in every era. Short of being stuck in hospital, or worse, there were no excuses for not getting in the ring. A business built on clashes between personalities meant that those personalities were what fans paid to see. Substitutions were a last resort.

Roddy had wrestled Wahoo McDaniel in Greenville, South Carolina, and during the match had badly hurt his right wrist. He put his arm in a sling to help it recover. On a flight to Savannah, Georgia, for the evening matches, McDaniel called him a sissy for wearing a sling. He shamed Roddy into taking it off, and he wrestled that night with an injured wrist. If he did it one night he could do it again. Before he knew it, he was just living with the bump on his wrist. For the next thirty-five years, until his death, Roddy had that lump, the size of a goose egg, because he hadn't taken care of the injury.

As if the injured wrist wasn't bad enough, on that same flight the plane dropped sharply when it hit an air pocket, sending the wrestlers onboard tumbling hard around the cabin (it was a small chartered flight). Roddy struck his head on the cabin roof and added the resulting neck strain to his list of untreated injuries. Stumbling disoriented off the plane, he had two very valid excuses now to sit out the evening's match. He didn't use either.

Maybe the wrestler who stood to lose the most from Roddy's success in Charlotte, Ric Flair was becoming a rival in the ring but a close friend away from it. He and Roddy partied mercilessly throughout the territory, dragging their peers out on the many towns throughout the Carolinas for nights they wouldn't remember. They got to be close enough that Flair could get away with the occasional swerve.

"We're in Asheville, North Carolina," began Flair. "I go up to Piper and I go, 'I promise, there's no way that Jack [Brisco] will find out, I'll bet you a hundred bucks that you can't take down Jack Brisco.'"

Roddy looked at him. "You mean to tell me that you're not going to say a word and you don't think I can take him down?"

"Not a chance."

"You're on."

As Roddy's getting ready to go to the ring, Flair found Jay Youngblood.

"Go over there and tell Jack that Piper's gonna try to take him down."

As Roddy and Brisco headed to the ring, the other wrestlers, all of them in on the rib by now, gathered around the dressing room curtain to watch.

After about ten minutes, Roddy finally got a grip on Brisco's leg. This was no small feat. Both Brisco brothers were excellent technical wrestlers. Brisco hopped around the ring on one foot as Roddy tried to kick his other leg out from under him until Roddy let himself get too close for his own good. Brisco grabbed him and the match was as good as over.

"Piper came back and said, 'I'm gonna kill you, Flair.'"

For all the work, and all the drugs and free-flowing alcohol, Roddy knew there was a hole in his life, and he knew only one person who could fill it. He and Kitty had tried to stay in touch after he left Portland, but both were moving around the country and had lost track of each other during the past six months.

In April 1982, Roddy picked up the phone and called Kitty's mother, hoping to track her down. "He called me out of the blue," recalled Kitty. She had moved on from working in

Washington, first to Kentucky and then home to Oregon, working with show horses in Wilsonville. "He said, 'I'm living in Charlotte, North Carolina. It's very good here, I'm getting successful, but it doesn't mean anything to me without someone to share it with. I've never met anyone like you and I want you to come move out here with me and we'll get married.'

"I said, 'Sure.' I knew I was crazy about him. The next morning I gave my boss two weeks' notice and headed out to Charlotte."

Roddy bought her plane ticket—along with passage for her dog and cat. She was taking a big risk. The risk felt even bigger when she landed in Charlotte and didn't find him at the airport. "Oh my god, he didn't mean it," she thought. "He's rethinking it. What am I doing? I'm stuck here."

Hours late, Roddy arrived, full of apologies. He'd forgotten the arrival time. He bundled her bags and small menagerie into the Yellow Canary and took her home.

The learning curve was steep for Kitty. Life with a professional wrestler meant, for one, many days and nights spent alone. His road schedule was gruelling, wrestling every day of the week, and twice on Saturdays. Throw Canada into the mix—Mid-Atlantic ran Toronto and Southern Ontario—and the travel schedule was relentless.

Kitty learned something else: not to say too much about her fiancé's past. She was approached one day by someone from Roddy's wrestling life—it might have been a fan or a journalist, maybe a colleague, she couldn't recall—who asked her what she knew about him growing up in Canada. Roddy and she had talked about his childhood, something he'd shared with few others, and she knew the answers to a few of these questions. Overhearing her reply, Roddy took her aside and asked her to be careful.

"I remember him saying, 'You need to separate what we know about how I was brought up from the story I built that I want people to know.' His wrestling persona." Roddy had learned to give audiences what they wanted, and how to get them to come back week after week for more. Now he was learning that this character needed depth if fans were going to continue caring about his fate. Roddy was building that depth one interview, one promo, one story at a time.

At the studio one Tuesday morning Roddy was introduced to Atlanta promoter Jim Barnett, because Anderson and Crockett had agreed to let Roddy work Georgia, too. This commitment would add two matches on Sunday to his already packed Mid-Atlantic schedule, in addition to frequent forays north to Toronto.

Toronto's Maple Leaf Wrestling was run by Frank Tunney and his nephew Jack, who partnered with NWA territories to fill the historic Maple Leaf Gardens for cards that regularly drew over 15,000 people.

"I wrestled in Maple Leaf Gardens a ton of times," Roddy remembered. "They had a bell. You'd hear a little bell shot and everybody's starting to get revved up. And that ramp that they had there. Ring high." After years of being punched, stabbed, sliced and burnt on his way to the ring, a ramp that took him from the dressing rooms to the ring was a much-appreciated luxury.

"We used to fly all the time from Charlotte to Toronto, work in Maple Leaf Gardens and fly back," said Roddy. Mid-Atlantic wrestlers would frequently work the matinee opening match in one city, then jet to another for the evening's main event. On at least one occasion, in July 1982, he drove back to North Carolina to fit in a few extra matches in Michigan. Given the sensitivities of the time and the company he was keeping, he was soon wishing they'd flown.

The 1979–81 Iran hostage crisis made the early eighties an awkward time to be an Iranian in America. Or at least it was if you were a professional wrestler working an Iron Sheik gimmick, and you kept up the ruse when crossing the border.

Hossein Khosrow Ali Vaziri was a former bodyguard of the Shah of Iran. The Shah had been overthrown by the same regime that had idly watched as more than sixty Americans were taken hostage in the capital city of Tehran. Vaziri had once been an avowed enemy of that government, but most North Americans didn't know the difference. Or care. And if Vaziri was crossing the border with a carload of buddies just as inclined to screw around with border officials as he was, and one of them happened to boast an unapologetic Soviet attitude, they might be in for a rough day.

Especially the young guy in the back seat.

Roddy didn't have a green card, and by this point wasn't bothering any longer with the H1 and H2 visas that allowed him to work in the US. Strictly speaking, he should have shown work visas when crossing the border, but this was twenty years before Canadians and Americans needed passports to travel between their countries. Unless a customs official really didn't like the look of someone, crossing the border usually meant slowing down long enough to smile nicely, show ID and say thank you.

"There are four of us in the car," remembers Roddy. "The gentleman driving was Rene Goulet." Goulet was a French Canadian who used to pretend he was in the French Foreign Legion. "In the front passenger seat was a man, a very nice man, but a very big, ex-Olympian from Russia, named Nikolai Volkoff. And the Iron Sheik, Khosrow Vaziri, was behind the driver in the backseat. And behind the large Russian gentleman was me, Rod."

As they approached the border, Roddy wasn't worried about his papers. He was worried about the quarter ounce of hash in his pocket. Figuring the stop would be a routine minute or two, he quietly tucked the hash in his cheek, like chewing tobacco.

They stopped and the US customs officer asked Goulet what his name is.

"My name is Rene Goulet."

"Where are you from?"

"I am from Quebec."

"Uh . . . citizen of?"

"I am from Quebec, Quebec, Canada."

"Do you have working papers? Do you have a green card?"

This was where the border crossing became complicated. Unless the customs official was a wrestling fan, all he saw were four large and in some cases strange-looking men packed into a single car trying to cross the border. No wives, no children. If they weren't such an openly odd collection of men, they might have made the official suspicious.

"I don't need a green card," said Goulet. "I come back and forth for years. I don't need it. They never ask me for the green card."

The customs official paused. He leaned down so he could see across to the front passenger seat.

"What's your name?"

"My name is Nikolai Volkoff."

"So where are you from?"

"Mother Russia."

"Do you have a green card, working papers?"

"I do not need working papers! I've been living in the United States. I go back and forth for years."

The official was sensing a theme. He went to the back window and knocked on the glass. The Sheik rolled down his window.

"What's your name?"

"I am the Iron Sheik, Khosrow Vaziri."

"Where are you from?"

"I am from Tehran, Iran."

"You got papers?"

"I live in the United States! I am the Iron Shiek, world's champion! I do not carry papers with me."

The official never got to last guy in the car, the quiet one in the far backseat whose mouth was starting to water.

"Everybody out of the car," the officer said, standing back. "Open the trunk."

They got out. Goulet opened the trunk and the official rustled around their four wrestling bags. He didn't say anything, though by this point he knew the four men in the car were—or claimed to be—professional wrestlers. Without a word or any display of temper, he turned around and started walking toward the office.

Volkoff went to the back of the car and slammed the trunk shut, saying as he did, "It's like the Gestapo."

The officer stopped. He turned on his heels.

"What did you say?"

Roddy continued the story: "Next thing I know, there's four of us in their little building. And in their little building they have an interesting room. It's all concrete. There's no toilet. There are no doors, just the one to get in and out. There's no window. No place to hide. It's just a room. And the walls were white."

Herded into the room with the others, Roddy was taking their circumstances more seriously than the rest. "I'm standing in the room. I've got Rene Goulet from Quebec, I've got Nikolai Volkoff from Russia, I got the Iron Sheik from Tehran, Iran, and

I got myself. I'm the only one who's illegal! I don't have working papers. I *know* these guys got papers. I don't have any. Plus, I got a quarter ounce of hash in my lip. I thought it was going to be a three-minute stop."

The other three, instead of thinking maybe they should start behaving themselves, started getting mad. Roddy, meanwhile, had yet to say one word. He was getting higher by the second.

"The reason I mention that the walls were white was that there was no place to spit, there was no place to place anything. It was a contained unit. If I spit, they woulda saw it. If I peed, they woulda saw it."

After maybe half an hour in the room, while officials checked the driver's licenses of the other three—Roddy didn't have one—an officer came to usher them to another room.

"Now they bring us out and got us in a line. We seem to have got the attention of a good eight, nine of them. And the other three guys, they're not showing any kind of serious respect at all. They got our backs against the wall and they're kinda surrounding the head guy, who's questioning us.

The other three wrestlers appeared finally to be coming to their senses. "Rene Goulet—he was a good man—he was saying, 'Listen, I have many years come back and forth, I work for Verne Gagne. I live in Charlotte, North Carolina.'"

Next, the official began questioning Nikolai Volkoff. "Nikolai's sincerely a really nice man, but 'the Gestapo'? Dumb. The Sheik, every night—they were a tag team—every night he'd come by and say, 'Nikolai, you are the stupidest man I know.' And this night he was correct. I used to feel sorry for Nikolai until this night.

"They're hitting Nikolai with the same things. Nikolai has an address, also in America. Rene was in Charlotte, Nikolai was in Pittsburgh, and I don't know where the Iron Sheik was living.

Maybe Charlotte also. So, they're not happy campers, but they're starting to get a sense of who they have in custody. But these officers are pissed from the Gestapo comment, and with the rather frivolous way they were taking these questions. And these officers' egos were being bruised a little bit. They're pretty powerful men when they want to be."

When the official questioned the Iron Sheik, astonishingly he came up with the same rant. "I am the Iron Sheik, from Tehran, Iran. I am the world champion."

For the first time, the official pointed his finger at Roddy and said, "Where you from?"

The senior officer had been grilling the wrestlers for about five minutes. Roddy still had remnants of that chunk of hash in his mouth. When the officer pointed at him, Roddy, whose attention tended to wander under the best of circumstances, found himself intensely focussed on getting out of trouble.

With the "chew" tucked far back in his cheek and in the best Southern accent he could muster, Roddy answered, "Charlotte, North Carolina."

The official didn't let a second pass before asking his next question.

"What school did you go to?"

In a split-second's inspiration, Roddy took a wild shot at an answer.

"Saint Mary's."

The official looked at him for a long moment. There's a St. Mary's school in almost every town in North America.

"That's the only one I believe," said the officer. "You, you can get out."

Roddy hiked over to the parked car while the other three squirmed their way out of trouble. Finally they joined him and crossed into Michigan. Relieved, Roddy picked up a newspaper that had been sitting the whole time in the middle of the back seat. Beneath it was a little bag containing an ounce of pot.

In October 1982, Roddy got on a plane with Kitty and took her home to Oregon. Kitty Dittrich would not be returning to the East Coast.

They'd lived in Charlotte for about six months, then relocated to Decatur, Georgia, where they lived in an apartment owned by one of the Brisco brothers, Jack or Jerry. From there, Roddy could make his dates for Jim Barnett without spending quite as much time on the road. "He was gone so much," Kitty said. "I didn't anticipate how lonely I would be. I had to get a grip on that and not let it crush me." She had spent so little time with Roddy before moving in with him, she was surprised to miss him so much when he was gone, except that now, of course, when he was gone, she was alone.

Kitty wasn't getting cold feet, though. "I definitely knew I had made the right decision," she said. "Especially when you're young, your feelings are just so intense for each other. I always felt very cared for, even though I was moved away from what I was used to and knew."

Near Portland, Roddy and Kitty assembled with a few close family and friends at the Tualatin Plains Presbyterian Church (also known as the Old Scotch Church) and got married.

Roddy often referred to the men who mentored him as his "dads." One of them stood up that day as his best man—Red Bastien, the only wrestling personality to attend.

Roddy's first choice had refused. It's difficult to get a handle on Roddy's relationship with his father. One moment he was reaching out to his dad, trying to rebuild burnt bridges between them, blaming himself for being a bad son; the next, he was reliving the horror of being six years old and thrashed with a vengeance for being a "pervert" in The Pas.

Roddy had asked his father to be his best man. Stanley Toombs had declined.

"Knowing his father, and the Victorian ways, I think that in his father's mind it wasn't proper for a father to be his son's best man. I would like to think that that was the reason," Kitty said.

Perhaps Roddy's request was too unconventional, or maybe there was too much bad blood between the men—it's hard to say why Stanley said no, because he and Eileen did attend the wedding. They were living on Vancouver Island by that time and once they ferried across the Georgia Strait to Vancouver, it was only a day's drive to Portland.

They met Kitty for the first time the day before the ceremony. She worried that they didn't approve of their son marrying her. "They wanted him to marry a Canadian," she said, with a laugh.

Being in Portland meant being in Don Owen's territory, and Roddy was hard pressed to take a day off, even to get married. He spent his wedding evening firmly in the sweaty grip of his old nemesis Buddy Rose. He wrestled several dates that week across the Pacific Northwest before returning to Georgia in the company of his wife, Kitty Toombs.

Marriage might have grounded Roddy, but the pressures on a top young wrestler in one of the hottest territories in the United States were relentless. Pressure was mounting on him also to provide for his family—his wife and the child they were soon expecting. Also mounting were the injuries and the temptation to bury all that worry and physical pain with something that wouldn't slow him down.

Promoters knew what kind of pressure they were putting on their wrestlers, and they understood that these bundles of testosterone and ambition were only human. Staff slipped painkillers, sedatives and uppers to Roddy, anything to make sure he made it to the arena, on time and fit to fight.

One of the young men who'd witnessed Roddy's first tour through Texas, back when he'd saved the national anthem by playing it on his bagpipes, was Tom Prichard, who had then started wrestling professionally himself. In time, he would also witness Roddy's ravenous need for pills and drugs to keep up the torrid pace.

Prichard first met his wrestling hero one afternoon at the Wilson Theater in Fresno, California.

"I'll never forget this 'cause I remember he was working with Andre that night," he began. The Fresno theater was well suited to wrestling: faces and heels used separate entrances and their dressing rooms were located on opposite sides of the building.

"Roddy came in and I can't remember the office guy but Roddy said to him, 'You left me last night, and I want my fuckin' money now!' And went off on this guy. Then once he stopped, he just came over and said, 'Hi, Roddy Piper,' and introduced himself."

For all the sweet talk about the way Roddy treated people with respect and dignity, he made sure nobody took that as permission to screw him over.

He and Prichard crossed paths again when Prichard came to Atlanta.

"I must be twenty-two years old around that time. Again Roddy was a great, great guy to everybody in the back. Never treated the young guys like some of the top guys did. If we go out to eat, which we did when we were on tour, he would usually pick up the tab. Of course he was top guy, but he wasn't making

WWF money back then, for sure. But he was making good money. He took care of the younger guys . . ."

Prichard hesitated here in the story he was telling about our dad. Wrestlers, even rivals, make a living by not crossing lines. There were lines in the ring that kept people from getting killed. There were also lines outside the ring, like not mentioning real family in their interviews (unless they were part of the work). But one line they cross frequently is privacy. Wrestlers aren't known for keeping each others' secrets. So when Prichard hesitated, we knew it was a sign of the genuine respect he had for our father. What he eventually told us was that Roddy was picking up the tab for more than dinner.

"If he had coke, he shared coke. If he had pills, he shared pills. . . .

"Piper was known for his consumption and being able to just function like nobody else could. I had a party with Roddy,"—Prichard mentioned another wrestler he was training with at the time, also known for his ability to handle uncommon quantities of drugs and alcohol—"I couldn't keep up with either one of them. But I tried my damnedest."

One night in Georgia, Roddy and a few of the other wrestlers pulled the ring truck into an empty parking lot. Everybody piled out and set up the ring and began play wrestling. "Everybody's drunk and just having a great time," recalled Prichard. Then Roddy climbed into the truck and started driving it around the empty lot with the ring down. "Just like a mad man," he said, laughing.

"Piper wrecked a couple rental cars when I was in Atlanta. With Nick Patrick and Brad Armstrong, Tommy Rich, that crew. It was a pretty wild time," he said. "You hear about rock stars partying, but in reality, wrestlers back in the seventies and eighties, even the nineties—I don't know that anybody could keep up with Piper or a lot of the guys back then.

"I never saw him mess around on the road with any women or anything like that. I never saw that. But he drank and drugged and lived his life the way he wanted to live it, that's for sure."

Whether he was living wild because he wanted to or was tamping down as much anger and pain as his limited frame would bear, Roddy mostly kept the lid on his duelling natures. The wrath of Rowdy had grown out of a timid son, a boy who'd been picked on at school and beaten at home. If he'd grown into a sort of avenging terror, fighting to set free a frightened kid who no longer existed, he was swinging wide of the real mark. Roddy didn't have the heart to turn on his father, but heaven help anyone who offered—no matter how unwittingly—to take his place, in the ring.

Between the roar of the crowds, the money (which was good, finally), and the importance a man can invest in himself when others around him are willing to break the law to keep him working, what happened next to Roddy was unthinkable.

Wrestler Tommy Rich had become a good friend. He and Roddy had wrecked a few cars and at least one boat together. But on their way to a match one afternoon in Chattanooga, they wrecked Roddy's career. They took a wrong turn and didn't realize it. By the time they got straightened out, they were hours late for the matinee. They got in the ring and had their match, thanks to some delay tactics by the other wrestlers, and afterward Ole Anderson fired Roddy.

Not only was Roddy out of a job, he was blackballed, his good name potentially struck from the rosters of every promotion across the United States.

Fortunately, Ric Flair was familiar with one place in the world Roddy had never wrestled: Puerto Rico, where the culture around the business and its fans was as wild as it had been in Mexico. In January 1983 Roddy asked, "Do you think I could start going to the Caribbean with you?" Flair got some bookings for himself and Roddy, packed his rival and friend onto a plane, and, as was Flair's custom at that age, got up, put on his wrestling robe and started serving the other passengers drinks.

Flair came by his ring name honestly. He turned every flight into a party bus, and he had a genuine knack for generating heat in the ring. Ric Flair could really piss people off, and he did it a little too well on that tour through Puerto Rico.

In Santo Domingo, Flair was booked against a local hero named Benítez. The crowd was so hostile to the visiting Americans—no one knew or cared where else Roddy might have actually been from—soldiers bearing short sticks with chains on the end escorted them to the ring. Astonished at the diminutive size of Benítez once he set eyes on him, Flair told Roddy to run around the floor beside the ring and grab at the Puerto Rican's ankles during the match. He knew it would infuriate the crowd. He was right.

Roddy's interference worked so well that the soldiers stopped holding the crowd back and turned on Roddy themselves. Even Flair, up in the ring, realized he would have to stop wrestling *professionally* any second and start punting for his life.

Another wrestler intervened and somehow ushered them to the dressing rooms. It was two o'clock in the morning before an ambulance successfully extricated them from the stadium.

As Roddy liked to say, just another day in paradise.

Back in the US, Roddy found work in Florida. He told Kitty he'd go alone, as it was supposed to be a brief stay, just a few weeks, maybe a month. But Kitty was seven months pregnant. She was by herself enough as it was. She wasn't interested in spending the final months of this pregnancy alone.

"I said, 'No, I'm not going to be left alone in Decatur.' So I went with him to Tarpon Springs," she says. When the Florida stay was done, they packed their belongings into a U-Haul and drove back to Charlotte, where their first daughter, Anastasia, was born in April. She arrived on a Monday night, and her dad went to work Tuesday morning.

Jim Crockett had faith in Roddy and ignored his blackballing. There was a job he wanted Roddy to help him do. Crockett had designs on much more of the American wrestling market than just his Mid-Atlantic territory. With Roddy included, he had one of the best rosters, if not *the* best roster, of wrestlers in the world. He set his mind to how he could put them to work expanding his territory and winning him the market he coveted.

Early in his Mid-Atlantic tenure, Roddy was introduced to the son of a wrestler he'd run into in Houston. Greg "The Hammer" Valentine, son of Johnny Valentine, was a stout, powerfully built wrestler from Seattle. He'd worked in Charlotte for some time before Roddy arrived, but had been on a run through the McMahons' New York territory until late in 1980, when he came back to Charlotte and fought a six-man tag-team match with Roddy and Bobby Duncum against Ric Flair, Sweet Ebony Diamond and Blackjack Mulligan (one of the Texans with whom Roddy had spent his first tour of Japan).

Roddy and Valentine worked well together, so Crockett had made them frequent tag-team partners throughout 1981 and early '82, usually lining them up against some combination of Ric Flair, Ricky Steamboat, Mulligan and Charlotte booker George Scott. Later in 1982 and into '83, Roddy and Valentine started working against one another until April in Greensboro, when Roddy won the NWA (Mid-Atlantic) United States belt from him. It was, said Kitty, "the only title he ever cared about."

In early May, Valentine won it back in a long, ugly match that looked more like a street fight than pro wrestling. Roddy spent much of the time against the ropes, taking hit after hit from Valentine while commentator Gordon Solie explained that Roddy had an ear injury that was keeping him from mounting any sort of a comeback. Eventually, Crockett himself entered the ring to examine Roddy, who on his hands and knees was trying to crawl after Valentine and continue the fight. Seeing the shape Roddy was in, Crockett called the match.

Those matches established something special about their rivalry. Few wrestlers could combine for such brutality in the ring as Piper and Valentine. They could pound on one another constantly and keep the crowd riveted. It was a talent that served them well, and would soon help vault both to the kind of fame nobody had foreseen for wrestlers.

Roddy left town for a week-long tour through the Pacific Northwest, where he faced yet another son of a wrestler who'd beaten him up in the past, Curt Hennig, son of Larry "The Axe." Then Roddy headed even farther west again, for the last time.

"I would go over to Japan and they would hate us," said Roddy. "Because they were still mad about the bomb—not kidding at all."

Whether he was kidding in retrospect, he was certainly not laughing at the time. Upon checking in with All Japan Wrestling, who had brought him over, he had to hand over his passport to them. The idea was that wrestlers were prone to getting drunk and losing things, and losing a passport was a major hassle. But to Roddy, it represented a loss of freedom. He might not have noticed if he'd been content with the tour, as he was when touring with Stan Hansen years earlier. But this time, his patience for life and work abroad was short. "Well, I got into this thing," said Roddy, "and I'm saying to myself, this is horseshit."

Dick Slater, who had been wrestling with Roddy off and on in Mid-Atlantic for a year, and Chavo Guerrero joined Roddy and a few other North Americans for the six-week tour. Roddy wasn't alone on the tour, but married and far from his family he felt like it. He was a father now—feeling all the anxiety that role carries—and he was an ocean and a continent away from his newborn daughter. Japan's entertainments—mostly drinking over Korean BBQ at night—had amused him when he was younger. Now they were just a means to express his frustration.

"I'm starting to get a little reckless. In Japan, where you'd see a soda pop machine, they have beer machines out on the street. You'd just put in, I don't know, two hundred yen or whatever it was, and you'd get a Sapporo or whatever. I'm drinking, trying to get through, trying to get my passport, trying to get out. Nobody's listening to me, can't get phone calls out, can't get nothing. Drinking.

"One night I got this bright idea when I saw this fire extinguisher, and I knew that this guy"—a trainer who had been making his life miserable—"I knew where his room was. I got that fire extinguisher about two in the morning—there were no cameras in the hallways then—and I let it go under the door.

"Next morning, even I was surprised. It looked like there was a blizzard—it had just covered the room in thick, white stuff.

The trainer confronted him. "I didn't do it," Roddy replied. "I don't know what you're talking about."

"Oh, I see, one of our Japanese boys did it."

"Anyway, give me my passport back."

"No."

At night, North American wrestlers stood out in a restaurant, and people started to figure out who they were. Some of those people were members of the Yakuza—the Japanese mafia, for lack of a better term.

"You knew who they were right away—one, they had tattoos all over them, but two, when they made a mistake, in front of the boss, they had to cut off a piece of their finger at the knuckle. Another mistake, a piece of the finger at the knuckle again. There were guys with three fingers and a thumb, two and half fingers, whatever. They all wanted to arm wrestle," said Roddy. "They didn't stand a chance."

Even if the Americans greatly outweighed the Japanese, the encounters could be unnerving. These were organized criminals, after all, who got a kick out of trying to prove themselves against the Westerners. But in the end they were mostly just like overly assertive fans back home, one of those things Roddy had to put up with.

"We had a lot of fun at night," remembered Chavo. Not surprisingly, Chavo recalled the tour more warmly than Roddy did. As was so often the case, Roddy went through life beneath a dark cloud that no one else could see.

"We tagged up that tour. Won a match," said Chavo. One habit of the Japanese fans got under his tag partner's skin. "They threw a roll of toilet paper and hit Roddy in the head. He was so pissed and I was laughing. He came up and says, 'Please, Amigo, please don't laugh.' I didn't think anything of it, but he took it as 'You stink,' or the Japanese people . . ." His voice trailed off, suggesting that the Japanese fans equated him with something normally handled with toilet paper.

Roddy wasn't in the mood. His third Japanese tour was about to become his final Japanese tour. He wanted his passport, and he wanted to go home.

"I started getting edgy and mean," Roddy said. "I made it real clear: I want out. A guy can get pretty desperate and nothing mattered anymore."

Making his way to the ring each night, Roddy kept noticing the silence of the crowd following a little polite applause when he was introduced. He tended to swear a lot in the ring, and had to watch himself there, where every word was audible. It gave him an idea.

"In the ring with these guys I'd say, 'Come on, you *okama*,' which is 'faggot' in Japanese." Even against their top wrestlers, like Fujinami, I remember, I'd say, 'Come on, you *okama*.' The promoters asked me to stop saying that. So I'd say, 'Give me my passport back,' and they wouldn't."

One night after work, Roddy went out by himself. It was late. He'd hit up every beer machine he could find. As he approached one of the Korean BBQs he frequented, he happened upon an empty taxicab parked at the curb. The door was open and the cab was running.

"Fuck it," he said.

He jumped into the car, threw it in drive and stomped on the gas. He hadn't realized the steering wheel was turned all the way to the left. The car jumped the curb and leapt across the sidewalk. "It went right through the wall, right into the restaurant. Next day, they gave me my passport back. I've been barred from the country ever since."

Chavo learned exactly what happened only after the tour was done. "The night that he did the damage, I had gone to my room. He was gone the next day. What happened to Piper? In Japan, nobody tells you anything."

Roddy's use of "barred" probably didn't reflect any diplomatic prohibition against his entering Japan. But it was pretty clear that the wrestling promotions were done with him. He was a very successful wrestler in the territories, and no doubt All Japan had considered itself fortunate to have him. It's hard to believe that with all he was about to accomplish in the next five years, no Japanese promotion ever asked him to return. But they didn't.

Back in the US, Roddy found himself in familiar company, wrestling Greg Valentine outdoors in Wilmington, North Carolina, in the rain. It was raining so hard, in fact, fans were climbing under the ring to stay dry.

The wrestlers locked up, punched, kicked and rolled around the sopping wet ring. "Go home!" Roddy urged Valentine. He wasn't enjoying himself wrestling a man who hit as hard as The Hammer while also getting soaked.

Valentine refused. "No. I ain't going home."

He thought it was funny, letting Roddy suffer in the elements. They were friends, and Valentine's insistence on seeing the match through was a rib, but Roddy wasn't happy and he didn't feel like having his nose pressed into puddles for any longer than necessary.

Roddy backed Valentine into a corner and punched him in the face. He punched him again. He did it twice more—"It looked like Muhammad Ali beating the hell out of Sonny Liston," said Valentine. He grabbed Valentine's head under his arm, turned toward the ring, empty except for the torrential rain bouncing off the canvas, and ran toward the opposite corner. Roddy hopped into the air with his feet out in front of him and crashed Valentine's head into the mat—a textbook Bulldog.

"Are we going home now?" said Roddy.

From beneath their tangled limbs, Valentine answered, "Yes."

After drying off in his own dressing room, Valentine came to Roddy's. Roddy looked up at him, a sheepish look on his face. He had been a little rough.

Valentine started laughing. "I deserved it!"

It's good that they both got accustomed to suffering in one another's company. In a few months, they'd be doing a lot more of it.

In Georgia, Roddy cut a particularly creative promo for a feud he had going with a Florida-born wrestler named "Mad Dog" Buzz Sawyer. In the video, Roddy crawls through a heavily wooded park, birds chirping in the background. He scuttles on all fours from behind one tree to the next, getting closer to the camera as if sneaking up on his prey. He's wearing a shredded jean jacket and a chain around his neck, since the upcoming match is a dog-collar match in which both wrestlers will wear a collar attached by this chain. His breathing is fast and shallow.

"I'm looking for you, Mad Dog," he says from behind a tree. The video cuts to him bursting through the surface of a swampy pond. "Where's that Mad Dog?!" he growls as he slaps the water manically from his face. It cuts again to a shot of an old truck while George Thorogood plays in the background. In a moment of very DIY video editing, the truck rolls forward fifteen feet and stops. Roddy jumps out and lights into more standard promo fare (two young women walk past in the background, looking curiously toward the shoot) before it cuts again, and the idea of standard fare goes right out the window.

Wearing a shirt that reads "Buzz Sawyer R.I.P.," Roddy bottles himself for what seems to be the third time in his career. Except for the suds running down his face, it's a bloodless example of the art, and he speaks clearly after pounding the glass against his forehead. It's a hell of a thing to get good at doing, but it gets attention, and that's the business he was in, which is maybe the only thing that explains where he takes the promo next.

Roddy reaches into the bed of the old truck and produces Kitty's Chihuahua, Feather, in a T-shirt that says "Mad Dog."

"By the time I'm finished with you, Sawyer, this is exactly what you'll look like!" He tucks the little dog under his arm as soon as he's made his point, and the dog looks bemusedly up at him. The dog is a funny touch, but the humour ends there.

One last time, the scene cuts to a shot of Roddy's legs, dangling above the park grass. The camera pans up and Roddy, still in the "R.I.P." T-shirt, has hanged himself using the chain and dog collar. He snatches a black bag from over his head to deliver his last line. His face is scrunched by the force of the leather around his neck. He is visibly straining and his face is red. "Move it on over, Sawyer, 'cause the mean old dogs are moving in." He tries to growl but can barely produce a sound.

That he didn't break his neck is a wonder, and testament to the shape he was in. But hanging himself at 230 pounds was tempting fate, tempting it to destroy him where nothing had so far succeeded—or tempting it to take its wildest gamble on him yet.

In another promo from this feud, Roddy chides Sawyer for going to college to become an amateur wrestler while Roddy was already fighting pro. He says, "The only thing that kept me out of college, brother, was high school. Went to the school of hard knocks. Black and blue's the colours, Jack!" From nearly killing himself in the promo to the language he used in others, he was aggressively writing the story of Rowdy Roddy Piper. (In fact, Roddy did finish high school.)

"Rod didn't like to let anyone else have the lead," Kitty said, to describe Roddy's self-mythologizing. He seeded that story every chance he got. "Just like the back of trading cards say born in Glasgow, Scotland, you build this image and it doesn't even need to be factual. Then it becomes *the* image and you don't change the image."

Those promos helped advance another narrative Roddy was building. His left ear was bandaged. "I can't hear outta this ear no more. It don't work!" he says. That ear would play an important role in his last hurrah for Mid-Atlantic, and in his grand return to the biggest territory of them all.

In 1972, Vince McMahon Sr. had put on a major card at Shea Stadium, home of the New York Mets, with a main event featuring Pedro Morales and Bruno Sammartino. He did it again in 1976, with the infamous Inoki/Ali match in Tokyo serving as a main event by closed-circuit television. Sammartino fought Stan Hansen in the undercard. In 1980 McMahon truly set a new standard for what was possible in the presentation of professional wrestling. He stuffed that year's Showdown at Shea with thirteen matches, showcasing some of the best wrestlers at the time, including many who'd worked with Roddy: Andre the Giant, Rene Goulet, Johnny Rodz, Chavo Guerrero, Inoki, and budding star, Terry Bollea, who'd been convinced by Vince McMahon Jr. to adopt the name Hulk Hogan (McMahon Jr. didn't take control of his father's New York promotion until 1982).

The 1980 Showdown at Shea was a major volley in a turf war to determine who in the old territories could expand his regional fiefdom into an international empire. McMahon Sr. had pulled his then-called World Wide Wrestling Federation out of the NWA, the national alliance of territory promoters that ruled the wrestling business in North America, thereby dismissing any boundaries on his promotion's potential for expansion.

Crockett fired back. He put together a supercard of his own for November 24, 1983, and to one-up the McMahons' gambit at Shea Stadium he arranged for the card to be available across the country on pay-per-view, a first in wrestling.

His main event would be the culmination of a long-standing feud between contender Ric Flair and champion Harley Race. Starrcade '83: A Flair for the Gold (today we'd call that title a spoiler) featured the title bout and seven others, including Piper wrestling Valentine.

Crockett approached Roddy and asked him to come up with the most brutal match he and Valentine could conceive. Fresh off his Georgia feud with Buzz Sawyer, Roddy had an idea.

"We talked about it for about five minutes and we went out and did it," said Valentine. "Because it wasn't planned, we were taking it off the cuff, and Roddy had worked with it before, so I followed him. . . . We just said screw it, we're hurt already, let's just go out and steal the show from Flair and Harley Race. And we did."

Their dog collar match became a classic.

The fifteen-foot chain had a black leather studded dog collar on each end. To ramp up enthusiasm, Crockett had the collars and chain showcased in the lobby of the Greensboro Coliseum before the evening started. Crockett had asked the wrestlers for brutal, and looking at that chain it would be easy to imagine that the result would live up to the request.

"I got this bright idea of putting sheep's wool inside these inch-and-a-half collars," remembered Roddy, with a groan. "The problem was, you get sweating with that inch and a half of sheep's wool . . ."

The match began with Roddy and Valentine pulling with their necks on opposite ends of the chain, because if they closed in on one another they could grab the slack and use it as a weapon. It's a great moment of ring psychology. The brief tug-of-war with their necks not only emphasized the danger to the most fragile part of the body, it gave fans a chance to clue in to the danger Roddy was about to exploit.

After a few moments of pulling against the chain, they advanced carefully. Roddy gathered a loop of chain and struck the first blow, lashing Valentine across the shoulder. After a few more sequences, Valentine took Roddy's lead and went to work himself, getting Roddy on the mat in front of him and wrapping the chain around Roddy's eyes. And of course, he hit Roddy on that left ear every chance he could.

"I can remember it getting to the point—it went a long time for that kind of a match—getting to the point where everything was numb," said Roddy, as he and Valentine reminisced about the match in 2015. "I remember getting hit by you, and I would feel the shot kinda, but you were numb. . . . You had that chain wrapped around me, twice, my teeth, my ears and my eyes, and you were pulling on it, and then you drop an elbow on my head."

Valentine suggested the dog-collar match was the first hardcore match—wrestling with no disqualifications and flagrant use of ultra-violent gimmicks and foreign objects—and Roddy elaborated on what a vicious match it was. "His fingers are like sausages, his hands are so big. And he had a chain around them.

And it was my left ear and it was bleeding and bleeding and he was working on it and working on it. It broke the eardrum."

The eardrum was already broken, though how much it had healed and how much worse it got after this is anyone's guess.

"Thank god I got a thick neck," replied Valentine. "And you always had one too, so we survived it."

By the end—in a bit of a replay of the match in which Roddy lost the belt to Valentine—Roddy was stumbling against the ropes, bleeding profusely from his injured ear, and commentator Gordon Solie was laying it on thick about Roddy's lost equilibrium. Roddy won the bout, but immediately after the pin, Valentine took off the collar and choked him with it.

"The orders that we had was, 'Go out and have the most brutal match possible so people would come back and see it.' I think I missed the last part," said Roddy.

"They were so happy with the results of it," said Valentine. "'You guys are going to do it in fifteen more towns!' There's no way those following matches were as good as that one, because we'd already beat the hell out of each other. They were good, but oh my god!"

Roddy and Valentine replayed that match in over a dozen cities. The pain they inflicted on each other every night was bad; the itching of those wool-lined collars was worse. They developed rashes on their necks that were rubbed raw every night. With a baby daughter at home, Roddy was putting baby oil on his. Valentine wore turtlenecks.

"I remember you being down on your knees, hitting me hard, and you were screaming at me," said Roddy. "And I can't tell what you're saying, and I pull the blood clot out of my ear, and you were saying, 'Only an idiot would put wool in a dog collar!'"

The booker George Scott suggested Valentine pour rubbing alcohol on his chafed neck. He did. Roddy meanwhile tried hydrogen peroxide. It was a rough few weeks. Both already had chests striped with welts and scars from Wahoo McDaniel's chops. "On the left hand side I got scars to this day where he just kept peeling the meat off," Roddy said. Both men were miserable with the constant itching and pain.

It took them thirty-some years before they could joke about it.

"Your ear looked like the ear on the Elephant Man," said Valentine.

The Yellow Canary was gone. Roddy had given it to a wrestler named Ron Ritchie. He was driving a Cadillac again and he was getting ready to drive it north. Vince McMahon Sr. had called Crockett to say that he wanted to use Roddy when he was done in Charlotte. Distinguishing himself from the run-of-the-mill promoter—the hated "P"—Crockett shared the news with Roddy of McMahon's interest.

He'd accomplished as much as he could in Mid-Atlantic. Flair was still riding high, much as Buddy Rose had been when Roddy had left Portland. And Flair wasn't leaving. New York had the added allure of being the one territory Roddy had failed to win over. There was no place else left to refine his trade. If he wanted to get over, truly over, it was time to step up to the bright lights of Broadway.

Many of Roddy's Mid-Atlantic peers were headed there as well, some with new gimmicks, others with the tried and true. Roddy wasn't changing, though. Whatever the magic of that kilt and the bagpipes that chimed him in (he didn't play them ringside anymore—too many whacks in the teeth from ornery fans), his brawling Scotsman persona had gotten him this far. He'd trust it to get him the rest of the way to the top.

Tom Prichard had watched Roddy with astonishment in Texas. He'd done the same in Georgia. He watched closely enough to realize the simplest secret to his hero's success: "Roddy got over by being Roddy."

Roddy was about to see if being Rowdy Roddy Piper was enough to take Manhattan.

7

A Despicable, Disgraceful Display

Canadians have a way of finding each other. Sure, Roddy was in Toronto, but the dressing room might as well have been in Charlotte. Never mind its distance from North Carolina, Toronto was Ric Flair country. The talent coming through Maple Leaf Gardens every week was largely American and the fans weren't much interested in locals, only greats.

A wrestler just a few years Roddy's junior was standing inside the entrance to the arena floor, just out of sight of the fans. The Gardens crowd was going crazy as Roddy and Greg Valentine beat one another into bloody messes with a fifteen-foot chain. It was December 1983.

The young wrestler wasn't well known yet, but his family was. Bret Hart was a son of Calgary promoter Stu Hart, who had trained many of the men Roddy had wrestled during his career. His Stampede Wrestling drew talent from all over the world.

"My conversation with Roddy was very brief," recalled Hart, "but very cute, in a way. 'Hey, little Canadian guy, how you doin'?'" In the Gardens dressing room that day, Roddy was pleasantly surprised to meet another wrestler from Western Canada, so close to where he'd grown up himself. For Bret, who was just beginning to build his name, meeting Roddy was a big deal. At twenty-nine, Roddy had been a star in the territories for several years. Very few names were placed higher on the marquee than Roddy Piper's. The two Westerners met again in the months that followed. This time Roddy let his infamous mouth get ahead of his judgement.

"There was a story that some wrestlers had made up about my dad," Hart said. "You still hear it sometimes from people." Repeating the stories in full—there were two—would be just another way of perpetuating a cruelty, so we won't. In essence, they involved Stu Hart not knowing or caring enough to wash his hands before he ate.

"Roddy told me this story," said Hart. "Wrestlers would howl at how funny it was."

It was never Roddy's way to mock somebody upon meeting them, let alone mock another man's father—that was our experience, anyway. Roddy was young still, though, and he had won the respect of his peers the hard way. Respect was a commodity he gave willingly to those who deserved it, but he didn't part with it easily.

"That's not funny. That's not even true," Hart said to Roddy.

Roddy tried to laugh it off, but Bret stayed serious.

"I know you're a big name, and you're a big star, but keep that stupid story to yourself."

After the matches that night, Roddy apologized.

"You know what, you're absolutely right. It was a stupid story."

Roddy had made one of his lifelong friends, maybe his first true friend, after fighting him in a garage. He made another when Bret Hart stood up to him in a dressing room. "The fact that I shot that story down and got offended by it," said Hart, "probably was the bridge to a respect and friendship that never, ever wavered after that."

By the time of their second meeting, Roddy had packed up Kitty and their infant daughter and relocated to New York, where he'd been hired by the World Wrestling Federation (formerly World Wide Wrestling Federation), whose owners' designs on dominating the wrestling market were accurately reflected in the promotion's grandiose name. The kind of expansion Jim Crockett desired in Charlotte was already underway in New York. It was the world's greatest media market and one of the world's most storied sports facilities: Madison Square Garden. If there was an ideal focal point for the territory to end all territories, New York was it.

After his blackballing in Atlanta, Roddy wasn't interested in signing another contract with a promoter. Vince McMahon—Sr. and Jr.—were gathering top wrestling talent like collectors buying up old comic books—and the nature of that talent was very comic book–like. Big men with outsized characters. The three-hundred-pound wrestlers Roddy had been dealing with for the past ten years were men who, despite their considerable muscle, tipped the scales with a healthy dose of body fat. But wrestlers like "The Incredible" Hulk Hogan looked like they'd just climbed out of the weight room at Venice Beach. Smaller men like Jimmy "Superfly" Snuka and Paul "Mr. Wonderful" Orndorff possessed chiselled physiques the likes of which eluded Roddy no matter how much time he spent in the gym. And then there were the giants: Andre, of course, Big John

Studd and King Kong Bundy. Roddy was right to worry about being a smaller man. He had the confidence now, however, to work without a contract. Thanks to his starring role in Starrcade and a strong endorsement from Sgt. Slaughter, the McMahons were eager to have him in New York, but he wasn't eager to belong to anyone.

Roddy and Kitty rented apartments in Connecticut—the actual home state of the WWF offices—and New Jersey, before settling in Woodbridge, New Jersey, where another daughter was soon on the way.

The loss of equilibrium that had followed Roddy's eardrum injury continued to hamper him in the ring, so upon his arrival in the WWF, he appeared as a manager to Orndorff and David Schultz. He was so good on the microphone that his new boss saw another opportunity to put Roddy to work.

Through 1983, the WWF had run several episodes of an on-set interview segment called Rogers' Corner. In front of a plain beige backdrop, the silver-haired sixty-two-year-old former champion Buddy Rogers played the babyface interviewer, staring down heels like "Magnificent" Don Muraco and Captain Lou Albano while bolstering the profiles of fellow faces like Snuka and Rocky Johnson. Rogers was the original "Nature Boy" and was a masterful manipulator of crowds in his prime, but he mostly let his guests speak, supporting their angles with mock offense or fraternal affection.

The idea of a wrestling talk show seemed right. The genius of Vince McMahon Jr.'s WWF was its ability to lampoon popular culture with a straight face and a thick neck. Johnny Carson was still a television staple after the kids went to bed while *Late Night with David Letterman* had just ramped up confrontational comedy in that television time slot. Roddy saw Buddy Rogers' Corner and had nodded off to his share of late-night television on the road. He made his pitch to McMahon Jr. If the kids were wondering what Mom and Dad were watching in bed every night, "Piper's Pit" would be exactly what the kids hoped was on TV. Pure trouble, setting up angles for upcoming feuds in the biggest, noisiest cartoon of them all.

"It's certainly a pleasure for me, and it's certainly a pleasure for you," Roddy began an early segment, during which he interviewed wrestler Eddie Gilbert, who was returning from a supposedly broken neck. Roddy corrected himself when Gilbert took issue with him calling Gilbert's father, also his manager, "stupid," and allowed that the senior Gilbert was only "ignorant." Roddy's arrogance set the tone of the show, which he accidentally called "Piper's Corner" during the inaugural segment, confusing names with its predecessor. But the segment immediately distinguished itself from anything that had gone before. The difference was, of course, Roddy. This time, the unrepentant heel was in control, and things were always guaranteed to go horribly, wonderfully wrong.

Jobber Frankie Williams was foisted on Roddy as another early guest. Roddy opened with a little revisionist history:

"I have never actually lost a match, because I figured once you were defeated one time that it would take that *oomph* away from you that you needed." Looking at the older, smaller Williams, with his unremarkable blue singlet and underdeveloped physique, Roddy no doubt saw his own worst fears looking nervously back at him. Of course Roddy had lost matches before, but a lie wasn't really a lie if it was doing a job for the camera. The way he mocked Williams revealed much about Roddy's ambitions and anxieties—and his strategy for remaining in control of his value as a top-drawing wrestler.

Roddy continued: "You're just the opposite. I have never seen you win a match in my whole career of watching you. . . . You lack the guts, you lack the authority to go in there. You lack the guts, and when you're against the ropes what you do is, instead of going after a man, you just back off from him. Maybe a little cowardism, maybe you should be making pizzas . . ." Williams kept grabbing the microphone, trying to defend himself. Roddy assured him, "This is verbal, this is *not* physical," then hit him with the microphone and threw him off the set. He then leaned into the camera, which picked up his closing line: "Just when they think they got the answers, I change the questions."

The line (which he'd also used in Portland) was a mission statement. Roddy Piper had arrived in New York, and as hard as his bosses might work him, they would be the ones trying to keep up with him. He was going to be relentless in his pursuit of novelty. If he succeeded, contract or no contract, the WWF wouldn't be able to imagine itself without him. And clobbering a career jobber, a poorly paid punching bag hired only to make other wrestlers look good, drew a clear line between Roddy and the kind of wrestler he wanted never to become.

He interviewed a wrestler of a very different stature in another early "Piper's Pit."

"I'm not that well acquainted with ya," he began his conversation with Andre the Giant. That wasn't true either. They'd wrestled dozens of times by 1984 and Andre was very fond of him. Years before, in Los Angeles, he'd taken Roddy out for breakfast and made him eat steak and a dozen eggs to pack on weight.

The segment immediately became confrontational, and Andre picked Roddy up by the shirt and threw him off the set. Roddy stormed back, shirtless, but the Giant was gone. Roddy screamed into the camera another of his signature lines, one he'd also employed in Portland: "You do not throw rocks at a man who's got a machine gun!"

Any threat against Andre was bound to sound hollow, but the riled-up conviction in Roddy's voice sold it. And that was exactly why Andre liked working with him. Andre either liked his peers or really didn't, and he'd immediately recognized in Roddy a wrestler who could use his relentless, manic style to convincingly punish the seven-foot-four Frenchman in the ring, all the while drawing enough heat himself to rile up the crowd in Andre's favour. Andre hated taking a bump for a wrestler who could never appear legitimately to hurt him. With Roddy, that was never a problem.

A few weeks later in Madison Square Garden, Roddy and David Schultz fought a tag match against Andre and Jimmy Snuka. That night, Andre did Roddy a great favour.

"Here was the thing with Andre the Giant," Roddy began, stating the obvious, "he was a giant! When he hit somebody, of course they'd fly, and it would make Andre look great. There was nowhere to go. It was just another short night. No one could get the Giant in trouble. You don't stand a chance."

After so many matches together, they'd worked out a few favourite routines. "What he loved to do was, he'd come and he'd take the T-shirt off me, because I had a different T-shirt on each and every week, and he'd put it on himself, like Baby Huey." Often, after Andre tossed him out of the ring, Roddy would abandon the match and walk off the arena floor toward the dressing rooms. Security would block the way, and with a disdainful wave in their direction, he'd return to the ring.

"So it comes to Madison Square Garden," continued Roddy. "Everybody, including Vince, tried to say no." Andre was proposing a unique turn of events in the match and refused to be denied by the WWF brain trust. Roddy had worked hard with him for several years and he wanted to return the favour.

"I'd get in there and I'd get my elbows up to his hair, and when he hit me, I'd hang on to his head and I'd go right in his eyes. And so he'd start to hold his eyes and he'd hit me, but I held on and I'd hit him again, and then the eyes," said Roddy, explaining how he'd learned to work with a man more than twice his size. "The first time doing this was really difficult. The second time, easy peasy. Finally he sat down in the second turnbuckle, trying to see. "I don't care if you're a giant or a polar bear, if you can't see"—and you've got somebody pounding on you and you can't get up—"it's uncomfortable. And then when he wanted to, when it came time, he'd explode. It's how he kicked me every time."

That night in the Garden, Andre didn't explode. In the epicentre of the American wrestling universe, the biggest wrestler in history decided he'd put his little friend over. Roddy said, "Andre the Giant allowed me to get on him, split him open, have him down to the point where he had to be taken out of Madison Square Garden on a fucking stretcher, bleeding." The stretcher was a farce, of course, because the people holding it couldn't conceivably carry Andre's dead weight.

"When you look at the tape, it couldn't really be said he was *carried* on a stretcher. They had him on the stretcher until they got out of the ring." Andre fell off on the way to the dressing rooms. "And you know what? He did that for me," said Roddy. "That's old code." Andre returned to the ring five minutes later, wrapped up and ready to chase Roddy and Schultz out of the building, but the favour was done.

"Nice, huh? I don't think he's ever done that for anybody else."

Roddy had a ringside interview with WWF host "Mean Gene" Okerlund a short time later. He was there with Orndorff and Schultz, whom he was still ostensibly managing. The promo was for an upcoming six-man tag match. Orndorff and Schultz used up all the time, leaving Okerlund to apologize to Roddy for not getting to him. Roddy replied, "Giant Killers don't have time anyway."

"Piper's Pit" worked. It became a staple of those studio taping days in Poughkeepsie, New York—and also Brantford, Ontario—when Roddy and the others taped three weeks' worth of television, including three "Piper's Pit" segments in a day. One of those segments is still remembered more than any other.

Jimmy "Superfly" Snuka could bring fans out of their seats with his acrobatic high spots and his strong-but-silent persona. He'd wrestled Roddy in the territories as far back as 1978 and had already been part of some iconic WWF matches in pursuit of the heavyweight championship. One cage match famously ended in a Bob Backlund victory followed by Snuka dragging the champion back into the ring, where Snuka climbed the cage and jumped off the top bars, about fifteen feet up, hammering the champion into the mat. Snuka's daring aerial drops inspired a generation of wrestlers to follow suit, but his second appearance on "Piper's Pit" would help inspire a cult following of the segment's host.

After setting up the interview by mentioning Snuka's previous "Piper's Pit" visit, during which Roddy hadn't let his soft-spoken guest get a word in, Roddy handed him the microphone and pulled out a paper grocery bag filled with pineapples and bananas for the Fiji-born Snuka.

"I wanna make you feel at home," Roddy said. He taunted Snuka with the tropical fruit, and then produced several coconuts and apologized for not bringing in a palm tree so Snuka could climb it.

"Are you making fun of me?" asked Snuka. He held the microphone so far from his mouth as to seem dumbstruck, like a child who doesn't have the nerve to stick up for himself.

"Am I making fun of you? Oh, no sir. No sir," said Roddy.

On television, the segment ran with a brief introduction by Vince McMahon Jr., who leaned over a supposed news desk with an air of grave concern to convey that he was the head of the WWF and he was taking responsibility for what viewers were about to see.

"We would like to caution you about viewing this piece," he said. "It is not a pretty sight at all. . . . Be forewarned."

As he said "No sir," Roddy turned slightly away from Snuka, pivoted and cracked a coconut against Snuka's head. It exploded and Snuka reeled backward, collapsing against the set wall, taking it all down with him. The backstage of the television facility looked as spare as an empty warehouse. The audience looked on in astonishment, as if they couldn't believe their luck. They had picked this of all days to get wrestling tickets.

For decades people have debated whether that coconut was real and whether Snuka knew Roddy was going to hit him with it. The coconut was real. Watch closely, though, and the segment reveals a few of its secrets. The first thing Roddy does is grab Snuka's hair with his left hand. That head is going to be in position whether Snuka knows enough to put it there or not.

Roddy brings the coconut around in his right hand, very quickly. Seeing him do this so deftly at thirty makes it easy to imagine him in his teens ambushing the man who'd flashed his billfold at a bar in Winnipeg. Roddy strikes so quickly and unexpectedly it's difficult for the eye to follow. As he'd learned from bottling himself: hit hard and don't let up.

The coconut connects with Snuka's head, but not directly against his skull. Snuka always wore a headband to control his frizzy long hair and the one he has on in the interview appears to be made of hard shells or some sort of white bead-like pieces woven together into a band strong enough that it doesn't break when the coconut is smashed against it.

Roddy spends the next minute kicking Snuka while he's down, mashing bananas into his mouth, whatever he can do to add insult to injury. Then, as Snuka rallies and slowly comes to his feet, Roddy, goading him the whole time, backs steadily closer to a steel door and finally slips through and slams it shut on a charging Snuka's face.

That escape was like Roddy's escape from most places in those days. It took some planning.

Television and film producer Mitch Ackerman had watched Roddy on television in Los Angeles and on MSG Network out of New York, where he'd grown up. Ackerman had already enjoyed great success with shows like *Knots Landing, Dallas* and *Falcon Crest,* and he thought wrestling's increasing popularity was making it prime for some sort of screen treatment. He and Roddy had a friend in common, so with no particular agenda Ackerman arranged to meet Roddy one evening at the Olympic in Los Angeles, while Roddy was on the road.

Ackerman got a quick education in life as wrestling's most hated heel.

"We set up for me to meet him after the matches by the locker room," recalls Ackerman. "He was the last match. This was when he was a bad guy and his program at that point was Jimmy Snuka. He was really beating the crap outta him. . . . Usually you see a back-and-forth in a match but this one . . . there wasn't any back-and-forth."

Roddy emerged from the dressing room and asked, "So where's your car parked?"

Ackerman had parked where the wrestlers parked, thinking that made sense, since he was collecting Roddy after the show.

"Okay, well, look," Roddy said to him, "when we get out we just make a beeline straight to your car, get in and just take off." Sure enough, when they left the Olympic, several dozen fans were waiting outside. They didn't want autographs. Roddy and Ackerman raced to the brand new Jaguar and the fans followed, booing and throwing garbage. Unfortunately, Ackerman had parked facing the building. He had to back out before he could take off, and that was impossible. The mob of fans surrounded them and started banging on the windows and climbing all over Ackerman's new car.

"Look, I'm gonna get out and I'll go back into the arena," said Roddy. "When you're able to get out of here, pull up to the door." Roddy opened the car door hard against the press of people on his side. As they went tumbling onto the pavement, he bolted into the Olympic. Ackerman waited until most of the crowd dispersed, then backed out and drove up to the door.

"I honked the horn and he jumped in. I put the pedal to the metal. I just took off. It was scary, and it wasn't the last time that something like that happened."

Fame—or infamy—was making life dangerous in New York, too. Greg Valentine had come to the WWF, and one night he was giving Roddy a lift home from Madison Square Garden.

"We couldn't get out," said Roddy, referring to the parking exit from under the Garden. "People were rocking the car. So

Gregory just puts the hammer down, slips over the curb, gets on the sidewalk on the other side. . . . I don't know how we didn't hit somebody."

"Just kept going like nothing ever happened," said Valentine. "I couldn't believe I did it either, without hitting somebody—or going down into the subway entrance."

"We have angels watching us, Gregory," he said.

"Cowboy" Bob Orton Jr., or "Ace," as Roddy had started calling him, joined "Piper's Pit" as Roddy's "bodyguard." Orton became a fixture in his cowboy hat and frilled vest, always manoeuvring himself to stand threateningly behind Roddy's guest.

"'Piper's Pit' woulda been nothing without Ace," said Roddy. "Ace was there for a coupla reasons. One is because he's one tough boy. Two, I don't know anybody that can outperform Bob Orton in that ring in any kinda way. We . . . complemented each other."

Having met in Charlotte, Roddy and Orton were now getting along famously in New York, even before Orton's run on "Piper's Pit." Both lived in Woodbridge and Orton was giving him a ride home after a long day of shooting in Poughkeepsie. Somewhere on the New Jersey Turnpike after midnight, they realized they were hungry and decided to hang a left for Japanese food.

"Bobby's driving. I'm just shotgun. We find a sushi place right in downtown Manhattan. We're so happy." After an hour of eating and drinking, they stroll contentedly outside into the cold, ready to go home. But they're greeted by an unexpected sight. Orton's car is double-parked, and there are police all around it. They've got a couple of men in handcuffs. Roddy's Halliburton, a kind of briefcase wrestlers coveted, was still where he'd left it in the back seat. But there was glass in the back seat, too, and the engine was running.

It was late and they'd had a few beers. They took a moment to catch on.

"We got up to the car," said Orton. "I must have left the car with the key in the ignition with the car running. I thought, 'Well shit, it was cold! I musta wanted to leave the heater on.' Then the cops wanted to know if we wanted the guys arrested."

It clicked. Two men had broken into the car, hotwired it and been caught by police when they tried to drive it away.

"I don't blame them," joked Orton. "I'da tried it too. Just to get out of the cold."

Orton and Roddy refused to press charges. It was late, and they didn't need the hassle. The swarm of police looked on in amazement as the arresting officers let the thieves go.

"These hundred-and-forty-seven New York policemen around the car," said Roddy, "are you shitting me?! We got in the car and went home."

Throughout 1984, Roddy was involved in another feud that exposed McMahon's colourful stable to even more fans. Pop star Cyndi Lauper was one of the biggest names in music, thanks to her album *She's So Unusual* and its Billboard chart–topping singles. With her multi-hued hair and New York accent, she fit right in with the wrestlers. She became friends with Captain Lou Albano, who appeared in the video for "Girls Just Wanna Have Fun." In his fifties then, Albano was known to WWF audiences as a manager, and his relationship with Lauper was the lynchpin of what became known as the Rock 'n' Wrestling Connection.

Lauper appeared on "Piper's Pit" in a segment during which Roddy mostly behaved himself. Albano, however, began arguing on camera that he was responsible for Lauper's success. She balked and the two had a falling out. To settle their differences, she challenged Albano to select a woman wrestler to meet the female wrestler of her choosing. The Brawl to End It All featured a main event in which Albano's pick, WWF women's champion the Fabulous Moolah, lost her belt—which she'd held for twenty-eight years—to Lauper's pick, Wendi Richter.

The women's match headlined a card filled with staples like Sgt. Slaughter, Hulk Hogan and Greg Valentine, but only the main event was broadcast, on MTV. In a stunning example of wrestling's new popularity, it earned a 9.0 Nielsen rating (the number represents the percentage of American television-viewing households tuned in to the show), MTV's highest rated program to date.

Lauper and Albano eventually made nice, with champion Hogan often in the mix. At MSG she appeared in the ring to give Albano a gold and platinum record, mounted and framed under glass. She then gave another to Hogan, who accepted it on behalf of the WWF. The feel-good ceremony went predictably wrong when Orton appeared ringside and Roddy barged onto the mat.

Before the assembly made sense of Roddy's presence, he grabbed the mounted records and smashed them over the manager's head. Lauper rushed to the fallen Albano, and found herself against Roddy's boot. With what would for years to come be called a "kick," Roddy lifted her off Albano and sent her sprawling across the mat. Then he body slammed her manager, Dave Wolff. Hogan returned to the ring (why did he ever leave it?) and Roddy slipped through the ropes on the other side, where Orton was watching. With the crowd exploding around them, they left for the dressing rooms.

The bit of extra-curricular theatre had set the table for a brand-new grudge, one that in turn would clear the way for a feast, the likes of which would eclipse the success of Starrcade or any event in professional wrestling.

George Scott, the Charlotte booker who'd brought Roddy to Mid-Atlantic, soon followed the country's top talent to New York, where he became assistant booker for the WWF. He had shown a lot of grace to Roddy, and it had inspired Roddy to reply in kind.

George Scott—Scottish born and raised in Hamilton, Ontario—had a son named Byron, and one night back in Charlotte, Byron had pulled his Cadillac up to Roddy outside a nightclub and said, "My dad's the reason you're here." Roddy took it as a slight and punched in Scott's windshield. The car lurched ahead, so Roddy ran to his own Cadillac to give chase, just as Jack Brisco, who had a cast on one leg, was trying to get into Roddy's passenger seat. As Roddy told it, he hit the gas while the door was still open, but the Cadillac's wheels were pointed hard to one side and it accelerated in an unexpected direction, ramming Byron Scott's Cadillac and sending Brisco tumbling out of the passenger door of Roddy's car.

The incident landed Roddy in court. There, George Scott said, "You know, I'm responsible for bringing Roddy in here." The implication was that he should take some responsibility for what Roddy did and the pressures he was under. That struck Roddy as about as solid a thing as a man could say.

"You're right, sir," Roddy said to the elder Scott. "I apologize." The matter was settled.

When George Scott came to New York, he didn't seem to hold a grudge. In a moment as inauspicious as it was crucial to the future of professional wrestling, Scott threw an invitation Roddy's way.

At the studios in Poughkeepsie, Roddy was walking down the hall toward the washroom. Scott was following close behind.

"You want to fight Mr. T?" asked Scott.

"Sure," said Roddy. "Gotta go to the bathroom."

It was as simple as that.

From Lou Thesz to Harley Race, professional wrestling had crowned many great technicians and tough-as-nails street fighters as champions. But no one had ever had a champion like Hulk Hogan. The bronze-skinned blond-haired muscle-bound giant towered over the old-school wrestlers who lingered in the new WWF—George "The Animal" Steele or Bruno Sammartino—and Hogan worked the camera like few of the new giants McMahon was bringing into his orbit—King Kong Bundy or Bundy's frequent tag partner, Big John Studd, for example. Matched with his new All-American image, urging kids to say their prayers and take their vitamins, the champion was an oversized bundle of kinetic energy, the perfect media darling to drive McMahon's promotion and avenge the humiliation of Cyndi Lauper and Dave Wolff.

In February 1985, the principals of this drama gathered at Madison Square Garden for the War to Settle the Score. The fact that it was Roddy's title shot was mostly lost in the larger narrative: this was Hogan's chance to defend the Rock 'n' Wrestling Connection. More than that, Hogan was defending the heart and soul that fans had invested into wrestling and its ascendance to the pop cultural promised land.

The main event looked a little like Roddy's first big match ten years earlier. He was escorted to the ring by the City of New York Emerald Society Police Pipe Band playing "Scotland the Brave." Doing commentary, "Mean Gene" Okerlund referred to them as "the clan, if you will, of Mr. Piper." The night had other echoes of Roddy's past, including an opening match featuring Johnny Rodz, who as Java Ruuk had not only thrashed a much younger Roddy in Los Angeles but provided the occasion for Roddy's first stint as a manager—the gig that had put him over in Southern California. Jimmy Snuka exacted a sort of revenge by proxy during the undercard by defeating "Cowboy" Bob Orton. Orton collided with a cornerpost during the match, after which he wore a cast, his forearm supposedly broken.

The cast, and his refusal to take it off long after any legitimate injury would have healed, gave rise to some great gags on *Tuesday Night Titans*, McMahon's own wrestling talk show. In one episode he welcomed a doubtful Roddy and Orton as guests, and surprised them with a visit to *TNT*'s "resident doctor," who examined Orton and revealed X-rays that clearly showed a healthy forearm. Valuing the usefulness of that cast in a fight, the heels rejected the doctor's opinion, questioned his education and called him a quack.

McMahon roped as many celebrities into his promotion as he could. Sports broadcaster Bob Costas joined the War as guest ring announcer. Mr. T, star of *The A-Team* and villain of *Rocky III* (which had opened with Hogan playing a wrestler called Thunderlips), was in the front row to pump up his "longtime friend," in the words of Okerlund, on Hogan's way to the ring.

"Cyndi Lauper is here!" Okerlund enthused before the match. "Gloria Steinem!" The match began with a flurry of punches in Hogan's favour, until Roddy turned it around and began to lay into the champion. As the action progressed, Okerlund exclaimed, "Danny DeVito . . . I see Joe Piscopo and Danny DeVito, both, standing on their feet!"

After Paul Orndorff crashed the match and double-teamed Hogan with Roddy, Lauper climbed onto the apron to protest.

"A hundred-and-four-pound little gal isn't going to do anything to these two men!" bemoaned Okerlund, his uniquely understated hyperbole in glorious display all night.

"She'll get killed in there! Get her out of there!" added fellow commentator Gorilla Monsoon.

Mr. T climbed onto the apron to defend Lauper, who had been trying to ward off the advancing heels while her hapless manager, Dave Wolff, was in turn trying to talk her down before Roddy and Orndorff got their hands on her. The rapturous din of the crowd swelled. When Hogan revived to save T and chase away the heels, the next and inevitable main event was obvious. The score had not been settled, but the job had been done. The crowd had been baited. When word got out that Roddy's feud with Hogan had just gotten even larger, demand to see it resolved would exceed anything Madison Square Garden could accommodate.

McMahon had seen Crockett's rejoinder to the Showdown at Shea, and McMahon's next volley would leave no doubt who had won the real war in professional wrestling.

"I'm the littlest and the last, Napoleon Rod." Roddy probably wasn't the very smallest wrestler in the WWF, but he was the hardest for McMahon to bring to heel. In the middle of March, a month after The War to Settle the Score, Roddy was still working without a contract. McMahon was insistent he sign one, but Roddy refused. He'd worked all over the country and abroad. His stock was high. He saw no benefit to swearing allegiance to a single employer. Anyone anywhere (except Japan) would pay him to wrestle.

Roddy sat down with Vince in a place he remembered looking like a warehouse, probably backstage at the Poughkeepsie studios. The contract in front of him filled only a single sheet of paper. Roddy said no. All the other wrestlers working in the WWF were under contract now, but Roddy knew that Vince had bet the value of the promotion, not to mention his own house, on the next big event. Fans were desperate for a resolution to the Piper-Hogan feud. Order had to be restored. But Roddy knew pro wrestling's greatest rule: never restore order. Order is boring, and boring doesn't sell tickets.

Then he thought again. There was going to be merchandise to sell, T-shirts and dolls and myriad other ways to earn money that weren't part of working in any other territory. And there was always the remote possibility that McMahon might get fed up and try to do without him. Roddy was ambitious. He wanted in on what was coming. So Roddy signed. Of course, that didn't mean he was going to accept without question whatever role McMahon had in mind for him.

"McMahon and Hogan and [Pat] Patterson were in the office and I'm on the phone," said Roddy, recalling how they'd planned the main event of WrestleMania—"The greatest wrestling event of all time," as its tag line went. He listened to how the others saw the match playing out, and he disagreed, vehemently.

As management saw it, the match went like this: "On the big comeback, bang their heads together. Typical match that you could think of, throw them together and they'll crash. Get down and roll their legs." In the finish they were plotting, Roddy would at long last be pinned and defeated by the heroes, within the rules. Deferred justice would at last be served. "And I'm saying, emphatically I'm saying, 'You're wrong, you're fuckin' wrong, all wrong! I'm telling you, it's the wrong way.'" Roddy had fought signing a contract, and now he wanted to run the biggest match in the history of professional wrestling. "Vince says, 'Hot Rod, there's many right ways to do a match.'"

Roddy was adamant. "I said, 'I'm telling you, you're wrong, wait, wait.' I'm screaming at them."

Roddy was concerned about two things. First, if Mr. T tried wrestling like the professionals, something he had never done, he'd make it look phony right when more eyes than ever were on their business. "Mr. T, he wanted to come in and bang heads around, make dolls and fun and then go home and laugh," recalled Roddy, the taste still sour in his mouth decades later. "That's why I didn't get along with him right away. I insisted with Vince, I said, 'No, there's only one right way to do it. Keep it amateur. He wants to go in there and throw punches and stuff, he is going to look like shit, I'm gonna get mad, it's not going to work. You got your house bet on this!'"

By this time, Roddy and Bret Hart had become the kind of friends who talked late into the night in hotel rooms and on the phone, sharing their concerns about work and family. Hart understood the second reason why Roddy was so worried.

"He was very defensive about the wrestlers and the business," said Hart, "and he was very distrustful of the office and their motives and their susceptibility to doing the wrong things. The way they used to push guys or make guys based on such flimsy logic sometimes. . . . Roddy was always the guy that earned everything he got and defended his position to the end. You couldn't get him to change his mind about something like that. With Mr. T, I think there was a lot of pressure on Roddy to comply and let Mr. T go over on him."

Roddy worried that if Mr. T pinned him—if a TV star could waltz into the ring and beat the WWF's top contender for the heavyweight title—then no gimmick or celebrity appearance could repair the damage that decision would do to the whole business of pro wrestling, never mind the WWF. Mr. T would move on, that feather forever in his cap, and the wrestlers would be left looking like pushovers.

Roddy was old school. If you wore a belt—and even if you didn't—when you were in a bar and tough guys called you on it, you fought them, plain and simple. And if they beat you up and the promoter found out, you'd lose the belt and probably your job, too. In the territories, the illusions of pro wrestling had to be maintained if the feuds and hostilities in the ring were going to keep filling arenas. For all the wilful blindness that went into watching pro wrestling, no fan should ever doubt that the wrestlers were genuine tough guys. Further, Roddy saw no reason to think the WWF was immune to the cycles of fortune and loss experienced by every other territory he'd worked in.

"Territories got red hot and then died. All the time," said Hart. "It's really hard to keep the momentum going."

Of course, there was another possible finish to the match: Roddy losing to Hogan. So long as Mr. T was a minor player in the defeat, wrestling would leverage his celebrity without losing its credibility as home to the toughest characters on the planet. Interest might not collapse the way it would if Roddy lost to T, but interest in Roddy as top contender, or at least as an ever-dangerous menace, would be done. Roddy wasn't sure how they'd finish the match, but he sure as hell wasn't taking the fall.

On the last Sunday of March, Madison Square Garden filled again. Mr. T's mohawk was the only aspect of his usually flamboyant self on display that night. No feather earrings or gold chains. He was stripped down to the essentials to fit in with guys who made their living in their underwear.

McMahon had brought in even more celebrities. Guest referee Muhammad Ali patrolled ringside in the event of extracurricular trouble (Orton). Guest timekeeper Liberace seemed like an odd fit save for the fact that he was one of the few stars in the country as camp as McMahon's wrestlers. He danced with the Rockettes in the ring and rang a tiny crystal bell to start the match. New York Yankees manager Billy Martin announced the wrestlers.

Orton was ringside and so was Jimmy Snuka, an ideal counter to Cowboy Bob, both quiet but excellent performers. McMahon took no chances with his referee. Pat Patterson, the former wrestler who played a crucial role in managing the WWF, made sure the pre-ordained chaos was convincing.

The opening moments—several minutes, really—of the match were as perfect an example of ring psychology as Roddy had ever staged. He had lots of help. Hogan and Orndorff were no slouches at working the crowd, and T was a television star. After a long standoff before the bell went, Orndorff grabbed a broom from an attendant who was trying to clean up debris tossed into the ring. He snapped the broom over his knee before he, Roddy and Orton finally retreated to their corner. With giddy embraces, they set up to begin, with Orndorff and Hogan in the ring. They could have started the match right there, but the stage was too big and too bright to settle for such a simple beginning.

Roddy became frantic, waving Orndorff over to tag him in. With a slow, high tag, Orndorff obliged. Roddy got in the ring with the champ, right where the crowd so badly wanted him. But then T started jumping up and down, hollering for Hogan to tag him. Sensing the poetic justice offered by the moment, Hogan complied. Suddenly, it was Roddy and T facing off. Roddy reacted with notable discomfort but then, with a creeping sneer, embraced the moment. He crossed the mat slowly, staring down T the whole way—the loudmouthed bully realizing the littlest guy in the match had just been offered to him on an otherwise empty mat. As they came together, Roddy pressed his forehead into T's, grinding into him until they exchanged slaps across the face. Roddy turned and signalled time out to Patterson, then spun and kicked T in the stomach, and the amateur wrestling began.

It quickly led to a moment Roddy loathed, when T picked him up across his shoulders in a fireman's carry. Cathartic for the fans, the moment where the actor had the wrestler at his mercy was immortalized on the front of newspapers all over the world. Roddy could stomach taking the bump for the sake of the match, but he couldn't get past the sense that this was bad for business.

From there, every potential breakdown of the rules was exploited to maximum effect. Orndorff and Roddy double-teamed Mr. T in the corner, Ali took a swing at Orton when he tried to interfere, Roddy led his entourage toward the dressing rooms before being turned around by security, while Hogan urged Patterson not to count the heels out during their absence from the ring.

At the end of so much theatre, Orton jumped off the ropes to finish Hogan with his cast, but instead knocked out Orndorff, who was holding the champion from behind in a full nelson. Hogan pinned Orndorff for the win, Roddy knocked out Patterson and stormed out of the ring in disgust with Ace in tow. "A despicable, disgraceful display," Monsoon once called Roddy's antics. They were on full display in Madison Square Garden. Orndorff woke up, abandoned in the ring, which set up a feud with Roddy and Orton to follow. The next plot started and the work never stopped.

"When you watch that match, you watch when T finally gets to Hogan," said Roddy. "I was waiting 'til I got just tired enough. I front facelocked him, then, *boom*, got over. You watch, he doesn't throw one punch. He doesn't do anything. Take him down, ride him and that's it. That's why that son of a bitch worked."

The match certainly did work. Over a million people watched on pay-per-view, eclipsing the success of Crockett's Starrcade. McMahon kept his house. Most importantly to Roddy, Hogan still hadn't settled the score between them individually. Fans would keep calling for Roddy's head—and paying to see the feud reprised.

"He never let Hogan beat him," said Hart. "He stood his ground on that, because once he beats him the power's gone. He protected himself that way. If you really look back on those days, that protection of his stock at that time is what protected him for his whole career. He was right about it. I remember him saying, 'I don't need a belt. Other guys need them, but I don't need them.' He was on a different plane. He understood that. This shows you how far Roddy's sense of worth went and how the business really operates, how dead-on he was about what he needed to do to protect himself.

"When there was Hogan and Piper—and that was it, just Hogan and Piper—there was nobody else. There was Junkyard Dog and there were all kinds of other names, Orndorff and this guy and that, but it was Piper and Hogan. Hogan sort of broke all boundaries, but whenever you picked up a Hogan doll you picked up the Roddy Piper doll, too. So Roddy had a lot of clout, he had a lot of power. He was very valuable to them. Vince needed him really bad."

Like Starrcade and McMahon's two previous supercards at Madison Square Garden, the WrestleMania undercard had been worth the price of admission, filled with talent Roddy had wrestled over the previous decade in all parts of North America and Japan: Andre the Giant, Ricky Steamboat, King Kong Bundy,

Junkyard Dog, Greg Valentine. Even Roddy's old Portland friend and nemesis Buddy Rose had been wooed to New York, appearing in a mask as The Executioner, versus Tito Santana. Cyndi Lauper was back, "managing" Wendi Richter.

The only question left to answer was where do you go from there?

The question became more pressing for Roddy when he tried to get out of Madison Square Garden. After he and Bob Orton had showered—the victorious Hogan and T were nowhere to be seen—they realized they were all but alone in the basement of the arena. The car they expected hadn't materialized. When they asked a policeman on horseback if he could hail a cab since so many fans lingered outside, he told them to hail one themselves.

Orton became Roddy's most visible friend in the business, given his role on "Piper's Pit" and ringside as Roddy's bodyguard. He didn't say a lot, which suited Roddy's style, since Roddy said quite a bit. Like Greg Valentine, Orton was the son of a wrestling legend, in his case Bob Orton Sr.

"Orton Jr. was a tough-ass pistol," says Len Denton, who'd worked with Orton in Charlotte. Roddy was of the same mind. He'd tried amateur wrestling with Orton and couldn't budge him.

Spending weeks travelling the continent was hard: Roddy and Orton were husbands and fathers now (Ariel, Roddy and Kitty's second daughter, was born in the months after WrestleMania). Substance abuse remained a response to the emotional rigours of their busy schedule and the relentless pain of their bouts, but on the road they tended to hang out in one another's rooms with a handful of other wrestlers they could trust, trying to stay out of trouble. As Orton joked, they "filled the tub with beer and told our lies." Bret Hart was one of the few new guys they let into their social circle.

"We were like a little gang," he said. "Roddy's gang would have been Roddy, Adrian Adonis, Cowboy Bob Orton, Don Muraco, Jim Neidhart and myself, and maybe the Iron Sheik would tag along. There was nobody else. They wouldn't let anybody else hang with us."

Roddy's gang would sit together in the bar after the show, watching each other's backs. Then they'd head to Orton's hotel room to tell stories and pass the night away.

As Bret recalled, "I was real honoured to be in that gang, allowed to hang around them. I learned so much, talking with Cowboy Bob Orton at three in the morning drinking beers. Bobby's always got beers in his bathtub. We'd just sit on the bed and talk wrestling. I would learn so much about psychology, who to trust, who's no good. Adrian Adonis would talk about territories. They would talk about, 'Oh, I went down to Florida and I worked with the Grahams . . .' Roddy would talk about Charlotte and Oregon, and I would talk about Stampede, and Don Muraco would talk about Hawaii and Japan. . . . We could stay up all night telling these old stories."

One of Roddy's best was still recent history during the months after WrestleMania.

Roddy and Hogan were pursuing their grudge in matches all over the United States, matches that weren't broadcast and no one but the audience in attendance that night would ever see. If one of those matches stands out still, it was for reasons that had nothing to do with Hogan and everything to do with just how much Roddy had gotten under the country's skin.

In September, he and Hogan met in Cincinnati. Before the match, Roddy was told that the youngest mayor in the history of the city wanted to make a presentation. The mayor—former mayor, actually, by this point—got into the ring before a packed house and said some nice things about Hulk Hogan, the usual all-American stuff, and then began lambasting Roddy, calling him every no-good, lowdown name in the book.

Roddy, looking on with a warmup towel around his neck, didn't appreciate the mayor inserting himself into the story. They were professional wrestlers doing wrestling business, and this skinny little mayor shouldn't presume he could step in and not pay his dues for shooting his mouth off. Even Cyndi Lauper had taken a bump for the business—no matter how gingerly applied.

Roddy charged the ring and beat the mayor with the damp towel, whipping him with it until he squirmed out of the ring. The politician, looking on in astonishment, had been given a lesson he'd soon put to work on his own wildly successful television show, one that took many cues from "Piper's Pit": *The Jerry Springer Show.*

Bret Hart hadn't been included in the undercard of WrestleMania but his star was rising, especially as a member of the Hart Foundation, his tag team with former football player Jim "The Anvil" Neidhart. Bret's star was about to rise a little faster. In April 1986 the Rosemont Horizon in Chicago hosted one of three main events in WrestleMania 2. The sequel was a bold next step for McMahon. Instead of moving out of his home base of Madison Square Garden into a larger facility, he expanded the sequel out from the New York area to stops in Chicago and Los Angeles. Each of the three locations would host a main event and a full undercard.

Hart remembered the mixed emotions in the lead up to WrestleMania 2. The wrestlers worried that lightning couldn't strike twice and the sequel would flop. "There were a lot people that thought maybe Vince was losing his mind."

McMahon knew he couldn't milk the Piper-Hogan feud forever. He needed his champion to be under threat from other contenders, and so he moved Hogan out of New York and into Hollywood, a natural fit, and paired him for the main event with King Kong Bundy. A steel cage with the bald-headed 450-pound Bundy was a dire enough threat to make the most jaded of wrestling fans nervous for the champ. But another threat lingered; if Roddy didn't have a shot at Hogan, he'd go after his friend.

Mr. T had boxed Orton at a Saturday Night Main Event in March, which ended with Roddy getting in the ring to whip T with his belt after Orton lost. Fans slavered for some violent retribution, so Roddy and Mr. T would box in New York as one main event in WrestleMania 2.

McMahon might have overshot, but he certainly hadn't lost his sense of showmanship. A twenty-man Battle Royal in Chicago featured a number of jumbo-sized NFL players, in particular William "Refrigerator" Perry of the Super Bowl championship–winning Chicago Bears, a three-hundred-plus-pound defensive tackle who was enormously popular with Chicago fans. The Battle Royal came down to Andre the Giant and the Hart Foundation, the match ultimately going to Andre after he tossed Bret out of the ring. And of course Hogan beat Bundy on the west coast. But it was the rivalry playing out on Long Island that has best withstood the test of time.

Each of the three main events had been pulled out of wrestling's bag of gimmicks: a steel-cage match, a battle royal and a boxing match. Only one of them had the benefit of a longstanding rivalry, two men whose personalities were not easily placed on the traditional axis of babyface and heel. Roddy was immensely popular, despite his crowd-baiting and badmouthing of opponents and fans, and Mr. T was ennobled by his proximity to Hogan but clearly relished the bad-guy role he'd taken on in *Rocky III*; even his B. A. Baracus character on *The A-Team* took morally suspicious pleasure when unloading on the bad guys. Further, in the boxing match with Roddy Mr. T would be alone. Hulk Hogan and his golden aura would be thousands of miles away. Fans had embraced T as a friend of their champion. Would they do the same when T was alone?

"I needed some—even if I could mistranslate—permission," recalled Roddy. He was hoping McMahon would give him some sign before the match, some hint that it was okay to break with the script and knock Mr. T out. Why not send T out the way Roddy had set up so many rivals when he'd left territories? Put them over with a resounding victory and move on. He didn't get the sign he was hoping for.

Roddy and T weren't friendly. That's never been a secret. But Roddy wasn't about to mess with the program. "Because here's the law," he said. "If you and I had a fuckin' problem, then [fine]. But in the ring, it's business. Don't bring your bullshit in there. Don't bring your stuff in the ring. That's cardinal law." No matter his feelings about the actor, or at least about the actor's role in the wrestling ring, Roddy wasn't going to try to settle any personal scores on company time. But he left himself a small opening. "Now, something happens *in* the ring, that's a whole different thing."

It had been a long time since Roddy had trained to box. So he got to work.

"Six weeks before that fight, fuckin' McMahon," he sighed. "Next thing I know I'm on a plane to Reno, in a ring with Holyfield, Braxton, Tyrell Biggs, Spinks and somebody I can't remember. Running five miles a day all of a sudden. Six weeks! And Lou Duva training me."

Lou Duva had managed and trained numerous champion boxers in his long career. It was his job to put some polish on Roddy's jabs. So there was Roddy, the mouthiest heel in wrestling at a time when everybody knew who he was, training with some of the greatest boxers in the world, all of whom were black. He had enormous respect for these men, but for the sake of business he'd done his share of racially charged baiting of competitors, even snipping a Mr. T–style mohawk into the hair of the black midget wrestler The Haiti Kid just in advance of WrestleMania 2. He was a good boxer, as wrestlers went, but this was intimidating company.

"Great White Hope!" he said with a self-deprecating snort. He'd taken some lumps for his craft.

In the Nassau Coliseum dressing room, WWF officials taped up Roddy's hands for the match.

"They said, 'Come here, mister, make a fist.' They put boxing tape all around my fist instead of wrapping my hand." Normally, a boxer's hand is taped across the palm and below the thumb. The bones in the hand come under great pressure during repeated punches and without support can easily break. "You got a boxing glove, you put your hand in, get 'er deep, and you kinda get 'er down to fingers, right, and then you curl your fist . . ." Roddy's fingers were curled into a fist and *then* taped, so the boxing glove would cushion his punches, rendering them less potent.

"But I can still take him out," said Roddy. He was sure he could beat T for real, if only McMahon gave him the nod.

In the end, Roddy took a bump when T threw a roundhouse at him that was supposed to look so devastating that the fight could have been over. T missed the punch by a greater distance than expected and Roddy, forced to sell the shot, became so frustrated he threw his stool at T during an intermission, scraping his leg. The match ended with Roddy body slamming Mr. T, which should have surprised nobody. McMahon surely realized by this point that Roddy's great drawing power lay in his open-ended brawling finishes, which never gave anyone, even the crowd, the satisfaction of seeing him beaten fair and square.

But it wasn't the end of the match that changed Roddy's career. Roddy went against script without even trying, and through his pure dedication to the art of professional wrestling, through perfecting the art of giving the crowds what they wanted, he won them over. In the second round, they began chanting his name.

At some point after the fight, he ran across McMahon, who smiled and said he'd thought Roddy would take out T in the second round. Roddy couldn't believe his ears; that was exactly what he'd wanted to hear McMahon say *before* the fight. He just shook his head and grimaced at the lost opportunity.

The celebrity count at WrestleMania 2 had again been impressive. But sitting wide-eyed beside Billy Crystal in one of the closest rows to the ring was a man whose time in the spotlight had ended. Cam Connor, Roddy's teenage friend from Winnipeg, had just retired after nearly a decade in and out of the NHL. He'd spent his final season as an assistant coach on a minor league team. They'd stayed in touch as much as any two constantly travelling athletes could and Roddy had secured him choice seats at Nassau Coliseum.

When Roddy had come into Connecticut to wrestle a few years earlier, he'd tried having Connor paged at the New Haven arena—Connor was playing for the New York Rangers' minor-league affiliate New Haven Nighthawks. Connor wasn't there, but Roddy had all the wrestlers sign his stick in the players' dressing room then tied Connor's laces into so many knots he'd need to cut them off. They'd gotten together a few times in New

York City, and Roddy had taken him out drinking with the other WWF guys. That had made for some punishing mornings, given Connor weighed barely two hundred pounds. But Connor noticed a more serious punishment taking its toll on his friend.

"He was a little man in a big man's game," said Connor, "and he paid a price." When Roddy visited Connor in New York, they'd sit and have a drink, then decide to go out on the town. "He'd go, 'Could you help me up?' I'd have to go over, pull him off the couch to get him up. He'd always be hurting."

Roddy wasn't just taking abuse in the ring. He was electrocuted around this time in Los Angeles. He slipped on a wet dressing room floor and, reaching out for something to break his fall, inadvertently stuck his finger in an empty light socket.

"I never saw anybody that had a higher threshold for pain than he had," said Mitch Ackerman, who had been waiting for Roddy outside the LA dressing room that night. "He was taking a really long time, and he finally came out, and he was dragging."

Roddy and Ackerman had become close friends, and Roddy bunked with him on occasion. Ackerman attended several WrestleManias as his guest, and they often met after matches for dinner.

"I said, 'You're alright to eat?' He said, 'Yeah.' So we went and had something to eat, but he didn't seem himself. He had to catch a seven a.m. plane. So I said to him, 'Let me take you back to your hotel.'" Roddy caught his morning flight, but was so disoriented he got off at the connection in Kansas City and went to the hotel he usually stayed in there. Staff found him wandering the halls and called an ambulance. It took him several days to recover, and for years he experienced numbness on the left side of his body.

"I knew that my body was taking such a beating," he said, looking back. Roddy was only thirty-two years old when he decided that maybe he'd taxed his body enough. He was about to make the most difficult decision of his young life.

WrestleMania's promise as the "Super Bowl of professional wrestling" was holding up. McMahon couldn't devise a third installment any more complicated than the second, but he could supersize it. WrestleMania 3 was going to take place in front of more people than all three events in 1986 put together. Hogan would once again take centre stage, and Roddy would do everything he could to steal the show.

Roddy took a break from wrestling for three months after WrestleMania 2. It was his first real time away since he'd begun in 1973, fourteen years earlier. In his absence, his old Twenty-Twos partner from Los Angeles, Adrian Adonis, stepped into the wrestling talk-show breach with a segment called "The Flower Shop" (Jesse Ventura also hosted, briefly, a segment called "The Body Shop"). Adonis, now known as "Adorable" Adrian Adonis and tipping the scales at over three hundred pounds, was working a half-hearted drag gimmick that saw him dressing in floppy sun hats, flowery dresses and comically misapplied make up.

"I loved him," remembered Roddy. "He would pump iron all day long. He looked horrible. But he could do anything in the ring. Then he'd eat tuna fish and he'd go, 'How do I look?!'"

At Adonis's weight, the gimmick went from strange to comically grotesque. Flowers hung off the latticework walls of the Flower Shop set and adorned the microphone. "Welcome to the highest-rated show on television today, 'The Flower Shop,'" Adonis boasts at the beginning of one episode.

Wrestling's main audience were middle Americans who exorcised their own misgivings about their rapidly changing world through the spectacle's weird and wonderful morality plays. Few were weirder or more wonderful than "Adorable" Adrian.

"Even when Adrian was doing 'The Flower Shop'—he had the Minnie Pearl hat with the price tag, big old dress on—he's the only guy that can go in drag and it's not a drag," said Roddy.

Positioning Roddy against Adonis's new gimmick solidified what the crowd had decided in New York. After setting the gold standard for heels, Roddy was about to turn babyface.

After his return to the WWF at the end of July, Roddy arrived on the set of "The Flower Shop" in place of the expected guest, Don Muraco. Surprised to see Roddy, Adonis welcomed him like an old friend. Roddy replied in kind, but not for long.

"I would like to say that you have been doing a tremendous job in my absence," Roddy said, "and I would like to thank you for taking it over. But I am here to take my show back, and the first thing that has to go are these damned flowers."

Citing a contract that makes the show his for good, Adonis shot back at Roddy: "I'm no summer rerun!" And then Orton appeared in his familiar bodyguard pose—but behind Adonis. His cowboy hat was now pink.

"Hi, Acey," said Adonis to Orton over his shoulder.

"Peanuts," Orton said to Roddy. "You were paying me peanuts compared to what Jimmy [Hart] and Adrian are paying me, man. It's money, plain and simple."

In the end, Roddy and Adonis agreed to a debate—their flimsy talk-show sets arranged side by side—to determine which show would continue, "The Flower Shop" or "Piper's Pit." Roddy's quick wit served him well when the day came—until it served him too well. His guest, Don Muraco, sensed he was being used as a stooge in a battle of egos and helped Adonis and Orton jump Roddy. Men who were in reality three of Roddy's closest friends held him down and smeared his face with red make-up while appearing to bang up his knee.

Roddy returned to the abandoned set later, on a crutch with his knee in a brace and carrying a baseball bat. "It's gonna take a hell of a lot more than that if they wanna keep me down," he growled at the crowd, before smashing "The Flower Shop" with the bat and declaring, "the war has just begun!" The crowd chanted his name as he hobbled away. The babyface turn was complete. "Piper's Pit" was back.

First on the Pit's agenda was seeding the drama for the WrestleMania 3 main event. One week, Roddy presented Andre the Giant with a trophy for his fifteen years without a defeat. Then Roddy hosted Hulk Hogan, with whom he had become friendly, and presented him with a trophy celebrating his three years as champion. Then Jesse Ventura appeared. Roddy called him "the Mike Wallace of professional wrestling," because he was always on the hunt for the next big story (Roddy eventually changed it to "Gravel Gertie, the Aunt Jemima of professional wrestling" for reasons that could only have had to do with his wardrobe). Ventura pointed out that Andre's trophy was smaller than Hogan's. Further, Hogan's "feels like real gold" while Andre's feels like "rotten old lead or something." Taking note, Andre crashed Hogan's celebration and challenged him to a title match. The feud was established and WrestleMania 3 was set.

But even with his match scheduled in the middle of a lineup of twelve, Roddy once again threatened to steal the show. He announced in February 1987 that his showdown with Adonis would be his final match. After fifteen years in the business of professional wrestling, he was retiring.

WrestleMania 3 lived up to its "Bigger, Badder, Better" billing by stuffing the Silverdome in Pontiac, Michigan, with a reported 93,000 fans. It opened with a tag-team match featuring Rick Martel, who had also found his way to the WWF. The Hart Foundation was on the card. Ricky "The Dragon" Steamboat had a career-defining match against another wrestler who could mesmerize a television camera, Randy "Macho Man" Savage. Volkoff and the Iron Sheik were there. The cream of Roddy's career had found their way to McMahon, and as a result to whatever corner of the continent McMahon wished them to go. His WWF was by then the undisputed champion of wrestling territories, and even Roddy had stopped refusing to wrestle for McMahon in the territories of promoters he respected, like Don Owen in Portland.

For a man who always wanted to leave a territory while he was still on top, 1987 was Roddy's ideal time. With nowhere better to go, an ever–forward thinking man could only leave the business if he wanted to keep growing his career. To say goodbye, there was no one he'd rather wrestle than Adonis in a hair match.

"He thought I was his brother," said Roddy. Adonis was an orphan and Roddy used to speak of himself in similar terms, thanks to his itinerant childhood: "I never had a home. I don't have a place I grew up." They'd bonded over much more than their common age and early starts in the business.

"He saved me, a couple of times," said Roddy. "But the one time, we were in Poughkeepsie and I was having issues, I was hot. He said to me, 'You know what's wrong with you? You need to buy a house. Put your kids in it.' He was right."

Roddy and Kitty had been talking about buying a house and putting down some stable roots for their young family. McMahon had tried to talk them into a house in Connecticut. He liked his talent close.

"They were offering to move us into very nice houses," said Kitty. "They couldn't have been nicer. I'm sure Rod would have loved to have done that." Kitty, though, was home alone with a small child, Anastasia, and Ariel then on the way. Roddy didn't socialize with the other wrestlers much when they weren't on the road, which left his wife without much of a social network on the east coast. Life at home was lonely.

"We could have a house out there and have no family and no roots, or we could buy one in Portland and have family and roots, which is something he had never had: roots," said Kitty. "We both wanted something a little more similar to what I grew up with for our kids than what he grew up with, which was constant change." Adonis, the orphan, opened Roddy's eyes to the impact his transient ways were having on him and his family. Even if he couldn't be at home for more than a few days at a time, knowing his kids were growing up in one place with extended family nearby and the spotlight far away would bring him some measure of peace.

"As nice as the houses were that they showed us," says Kitty, "we said no thank you."

With Adonis's words ringing in Roddy's ears, he and Kitty moved to a house in the countryside just west of Portland, Oregon. Roddy never forgot his friend's wise counsel.

"I always used to tell Adrian, 'I love ya.' And I meant it. He'd say it back to me and [his wife would] say, 'What's wrong with you guys?'"

The floor of the Silverdome was so large, the wrestlers involved in WrestleMania 3 travelled on a motorized platform from the dressing rooms to the ring. It malfunctioned when Roddy was being announced, so he trotted out into the crowd and then, filled with the desire to live this moment to its fullest, broke into a run and didn't stop until he was on the mat, arms open wide to embrace the audience's roar. It was the same gesture he'd used to mockingly invite the fans' disgust, welcoming their tossed drink cups and cigarette butts, their popcorn and toilet paper. But this time the smile was genuine, and so was the applause.

The ovation continued for a minute. The surprising endorsement that had welled up from the Long Island crowd a year earlier now overflowed in a deafening roar. Roddy's tactics hadn't really changed (he began the match by taking off his leather belt and whipping Adonis with it), but the fans had. Their hate was always a form of love refused, and now, they realized, so was his.

The match featured some spectacular flops over the ropes by Adonis, who was intent on making his friend's farewell match a memorable one.

"In WrestleMania 3, he made sure that I got over," said Roddy. "It's him that did it, not me. It's him that did it."

They traded sleeper holds—known as the "Goodnight Irene" in Adonis's arsenal. Brutus Beefcake snuck onto the mat, first to wake up Roddy from Adonis's sleeper and then to shave the prone Adonis's head after Roddy knocked him out with a sleeper of his own.

"I learned one thing," Roddy said of all those hair matches he'd lost to Chavo Guerrero in Los Angeles. "It's really hard to cut a man's hair when it's wet. So, as much as they think I was being a nice guy, I go, 'Brutus, *you* cut his hair.' And that's how he became Brutus 'the Barber.'"

The crowd wrapped Roddy in a blanket of noise as the clipping of Adonis wound down. Roddy had been expertly put over by a friend, but he wouldn't get many chances to thank him.

On July 4 of the following year, Adonis was travelling in a van to a match in Gander, Newfoundland. The Trans-Canada

Highway that crossed the island attracts almost as many moose as cars. Wrestler Mike Kelly was driving when one of the massive animals appeared on the road ahead. He tried to steer around it, but lost control. Mike's brother Pat Kelly, Dave McKigney and Adonis were killed.

Adonis had once said to Roddy, "You know, Pipes, when I die, I don't want a funeral with people crying and weeping. I want a party." The comment stuck with Roddy, and he thought of it when he was asked to give the eulogy at Adonis's funeral in Bakersfield, California.

"So I'm up doing the eulogy, and I'm having a bit of a tough time. But I got a pretty good game face on," remembered Roddy. "I got up there to do the eulogy and I was nervous. Really nervous. Adrian's family had a curtain drawn in front of them and Adrian's casket was closed. I got around to what Adrian had told me: 'I don't want people feeling sorry for me—throw a party.' This sound came out of his wife," he said, still haunted. "I can't mimic the sound."

Roddy finished his eulogy and took his seat. When the funeral was over, Bea Franke, Adonis's widow, approached him. Thinking of Roddy and her husband's saying "I love you," she said, "Now I know why you guys said that.'"

A pastor had been in the ambulance that arrived at the scene of the crash. He wrote Roddy a detailed letter, explaining the accident. Nearly a year later, Roddy made the trip to the spot on the highway where Adrian had died. Roddy wasn't thirty-five yet, but the roll call of wrestlers who had died young was growing fast: brothers David and Mike Von Erich, Bruiser Brody, Moondog Mayne, and now Adonis and the others in the car.

"That's the last funeral I went to," Roddy said. He couldn't bring himself to sit through the death rites of another friend.

WrestleMania 3 felt like the end, but true to Roddy's way, his final match was the beginning of something else. "To stay on top," he said, "I needed to get out of the business completely, do something in another form, and walk back in the front door." Something that wouldn't add to the injuries, something that shouldn't lead to so many lost friends. And if he ever decided to come back to the ring, this next stage in his career would make his fame too big for a wrestling promoter to diminish or outright ruin, should any try.

8

All Outta Bubble Gum

"There was a time in my career when I had a limousine, Learjet, red carpet going to it, suite, a dressing room catered, I swear to you," said Roddy, looking back at the moment when he knew he needed a change from the wrestling life. "I'm in the suite, and there's everything a guy could ever want. I was thinking to myself, 'I can't think of another thing to ask for. That's not good. We're downhill from here.'"

He laughed as he said it, but the decision was a big one. He'd chosen to retire while still on top. His renown as one of the best talkers in the wrestling business made him a potential box office draw, and Hollywood needed to sell tickets, too. Roddy had been wrestling as many as three hundred days a year since he was nineteen years old. He knew every day where his pay was coming from, even if he had to scream at someone to get it. Now, in Hollywood and aiming to shift into acting he had to learn a whole new set of rules.

During that short break after WrestleMania 2, Roddy had taken on the role of fictional wrestler "Quick" Rick Roberts in a comedy called *Body Slam*, about a music manager (Dirk Benedict of *The A-Team*) who accidentally finds himself managing a professional wrestler (Roddy). The film is a bit of silly fun, but Roddy is surprisingly at ease delivering his lines. Then, the following year, after WrestleMania 3, Roddy acted in a low-budget movie that finally took him out of the wrestlers-playing-wrestlers casting ghetto: *Hell Comes to Frogtown*.

"Unfortunately, the movie really got a lot of attention," he said. "I guess some people have actually bought it. I try to tell them, 'Listen, you're wasting your money.' But the more I try to talk them out of it, the more they buy it." Cyndi Lauper's manager, Dave Wolff, the man Roddy had thrown around the ring to set up The War to Settle the Score, was trying his hand at managing Roddy, and persuaded some producers to let him read for the lead in a sci-fi movie.

"I walked in there and it was horrible. I can't read . . . there was no inflection, nothing. Basically, Dave looks at the casting director, 'What do you say? Let's go?' They just got pressured into giving me the part. At the same time, I had a name, so they were getting something."

In the film, Roddy's character, Sam Hell, is the last potent male left after a nuclear holocaust. The authorities—composed of a group of tough nurses—capture him to breed with their collection of fertile virgins (how they know the virgins are fertile is anyone's guess). When frog-headed mutants, led by the evil Commander Toty, capture the women, the nurses—led by six-foot-tall dancer Sandahl Bergman, who had starred with Arnold Schwarzenegger six years earlier in *Conan the Barbarian*—put Sam Hell to work helping track the women and save them.

Just thinking about the film got Roddy wondering again why he'd ever agreed to take the role. "It was ridiculous. Out in the desert. I had this chastity belt on. If I tried to run away, they'd hit a button and it would zap my nuts and drop me to my knees," he said. "There was a frog I needed to breed with. She had a crush on me. So I put a bag over her head before I bred with her. Baby Jesus . . ."

The memory annoyed Roddy for reasons other than just the film's substance. He didn't get along well with the creator and initial director, Donald G. Jackson (he was eventually replaced by R.J. Kizer). Jackson died in 2003, so it's unlikely we'll ever know the whole story, but from the outset, he was bitter about having his lead actors foisted on him. Jackson had other actors in mind until the production company came in with a significantly increased budget and gave the roles to Roddy and Bergman for their added star power.

"The director hated me," said Roddy. "And I hated him, actually. There was one time when I was tied up, and somebody was worried about me being comfortable. The director says, 'He's getting enough money.' I said, 'Listen, I could kick your ass from here.' That was the temperature on that movie."

At one point in the story, Bergman is forced to do the "Dance of the Three Snakes" for the mutant leader. The dance, like the rest of her role, required the statuesque actress to wear a number of skimpy outfits. Bergman had a little fun with one of those outfits when the wrestler's wife paid a visit to the set.

Kitty was having lunch with Roddy in his trailer when the door opened. It was Bergman with one of her tiny outfits on. "*Barely* on," Roddy said. "She looks over and goes, 'Oh, Rod, I didn't know you had company today,' and walks out. She had never been in my trailer before. Never. "

Bergman's swerve didn't help make the night of the film's premier any more comfortable.

Before the screening started, a producer addressed the crowd. "He stood up in a Quaker hat and a jacket with a kind of a Nehru collar to it. The place was packed. He said, 'You're going to love this movie. It wouldn't have been possible without Roddy.'" In reality, Roddy had bickered with the director and had his marriage pranked by his co-star, all for the sake of a movie he didn't even like. Now the producer was thanking him for making it happen. Hollywood really was a complicated place.

The situation was going to get better before it got worse. And better started with an introduction to director John Carpenter.

"In *Hell Comes to Frogtown*, there was a scene that was cut—I don't know how John Carpenter saw it—and he saw the director saying, 'Roddy could you do this? Roddy, could you do that?' John determined, 'Yeah, he's directable. I'll go with him.'"

John Carpenter was coming off a successful run at the box office directing films like *Escape from New York*, *Halloween*, *Big Trouble in Little China* and his remake of *The Thing*. On his new film, to be called *They Live*, Carpenter asked a Juilliard-trained actor named Keith David, who'd had a key role in *The Thing*, to co-star with Roddy.

David was a big man who wouldn't look physically out of place on screen beside a pro wrestler. Roddy was barely experienced as a screen actor. Pairing them would help Carpenter coach Roddy on set. In turn, Roddy could help David with the rough stuff, which the director knew was going to be a big part of his film. In Roddy, Carpenter knew exactly who he was dealing with. Roddy, on the other hand: "I'd never heard of John

Carpenter. I didn't know who he was. I was still watching *Leave It to Beaver*!"

The night before WrestleMania 3 in 1987, John Carpenter had travelled to Michigan with an executive from Warner Bros. to have dinner with Roddy. Roddy brought along his friend Mitch Ackerman, the producer from Los Angeles, showing the filmmakers that he wasn't completely adrift in their world.

Ackerman had been mulling over the idea of a dramatic wrestling movie, and also a comedic one about a group of pro wrestlers going to college. Neither idea had gone anywhere, and Roddy's invitation to have dinner with Carpenter was very appealing.

Carpenter had grown up a serious wrestling fan, even wrote a column for *The Ring's Wrestling* magazine while growing up in Bowling Green, Kentucky. According to Ackerman, Carpenter and the executive were also fans of the annual Jerry Lewis Telethon for muscular dystrophy. They would watch it for the whole twenty-four hours each Labour Day. When the subject came up at the table, Ackerman told them he'd worked on the telethon during college. "That drove them nuts," he said. "It was a great icebreaker."

Though congenial, the dinner didn't seem particularly focussed on asking Roddy to try out for a role.

"Not a lot happened," Roddy said. "Someone passed me a bottle of Cristal and I poured orange juice into it. John asked me to pass the rolls and butter, and at some point asked me to be in a movie. Simple as that."

Carpenter wanted to make a film that was both a political statement and an action-filled sci-fi thriller. He was inspired by a 1963 short story called "Eight O'Clock in the Morning" by sci-fi writer Ray Nelson, the main character of which is named

George Nada. Under Reaganomics—shorthand for the economic policies of president Ronald Reagan—Carpenter felt America was leaving too many people out in the cold to the benefit of a wealthy and powerful few. Roddy fit the idea Carpenter had for his protagonist, a drifter with no past and little future looking for construction work in the poorest corner of Los Angeles, with the gleaming towers of wealth and privilege looming in the distant background.

Carpenter had considered making his character a television executive but figured the drifter who sees America changing from the perspective of its lowest strata was a better fit—a science fiction *Grapes of Wrath*. Being a fan of folk singer Woody Guthrie, Roddy understood exactly what he was going for.

"He wanted an actor who actually might have worked with his hands in his life," said Roddy, "but also a guy who, when he saw something strange was happening, he'd figure it out and kick some ass. That was me."

Carpenter described the main character, credited in the film only as "Nada," as a guy without a place in society, but perhaps because the place for his core values had diminished, not because there was anything intrinsically wrong with him. "He's a loner and he's tough, and he's ugly but he has dignity," Carpenter said.

Roddy always expressed surprise that the director saw him as an actor, since to his mind he was "so coarse" at the time. Carpenter cited Roddy's role on "Piper's Pit" as more than enough acting to know that he'd found his man.

"This is what I wanted," Carpenter said to Roddy in 2014. "*You* were the character. You weren't polished. That was what was so appealing. I didn't try to make you into something you weren't. I tried to take what you were and bring it to the screen in this character. It was your talent and your ability and your past knowledge. You knew how to wrestle, knew how to fight. And you'd lived life, I could see it on your face."

For all the lunatic violence that audiences associated with Roddy, in Nada's jeans and plaid shirt he looked like the man he had actually been not so long ago: a quiet guy who was willing to work for his supper. Swap the construction gear for wrestling trunks, and Nada's nomadic character is pretty close to Roderick Toombs when he'd first come to wrestle in LA.

As well as being a great fit for the role, Roddy also was massively popular with the same demographic that liked clever sci-fi movies. Carpenter didn't need Roddy's drawing power as much as the *Frogtown* producers had, but it didn't hurt. An ideal fit or not, though, Roddy still had to audition for the part.

Roddy had resented having Mr. T parachuted into the WrestleMania script. He didn't want Hollywood actors feeling the same way about him. To be sure that he could carry his weight in front of a movie camera, he began studying with a renowned Los Angeles acting coach named Sal Dano. Dano videotaped Roddy reading lines so the filmmakers could assess his delivery. Proud of the resulting clips, Roddy shared the results with Carpenter. When Dano realized Roddy had jumped the gun, he was furious.

"What if he didn't like them? You'd be out of a job!" he said.

Roddy hadn't thought of that, but ignorance was bliss. Luckily, Carpenter thought the tapes were fine, and Roddy got the part. What he couldn't have known was that the project he was about to embark on would become a cult classic.

They Live was shot in downtown LA, but life on set wasn't cushy.

"Every morning while we were shooting, I'd be up at four a.m. I'd climb in the sauna." Roddy used his time in the sauna to reflect, thinking of himself like a car in the shop, sweating out the old oil and putting in the new. "Then I'd go back to my trailer and John's wife, Sandy, made me stick my head in a bucket of ice water. When I came up from that I was ready to go."

Roddy wanted this to work. As a wrestler, he'd ask himself every year: Am I getting better? If the answer was no, he wouldn't continue. "I felt the same way about making movies," he said. "*They Live* was going to be my third. If I wasn't becoming a better actor, I would have quit." Still, *They Live*'s most memorable scene came straight out of Roddy's old wrestling playbook.

Carpenter had Roddy and Keith David watch *The Quiet Man* starring John Wayne and Maureen O'Hara, about a boxer who retires to the Irish village where he was born. It contained what was then the longest fight scene in cinema. Carpenter wanted to one-up that scene with an even longer one, and he wanted more than just a bigger, longer punch-up.

"You usually see guys stand up and the hero just quickly whacks the bad guys and moves on," says Carpenter. "It seems like in the eighties especially, heroes are invulnerable. They just run with a machine gun, they kill everybody and off they go." What keeps the fight scene in *They Live* tense is that it's a fight between two friends, one so desperate to show the other something crucial to their survival that he'll punch him out rather than let him refuse to look.

When Nada discovers a discarded box of sunglasses and tries on a pair, he suddenly sees the world as it really is (the box of glasses was left over from *Big Trouble in Little China*). It's a startling moment that wouldn't have worked if Roddy couldn't tone down his normally arena-sized reactions.

Seen through the glasses, a billboard for computer equipment reads "OBEY" and another advertising Caribbean vacations says "MARRY AND REPRODUCE." More worrisome is that the successful and wealthy types Nada crosses paths with on the street—"yuppies" in the parlance of the time—are actually skull-faced, bug-eyed aliens. Determined to share what he's discovered with Frank, his friend from the construction site, played by Keith David, Nada tries to force him to put on the glasses.

For two weeks (some people have said three), Roddy and David blocked out the six-minute fight in Carpenter's backyard, under the careful eye of stunt coordinator Jeff Imada, who had also worked on *Big Trouble in Little China*.

"I brought Jeff Imada in and I brought Roddy in," says Carpenter, "and we talked about it. About what would make a fight unique. . . . I wanted to use some of Roddy's professional wrestling techniques and knowledge."

There are moments in the fight that clearly have their roots in the physical aspects of professional wrestling. Both actors were proud that they'd shot the scene without stunt men. But it's the moments rooted in ring psychology where Roddy really shines, and he always called that part of the movie his favourite.

"There was a place where I took a two-by-four and Keith was by a car and I swung the two-by-four at his head," said Roddy. "I remember telling him—this is an old wrestling thing—'Hey, brother, you need to move because I'm coming.' And he was good about moving! It broke the windshield of the car. At that time, the character, Nada, went, 'Ah, what am I doing? This is my friend, I coulda hurt him.' At the same time, that pissed Frank off . . . and he grabs a wine bottle and breaks it to come back at me. He cuts his own hand, and that makes me, as his friend, laugh from concern. Which is a dumbass thing to do, which makes him even more angry, and he comes charging, and we go backwards over a couple cars."

After the weeks of rehearsal, Carpenter shot the scene over three days. Initially, he let the actors fight as far into the scene as they could without stopping, an approach that Roddy credited with giving the scene some of its energy. The night before they started filming, *Entertainment Tonight* showed up on set. Roddy making a major film with one of the hottest directors in Hollywood was newsworthy, and of course people wondered if the infamous heel (his farewell babyface turn had changed no perceptions about his unhinged persona) could restrain himself when fighting on set with a refined actor like David. David called it the most fun he'd ever had, and credited Roddy with teaching him how to react convincingly to a punch. As for getting hurt, David wasn't the one who needed to worry.

"When you're choreographing for fights on film, it's all about angles," David said. "I can be ten feet away from somebody; if the camera's behind me and I swing right and they react right, it looks like I hit him. It was always about the distance. That was always being stressed. So he never hit me. And I almost never hit him.

"As soon as the camera rolled for *ET*, the first move was I punch him in the face. And I was standing too close, and I go bang! 'Oh, shit, I'm sorry, I'm sorry!' He goes, 'It's okay, it's okay. Let's just start again.'"

By the time *They Live* was being filmed, Arnold Schwarzenegger's loadbearing little sentence from *The Terminator*—"I'll be back"—had permeated popular culture. More than thirty years later, the line still resonates. In *They Live* Roddy delivered an enduring line of his own. People have often speculated that

Roddy improvised it on set. Not quite—not that Roddy helped clarify where it came from.

"I've told it many different ways, the line," confessed Roddy, "but sometimes, when you do as many interviews as I do, you gotta craft!" Until he'd sat down and discussed it in 2014 with Carpenter, he couldn't actually recall how he'd come up with his memorable sentence.

Roddy had kept notebooks full of one-liners and ideas for wrestling interviews and promos—"Don't throw rocks at a man with a machine gun," etc. He handed the book over to Carpenter and said, as the director recalled it, "Take a look at this. Here's who I am. Here's what I've written. Here's where I came from." The best of the bunch was written for a match in Portland against Buddy Rose.

As part of his heel act, Roddy often sauntered to the ring chewing bubble gum, displaying a juvenile's lack of respect for the guy he was about to wrestle. It raised the ire of his opponents and their fans. In the movie, Nada, carrying a shotgun stolen from the police as the aliens pursue him, runs into a bank. The bank, of course, is also full of aliens. He decides to put a little fear into the invaders, and before shooting up the tellers' booths declares, "I have come here to chew bubble gum and kick ass, and I'm all outta bubble gum."

Carpenter loved the line and put it in the film.

Much of *They Live* takes place in a shantytown, which in one scene is razed by the authorities who suspect there's rebellion brewing there. Filming in and around Los Angeles's less prosperous neighbourhoods came with its challenges. But Roddy and Carpenter both had a lot of sympathy for the kinds of people they encountered there.

"We had to pay off two different gangs to leave us be," said Roddy. To get to the shantytown location every day, he walked down a lane filled with homeless people and always stopped to talk with a few of them on the way. "I gave a guy a few bucks—that I'd borrowed from John," he said with a snicker. For a scene where the police raze the shantytown with heavy equipment, Carpenter hired some of those homeless people for the day.

Carpenter felt an affinity with working-class heroes. "I think everybody is potentially heroic," he said, "depending on what they're presented with in life. A lot of people who commit themselves to an ideal, raise children, work loyally, are heroes. I think we all have a little bit of that in us." He was charmed when Roddy, his working-class star, wouldn't take off his wedding ring while shooting.

"The thing that was interesting with Nada staring over the LA skyline," said Roddy, "was you didn't know anything about him, you didn't know where he came from, he wore a wedding ring, you didn't know why, you didn't know where he was going. He was that lost America."

In a quiet moment, as Nada and Frank speak reflectively in a dark hotel room while drinking a beer, Nada gives a hint about where he came from. Exactly how much of this background came out of Roddy's notebook is hard to determine, but Carpenter revealed that he came up with the scene after long conversations with Roddy about his past, and he guarded Roddy closely on set in the hours before they shot it, sensing his star's discomfort with the character's emotional openness and vulnerability. It's easy to imagine hundreds of nights on the road with Roddy's gang or on a hotel window ledge with the likes of Kerry Von Erich that looked a lot like this scene. Men whose unrelenting days don't allow them to look anywhere but forward, who gather late at night in their hotel rooms to share stories over a quiet drink. Sleep is best postponed until they're exhausted and pass out so quickly their demons can't catch up to them in the unguarded twilight that comes before dreams.

"My old daddy took me down to the river," says Nada, "kicked my ass, told me about the power and the glory. I was saved. He changed when I was little. Turned mean, started tearing at me. So I ran away when I was thirteen. Tried to cut me once. Big old razor blade. He held it up against my throat. I said, 'Daddy, please.' Just kept moving it back and forth, like he was sawing down a little tree."

Frank wonders aloud if the aliens like seeing humans tear into one another.

"I got news for them," answers Nada. "Gonna be hell to pay. 'Cause I ain't Daddy's little boy no more."

Roddy hoped to take fewer bumps in the movie business, but in filming the finale of *They Live* he learned pain wasn't so easy to avoid. Standing on the roof of the Bank of America Plaza in downtown Los Angeles, where Nada would have his final confrontation with the alien-directed police, a special-effects technician was hooking Roddy up with squibs, tiny explosives filled with gunpowder and fake blood to make him look like he'd been shot.

"This guy warned me the charges might sting and said he was worried I might black out," said Roddy. "Black out? Not a chance. So the scene starts and these things go off on my arm and he's not kidding—they hurt. Even more than I expected."

Carpenter yelled "cut" and the dust settled. The guy who rigged up Roddy's squibs looked surprised when he sees a tear in Roddy's sleeve but no "blood."

"Damn," he said, "I must have put them on backwards."

They Live debuted as the number-one film in the United States.

"After the two weeks, you couldn't find it anywhere," said David. So he asked one of the producers—Carpenter's wife, Sandy King—why she thought that was. "She said, 'Obviously it pissed somebody off.'"

When David tells that story today, he's no doubt playing to his audience. Part of the reason the film continues to be screened is its appeal to conspiracy theorists. With its portrayal of a secret power running, and ruining, America (at one point, Nada gazes over the LA skyline and says, "I still believe in America," a line Roddy loved), it's easy to see where that appeal comes from. Roddy himself took to calling it "a documentary," a sentiment with which Carpenter agreed. Neither thought the film was literally true, but its portrayal of power and the wilful blindness of runaway consumerism cleverly reflected forces that were undeniably at work in America.

They Live lives on. Roddy's bubble gum line has been echoed in many places, possibly first in the popular 1996 video game *Duke Nukem 3D*. The cartoon *South Park* mimicked the fight scene, blow-by-blow, in a 2001 episode called "Cripple Fight." Roddy wouldn't watch the parody for ten years, thinking it too cruel, until a child on crutches in an autograph line mimicked the *South Park* scene while mugging with Roddy for a photo. Provocative artist Shepard Fairey (designer of the iconic "HOPE" poster for Barak Obama's 2008 presidential campaign) based a public art campaign on the film's use of "OBEY," pairing it with an illustrated close up of Andre the Giant's face. Stickers of that design slathered streets across the globe.

"That was a movie that really could have made him a big star," said Ackerman. "He got really good reviews. I remember,

I think it was *Film Comment* magazine, just wrote this rave about him. One of the reasons he did shine in *They Live* was he had a major director, and a director that was major in that genre also. . . . The rare times that he would work with a good director, you could see it in the film that he did. He was a really good actor." Despite this, Roddy struggled to find the right next role to build on his success with Carpenter. "The problem was," said Ackerman, "that he didn't have the right people surrounding him in order to use [*They Live*] as a stepping stone towards the future."

They Live was a slow burn. It has remained a cultural force—but not of the kind that earns a man a living. Some kind of a return to wrestling was the inevitable result of projects that capitalized on the casting of Rowdy Roddy Piper and not Roddy Piper's evolving talents as an actor.

At home, Roddy's evolving talents as a parent were getting him further.

Roddy was away working so much that to his daughters he was often reduced to the voice on the other end of the phone or the reprimand on the other end of the old threat: "Wait 'til your dad gets home!" But his oldest daughter really couldn't wait. His reprimands rarely lived up to expectation anyway.

"My father and I were born two days apart," recalled Anastasia. "We're pretty much the same." At heart Roddy was a homebody and an independent thinker, and his oldest daughter was turning out just like him. She was still a child, but already other kids and their parents understood who little Stacia's father was. Even as a child she didn't care who her dad was on television or what other people knew or thought about him. She just wanted him there.

As one birthday approached, Roddy had an idea about how to

be there *and* keep Rowdy Roddy Piper from intruding on his daughter's big day.

"My mom invited my entire kindergarten class for my sixth birthday and everyone was so excited to come over because," Anastasia paused, feeling the old disappointment, "of my dad." Roddy made an appearance at the party, but not the one anyone was expecting. "He dressed up as a rooster and played the piano in front of my entire class."

Roo-Roo-Rooster became the stuff of legend throughout Anastasia's school years. She has no idea why Roddy dressed like that—it was likely just the costume he could get his hands on most quickly. But even if it sometimes seemed like the Toombs kids down the road had a superhero for a father, truth is, Roddy really did have a knack for saving the day.

The Morton Downey Jr. Show lasted only three years (Downey was bankrupt by 1990), but while the talk show was on the air, its chain-smoking reactionary host was hard to ignore. Blowing smoke in his guests' faces, Downey noisily excoriated whatever and whoever caught his interest, and viewers loved the controversial racket he generated about politics, social issues and, yes, even professional wrestling. Somewhere between "Piper's Pit" and *The Morton Downey Jr. Show*, the line between irony and reality was crossed. A collision between the original and the imitator was a tempting prospect to Vince McMahon.

Here, Roddy's story intersects with the other one of those teenage brothers who had watched him wrestle as a twenty year old in Houston. The younger brother, Bruce Prichard, was hired by the WWF after WrestleMania 3 as a producer. In yet another "Piper's Pit" knockoff, Prichard portrayed a southern-preacher -like character, Brother Love, host of "The Brother Love Show."

With his face painted red as if his blood pressure were going through the roof, and dressed in a starched white suit, he cozied up to the heels and mocked babyfaces with his dragged-out opening phrase, "I loooove you," spoken in an exaggerated southern drawl. Early in 1989, Roddy returned to the WWF. Like Adrian Adonis before him, Brother Love was waiting in the bully pulpit Roddy had once called his own.

"Roddy had been gone for a while at that point—it had been two years. The Jim Bakker thing was hot, and we were looking for the perfect guest for Brother Love for WrestleMania," remembered Bruce Prichard. "Vince calls me into his office one day, and he says 'I'm not going to do Brother Love at WrestleMania,' which broke my heart. But he says, 'I've got another idea. What if I had the three biggest mouths out there? What if I had you and Morton Downey Jr.'—and I'm thinking wow, because Morton Downey Jr. was the hottest thing on TV at the time—'But wait,' he says. 'And what if the biggest mouth was the host—we bring back "Piper's Pit" for one night?'"

Prichard thought, "Holy shit, I get to work with Roddy!" He had missed out on Roddy's first run in the WWF by just a few months. When Vince told him to go meet Roddy and sell him on this idea, maybe do a little test run to see if they had chemistry, Prichard got worried. He didn't know Roddy personally. His brother, Tom, had gotten to know him a little in Charlotte, but Tom's crazy stories about his encounters with the wrestler only made Piper's legend more intimidating.

"Aw, you'll all get along fine," said McMahon. He'd booked Roddy for a show in Denver, and Prichard flew out to meet his new colleague. When Roddy arrived at the arena they chatted for a few minutes, and Prichard explained the Brother Love segment he wanted to do with him. He tried to break the ice with something he'd become good at and was pretty proud of, his imitation of Roddy.

"I had this whole scenario worked out where I would interview him but I would answer in his voice with his kind of stuff while he sits there with his thumb up his ass in the ring. And I'm pitching this idea to him, and I'm looking at him, and he's just kind of smiling." He didn't know Roddy hated to be mimicked.

Roddy didn't just smile at Prichard. He petted him. It was an old habit. If you were talking to Roddy and he liked you he would absent-mindedly put a hand on your arm or your shoulders and gently pat, like you were a cat gazing up at him in hopes of a treat. The impulse was meant to be reassuring, but it could be intimidating instead. Roddy's hand on your arm made you think very carefully about what you said next.

"So really cool, okay, so you're gonna do that. And I'm doing what?" asked Roddy, staring at him. "I'm just . . .? I'm just watching. Okay, okay. Go ahead."

A little spooked, Prichard tried to explain further before Roddy interjected.

"Ya know, let's just go out there and have some fun," said Roddy. "You do your thing; I'll do my thing. Let's just see what happens."

Roddy and Prichard worked out a finish for the segment, but they left it up in the air how exactly they'd get there. They got in the ring and Prichard, in his glaring white suit and red makeup, his hair slicked back, started asking Roddy questions. Roddy tried to answer but each time, Brother Love pulled the microphone away and answered the question himself, in a full-out imitation of Roddy.

"And right in the middle of the damn thing," said Prichard, "the third time I did that, he hauls off and knocked the *living fuck* out of me." He laughed to remember it, but he wasn't laughing at the time. "I caught myself on the second rope, and I'm looking up at him, and he's smiling. I was pissed." Prichard got back on his feet and came back with more questions and they finished the segment. Afraid Roddy had thought the idea was terrible all along and had just used the segment to tell Prichard to get lost, he approached Roddy backstage.

"I'm thinking he's gonna just be a raving maniac," said Prichard. "And instead he gives me a big hug, and he goes, 'I thought that was great!'"

The Denver show warmed up the duo for the in-ring return of "Piper's Pit" at WrestleMania V in Atlantic City. There, Brother Love appeared in a kilt, held up with bright white suspenders, but the segment quickly turned into a confrontation between Roddy and the second guest, Downey. Roddy asked the talk-show host repeatedly to stop blowing smoke in his face, then when he kept doing it, blasted him with a fire extinguisher. The boss was back—again.

McMahon booked Roddy to do match commentary through autumn of that year. After WrestleMania he sent Prichard to meet with Roddy and start planning more segments and storylines.

"Vince had a love/hate relationship with Roddy," explained Prichard. "While he loved his talent and appreciated him, sometimes Roddy could be a little difficult to work with. But to me, he was never any more difficult to work with than anybody else." In Prichard's experience, if you told Roddy straight up that an idea wouldn't work, he'd respect your opinion and move on. Following up on McMahon's order, Prichard was about to get a whole lot of that experience.

He called Roddy, who was staying at the Westin Hotel in Stamford, Connecticut, to meet for a drink. Roddy asked him to come to the hotel.

"I get there and he's in his jammies, and he doesn't want to go out. He says, 'Why don't you just come up to the room. I've taken the liberty to order some refreshments.'

"I go up to his room and he's got a case of beer—light beer—on ice, and he's got shots, and about a dozen hits of a white substance, lined up," recalled Prichard.

"We can always get more, but this should get us started," said Roddy.

Wide-eyed, Prichard suggested they just smoke a joint to break the ice. Marijuana helped Roddy with his aches and pains, not to mention anxieties, so he gladly agreed.

"I break out what I had, and he looks at me and kind of pets me, 'Son, you go ahead and put that away. You save that for when there's nothing else in the world to light up. I visited the old man on the hill.' Roddy always had the best pot. So we sat there. I smoked this shit with him, and did shots, and I looked at him and said, 'What is this?' He goes, 'Aw, it's nothing that'll kill ya, son, just go ahead. Cheers!'

They drank and smoked and got obliterated. The time together wasn't wasted, though. Roddy didn't easily trust his bosses or the people who worked for them, and the long day and night in the hotel room with Prichard helped him get over those reservations. "I think he was used to getting the con and the bullshit and people trying to swerve him," said Prichard. "We just slowly built up that trust, and built up that relationship." Roddy even coaxed him into the Gold's Gym in Stamford, where the wrestlers went. Prichard was a big man, but he didn't possess the kind of physique typical of McMahon's top talent. Roddy got him up at five a.m. to work out. "He was the only person ever to get me to where I could actually do chin-ups."

That fall, Roddy made several appearances on "The Brother Love Show," setting up a feud with "Ravishing" Rick Rude and introducing his Survivor Series' team Roddy's Rowdies, which included the Bushwhackers and Jimmy Snuka (who was still wary around a semi-conciliatory Roddy). Roddy even took over one segment, leading Prichard, bound and gagged, onto the set with a rope, a sheet thrown over him and a diaper on.

"Doing anything with that maniac was fun," said Prichard. "He loved it when you threw shit at him that he didn't expect, because you knew you were getting it back . . . that was the beauty of working with him. . . . I never was quite sure what he was going to hit me with."

Sometimes literally. And sometimes Roddy didn't pull his punches, which wasn't helping with his ongoing effort to make a living outside of wrestling.

One of the less-helpful screen roles Roddy took was that of a wrestler-turned-henchman on *The Love Boat*. The movie-length special, "A Valentine Voyage," was filmed in June 1989. It was a payday on a popular television franchise, but playing a thug named Maurice "The Beast" Steiner wasn't going to improve anyone's sense of Roddy Piper as an actor. The role exemplified the sort of typecasting that hindered his career.

"A man can drink a lot on a boat," Roddy said, recalling the weeks at sea, shooting the episode. One night he was wandering the ship and happened upon a dance hall. A live band was performing and, with a few drinks warming his belly, Roddy decided to check it out. As he was walking in, someone took exception to him.

"I don't know what I did wrong. I kinda walked in and I'm looking—all of a sudden, boom, somebody kicks me in the ass. I turn around. Seriously?! I don't know if I got in front of him or something. But I didn't care."

Roddy dragged the hapless passenger outside to the railing.

"This is nighttime, and I said to him, 'You're going to apologize to me, and if I don't like it, I'm throwing you overboard.'"

Roddy didn't realize it, but one person was watching closely—the show's director of photography.

Facing the cold black waters several storeys below, the offender apologized.

"Ain't good enough," said Roddy. He hiked him up the railing and the apologies piled up quickly. Roddy wasn't trying to fake him out. But he hadn't considered that if he did toss the guy over to teach him a lesson, the ship couldn't just turn around and collect the man from the ocean. "Woulda killed him."

He eventually let the man walk away.

"The next morning I'm in the sauna, trying to get some of it out. Aaron Spelling comes into the sauna with his clothes on. 'Hello, Roddy.'" One of the biggest producers in Hollywood, fully dressed, was visiting him in the sauna. This could only mean trouble.

"'So, were you going to throw somebody overboard last night?'" Roddy recalled him saying.

"Yeah . . . yeah, I was."

Spelling asked if he realized it would have taken a mile just to stop the ship, and even then the man would have been impossible to find in the dark, if he hadn't already drowned.

"No," answered Roddy. "But I'll tell you something. He kicked me in the ass."

"What?"

"He kicked me in the ass." Spelling let the matter drop. Roddy went home after the filming ended.

In August that year, Colt was born. Roddy now had two daughters and a son, the same family structure he'd grown up in. The parallels didn't end there. Not only had Roddy and Kitty decided to give their son his paternal grandfather's middle name,

Baird, Colt was born on August 5, Stanley Toombs' birthday.

We rarely saw that side of the family, and our father was always anxious when we did talk to them. But whatever bad blood lingered between Roddy and his father, Roddy respected the institution of family too much to break the tradition of passing down family names. Even if affection had eluded them, he found it in himself to respect what Stanley had endured to provide for his family.

Twenty-nine-year-old Len Denton began booking in Portland for promoter Don Owen in 1987. Owen hadn't had a strong run of sell-outs since Roddy left for Charlotte in 1980 (where he'd first met Denton, aka "The Grappler"). McMahon had stayed away from Portland for longer than most parts of the country out of respect for his father's long-time friendship with the Oregon promoter, but the WWF soon encroached on the old NWA territories, so it was tough to draw wrestling fans to anything less sensational than the New York–based big league.

"Don's a big ol' bastard," said Denton, his Texan twang still evident nearly three decades after moving to the Pacific Northwest. "Don't get me wrong, I loved him to death. But he'd just get under your skin. 'Hey, you sawed-off Texan, I thought everything was big in Texas. You got this big reputation as a booker. Harley Race taught you and all this. How come you can't sell out the Sports Arena?' I go, 'Damn, it hasn't been sold out in ten years.'"

Like most of the promotions around the continent, Owen's promotion had its own weekly television show, which set up storylines developed at the live shows around Oregon through the rest of the week. So I say, 'Tell you what'—'cause he and his son Barry would monitor everything I did on TV—I said, 'You let me run the TV show for six weeks and do whatever angles I want to, and if I don't sell it out . . . I tell you what, I'll shake your hand and go back to Texas where I belong.'"

It was a deal. Denton not only sold out the Portland Sports Arena, they turned away six hundred fans at the door. Afterwards, Denton figured he was due an extra cut. Owen handed him his regular pay only. "I go, 'You owe me at least another grand, come on. There were three thousand people here.' He says, 'You take that money and be happy with it or kiss my ass.' I said, 'You know what, Don, that's fine if that's what you want to do. But I'll get my money one way or the other.'"

A few weeks later, Owen sent Denton to wrestle a three-week tour in Japan, including a world title match against Tatsumi Fujinami. "I called my lady three times a day from Tokyo on Owen's bill." When Denton got back to Portland, Owen told him to meet him for lunch. Denton arrived at the restaurant to find him sitting with the phone bill in his hand. Also at the table were his son Barry and Roddy. Seeing him here with a furious Don Owen, Denton knew he was about to get fired.

"Don starts saying, 'Let me tell you something, Roddy Piper's taking your place. You think you're funny, you sawed-off Texan? You think you got even with me, huh? Your ass is fired.' I go, 'All right.' I start to leave and he goes, 'No, sit down, you can eat lunch with us.'"

Lunch wasn't a courtesy. It was a chance to continue lambasting Denton for his act of subterfuge. He remembered it going something like this:

"Roddy's going to take your place, Roddy's a better booker. He looks better than you, he's more popular than you—"

"You guys, stop," said Roddy. "Don, you know I'm working for Vince. I got a contract. You know I'm doing movies in Hollywood. You know I got a lot of irons in the fire and tons of obligations, and you want me to be a booker here and run this TV show?" Roddy was willing to moonlight for Owen. So long as he kept a low profile, McMahon would turn a blind eye to the side work, not least because Roddy was wrestling only part-time for the WWF. But Roddy couldn't do all Owen wanted by himself. He told the promoter that he needed an assistant.

Like a man attending his own funeral, Denton finished lunch as Roddy worked out his deal to take over his job.

"Good," said Owen. An assistant made sense. And they agreed on the assistant's pay.

"I'd like to hire Len Denton."

"Son of a bitch," muttered Owen, realizing Roddy had pulled a fast one on him.

"That's Roddy Piper," mused Denton. "I loved him to death. He didn't need that job. But he made Don keep me on. We did good houses after that for years."

By the end of 1992, Don Owen had sold Pacific Northwest Wrestling and retired. At a Christmas farewell in the Crow's Nest, Roddy joined the festivities to honour Owen, who was led onto the stage by Denton. "The Grappler" had already started celebrating, and after he popped a bottle of bubbly, he leaned into Roddy's microphone and launched into a breathless plug for a venture that would pay his bills in lieu of Portland Wrestling.

"Hey, this is the festive season. Everybody knows it!" yelled Denton.

"Get out of here," Owen grumbled from behind his scene-stealing assistant booker.

"It's just like at Piper's Pit Stop transmission centre, 156 and Division, brother!" continued Denton. "We're always having a good time. And we'll treat you so many ways, you're bound to like one of 'em!"

With Portland wrestling changing hands, Denton had figured

he was headed back to Texas. Then Roddy approached him with an alternative. He was making a lot of money and wanted to invest some of it in a small business. He trusted Denton and knew Denton had a young family that might not hold together if he hit the road again, living out of his car on a wrestling circuit in whatever part of the country wanted him. So Roddy told him to pick a small business that he'd like to run and let him know what it would cost.

Denton had been doing commercials for a local transmission shop and saw the money was pretty good, so he suggested they open one of those. They shook hands on a deal to co-own the venture. Roddy paid for it and Denton would run it. "I said, 'Roddy, I promise you one thing, I won't take off until I have this place paid for if you invest your money in it.'" He didn't take a day off for two years. Finally, he asked Roddy if he could take a break.

"He says, 'Okay, I'll handle it. How long you going?' I said five days."

Every morning, the shop put a call in to its local supplier for auto parts. The guy who made the parts run called Denton during his vacation. "'Lenny, you need to get home. Roddy's sending cabs to get parts.' I said, 'What?!' You had to be there at eight forty-five in the morning to call them in so the shit comes on time. Roddy'd get there at nine or ten, he done miss it. 'Send a cab to get it.' He was doing it like he was at the five-star places. This is a podunk, trying-to-make-it transmission shop, friend!"

Denton's vacation lasted three days.

Mitch Ackerman continued to help Roddy find film and television work. But with all the wrestling and "Piper's Pits" he was doing, his public image was stuck firmly to his wrestling roots.

One project that held some promise was a Disney-backed buddy-cop TV series with Jesse Ventura called *Tag Team*. They'd play wrestlers—"Tricky" Rick McDonald and Bobby "The Body" Youngblood—who are blackballed after refusing, of all things, to fix a match. Breaking up a robbery in a grocery store inspires the unemployed wrestlers, and they enroll in the police academy. Ventura was signed already, and the network expected to pair him with an actor. Ackerman caught wind of this and went to the casting director and creator. "I've got a wrestler who's an actor who'd be great for this," he said. They agreed to meet Roddy, liked him and gave him the part.

Before filming the pilot Roddy went for his insurance physical. The doctor had a grip-testing gadget. "It's an old thing that you squeezed and a needle went up and it told you how much strength you had," Ackerman said. "Roddy broke it." Hollywood doctors hadn't seen many wrestlers yet.

Ackerman called the WWF and McMahon allowed the pilot's "fixed" match to be filmed before an actual WWF card at the LA Sports Arena. When it was announced to the audience that the opening match would be Roddy Piper and Jesse Ventura against the Orient Express, featuring Pat Tanaka and Akio Sato managed by Mr. Fuji (playing Tojo Samurai and Soji Samurai, managed by Mr. Saki), the crowd went wild.

"Roddy was really close with Mr. Fuji, and he asked me afterwards if we could try to get him a SAG card," said Ackerman. "I don't think he ever worked again, but we got him a SAG card."

The pilot was picked up to go to series, with a minimum of twelve episodes. To celebrate, Roddy and the rest of the cast, producers and executives gathered at The Palm restaurant.

"Roddy was always famous for going to The Palm and ordering a seven-pound lobster plus a steak," said Ackerman. Roddy loved shellfish, but he wasn't keen on the muck and guts of pulling one apart. "You guys cut up the lobster," he said. "I don't want anything to do with that."

In July, the cast and crew were in LA to start shooting the series. At 4:30 the afternoon before shooting was set to begin, the phone rang. The head of ABC, Bob Iger (now CEO of Disney), had read the scripts and didn't like them. Shooting was postponed. For several days, the cast and crew stewed, until the network pulled the plug and cancelled the show.

"We had spent all these weeks preparing. Directors were hired, writers were hired, cast members were hired," said Ackerman. "The network had to pay us seven million dollars of money that we had already spent—*not* to do the show. We said, 'We don't understand it. At least do one or two shows and see how it comes out. As long as you're spending that much money.' But they didn't. It really was one of the big disappointments of all of our lives, me, Roddy, Jesse." Ackerman still bemoans the opportunity lost. "I've talked to Jesse," he said. "If that series had gone on and been a success, he may never have been governor of Minnesota."

And we both have sometimes wondered, if our dad had enjoyed a few successful seasons with a prime-time television hit, would he—like "Tricky" Rick McDonald—have walked away from wrestling and stayed away?

By the time Roddy had arrived in the McMahons' New York promotion, he'd set a high bar for himself. WrestleMania VI in Toronto, April 1, 1990, was as close as he came to not clearing it.

"Oh, Rod. What were you thinking?" he said, casting his mind back to a meeting in 1990 with McMahon, Pat Patterson and Allen Coage, a wrestler who went by the name Bad News Brown. Coage was from New York City but became a Canadian citizen and adopted Calgary as his hometown. A top judoka (he won gold as a heavyweight for the US at the Montreal Olympics in 1976, and gold at two Pan-Am Games), he became the first African American to win a solo Olympic medal outside of boxing or track and field. He quit amateur judo after the Montreal games, citing his distaste for the sport's internal politics and found his way into pro wrestling.

Already into middle age, Coage hadn't taken the usual track toward wrestling fame. His sense of being an outsider, alone in a world that didn't give him the respect he felt he deserved, played into his wrestling persona: an angry heel who refused alliances and picked fights with anyone, babyface or heel. The obvious differences aside, he sounded a bit like the guy he was supposed to wrestle in Toronto.

Maybe it was the parallels between Harlem and rough-and-tumble Glasgow that jumped into Roddy's mind. Or, given his own background, maybe he couldn't stomach attitude about growing up hard from a guy who had spent time in the US Olympic program. Either way, Roddy had a problem to solve. How do you play the babyface against a heel who identifies himself as a black tough guy with a racially charged chip on his shoulder without appearing to position yourself against black people generally (especially when your own gimmick is grounded in your own Gaelic and Caucasian identity)? The answer that struck Roddy in that meeting was to paint himself half black, expressing his desire to champion *all* people. Besides, in his words, Brown "wasn't a real pizzazz-y pro wrestler." With numerous promos to do in advance of the match, they'd need something to fight about.

"Bad News Brown wasn't real happy with me," he said, thinking back to the moment he suggested the paintjob. But McMahon responded positively and they went with it. During one promo, Roddy said he could be black and sang Michael Jackson's "Beat It," then turned his face to the unpainted side and said he could be white and sang Tiny Tim's "Tiptoe through the Tulips" in mock falsetto. Conscious that this whole effort could easily be misinterpreted, he tried to be an equal-opportunity offender. Then he got in the ring and tried a few Michael Jackson dance moves. It didn't fly.

Roddy was a great heel because he wasn't afraid to go to any level to piss everyone off. But how do you piss off a black opponent by painting yourself black without understandably pissing off every other black person watching you? Times were changing, and anything so reminiscent of blackface (and oddly prefigured the Scottish war paint made famous in Mel Gibson's film *Braveheart* just a few years later) wasn't a tool that could be wielded well, no matter Roddy's intentions. As a heel or babyface, Roddy's strategies didn't change much, but this was one way to antagonize his opponent that was unappealing any way you looked at it. When he'd baited the largely Hispanic crowds in LA and they flocked to the Olympic Auditorium to see him take his licks from their hero, Chavo Guerrero, Roddy had been vulnerable. Fans rushed the ring to get at him. They stabbed him and threw cigarette butts at him. Then to their delight Chavo beat him up (sometimes). Playing fast and loose with racial politics wasn't the same when the crowd was supposed to be on your side.

Ultimately, the gimmick sucked the life out of the match. Promoted as a battle of two brawlers, it contained little wrestling artistry or ring psychology. The crowd struggled to get into it until both wrestlers were counted out of the ring and took their brawling all the way to the dressing rooms. But Roddy wasn't content to just walk away from a bad idea. He couldn't walk away from it even when he tried.

Vince McMahon had provided him with a black paint that wouldn't run when he sweated, but would wash off with a particular solution of solvents. Roddy went to the dressing room after the match and started scrubbing the paint. The black didn't budge. He scrubbed until he was raw. His skin was going to come off before it came clean.

In one of the cruellest ribs in wrestling history, Andre the Giant and WWF staffer Arnold Skaaland had dumped the solution and replaced it with water.

"I'm half-black and half-white, and there's nothing I can do about it. So I went out drinking," said Roddy. He woke up in his Toronto hotel room the next morning unsure what he'd done the night before. His clothes were on his bed and his door was off its hinges. A cowboy hat he'd never seen before was sitting in the middle of the floor. A giant souvenir he'd bought for one of his daughters was sitting in the corner. He'd woken up in worse circumstances. Roddy packed his bag and headed to the airport, still unable to wash off the paint.

"I'm half-black with a cowboy hat on, about two hundred and forty-five pounds, a four-foot Mickey Mouse under my right arm and a Halliburton in my left hand," he said. "Even customs, they just want you to get the fuck outta there."

As he boarded his connecting flight to Portland in Chicago, an airline attendant told him he had to check the doll. Whatever contrition he had been feeling melted into petulance. He bought the doll a first-class seat. "Me and Mickey, we drank all the way to Portland, Oregon. It took me three weeks to get that shit off."

Roddy wasn't done with racial politics. It took a lot of nerve to wade back into those waters, but if he was going to draw from his own past as a social outcast to identify with others, he had to drop the funny stuff. Instead, he'd cut to the heart of the matter: wealth, power and privilege. Fortunately, the WWF had a heel whose character positively dripped with these qualities, as well as his recently fired black bodyguard who needed a little help getting over.

Not since "Ace" Orton had watched his back had Roddy been anyone's idea of a team player. His character didn't fit neatly into group storylines. He worked best alone. So when "Virgil," the bodyguard of "Million Dollar Man" Ted DiBiase, turned on his arrogant employer and the two were slated for a master-and-servant showdown at WrestleMania VII in LA, Roddy got the call to tutor the former servant on how to be a solo act.

On "Piper's Pit," DiBiase described the feud from his perspective, saying of Virgil, "He's a gutter rat, that I took out of the gutter. I put clothes on his back. I put money in his pocket. I made him somebody . . . Virgil only could respond to orders."

Virgil—born Michael Jones—wasn't a great talker. For McMahon to cast him adrift of a veteran partner like DiBiase was a risk. Putting Roddy in his corner as a sort of friend/mentor/unofficial manager loaned the feud some verbal creativity. In an interview with Virgil and Gene Okerlund, Roddy got started with "a lesson in human rights."

Discussing later the WrestleMania VI debacle, Roddy often mentioned how much he respected Nelson Mandela, who had been released in 1990 after serving twenty-seven years of prison time. The fact that Mandela had greeted his guards every morning by shaking their hands and thanking them for their care had mesmerized Roddy. Mentioning Mandela could sound like a wild swing by a man trying to talk his way out of politically incorrect trouble, but his "lesson" for Virgil revealed that he understood more about human rights than people might have guessed.

"There's a difference between being a friend and a fool. And I does hate a bully," he began.

He asked Virgil to repeat after him: "Roddy, my back's hurt. Would you mind, friend, shining my boots for me?" Roddy handed him a cloth to hand him back as he delivered his line. Virgil did, and Roddy got down on one knee and shined his shoe.

"It's a pleasure, you know why?" Roddy asked him, looking up. "'Cause I'm your friend."

The next step of the lesson was for Virgil to say, "Roddy, kiss my feet." When he did, Roddy jumped in his face and yelled at him, "Stick it in your nose!" and then urged Virgil to slap him in the face.

They went back and forth like this, becoming ever more heated, until Virgil shouted a forceful NO into the mic.

"What are you?!" yelled Roddy, like a coach firing up an athlete.

"A man!" he responded.

"When I see you, I don't see a black man, I don't see a white man, I don't see a yellow man. I see here a man!" said Roddy.

At the end he asked Virgil how he felt. "I feel like a million bucks," replied Virgil.

Until Roddy's "lesson," the racial aspect to the DiBiase-Virgil relationship was mostly implied. But as soon as Roddy opened that box full of trouble, he slammed it shut with his closing line, citing the classic Sidney Poitier–Katherine Hepburn film about race in America.

"Hey, DiBiase, at WrestleMania, guess who's coming to dinner?"

On WrestleMania VII's massive fifteen-match card, McMahon held back the Virgil-DiBiase fight until the thirteenth slot, treasured real estate for any wrestler, and deeper in the card than he'd placed Roddy since WrestleMania 2.

Roddy had made lemonade out of the previous year's lemon, suggesting that even at the age of thirty-six his best moments in the ring might still be ahead of him. In a year, he'd prove it.

9
Frats

Wearing a tuxedo jacket, bow tie and no shirt, with his hair slicked back and dark sunglasses, Rick Martel looked more like a Chippendales dancer than the champion wrestler he'd always been. If the gimmick wasn't clear to everyone, an enormous button hung from his jacket reading, "Yes, I am a model" and he carried a DDT sprayer–sized cologne dispenser into the ring, with "ARROGANCE" printed down its length. With his genial disposition, good looks and bright smile, Martel was a tough man to dislike, but it was as a heel that "The Model" finished his distinguished wrestling career in 1990. Or so he thought. In early 1991, Vince McMahon asked if he'd wrestle one more time, to put Roddy over.

"Business-wise, I had no advantage in doing that," recalled Martel. But he didn't think about his own business. "I said, 'For Roddy, whatever I can do, I will.' I came back for that one show."

After WrestleMania VII, Roddy had filmed an episode of *Zorro* on location in Spain, his second guest spot in the TV series. He was still wrestling part-time, including one run through Ireland and the UK, where he also filmed the video for his upcoming single, "I'm Your Man" and then filmed a fitness video, "Fighting Fit." For all his extracurricular activity, Roddy's star still shone bright in the firmament of WWF stars, and McMahon wanted to make a statement with him on television before beginning a new storyline.

So, in May, 1991, Roddy wrestled Martel—the two had rarely worked against one another, and there was no mention of their youthful history in McMahon and Randy Savage's commentary that night. This match wasn't about Roddy's past. It was about sharpening his wild image for what was yet to come. "Look at those eyes," commented the "Macho Man" after Roddy had decisively won the match. "Those aren't the eyes of a sane individual."

Rick Martel and Roddy didn't see much of one another after that match. But whenever they crossed paths, it was immediately like old times, something many of the wrestlers we talked to noted about our dad. A decade could pass, but the warmth of his presence made the years apart dissolve in an instant. "It was a pleasure for me," Martel reflected on his final match, "to do that for my friend."

The match helped set up Roddy's feud with Ted DiBiase—a carryover from the work with Virgil—but the long game revolved around another old friend of Roddy's, one of his gang. Bret Hart and Jim Neidhart had wrestled their final match as the Hart Foundation at WrestleMania VII. Despite winning the Intercontinental championship, Hart found himself in a position a lot like Roddy's during his early years in LA (though on a much grander scale); he had a belt, he could wrestle main events, but he just hadn't yet cracked that top echelon that drew fanatical audience interest. The following year, Roddy would be enlisted to help get him there. The months in between threatened to be interesting for another reason, one that began in a doctor's office in Hershey, Pennsylvania.

In June 1991, the recently retired "Superstar" Billy Graham walked into a Pennsylvania courtroom, leaning on a cane. He had come to testify in the trial of urologist Dr. George Zahorian, indicted in July 1990 on multiple counts of distributing controlled substances—most notably anabolic steroids—to wrestlers and weightlifters. Having recently undergone ankle and hip surgery due to degenerating bone and muscle tissue, Graham was there to speak about the debilitating long-term effects of steroids. The drugs not only helped build more impressive physiques, they sped up recovery times for sore and injured muscles—crucial for aging wrestlers who needed to perform night after night. But as Graham's crumbling joints attested, steroid use came with a terrible price.

The Zahorian trial was small news until the doctor's attorney hinted at the stature of the athletes who'd been buying from him. "[Steroids are] used throughout the WWF," he said. "Wrestlers either use them or they don't participate." Suddenly every news outlet up to the *New York Times* was reporting on the trial and several WWF wrestlers were subpoenaed to testify.

WWF headquarters urgently produced a legal argument to keep the most famous of those wrestlers, Hulk Hogan, from having to appear, citing potential personal and professional damage. They got the face of the WWF off the hook, but not Roddy. Compelled to take the stand, he was angry that the WWF didn't extend the same effort to protecting him as it had Hogan.

For a few years, Roddy had been calling Zahorian's office when he was struggling with injuries or severe muscle soreness. He had always worried about being a smaller wrestler in New York, so the bulk added by anabolic steroids was a major plus. Accounts of how the many different drugs were delivered to wrestlers vary—some say they picked them up at his office in brown paper bags—but it was FedEx records that ultimately connected the doctor and a few patients' home addresses.

The day Zahorian's lawyer let the cat out of the bag about the WWF connection, Roddy was wrestling The Undertaker. The office told him to lose. Roddy hadn't been pinned since before WrestleMania in 1985. This was a minor match in a small venue—not the sort of situation in which a wrestler of Roddy's stature would be asked to take a fall. The order aggravated his suspicion that he was being hung out to dry.

He told The Undertaker to piledrive him on the floor—off the mats. The Undertaker complied, aware that Roddy was known for handling some hard knocks. When The Undertaker picked him up, Roddy manoeuvred his head toward his opponent's knees, where it would be less protected when he was dropped to the floor. His head struck the concrete and he collapsed, and he was counted out; appearing legitimately injured, he avoided the pin. Later, he had to be helped to the plane that was waiting to fly him to Harrisburg for the next day's testimony. He was stumbling and seemed to experience multiple seizures on the flight. The next day, he gave his deposition in a fog from the "accident," exhibiting difficulty focussing on the questions asked, much to the chagrin of the prosecutor. Roddy wasn't obstructive on the stand, but he wasn't eager to co-operate. He believed that the doctor had helped a number of wrestlers cope with the very real pressures and damage of their business.

Outside the law or not, Zahorian hadn't preyed on wrestlers any more than the business had.

"Did you have occasion to call Dr. Zahorian on March 23 of 1990 and ask him for anabolic steroids?" asked the prosecutor.

"Yes," Roddy said. "I did."

"And what did you ask him for?"

"I asked him for some Winstrol, and I believe some Deca Durabolin, and I'm not sure, maybe an anti-inflammatory, too."

"Did you receive the anabolic steroids you ordered from Dr. Zahorian in California?"

"Yes, sir."

Zahorian was found guilty on twelve charges, including the illegal distribution of steroids, and then acquitted on two counts of possession with intent to distribute. After the trial, the WWF began testing for steroids. Roddy never failed a test (Vince McMahon later admitted trying steroids himself and said 50 percent of the WWF wrestling stable initially tested positive), but he hated taking these tests. When the office sent someone down to watch him fill a cup for a urine sample, he drove the man's head into the washroom wall.

In 1992, a pair of veteran wrestlers—one having left the WWF at the time, the other retired—came forward in the *LA Times* to point fingers: Billy Jack Haynes at the promoters, Ivan Putski at the hazards of the profession. "Valium, Placidyl, acid, pot, steroids, cocaine, alcohol are all a major part of professional wrestling," said Billy Jack Haynes. "It's all brought on by the promoter because he asks too much of you. You're only a human being, but you're just a number to him."

Ivan Putski: "It's something you have to do. I didn't want to take them but I had to because I didn't want the other guy to look better than me. . . . It's a vicious circle until you retire."

It's hard to say how much the steroid scandal increased tensions between Roddy and his primary employer. With a sexual abuse scandal erupting (young men who worked around the rings were coming forward with stories of being exploited by office staff), Roddy might actually have been one of McMahon's most reliable assets. Either way, the boss put a good portion of the business on Roddy's shoulders—or more accurately, around his waist—in the all-important lead-up to WrestleMania VIII.

In January 1992 Bret Hart lost his Intercontinental Championship belt to a heel known as The Mountie. The kitschy French Canadian held the title for only a few days before Roddy won it away from him. The ensuing storyline played into the real-life friendship between Bret and Roddy. Far more memorable than how Roddy won the belt was how he would soon lose it. For all the wrestling knowledge he had taken with him to the movies, something he'd learned filming *They Live* was about to pay dividends in his wrestling life: the high drama of a fight between friends.

At an out-of-the-way table in a quiet restaurant in Moncton, New Brunswick, Roddy and Bret Hart sat down to a salmon dinner. More than sixteen years earlier, Roddy had separated himself from the wrestling flock as it migrated west from here for the winter to wrestle for Stu Hart and his sons in Calgary. Roddy had gone to LA instead, missing Bret entirely during his formative years. Tonight, he and Stu's most famous son put their minds to a spectacle that would be worth the wait.

Almost since that first meeting in Toronto, Roddy had been encouraging Bret and advising him whenever asked. When Bret and Jim Neidhart were not getting the recognition they deserved as a high-energy new tag team, Roddy had told Bret to ask

McMahon for more promos; if they didn't learn how to talk, they'd never convince the WWF brain trust they could play a major role. Bret asked, and they got the chances they needed. They won the tag belts, which was nice, but not considered terribly prestigious. Roddy's encouragement continued. "It's a step, it's a big step," he'd said. "It's not a small thing. It's an accomplishment. You're one of the main events."

"He pushed me to work hard," said Hart, "to be conscientious of being tag champions, even though it's not like the big matches." Bret was getting into those big matches now, solo. In April, he would reclaim his Intercontinental Championship belt from Roddy at WrestleMania VIII. That he was going to take it away from a friend and mentor should have been reassuring. Bret's stock was rising rapidly in the WWF, and Roddy's insights had helped him make some of the decisions behind that rise. But Roddy's participation also worried him. They had to plan this match together, and Bret had been giving it a lot of thought. What if he didn't like Roddy's ideas? What if Roddy—whom he loved and respected—envisioned a match that served Roddy's interests more than Bret's? Roddy was smart enough to lose a belt and still leave the ring looking like the better man.

As they tucked into dinner, Bret asked Roddy how he thought the match should go. Roddy spoke for about twenty minutes, explaining the attitude of the match and its shifts in momentum, how it would favour one guy and then the other. Hart never interrupted. He didn't have to.

When Roddy was done, he looked expectantly across the table.

"That's exactly what I was going to tell you," said Hart. The only thing he hadn't imagined was the finish, which Roddy had seen in a match a long time ago and filed in the back of his mind. The reason he hadn't used it yet was obvious to Bret. It would end with Roddy's shoulders pinned to the mat, something he hadn't allowed since before those early debates over his feud with Hogan.

Roddy knew when he won the belt that one day he'd need to give it up. You can't lose a belt by being disqualified or counted out while unconscious or bashing someone's manager over the head with a folding chair, which were Roddy's usual ways of losing. He didn't value a WWF title as much as he valued the cachet that came with having never lost by pinfall. Taking the belt while knowing full well that he'd have to let Bret pin him was a gift, "a very generous act," in Hart's words.

"He was still a main character and a valuable character," said Bret. "But I think he recognized, 'Here's an opportunity for me to insert myself and lift this guy up. I can see the future and I know this guy needs someone to elevate him, give him credibility, to give him a little boost right now at an early part of his career.'"

There was just one thing that would make the fight really pop, Roddy added. He suggested it to Bret, but left it up to him to decide; a guy could get himself in trouble.

"I can do it," said Hart. "It'll look like an accident. No one's gonna know."

Roddy needn't have worried. Once again, Bret was thinking the exact same thing.

The promos and interviews ran through late March. "Bret Hart, nice guy. Don't particularly wanna fight ya," Roddy says in one. Then he breaks one of his cardinal promo rules: don't say you're going to do something to your opponent that you can't literally do. "But I'm telling you right to your face, I'm gonna rip your throat out if you show up April 5 in the Hoosier Dome."

The fighting-friends storyline meant Roddy couldn't engage in his usual creative character assassination. The reason for the match had to be business, plain and simple. "I feed my kids this way. I made it real clear to ya, I like ya. I like everything about ya. But this is what I do for a living!" Fury and disrespect were Roddy's baselines. He usually began his promos already in a lather over his opponent. Could the wrath of Rowdy be turned off?

In an interview with Bret and Gene Okerlund, Roddy shows up wearing pants: "The only time I wear my kilt is when I'm gonna fight." He and Hart sit down and Roddy tries to explain that he doesn't want to fight him. He says he's known Bret so long he might have changed his diapers. Hart briefly but visibly struggles to keep a straight face. Then Roddy says he's going to back out. "I can't find it in my heart to go out there and fight you. So I'm not gonna." Bret makes the point that if Roddy won't fight, he has to forfeit the belt. Roddy refuses, the temperature rises and the fight is on.

When the day arrived, the match went back and forth from one's favour to the other's. It got dirtier as it progressed. The crowd cheered when, after both went over the ropes and fell on the floor, Roddy held the ropes open for Bret to climb back in. The audience bought into the sportsmanship of the contest; they loved seeing two bad boys play nice out of mutual respect. As they were applauding Roddy's act of grace, the referee pointed out to Bret that one of his bootlaces was undone. He bent down to tie it up and Roddy reached around the ref to give him an uppercut. Then he kicked him in the face while he was down. By the time Bret was getting back up blood was running down his face and across the mat. Gore smeared both wrestlers as the street fighting took over. Roddy had made a show of keeping up with Hart's exalted scientific wrestling skills but suddenly the match was looking like a typical Piper brawl.

Hart changed the momentum of the match with a series of high-energy moves, ending with a backbreaker. He climbed to the second rope while Roddy lay prone in the middle of the ring.

"I jumped off and Roddy stuck his foot up and caught me in the jaw with a straight leg," said Hart. "I took a good bump. But I think I jammed Roddy's hip. If you ever watch it, you can see Roddy grab his hip right away."

Genuinely smarting, Roddy shoved Hart at the referee, knocking him temporarily out of action. Roddy left the ring and returned with the timekeeper's bell. Holding it above Hart's head, he scanned the audience, picking up on their disapproval, encouraging their feedback. Never mind sportsmanship, this was the old Rowdy Roddy Piper, reaching into his bag of dirty tricks, heedless of the damage he'd cause his friend in the name of victory. He waited, let the crowd give voice to what they were feeling, that two friends should have an honest match. "Don't do it, Roddy!" people screamed. Roddy was more of a babyface at the time than Bret, so as he looked over the crowd, their pleading grew louder. He tossed the bell out of the ring and the crowd cheered. Of course, the brawler's concession to grace was his fatal mistake.

Roddy next applied a move that had rarely failed him, his signature finisher, a sleeper hold in the middle of the ring. Hart had nowhere to go and was too badly beaten up to believably turn the match's momentum again. But then, even as he faded in Roddy's grip, Hart inched them both toward a corner post. In a last-ditch burst of energy, he ran his feet up the post and flipped over Roddy's head, crashing them both to the mat and turning Roddy's sleeper into a pin of his own shoulders. The match was over.

Still playing with the crowd's desire, Roddy placed the belt around Bret's waist and raised his friend's bloodied hand, then helped him stumble out of the ring and back to the dressing room. The match and the narrative around it were a resounding success. But the storytelling wasn't over.

Behind closed doors, Bret straightened up, and in front of their peers, he shoved Roddy. He yelled at him for being too aggressive, too reckless, kicking him in the forehead and breaking his brow open. Before their good sportsmanship in the ring could degrade into an old fashioned punch-up in the dressing room, Jay Strongbow grabbed Hart by the arm and pulled him away.

"You got some fuckin' problem? Let's settle it right here!" Roddy yelled back.

After several minutes of shouting and threatening, the other wrestlers calmed them down. Roddy's temper lowered, and he apologized. It was an accident; he would never have cut Bret open on purpose. The matter seemed settled. The others left them.

Roddy and Bret sat down. They looked at each other. As they made certain they were alone, smiles crept onto their faces. They burst out laughing.

"It was a little drama for everybody in the back," said Hart. The fight in the dressing room had an important purpose. "We went to great lengths to make it look like it was real"—first the cut, and then the argument backstage.

"Colour"—intentionally causing yourself to bleed in the ring—was forbidden. The WWF wanted to keep its product family-friendly, and in the midst of AIDS paranoia the transmission of a blood-borne illness between competitors was potentially a major legal liability (Abdullah the Butcher was successfully sued after infecting another wrestler with hepatitis C in 2007, after cutting himself and his opponent with the same blade). "Vince asked me, 'Was that on purpose or an accident?' I said, 'He kicked me and it busted my forehead open.' I had a little tiny cut about an inch long on my eyebrow, and he believed me," Hart said.

The other wrestlers had left the simmering friends to watch the next bout, a heavyweight title match between Randy Savage and Ric Flair. They were either inspired after seeing the bloody mess left by Roddy and Bret, or they'd had the same idea. Where Hart had been as discreet as possible in cutting himself with a small blade (in front of sixty thousand pairs of eyes), Flair cut himself in full view of the cameras. McMahon fined him and Savage five hundred dollars each.

"Roddy's always told me that it was his favourite match of all time," said Hart. "I love the story. I love the match. I love the intensity of it." The psychology of the match had brought out the best in both their characters while still transferring the belt. It accomplished another goal: raising Hart's stock with the audience. "Roddy was one of the only guys, maybe the only guy, that comes to mind from that generation that reached down and grabbed my hand and said I'm going to help pull you up." Roddy hadn't known when he'd planned the match that it would become a classic. He'd just wanted to pay forward the favour Andre the Giant had once done for him. "A huge leap in my stock," said Hart, "and he did it all for nothing where he was concerned. Just for being a guy who wanted to help."

Looking to stay sharp on the mats while spending many of his days on movie sets, Roddy called Gene LeBell. He was going to visit the dojo. LeBell recalled, "Roddy wants to work out. He says, 'I don't have a gi,' which is the uniform. I say, 'I'll give you a uniform. I got a size six uniform, brand new, and you can wear it.' He says, 'That sounds good, but let's have some fun.'" Roddy didn't explain any further.

A half dozen judo students were working out when Roddy arrived. They weren't wrestling fans and didn't recognize him, even in his kilt and carting his bagpipes.

"I want to fight!" Roddy said in his best Scottish brogue. "I want to wrestle!"

The students looked on, wondering who the crazy guy was. Roddy produced a photo of a highland games competitor tossing a caber. "This is my last opponent!" he said of the twenty foot wooden pole. "I wanna get on the mat and wrestle." LeBell took training his students very seriously, but this was too rich to shut down.

"You gotta take your shoes off," Gene said, playing along.

Roddy kicked off his sandals and stepped on the mat.

"Wait a second," said LeBell. The students in their gis looked on, bewildered that this Scottish madman hasn't been shown the door. "You're not going to wrestle in that."

"That's what we do," insisted Roddy, and he showed the picture of the caber toss again to the students. "This is my last opponent. He weighs two thousand pounds and I threw him down!"

LeBell offered him a gi to wear, but Roddy turned his nose up at the idea. "What's a gi?! This is a kilt, and this is what I wrestle in."

LeBell turned to one of his black belts. "Ask him if he's got anything under the kilt."

"You do it!" replied the student.

Roddy finally agreed to put on the gi and then drove the students to distraction by consistently besting them on the mats. LeBell didn't say a word. After changing back into his kilt, Roddy marched back into the gym from the change room and said, "When you really enjoy yourself, you gotta give them a goodbye." He played the bagpipes as a thank you to the perplexed judokas.

"That guy's a great wrestler," they said when Roddy was gone, "but he's strange."

LeBell looked unfazed by the visit. "I didn't see anything strange about him."

As January 1993 passed, one of wrestling's most important names faded into history. Andre the Giant died in his native France. The tally of Roddy's lost friends continued to grow. With each fallen wrestler, he had one more reason to get away from wrestling and stay away.

Two years earlier, Roddy had met a British talent manager at a reception in Los Angeles. Freya Miller said that next time Roddy was in the UK she would arrange some non-wrestling business for him. Included in that was her promise of a recording deal. She was the one who convinced Sony to take a chance on recording Roddy's single, "I'm Your Man."

When Roddy went to London for SummerSlam in 1992 Miller continued making good on her promises. He didn't wrestle, but played "Scotland the Brave" with the Balmoral Highlanders pipe band before Bret Hart's Intercontinental title match against English wrestler Davey Boy Smith—and he extended his stay for the release of the single, which made a brief appearance on the UK and Irish music charts.

"In Ireland they loved Roddy," remembered Miller. "North and south. We went there when we were promoting the record. Roddy wanted to go out and have a few drinks. I lost him completely one night—he was out drinking with a leprechaun." Miller explained that she was tired and didn't feel up to drinks, so Roddy offered to take out their diminutive driver, whom he'd taken to calling his leprechaun. "I said, 'Right, but don't come back late.' About seven o'clock in the morning, the two of them come back, and he's holding the leprechaun under his arm. . . .

He couldn't drive. The leprechaun couldn't even remember where he'd left the car."

Miller—whom Roddy took to calling "Buttons" and who responded by calling him "Grumps"—estimates she arranged roles in a dozen movies for Roddy during the nineties. It was a prolific time for his acting career. He started taking classes again with another Hollywood acting coach, Ivana Chubbuck, determined to hone his craft.

Roddy had worked with many tough guys, but few as truly deadly as Japanese martial artist and actor Sonny Chiba. The film star had been working on his English in hopes of breaking into American films. "He was *right there*," said Roddy, "the words just couldn't come." Casting Roddy alongside Chiba in *Resort to Kill* (released on video as *Immortal Combat*) gave the film and its action star a practiced actor who could also keep up physically with Chiba—and his posse of ninjas.

"Real-deal ninjas," said Roddy. "No bullshit. I watched these guys, they did a scene, real-deal samurai swords, Sonny fighting them. These guys"—he mimicked the sound of blades slicing through the air in front of his face—"that close, a minute and a half, full bore. Holy cow, if Sonny Chiba had a broomstick in his hand, I'd fuckin' run."

None of the ninjas spoke English, but one realized he and Roddy shared an interest.

Roddy was working out on a rowing machine one day when Chiba approached and offered to share some tea. They settled in for a cup and a few of the ninjas joined them. Eventually Chiba and the ninjas left, except one. "I spoke zero ninja. Zero. He spoke zero wrestler, zero English; me, zero Japanese." Roddy tried to communicate that he was going back to the hotel to smoke a joint.

"He figured it out and he came to my room." Roddy had security watching outside his door, making sure nobody bothered them, and ready to give a head's up if anyone important approached.

"We start to smoke a joint, you know. Going on maybe twenty, twenty-five minutes, back and forth, you know, and we're talking. He's going to have a drink of beer and I'm having a Coke, and we're talking about the difference between Japan and America. And about thirty minutes in I'm talking to him about some stuff I got, whatever was going on. And all of a sudden out of the clear blue sky he goes, 'Why are understanding each other?' And then we couldn't understand each other." However they had been able to communicate—if in fact the joint hadn't just relaxed the martial artist enough to try his English—the experience had made Roddy a friend. "He had my back after that."

Younger than the reigning action heroes, Stallone and Schwarzenegger, Roddy was in a good spot, demographically, to take the next step in his acting career. "He was in great shape and he looked good and everything was right," said Miller. But the next step collected dust. "We'd have a really good run with films, and then he'd go back and do wrestling and then we'd be back to square one with the films," said Miller, leaving Roddy unable to shake the wrestler-slash-actor label.

Miller thought Roddy was taking career advice from too many wrestling fans who wanted him to keep wrestling without concern for his best interests. But those people were frustrated that he wasn't finding roles with more established filmmakers, which in turn forced his lucrative returns to wrestling.

He loved to work and, rather than idly wait for the perfect project, he would take what was in front of him, like his guest spots on the TV show *Highlander* (filming his final scene with the star of the show, Adrian Paul, Roddy broke Paul's sword and badly cut the actor's finger—or as Roddy put it, "cut his finger off with a sword"). Most importantly, he couldn't forget what it was like as a kid to scramble for his next meal. Income, no matter the source, was a greater investment in his family's security than no income. Sometimes, it was as simple as that.

Bret Hart was right about Roddy's hip.

"What finished it was the match with Bret," Roddy said. "He came off that turnbuckle and I put my foot up. You can see me grab my hip."

The pain had become so intense that during the subsequent filming of a movie called *Marked Man* he needed to support the joint to be able to move properly on set. "I literally took white jock tape, tried to tape my leg to my body. The pain . . . un-fuckin'-believable."

In 1994, Roddy scheduled a titanium hip replacement. He allowed himself enough time for something more important to happen first. Kitty was pregnant with their fourth child. Falon was born December 1, giving Roddy a perfect record of attendance at his children's births. But he couldn't stay in Portland long. He had the surgery two days later in Los Angeles.

While Roddy was recovering in the hospital, two rehabilitation therapists entered his room, a younger and an older one. "One said, 'You're Roddy Piper. I hated you my whole life.'" The physiotherapist might have meant it as a compliment, but Roddy was in no mood. He grabbed his lunch plate and threw it toward the younger man's head. The plate continued out the door and crashed loudly in the hall. The physiotherapists got out of the room.

"The doctor comes in, 'What the fuck?' The guy came back in, the older guy, and I said, 'Hey, bud, let it go. Fuck it, come on.'"

Ground rules established, Roddy went ahead with his physio. It didn't last long. "I was the fastest guy ever to get out of a hospital."

For all of Roddy's strengths, his record for hiring personal assistants was questionable. Most were aspiring wrestlers for whom life with Roddy went more or less wrong. His assistant at the time joined him for the trip home—less than a week after the surgery.

"We're on first class Alaska Airlines, LA to Portland, Oregon, to get my ass home. I got the crutches, hips. He starts drinking." By the time the plane began its descent, the assistant was drunk enough to stand up and start pulling their bags out of the overhead compartment before they were on the ground.

"Sir, sir, sir . . ." The flight attendants begged him to close the compartment doors and sit down. Roddy grabbed his tie and pulled him into his seat.

Upon landing Roddy awkwardly took their bags and hobbled to an escalator himself. He was furious. The assistant followed. "He tumbled all the fuckin' way down to the bottom of the escalator. I'm so fuckin' mad. I get to the bottom, I got the crutch and I'm stabbing it in his fuckin neck. 'You stupid, fuckin' . . . Get up, you buffoon!'"

When Roddy realized someone was calling the police, he hobbled out the door of the Portland airport, hailed a cab and went home, leaving the assistant to sober up and find his own way to the house, nearly an hour outside the city.

Roddy was in his forties now, and apparently middle age looked good on him.

WWF president Gorilla Monsoon was getting over an injury, so Roddy was brought in as acting president (mostly just a reason for him to return to the fold for a while). When early in 1996 wrestler Razor Ramon (Scott Hall) got into a contract dispute with McMahon, Roddy stepped into his role in an upcoming storyline. The pending feud was an important one, as it was crucial to setting up WrestleMania XII. It started, as Roddy's feuds usually did, when he was in front of a microphone.

A younger wrestler named Goldust (Dustin Rhodes, son of wrestler Dusty Rhodes, working a gold-painted transvestite gimmick far more lascivious than anything wrestling had seen in a very long time) became smitten with Roddy's new-found authority. When Roddy refused his interest, Goldust slapped him in the ring. The feud was on, but its culmination at WrestleMania wasn't going to be a simple affair. Fans wouldn't even see the first half of the match live.

The Hollywood Backlot Brawl was exactly what it sounds like: a fight in a parking lot. Three weeks before WrestleMania, with a few dozen Disney employees watching, Roddy waited behind a building at the Disney Studios in Burbank, gripping a baseball bat. In jeans and a black leather jacket, he looked the picture of straight, red-blooded American self-assuredness. In fact, he was anything but sure on his feet. He'd recently broken both feet in multiple places while jumping off a lifeguard stand for a TV movie called *Daytona Beach*.

When Goldust pulled up in a gold-painted Cadillac, Roddy smashed its windows and dragged him out of the car. He landed a pair of audible punches to Rhodes's bleeding scalp and immediately flexed his right hand in pain. The second punch had broken a knuckle.

Goldust got the upper hand long enough to jump back in the car. He accelerated straight at Roddy. Standing in front of a dumpster with the bat, Roddy watched Goldust's eyes widen in disbelief. Roddy was supposed to be getting out of the way.

As the car slammed into the dumpster, he jumped just high enough to land on the Cadillac's hood. The Disney people looked on in shock. They couldn't imagine why Roddy had let himself get grazed by a car, but he was just returning a favour.

Before the shoot began, Roddy had handed six-year-old Colt off to a senior member of the WWF office who was on location. The executive walked the child to a chair in front of several monitors from which they could watch the proceedings together. The executive was Vince McMahon. For all the friction between him and Roddy, McMahon had offered to babysit. The wrestler returned the favour by taking a bump from a gold-painted Cadillac—an outrageous idea that Roddy knew full well would keep tongues wagging about the match for years.

Roddy rolled off the car. Goldust sped away. The titanium hip groaned from the impact. He climbed into a white Ford Bronco and tore away in pursuit. Using footage from the actual OJ Simpson highway chase—in which Simpson tore through Los Angeles in a white Bronco—WWF producers pieced together a chase scene that would appear on-screen at Arrowhead Pond in Anaheim during WrestleMania XII, followed seamlessly by Roddy chasing Goldust through the arena to finish the fight in the ring, without a referee. No one would know the parking lot scene had taken place nearly a month earlier.

After shooting the backlot scene, Roddy came up to Colt. "Hey, champ. How are you?" he asked. "Do you need a drink? Do you need anything?" Dripping blood, his own and Goldust's, with a broken hand and a throbbing hip, he was worried first and foremost about whether his son wanted a juice box.

The storyline of the match meant also shooting a scene in which the Bronco catches up to the Cadillac behind the Anaheim arena. Roddy had taken the extra hit for the match, but he took it easy on the Bronco. Instead of ramming the Cadillac straight on, he ran a corner of the front bumper along the Cadillac's length, doing more damage to the car than the truck. He liked the Bronco, and after WrestleMania was over he asked McMahon if he had any plans for it. He didn't. Roddy drove it home to Portland, where he'd treasure the clunker for years.

Because he also needed to wrestle Ramon's scheduled matches ahead of WrestleMania, Roddy didn't put his injured right hand in a cast. The impact had sunk the third knuckle a half inch below his others, which is where it stayed for the rest of his life.

The Backlot Brawl was one of the earliest appearances of that leather jacket, which over the years would become as much a part of Roddy's image as his kilt. The coat wasn't as it seemed. Lined with Kevlar, it weighed as much as a small child (when we were acting up he'd put it over our shoulders as a "favour," effectively immobilizing us). Ever nervous about getting stabbed, he was always relieved to have it on in public. Not only was it nearly impenetrable, it hid a multitude of zippered compartments—one for his money, his passport, his knife, his keys, his gun (back when he carried one). Living on the road, wrestlers knew the value of being able to get out of someplace quickly. With that jacket fully loaded, if worse came to worse he could throw it on and go.

After WrestleMania, Roddy went far afield to film a movie called *Last to Surrender*. Filming in Indonesia meant facing one of his least favourite things: snakes. In a dressing room, he'd once pulled a gun on Jake "The Snake" Roberts when Randy Savage told Jake that Roddy loved snakes and he should introduce Roddy to his python, Damien. When Roddy looked up to see the snake a foot away from his face, he jumped off his seat and grabbed his handgun out of his Halliburton. Roberts' python made many of the other wrestlers nervous as well, though it wasn't really big enough to harm most of those men. The same couldn't be said about the cobra Roddy met in Indonesia.

The shoot in Indonesia was all creatures and none of the creature comforts Roddy was accustomed to. He almost drowned in a scene shot in a river—a river filled with dead rats. At dinner one evening, someone brought a monkey. Roddy might have got a kick out of that one, if they hadn't stuck it through a hole in the middle of the table, cut off the top of its skull and started serving its brain. "I don't care how tough you are," he said when he got home, "no one wants to eat that!" He was also served a snake-based wine, which he was equally uninterested in consuming. For whatever reason, Roddy just hated snakes.

With political unrest causing riots across the country, his hotel had the brief distinction of being the second most bombed hotel in the world. He was so afraid that he'd die he faxed Kitty a hand-written will. But still, snakes worried him even more. He had a scene in which he's running and falls down and a cobra rises right in front of his face. He had to shoot the scene repeatedly because he kept jumping up so quickly the camera couldn't follow the expression on his face. "Roddy," the director shouted at him, "we need the reaction to the snake on camera."

Everybody wanted to challenge Roddy Piper. It was tough for Dad to go to restaurants or bars. Sometimes when he was in Portland he'd take Colt out, just to get out of the house for a bit. Colt would sip a root beer and they'd talk, and sometimes men would approach and pick fights. Roddy wouldn't fight in front of us. He'd let the aggressor yap and yell and even push. He'd quietly walk Colt out of the restaurant. Then, if the car wasn't close to the door, he'd pull it into the handicap spot. It wouldn't be there long. Before Roddy went back into the restaurant alone, he told Colt not to unlock the car door for anyone but him and to honk the horn if anyone bothered him.

Colt loved sitting in the front seat. He'd pretend to drive the car, turn on the seat warmers, change the radio station. He had no clue what his father was up to. Then Roddy would come hustling out of the restaurant, jump in and drive them away, leaving some corrected attitudes in his wake. Those tense situations from Roddy's private life might seem familiar to wrestling fans. They witnessed him caught in the same bind, once with much the same result.

In the late nineties, World Championship Wrestling (WCW) was stealing the WWF's lunch money by stealing its great personalities. WCW even resurrected wrestling's signature feud in the form of a running argument between Roddy and Hulk Hogan—their babyface/heel positions now reversed—over who was wrestling's greatest icon. McMahon hadn't been thrilled to see Roddy wrestle for a rival (the WWF's first real competition in over a decade), but he'd been on short-term contracts for so long now that McMahon had little recourse.

During a segment where Roddy brought Colt into the ring for a chance to experience his father's world from the inside, Hogan—accompanied by members of his gang, the NWO (New World Order)—crashed the happy moment. Surrounded by friends, he threatened to beat up Roddy in front of his son. The result was testament to just how well the two veterans could play together.

Compromised by his responsibility for his child, Roddy—the most determinedly old school of wrestlers—cleverly broke kayfabe in order to preserve it. "I'm not out here to do anything. Terry, I'm asking you from the bottom of my heart, don't do nuthin'. Just let me go home." Calling Hogan by his real name emphasized for the audience just how serious the situation was and how genuinely he wanted to get his son to safety. It appealed to a relationship fans had to presume existed behind the scenes, no matter the years of antagonism between the two stars. Colt snugged close against his father's hip.

Earlier in the day, Roddy had asked Colt, "Hey son, would you be comfortable going in the ring with me?" Excited, Colt agreed, but as the moment drew closer he got nervous, so Roddy sat him down. "Son, would I make you do anything where I thought you were going to get hurt?"

"No, sir."

"If you're scared, just get close to me. Okay?"

Colt got very close, very quickly. He had met Hogan once or twice in dressing rooms, but he hadn't talked to him that day. So he was not comfortable when Hogan started berating Roddy, forcing him to concede that, yes, Hogan was the real icon, even slapping him in the back of the head twice as Roddy gingerly led his son toward the ropes. Of course, Roddy talked Colt's way out of the situation without violence, then came back on Bischoff and Hogan with a leather belt and cleared the ring, setting up a future moment fans thought they might never see.

As for Colt, he didn't need kayfabe broken to think the matches were real. In another encounter, members of the NWO beat up Roddy and spray painted "nWo" on his thigh. We all bawled our eyes out watching it on television. We had just watched him go through four months of excruciating rehabilitation from the hip replacement.

Falon walked in on Roddy one morning after he'd returned on a red eye from a Friday spent wrestling for WCW. She wasn't usually allowed to watch wrestling on television but had somehow caught one storyline in which the NWO hit him over the head with a chair and spray-painted his back in silver paint. It upset her, but it was on television, it wasn't real, and the upset didn't last.

"I remember running into the room the next morning and he wasn't wearing a shirt and he was turned around looking out the window and he still had the spray paint all over his back. I broke down crying, because it clicked in my head that my dad was just beat up on TV."

Roddy hugged her and told her not to worry, he was "a box of fluffy ducks," as he liked to say to mean he was fine. "Don't worry, I'm tough," he assured our little sister.

At some point, Kitty had to make each of us stop watching wrestling.

After the confrontation in the ring, Hogan came by to shake Colt's hand and said, "Good job, champ."

Colt had done a good job outside the ring, too. At his father's direction (and possibly also his father's pre-arrangement) he negotiated his own appearance fee with the WCW office. When officials offered him a thousand dollars, he refused and asked for three thousand. He got it.

WCW had absorbed the old Mid-Atlantic Wrestling and turned Jim Crockett's Starrcade into its own premier annual event. It took place in December, far from McMahon's early spring WrestleMania. In the 1996 edition, Roddy Piper settled the old score once and for all. He caught "Hollywood" Hulk Hogan in a sleeper and won Starrcade's main event. During the bout, Hogan had put him in an abdominal stretch, which made Roddy's large hip-surgery scar fully visible to the cameras. Roddy had asked him to do that, and also to hike up his trunks to show it off clearly. At another moment, Roddy hopped around on that leg to further make an important point. Not McMahon nor any other promoter could ever cast doubt on Roddy's ability to wrestle on that titanium hip.

Before Roddy put the sleeper on Hogan, an imposing new member of the NWO had tried to interfere in the match, attacking Roddy and lifting him several feet off the mat for his signature chokeslam. The Giant was the biggest wrestler to hit the big time since Andre (in fact, Roddy escaped his grasp by dipping into his old giant-fighting toolkit, biting him on the nose to make him let go). Behind the scenes, the seven-foot rookie and the much smaller veteran had made fast friends.

"There's a story Big Show tells in front of God and everyone," said Roddy (The Giant would change his name to Big Show when later wrestling in the WWE). Big Show told us the story himself.

"I was green as grass. I was driving in on a Sunday night into Wisconsin and I got in really late." Tired from the road, he went to the hotel's front desk. The lady working the night shift said, "You're so big, I'm going to give you a suite." Grateful, he went up to the room. It was large and full of amenities. He went to the bathroom and splashed his face with cold water. "I was drying my face and I look and there's a leather jacket hanging on one of the chairs." Figuring a previous occupant had left the jacket, he dismissed it and went to the bedroom. As he opened the French doors he heard somebody snoring, "like the entire room was being sawed in half." On the nightstand was a bottle of NyQuil, and face-down on the bed, butt naked, was Roddy Piper.

Oh my God, he thought, *that's Roddy Piper. This is awkward.* They'd never met, but he'd grown up watching Roddy on television.

"So I quietly shut the doors, took my bags, meandered back downstairs. I said, 'I'm sorry, ma'am, but there's somebody in that room.'" She apologized and gave him another.

The next day he went to the WCW Nitro set and saw Roddy backstage.

"I think nobody understands what an incredibly nice guy he was all the time," said Show. "I mean so very humble, so very polite, and just set an example of what a superstar should be . . . the kindest, nicest person you could ever be around."

"Hi, I'm Roddy Piper," he said to the towering kid.

"I met you last night," said The Giant.

"You did?! When?" said Roddy, slapping his head in embarrassment for forgetting.

The Giant told him the whole story and Roddy smiled at him. "Ah, brother, you could have had me last night!"

"I remember thinking to myself as a young kid, about twenty-four years old, I go, 'Oh . . . whaaat?'" As The Giant settled into the business and got to know the habits of his fellow wrestlers, he realized what Roddy had meant. "I could have ribbed him to death. I could have stolen his jacket. I could have written all over him with a Sharpie."

Every time they saw each other for the next twenty years, Roddy would wag his finger at him and smile, "Brother, you could have had me!"

"As I got older in the business, there's no way in hell I would have ever ribbed Roddy Piper anyway," he said, because the payback "would have probably put me in therapy! You don't mess with the old-timers like that."

A middle-aged wrestler, now, the kind of star who used to beat him up many years ago, Roddy was instead winning fans among the new generation, even as he was losing the very first of the generation that raised him.

In 1997, Stanley Toombs was dying. Roddy went to BC to see him in the hospital. Roddy never forgot leaning over his father, who had wasted away to nothing from cancer. He never forgot how the tiny gold cross Roddy wore around his neck came to rest on his father's skin as Roddy leaned down to say goodbye. For all the tension between them, for all the pain they'd caused one another, Roddy respected the man who'd fought his way across Canada for the sake of his family. He never lost a fight, Roddy often said, and he'd had his fair share of them. Roddy learned from his father's unintended example to never lay his hands on his children in anger. He also learned that there was never an excuse to not provide. When he could afford it, Roddy paid off his parents' mortgage.

In October, after a long and brutal bout with the disease, Stanley succumbed to the inevitable. After his funeral, his ashes were spread in several different places. That his father had no gravesite troubled Roddy. He thought a family should have someplace to visit their father.

A week after the funeral, Roddy was back in the ring for WCW's Halloween Havoc, where he was fighting Hulk Hogan in a cage match. Roddy won, strictly speaking, but Randy Savage got involved before it was truly over. He jumped off the cage to drop his famous elbow on Roddy with the full force of his 240 pounds. He missed his mark and broke Roddy's ribs.

Just another night in paradise.

In the WCW, Diamond Dallas Page famously returned to the dressing room after his matches by hopping the ring-side barrier and walking right through the audience. After a match one night, he suggested Roddy join him. He didn't consider how many times Roddy had been targeted and stabbed by fans.

Roddy followed him through the crowd anyway, luckily without incident.

Fate had come for so many of his friends. If fate had its eye on him, he'd prefer that it take its shot sooner than later. He used to say that if someone threatened him, he'd never let the person walk away. There was no better way to confront fate than to wade right into a riled-up crowd of wrestling fans.

Roddy played with fate outside the ring as well. He was still driving the white Bronco from the Backlot Brawl, but Kitty wasn't fond of it. She had a new GMC Yukon Denali better suited to schlepping four kids around the countryside near Portland. Roddy liked the Denali as much as she liked the Bronco.

"I'm driving it and I got in one of my moods," said Roddy. "I'm going through a place called the Slough. It's a swamp on both sides. I just took a hard right with that Denali. It went off about ten feet in the air."

The SUV crashed through a stand of trees and splashed into the water. Roddy climbed out of the half-sunk truck and started swimming for shore. It took him a little time; he tended to underplay the debilitating effects of being in a car crash. "All of a sudden police are up there. 'You okay?!' 'Yeah, I'm fine. Thank you very much. I'll be fine.'" At first he couldn't imagine how police had discovered that he'd swamped the truck. "Damn thing had OnStar."

In 2000 he crashed another car only half a mile up the hill from home. Kitty was called by a neighbour who realized whose car was surrounded by police and paramedics. Falon was too young to leave behind, so Kitty took her with her to the scene. When they arrived, Roddy's bottom lip was nearly torn off. He didn't like wearing a seatbelt because it meant somebody telling him what to do. Independence came with a price that day.

"That was a horrifying experience to see," said Falon. "His face was ripped off. His lip was hanging."

It took extensive plastic surgery to put Roddy's bottom lip back in place. Unpleasant as the experience was, Falon had grown up with Roddy's sense of humour. "Forever after that, he and I would joke. I'd go up to him—'Ugh! Look at me!'—and pretend my lip was hanging off."

As Roddy's wrestling career wound down, he had the luxury of a little more time at home, which meant more time for his kids. Two weeks before baseball season, Roddy took Colt to a batting cage. Roddy had liked the game as a kid; Colt was eager to give it his best.

"Hop in there, son, you can do it." Roddy set the machine to throw fastballs.

To his father's delight, Colt connected on the first pitch. But it nicked his hand and really hurt. Roddy encouraged him to keep going. Of the twenty-five pitches he hit four. Not bad for a nine year old.

"My thumb really hurts, Dad."

The thumb was blue and swelling quickly.

"Ah, yeah, you mighta broke it."

Colt had to sit out the first half of the season. Kitty never let Roddy live it down. "Don't break his thumb this time, Roderick," she'd say, whenever Roddy took him somewhere.

Life with Roddy as a father could be rough, in an enjoyable way. That year Colt realized the upside of everything he'd learned from his dad—even when Dad was the reason he needed to know it.

In fifth grade the biggest kid in school decided something Roddy had done on television needed to be sorted out with Colt and confronted him. Bullies often gave Colt a hard time, but he could usually shrug them off. He'd never even been in a fight. That was about to change. When the kid pounced, Colt hip tossed him, and he landed him so hard on the ground he was stunned into silence. Colt's first fight was over as soon as it had begun. Strangely, before this he hadn't really connected what his father was teaching him on the basement mats with actual schoolyard scrapping.

"Colt," said Roddy that evening, when his son told him what had happened, "that's how you stand up for yourself." Violence was a last resort, Roddy taught him, which was maybe why all that mat work had seemed like just abstract exercise. A gentleman might have violence in his playbook, but he avoided using it. He should speak, and speak well. "Cussing is for the illiterate, it's for the dumb man," Roddy lectured. "It's the dumb man's weapon. Smart men talk."

After dinner, Roddy took Colt out and they talked over ice cream.

Being on the road as many as three hundred days a year meant home had to run smoothly without Roddy around. Our mother managed that so well that when he did have time at home he could spend it making up for his absence. He used it to bond with us the way wrestlers usually bonded—practical jokes. Late one night when Ariel was in her teens, she walked home along a mountainside road after spending the evening at a neighbour's house. She passed a deer in the pitch black without seeing it until the last second and was still jittery as she made her way up our long driveway. As she passed the cars parked outside, three figures wearing ski masks raced at her out of the dark. She screamed. She screamed as loud as she could for ten seconds or maybe longer. Long enough, anyway, that her father and brother and his friend were rolling on the ground laughing by the time she stopped.

A few years later, Roddy took Ariel to Las Vegas for the annual gathering of Cauliflower Alley Club, a get-together of professional wrestling alumni where retirees and veterans of the business celebrate their peers and accomplishments—and eat and drink for a few days like they're back on the road in their prime, tearing up every highway from Raleigh to Roseburg, Orlando to Oshawa. Still a teenager, Ariel hadn't often been out of Oregon. It was time, Roddy thought, that she experienced a bit of the luxury to which he was accustomed.

When they got to their hotel room, she asked what the second porcelain fixture was in the bathroom. He said he didn't know; maybe she should turn it on to see what it does. To his teary-eyed delight, the bidet soaked her to the bone.

Being the fun parent was a break from the stresses of work and the ghosts that lingered in the back of Roddy's mind, but there were moments of frustration and anger when the strength of his own hands was hard to restrain.

We were forbidden to be disrespectful to our mother, and when he thought we had broken that rule he'd call us kids to the table for a blistering talking-to. The power of our father's voice froze us in our seats, but his lectures could wander away on tangents. We'd become petrified that he'd ask one of us a question, because we couldn't always follow what he was angry about. He did punch a hole in a wall, once, and pulled a bedroom door off its hinges when one of us kept locking it. These might not be extraordinary events in the life of the average American family. But there's one other moment that stands out in memory, something most dads couldn't do.

When Roddy came home from wrestling trips, he often went straight to bed to sleep and recover. When he emerged, sometimes days later, he was usually the playful father we've described. There were days, though, when all that butting heads with wrestling promoters and trying to figure out Hollywood producers weighed on him. He got up one day and sat down with us at the kitchen table, cranky for some reason he didn't explain. We were goofing off and arguing, and we could see the annoyance creeping into his face. He raised his arms and slammed them onto the table. It broke.

We froze and stared at him for a long moment. He looked back at us, just as shocked. Like the proverbial bull in a china shop, a wrestler in a family home could do a lot of damage if he wasn't careful. "Well that was extreme," someone said, and we all just started laughing, Roddy included.

Kitty didn't replace the table right away. Roddy's place at the table was the sharp, jagged end, a reminder of how careful he needed to be.

These moments were blips, though. Affection was the norm with Roddy. No matter how old we got, he'd take our calls anywhere short of on a stage or in a ring. He hugged us every chance he could. What could be more reassuring for a man who spent his working life pressing his face into the enormous biceps of his friends and enemies than wrapping his own big arms around the people he loved? Our heads got petted, our hands were held. It was embarrassing in high school, but we loved his affection.

Hug your kids, he urged his friends and people he met. Because you never knew when it might be your last chance to tell them you love them.

Roddy and Bret Hart used to call it shining the batlight. When one of them wanted to talk to one of the few people in the world who would understand the anxieties of their business and lifestyle, he sent up the signal. When Hart won the world title, Roddy was the first person he called. Roddy reminded him that every guy in the dressing room—good guys though they may be—wanted what Bret had. That was treasured counsel.

In 2002, Hart couldn't send up the batlight. He suddenly couldn't do much of anything. While riding his bike home from the gym in Calgary, he suffered a massive stroke. A local wrestler visited regularly, but otherwise Hart saw only one of his WWE peers while recovering at the hospital. And it was a major recovery effort. "I lost everything on my left side," said Hart. "Right from the top of my head. It just cut my whole body in half, like a chain saw. My whole left side was dead." Within a week of the accident, Roddy showed up. Bret was in a wheelchair, and he was already sick of it.

"I burst into tears. I couldn't live like that," recalled Hart. "When I saw Roddy, I was pretty fed up with that wheelchair. 'I don't care what happens, I gotta get out of this wheelchair. . . .' We talked about that. It was pretty emotional for me to tell him, show him, the heartache that I was feeling from my stroke and how devastating it was. . . . Through that whole time he was a big source of comfort and inspiration."

"You can beat this, cuz," Roddy told him. "Don't quit."

Roddy had called Bret "cuz" since they figured out they might be cousins. Generations back, the Harts were related to a family with Roddy's last name in the northwestern States, but the name turned out to be spelled "Tombs," not "Toombs." Roddy liked the thought of Bret and Owen being his cousins, regardless, and continued using the nickname. (Given how inconsistently family names were spelled in the 1800s, they might have been related after all.)

"He gave me all kinds of support that I never got from anybody else," said Hart.

Bret was down, but he wasn't going out. Still, the reminders of a wrestler's mortality were constant.

Roddy was in the passenger seat of a Volkswagen Jetta, an assistant's car. He was thinking about the book he was working on, telling the story of his life. He'd never met the writer. There had just been many phone calls, stories being shared, opinions being given. They were a long way from finished.

Driving through LA, he and this personal assistant weren't getting along. They approached an underpass. "Should I hit it?" the assistant asked. Roddy thought he meant the gas. "Yeah, hit it," he said. The car swerved hard off the road. They collided with the concrete wall. The passenger side took the brunt of the damage.

When the dust settled, Roddy took stock. "My foot literally went through the floor to the cement," he recalled. By the time police showed up at the scene, he was leaning against a telephone pole. He couldn't stand on one foot and a pain in his gut made it hard to stand at all. Emergency crews got the driver out of the car and into an ambulance. Roddy leaned against the pole and watched. A tow truck came and collected the wrecked Jetta. He asked the police for help getting home, but with no visible injuries suggesting how badly he was hurt, the police told him sorry, but we're not a taxi service.

He finally hailed a cab and got himself the two miles back to the Oakwood Apartments, where he was staying. The cab driver went inside and asked an assistant in the apartment to come out and help collect Roddy. Roddy had been injured before, so he fell back on the tried and true.

"I said something like, 'Leave me alone. I'm going to take a shower.' They fix everything, right?" he said. He couldn't remember much about the accident or the hours after. But he remembered that once he got in the shower, standing on one foot, he couldn't compartmentalize the pain.

"Hey, hey!" he shouted from the bathroom. "I'm going down!"

The assistant at the apartment called 911. Another celebrity passing out in the bathtub didn't inspire much hustle in Hollywood paramedics. They came in and took his blood pressure. Then everything changed. He was 60 over 20. He was going down all right. The paramedics rushed him to Cedars-Sinai hospital.

"I died on the table," said Roddy. It would be days before he was fully aware of what was happening. Mitch Ackerman snuck into his room. They had a conversation, but Roddy was in and out of consciousness. He didn't remember the visit. The tally of injuries, though, was burned into memory. "It busted my right ankle, four ribs. One rib went into my liver, my spleen and my back in two places."

You can see why we thought he was invincible.

The book, to be called *In the Pit with Piper*, was finished while Roddy recovered. It adhered closely to Roddy's kayfabe version of his early life. When it was published in the fall of 2002, he bought Colt a PlayStation so he could join him on the promotional tour bus. "I did a hundred and seven pieces of media in thirty towns in twenty-five days," said Roddy. By the time he went home, he was ashen from the effort, coming as it did so quickly on the heels of his injuries. "They said I was grey."

Much of that book focussed on something Roddy called "the Sickness." The term referred to a state of mind in which wrestlers' sense of self became unhealthily consumed by their comfort with violence and pain, and by the belief that the show must go on at any cost—costs to themselves and those around them. Fuelled by drugs, alcohol and the relentless pressure of the "P," the Sickness was fatal for many wrestlers. Roddy replaced the Hot Rod shirt he'd made iconic back in 1986 with one that said "Frats"—a reference to the fraternity brothers (wrestlers) who had died from the Sickness.

A list on the back of the shirt named ten wrestlers who'd died before their time: Art Barr, Rick Rude, Brian Pillman, Rick McGraw, Adrian Adonis, Andre, Owen, Kerry Von Erich, Bruiser Brody, Junkyard Dog. "Owen" was Owen Hart, who fell to his death while being lowered from the rafters above the ring in Kansas City, Missouri. The book lists even more, including Dino Bravo, Jay York, three more Von Erich brothers—David, Mike and Chris—and Wahoo McDaniel.

Roddy also abandoned the custom tartan and started wearing a solid-black kilt in commemoration of these men and all wrestlers who'd suffered from the outsized expectations placed on them. He had entered a dark phase, into which he gave some insight during an HBO Real Sports interview in 2003.

"Tuinals, Seconals, Tylenol 4, Demerol, testosterone, Placidyls, Valium. You get this going and then you start drinking alcohol. Deadly combination. You bring cocaine into the picture. Does a line. It's time to fight. No downers there. But it would be nice to have a little painkiller in you as you go in. Or a lot." When a wrestler with this chemical stew in his veins came out of the ring after a show, his head still full with the roar of ten thousand fans cheering or jeering him, trouble was inevitable. Why then did he keep returning to the ring? "What would you have me do at forty-nine when my pension plan I can't take out 'til I'm sixty-five? I'm not going to make sixty-five, let's just face facts, guys. . . . Everybody's dead. They're all dying early. And nobody cares about it."

HBO hadn't yet aired the interview when Bruce Prichard was discussing the lineup of WrestleMania XIX with Vince McMahon. McMahon—an amateur bodybuilder—had begun wrestling some of his stars as a heel, the ultimate corporate villain. At WrestleMania in Seattle, he was scheduled to wrestle Hulk Hogan in a "street fight."

"He was on the outs at the time," said Prichard of Roddy, "and I remember talking to Vince going, 'You know, he's sitting at home, he's not dealing with anybody right now.' What a kick, what a surprise if you put that son of a bitch out there in the middle, with Vince and Hogan." McMahon agreed and Prichard called Roddy at home in Portland, a short drive from Seattle. His insinuation into the storyline was a secret. Fans and staff expected to see him backstage, signing autographs with some of the other retired stars. "Even when he was in the locker room, people just thought he was there to do an appearance or something. It never got out."

While McMahon and Hogan were fighting a match with more colour in it than Roddy and Bret Hart had produced (pro wrestling had changed, favouring the "hardcore" blood-and-guts approach), Prichard walked Roddy down the aisle in a big hat, long wig and black trench coat. Roddy was well enough hidden that a security guard tried to stop them. They hid under a camera position and waited until McMahon had brought a metal pipe into the ring. Roddy climbed through the ropes, tore off his disguise and went after the pair, kicking McMahon onto his face while calling him "Junior!"—a shot he never stopped taking at the son of the promotion's founder—and clubbing Hogan with the pipe. The crowd popped. Who came more naturally between Hogan and McMahon than Rowdy Roddy Piper?

In the weeks that followed, that bottomless feud resurrected itself with Hogan appearing in a mask as Mr. America. It ended quickly, because that HBO special finally aired.

"They released the damn thing," said Prichard. "I guess it was the first time Vince had heard it, even though I know Roddy had told us about it ahead of time. They had their disagreement, and it was all *my* fault, because I had brought him in!"

McMahon already knew Roddy wasn't happy. In an interview with Vince, HBO reiterated Roddy's claims about the promoter's unreasonable demands on wrestlers. McMahon pointed out Roddy's enduring anti-promoter attitude and summed up their relationship, in a way that said everything about how he had managed Roddy's push to his own pull for so many years: "That's okay. I don't mind being who I am and I guess he doesn't mind being who he is."

Roddy was out again. This time from the WWE—the mighty World Wrestling Federation had been bent to the breaking point by the fallout from the steroid trials (McMahon was himself put on trial in 1994 for peddling steroids to his talent; he was acquitted of all charges). It was time to fess up to pro wrestling's worst kept-secret, that it was all work. McMahon's promotion was now called World Wrestling Entertainment.

Colt spent a lot of time on the mats in our basement, learning how to grapple, box and stretch. Roddy's assistants, who were usually wrestlers, often joined in, giving Colt, who wasn't as tall as Roddy, experience wrestling with bigger bodies. Then, in 2003, during his freshman year at high school, Colt went to LA to train with the one man Roddy always said he'd never want to fight.

In his seventies, Gene LeBell didn't like to take a bump while training students; even a controlled fall on the mats left him aching for days. His reluctance was simply a matter of age. So while training Colt, LeBell took the lead and Roddy subbed in as his son's sparring partner.

Colt won a number of martial arts tournaments through high school, but it was later, on the road in Chicago, sitting in the sauna with Roddy after one of their early-morning workouts, that Roddy asked if he'd ever considered becoming a professional fighter. Not many people come out of high school with the kind of training in any discipline that Colt had received in martial arts. Colt knew he didn't want to live our father's nomadic existence as a professional wrestler, but there were options now beyond grinding through the territories. The conversation stuck with him. And then he did something about it.

"Oh, God. I'm gonna die." Colt had never been so scared in his life. He'd been cleaning mats, getting stretched and beaten up for years in preparation to fight competitively. He was thinking he probably should have gone to college instead.

With Roddy pacing nearby, Colt was waiting for his first amateur MMA (mixed martial arts) fight. He was seventeen years old. His opponent was a thirty-year-old firefighter from New York City. Roddy was trying to keep him calm without intruding too much on his experience. Colt had paid his dues. He deserved his own time in the spotlight.

"Okay, kid, get out there," came the order. Colt was making his way to the ring when the announcer introduced him as the son of Rowdy Roddy Piper. He didn't even say Colt's name. His heart sank.

Like the fight Roddy always referred to as his own first, Colt's first bout was short. He scored a technical knockout in forty-seven seconds. Proud as Roddy was, he was incensed that the announcer hadn't called Colt by name and gave him hell afterward.

Roddy spent most of Colt's MMA fights in the audience, but he didn't always stay there. He rushed the corner, pushing past security, to stand with Colt's coach. Sometimes he shouted from the audience in a voice that couldn't be mistaken. Well back from the ring, he yelled one night, "Knee him!" Afterward, Colt listened to the audio from the fight but couldn't hear Roddy on it. He asked Roddy if he'd imagined it. No, said Roddy, he'd really yelled it. Colt had done what Roddy said and won the fight.

When two men fight each other, bleed on each other, break each other down to a point that would make most men cry, a rare bond results. It was also a familiar one to Roddy. It was one of the only places where he felt truly comfortable with others—and it pleased him to no end to share that hallowed ground with his son.

With the help of manager Freya Miller, the UK was continuing its crush on Roddy Piper. In 2005 ITV invited him to co-host a British reality show called *Celebrity Wrestling*, on which chefs, rugby stars and actors were pitted against one another in a series of competitions. Roddy flew to England and brought Len Denton with him as an assistant. "The Grappler" knew as much about wrestling as anyone, and Roddy liked to have a trusted friend for company.

On their first day, they walked down the studio hall to Roddy's dressing room. A sign with Roddy's name hung on the door.

"Look at that, brother!" said Denton. They also found fresh fruit and flowers inside. A veteran of the old territories, Denton wasn't used to this kind of treatment.

"Lenny, you see that sign?" said Roddy. "You see this food and these flowers and all this pretty stuff? When we do the last shoot and we come back, that sign will be gone and there won't be one flower in this room or any food."

"Come on," said Denton. He figured Roddy was kidding.

MMA star Ian Freeman was the show's referee. American D'Lo Brown and Canadian Joe Legend trained the competing teams; but you didn't have Roddy Piper and The Grappler in the building and not ask their advice. They weren't sure how to advise the competitors, though.

"They came up with these crazy games," said Roddy. "They had poles with big humps on the end of them. And they just beat each other like Fred Flintstone and Barney Rubble."

Denton gave the only piece of advice he knew to be universal. "Hit him harder!"

As filming continued, Roddy's voice started to give out, so he drank tea with honey. Denton was happy to make him a cup when asked, until something occurred to him.

"Listen, does your throat hurt or do you just like the drink?" he asked Roddy. "'Cause if you just like the drink, get your ass up and go get it!"

Lunch was difficult because the celebrities wouldn't leave Roddy alone to eat, so they started taking their lunch in the dressing room. Roddy needed the downtime.

A young man came to the room to take their lunch order.

"And for dessert, what would you like?" he asked.

"What do you have?" asked Denton.

"Well, we have spotted dick."

Denton was a Texan. He had never heard of spotted dick, and he sure didn't like a wise guy, especially one with a fancy accent.

"Hey, asshole! What'd you say? You trying to be a smart ass, boy?"

Roddy had to intervene and keep his old buddy from teaching the kid American manners.

Celebrity Wrestling didn't do well. Wrestling fans wondered where the wrestling was. So the show was moved from its Saturday night primetime slot to Sunday morning.

"Loads of accidents happened," explained Miller. A chef broke his arm. "So that got cancelled."

After the final shoot Roddy and Len headed back to the dressing room to clean up and collect their things.

"We're walking down the hall and I look up," said Denton, "and the sign's gone."

Fame's hard finishes struck Denton as a slap in the face, but Roddy didn't let it bother him. By his count, he'd wrestled nearly ten thousand matches. There was always the hope and promise of another dressing room, another entrance, one more crowd wanting to say thank you.

10
Finish

In 1982, Georgia Championship Wrestling commentator Gordon Solie went deep on the character of Roddy Piper, this wild young wrestler who'd arrived on the east coast from the west, blowing up wrestling rings wherever he went.

"I thought it might be interesting to try and get a look at this man, and try and find out what does make Roddy Piper tick," said Solie. "Piper is a totally unpredictable competitor . . . a man who issues pain like you would a traffic summons. He appears to be totally and completely fearless. He doesn't worry about his physical health at all. He also has the capability of forgetting about law and order, of taking it into his own hands. . . . The man is such a series of interesting conflicts, and I can't help think that he has a lot of conflict within himself. Be it because of his environmental background or what, I don't know, but he is a man of many inner conflicts, I do know that. . . . Such an enigma in his own way."

Around the time he turned fifty, Roddy began to wonder about some of these same conflicts himself. He'd outlived many of his friends and peers. (In 2003, "Mr. Perfect" Curt Hennig died at forty-four from a drug overdose. "Big Boss Man" Ray Traylor Jr. died in 2004 of a heart attack, aged forty-one.) Roddy had raised the bar for his profession and also for wrestlers looking to branch out into acting careers. (By 2005, wrestler Dwayne "The Rock" Johnson had starred in a big-budget sequel and spin-off of the box-office hit *The Mummy*.) Roddy had worked non-stop for thirty-two years. He was still working hard. He'd spoken out about the business and his place in it, but he'd never stopped to take stock of who he really was and where he'd come from. A special event in 2005 marked the beginning of a more reflective period. He'd play down what the honour meant to him, but Roddy was proud to be inducted into the WWE Hall of Fame, along with several of his greatest peers from the eighties: the Iron Sheik and Nikolai Volkoff, Paul Orndorff, Jimmy Hart, Bob Orton and Hulk Hogan. He knew his acceptance speech at the ceremony in Los Angeles would be remembered, for better or worse, so he enlisted the help of Barry Kolin, or "Coach," as Roddy called him. Kolin owned the Portland comedy club Harvey's. A mutual friend in Portland had introduced them a few years earlier, when Roddy expressed interest in developing a stand-up comedy routine.

"I've got some stories I've told. I've taped them at home in my basement," Roddy had told Kolin. "Would you take a look at it and tell me what you think?" Kolin did and he was impressed with the stories, but Roddy's delivery was so scattered they fell flat. Kolin read Roddy's book and realized the stories—Victor the Bear, Andre the Giant staring down cops in small town bars—were potentially a comedic goldmine.

Roddy took a few test runs at Harvey's, but he wasn't getting over by telling jokes. It was his incredible warehouse of stories that was making audiences laugh. The stories worked, as did another resource that had made his foray into film so memorable. Kolin said, "He's got his stock lines. 'Hey Piper, what's under your kilt?' [Answer:] 'Your girlfriend's lipstick, asshole.' They were good. I said, 'We'll put those in your show. I love those.'"

And now "Coach" helped polish that stock of one-liners for Roddy's Hall of Fame induction speech. Kolin sat down with him and they put together the speech Roddy delivered that night, with all of us and our mother sitting near the front, beside Hogan's kids. Ric Flair introduced Roddy and then handed over the stage. Hogan was the target of a few gentle zingers in that speech, though Roddy made more pokes at himself:

"I gotta admit, I was jealous of Hogan. It had nothing to do with the hair. However, I would listen to him, because I would train just as hard . . . I would listen to his interviews and he would say, 'Say your prayers and take your vitamins.' And folks, I took some serious vitamins. Never got them twenty-four-inch pythons."

It was how he ended his speech, though, that pointed to the unceasing drive that would push him through the final decade of his story. "I guarantee you this, my name is Rowdy Roddy Piper, and you ain't seen nothing yet!"

Aside from a few special appearances, Roddy hadn't wrestled much in the five years leading up to his Hall of Fame induction. And it was around this time that he also ended his career as a small-business owner. Piper's Pit Stop had been keeping Portland's transmissions operating smoothly for fourteen years and, as

Len Denton was proud to tell, the owners had paid off the initial investment in half the time. But Denton had seen enough car parts, and it was time to move on.

"The place is sold," recounted Denton. "So they issued a cheque to Roddy's accountant." He and Roddy were in Toronto at the time at a fan convention, where Denton was assisting Roddy. "Roddy goes, 'Listen to this, Lenny.'" He held up the phone in their hotel room as she confirmed the amount received. Then she mentioned the cheque was in Roddy's name alone. Legally, Denton wasn't entitled to a dime.

Roddy wasn't working as much as he used to, and he wasn't as flush as he once was. Without hesitation, he told her to send a cheque for half the money to Denton's house that same day.

"That's the kind of guy Roddy was. He wanted me to hear it," said Denton. "It was a handshake. That don't happen no more, I don't believe."

At the convention, which took place on the playing field of the Rogers Centre, home of the Toronto Blue Jays, Roddy was due to spend three days signing autographs and having his picture taken with fans. Old friend and former NHLer Cam Connor flew into town to help out.

"Well, I didn't know who Cam Connor was," said Denton. "He comes in the room. Roddy's in the shower. He said, 'Yeah, Rod's a school friend of mine.' That's all I knew. I didn't know he played for the Rangers.

"So he comes walking in the room and both his knees are torn. I said, 'What the hell happened to you?'"

Connor had got cut off in the parking lot and the other driver had given him the finger. Then, Connor explained, he and the driver got out of their cards and had a chat about the incident.

Damn, thought Denton. *He's my age!*

They'd been sitting in the room talking for five minutes before Denton noticed Connor's Stanley Cup ring.

"Hey, where'd you get that ring?" he asked, doubting Connor could have really won a professional hockey championship.

"What do you mean, where'd I get that ring? I won it," replied Cam.

"You ain't won no Stanley Cup ring!" said Denton, as offended by what he presumed to be a lie as Connor was by Denton's disbelief.

"What'd you say?!" said Connor.

"Roddy had to come out and break us up," recalled Denton. "'Stop, assholes!' First time I ever met Cam, almost got in a fight. 'Quiet down, quit screaming at each other. This is a real Stanley Cup ring!'" Connor and Denton's tempers dropped quickly after Roddy's intervention and they had a good laugh. It was the beginning of another friendship.

Denton continued working with Roddy, selling merchandise and generally assisting while he was on the road. After a week at a similar convention in LA, they were preparing to go to England when Denton received an unexpected call in his hotel room. His daughter was pregnant, and when her water broke she wouldn't be consoled until she knew her father was on his way home.

"I packed my bags and I went down and I knocked on Roddy's door and he goes, 'What are you doing? Are you leaving?!'" Apologetically, Denton explained why he couldn't continue on the trip. Roddy looked at him for a moment. "He goes, 'You know what, Lenny, brother? Family comes first. Go see your grandbaby be born.' Gave me a big hug and says, 'God bless you. Get your ass outta here, boy.' That's the kind of guy Roddy was."

The other kind of guy Roddy was, was a wrestler. And when

an opportunity arose for him to get in the ring again, he was hard-pressed not to answer the bell.

Before WWE's annual Cyber Sunday event in November 2006, fans had voted online for who would join Ric Flair as his tag-team partner against members of the Spirit Squad to contend for the championship. Dusty Rhodes, Sgt. Slaughter and Roddy were their options. Roddy was declared the winner, receiving just under half of the announced fourteen million votes cast from around the world. He climbed in the ring and won the title with Flair. That night in Cincinnati began a short reign—one that in a weird twist of fate saved Roddy's life.

Winning this championship meant hitting the road to defend it. Roddy was fifty-two years old. His physical conditioning had slipped. But he was with an old friend, and some other good company, each familiar in their way. The night after they won the title, Roddy and Flair travelled up Highway 71 to Columbus where they wrestled Edge, a young Canadian, and Randy Orton, the son of Roddy's old bodyguard, "Ace." From Ohio, they went to the UK, where Roddy and Flair defended their belts in Glasgow.

Roddy Piper in Glasgow, his professed hometown, was a special opportunity. The intense rivalry between Glasgow's two soccer teams, Celtic and Rangers, reflected the city's troubled history of Catholic-Protestant antagonism. Roddy decided to bring a little unity to the Old Firm, as the rivalry is collectively called. He hiked down to the ring wearing two scarves: one was Rangers red, white and blue, and the other Celtic green and white. When he joined Flair in the ring, Flair shed his usual sequined robe to reveal he was wearing a kilt, too. If ever there was a moment when Roddy proved he was as adept a babyface as he was a heel, this was it. They were joined by the Highlanders to wrestle the full complement of Spirit Squad in a four-man tag match. The crowd was manic.

Wrestling hurt. A dull pain in Roddy's back grew sharper and more intense every night after Glasgow. As they worked their way through packed houses in England, he could barely stand up straight. His ability to compartmentalize pain had astonished friends and colleagues for decades, and he made a good show of each match on the tour. But as they pulled into Manchester, he couldn't rally himself past the agony. He had to back out of the match.

Adam Copeland had grown up near Toronto in the eighties as a Roddy Piper fan. As "Edge," Copeland, in his early thirties, was in the prime of his pro wrestling career in 2006 and would go on to set records for the number of times he held certain titles. That morning he and Randy Orton got the word: they were taking the belts that night. Roddy couldn't wrestle—but he also couldn't leave town without a fight.

Edge had enjoyed seeing the veterans wear the belts. It had been a long time since men in their fifties had enjoyed such high stature in professional wrestling. He was surprised they didn't run with the title for longer than the two weeks since they'd been crowned. He was told Roddy was hurt, but he hadn't noticed him complaining or showing any sign that he was injured. He and Orton knew the work would be delicate, because whatever was bothering Roddy had to be serious. Wrestlers didn't drop out of a tour unless they were in real danger.

"Roddy felt comfortable with us," said Edge. "He knew we wouldn't do anything stupid to put him in jeopardy."

"I completely trust you guys," Roddy told them before the match. "I know I'm in good hands."

"When someone who's injured, especially at that stature and at that point in their career, says they'll be okay with you," said

Edge, "it's pretty much the biggest tip of the hat you can get."

That night, when Roddy was announced, Edge and Orton (collectively, "Rated-RKO") were waiting for him in the ring. As Roddy neared, they jumped off the mat and surrounded him on the floor. A few quick blows followed, including one with a chair from Edge into the back of Roddy's thigh.

"I remember specifically trying to stay away from his upper body," said Edge. How, then, to take Roddy down? They had to make some form of contact without getting close to his injured back. The blow to the leg knocked him to the ground and then it was all up to the boots. Flair fought the match alone—and lost—while Roddy was helped back to the dressing room.

Later Edge and Orton caught up with Roddy behind the scenes.

"My first concern was, is he okay? Especially when you know going in that somebody's dinged up," said Edge, "your first stop is to check and make sure everything's good."

"Nah, you guys you took care of me," said Roddy, "Thank you. I love you."

"He was super gracious," said Edge. "You hear 'I love you' from Roddy Piper and your heart just goes, 'Aw, man . . .'"

Roddy said he was going home, but Edge had a job to do first. He and wrestler Tommy Dreamer snuck into the props collection, pried the nameplate off Roddy's belt and gave it to him.

Without treatment, Roddy flew back to Portland, where he went to St. Vincent hospital. A surgeon noticed him in the ER waiting room. He asked the registration nurse why Roddy Piper was there. Something more than Roddy's celebrity had caught the doctor's eye, and he had Roddy brought in immediately. An MRI revealed just how close Roddy had come to permanent damage.

Three pieces of bone had broken away from a fracture high in Roddy's spine. The fragments were so close to his spinal cord that they were threating paralysis. One hard bump in the ring from the wrong direction and he could have spent the rest of his life in a wheelchair—and the rest of his life could have been very short. While Roddy was on the operating table, the surgeon noticed an odd-looking lymph node. He ordered tests. The results came back: non-Hodgkin lymphoma. Roddy had cancer.

There was no telling when the initial fracture had happened. Roddy's high pain threshold meant he could have been putting up with the fracture for weeks. Getting back in the ring either caused it or made it worse, pushing those chips inward and turning the dull constant ache into pain he couldn't ignore. Had his fans not voted for him, getting him into the ring again, the cancer would have gone unnoticed much longer, maybe long enough to spread beyond the reach of treatment.

Ariel, twenty one at the time, flew to Portland from her new home in Los Angeles. Her siblings were at the hospital already, visiting their maternal great-grandmother, who was on another floor with a bad flu that at her advanced age was very dangerous. Kitty ushered Ariel straight in to see her ailing grandmother. Within moments she died. Shocked at the suddenness of her passing, they all went upstairs to their father's room. He had something he wanted to tell them. The timing couldn't have been worse, but it couldn't be avoided. He told them about the cancer.

Colt, seventeen, looked at his father. "No, you can beat this, Dad," he said. "This is nothing."

A tear welled in his father's eye. Roddy looked at his son, then at all the members of his family. "Yes, we will, champ."

Over the months to come the disease would barely slow the patient down, and it was yet another Canadian who kept him busy.

An ex-pat Canadian named Noelle Kim worked in the office for Gene LeBell. She'd gotten to know Roddy because Gene talked to everyone on speakerphone, and she and whoever else was around would get drawn into his calls. Being more aware of the online world than her boss and his cohort, she was on an MMA message board one day when someone opined that wrestlers weren't really tough. She used Roddy as an example to prove him wrong, and he replied by asking what level belt he had. She'd been told he'd gotten his black belt from Gene, so she asked Gene over her shoulder when he'd awarded it to Roddy. Unsure, he hit autodial and got Roddy on the phone.

"When did I give you a black belt?" LeBell asked.

Roddy didn't answer for a moment. "Either you choked me out too many times or I really have lost my mind," he finally answered, "but I didn't know I was a black belt with you, Gene."

"That's terrible!" said LeBell. "I've been telling people for years you're a black belt with me."

Kim started writing up the diploma then and there. She had a background in television (she started as the matchmaker on *The Dating Game*) and in talent management. As she got to know Roddy, she began noticing roles in the theatrical breakdowns—a sort of industry news wire that shares descriptions of upcoming projects—that she thought suited him. Kim knew his wrestling, of course, but admired him primarily as an actor. So she started sending him parts she thought he should audition for, only to realize that no one else was doing this in North America. Roddy said if she could find him roles, he'd make sure she got a management cut. On that informal arrangement, Roddy had the American film-and-television agent he'd always needed—keen, connected and utterly convinced that his potential as an actor had barely been tapped.

In 2007, while Roddy recovered from his spinal fracture and surgery, and radiation treatment for his lymphoma, he remained eager to work. He loved acting in particular and didn't want to slow down any more than he needed.

For four months after the surgery, Colt remained glued to his father's side. He drove him to the hospital every Monday for his treatment and waited beside the radiation booth. Roddy would emerge, groggy and weak, grateful for the shoulder to lean on—more grateful yet that it belonged to his son. He'd be on his feet by Tuesday morning, when they'd fly to wherever he was shooting or doing a "Piper's Pit," then fly home Sunday. Monday the routine would start all over again. They also had a morning ritual of getting up early and going to the gym before the workday got started. Roddy took only two weeks off work once his treatments began and he kept up his gym schedule, too.

After the months of treatment and then a year-long wait to ensure the cancer was in remission, father and son celebrated with root beer floats and filet mignon.

"We did it," said Roddy.

Colt was proud to have helped. His days of celebrating with root beer floats, however, were just about done.

In 2008 Roddy found himself back in a Winnipeg bar. He had one more day of shooting a film in town and he and Colt settled in for a relaxing evening at the Viking Inn. They played pool with the locals, talked to fans and thoroughly enjoyed themselves.

At around eleven, they climbed into their car. Colt had been making good use of the lower drinking age in Manitoba, but Roddy was sober because he had to work in the morning so he took the wheel. The rental was a two-seater sports car, and he hadn't had a chance to open it up. His belief that rentals were essentially disposable hadn't much changed since the mid-80s, back when New Jersey rental companies had stopped renting to wrestlers. On the way back to their hotel, Roddy stepped on the gas. Hard. The needle soared past the speed limit. They saw no other cars on the road, so when they pulled into the hotel parking lot he was surprised to see red lights flashing behind them.

"Sir, have you had anything to drink tonight?" asked a police officer.

"No sir, I haven't," said Roddy.

"You were speeding back there, you know that?"

"I'm just real tired and trying to get home in a hurry."

He looked at Roddy for a moment. "Sir, are you Rowdy Roddy Piper?"

"Yes, sir, I am."

"Do you realize you were going over a hundred kilometres an hour?"

"Yes, I do."

"Do you realize you blew through about a dozen stop signs?"

That one got Roddy's attention.

"I did not know that," he said. "I apologize, sir. I did not see a single stop sign."

"You were probably going too fast to see them."

The officer decided to forego a ticket in favour of a picture and an autograph.

As the police car pulled away a guy was watching from his balcony a few floors up. "Damn," he called down. "I thought he was going to give you a medal of honour."

The officer wasn't done with Roddy and Colt. The next afternoon, after Roddy's final day on set, they drove down the same road. From each stop sign along the way hung bright orange streamers, flapping in the breeze. Their appearance didn't seem to be a coincidence, a suspicion confirmed when Roddy and Colt got to their hotel room. On the door was a note: "Thank you so much Mr. Piper for the picture. I hope you'll notice the stop signs now."

Tammy Perschmann came home from work late the afternoon of April 28, 2009, and found her husband dead. Diabetic and overweight, "Playboy" Buddy Rose had retired to Vancouver, Washington, just across the Columbia River from Portland, where he'd worked the majority of his career as a professional wrestler. The Pacific Northwest was one of the few territories small enough that a wrestler could sleep in his own bed almost every night.

Roddy missed another funeral.

Giving the next generation a boost was a gesture Roddy didn't reserve just for wrestlers. With Ariel pursuing film work in LA, he knew she could benefit from the exposure she'd get accompanying him to industry events. So one night at the Kress nightclub in Hollywood, she arrived on her father's arm, and they headed to the rooftop bar, where they were expected.

Ariel hadn't spent much time in public with her father. She hadn't really seen Rowdy Roddy Piper up close and in person. At the Kress, when an older producer-type with hair slicked back in a ponytail started talking her up and put a hand on her leg—an annoyance she was becoming familiar with in Hollywood—she got her first good look at her father's alter ego unleashed.

As Ariel was hoping her eager suitor would get bored and go away, she heard someone say her name then pull her off the couch and out of the way just as her father caught her eye. He was approaching, fast.

Roddy grabbed the man by the collar while uttering a full-throated roar like she'd never heard from him. Roddy threw him hard against the glass wall that surrounded the rooftop patio. As she watched, dumbstruck, Ariel saw some kind of realization suddenly wash over her father's face. As he later confessed, it hadn't occurred to him that the glass was there.

She had witnessed Roddy before in what the family called "pitbull mode," when someone he didn't like the look of came too close to his kids and he'd start to growl without realizing it. If she ever met with a casting agent or director who had a bad reputation, he'd call her after to make sure he didn't need to pay a visit to the agent's office. She knew mentioning her father was a good way to shut down unwelcome interest, too, but she hadn't thought his reaction would be this extreme.

Security staff intervened within seconds, with apologies to "Mr. Piper," and hustled the man out of the nightclub. Like a switch had been thrown, Roddy turned to her and smiled. She was shaking and near to tears. It was upsetting to see a parent lose his cool like that. She apologized for the drama.

"You don't have anything to be sorry for," he said, his good cheer restored. "Do you want to get another drink?"

When Roddy was a young wrestler driving through the territories day and night, hard drinking was the norm. Police had treated drinking and driving on a no-harm-no-foul basis. But as the first decade of the new century neared its end, Roddy's taste for alcohol was increasingly at odds with the world around him.

Noelle Kim had secured him a role in a Las Vegas production of *Tony n' Tina's Wedding*. One night in Vegas, over dinner, she watched as doubles of Grey Goose darkened his ebullient mood. Memories of his childhood spilled out, memories of being hit so hard with a belt he went to school for two weeks with a bruise across his face and no one said a word about it. Alcohol subdued the physical pain that racked him constantly in his fifties, but allowed the old ghosts to occupy his thoughts.

Ariel got in an argument with him one night when he wanted to drop her off on the way home from an evening out. She hadn't been drinking and wanted him to let her drive. He refused and she eventually got in. The car was swerving as they headed to her apartment, and she got pissed off. He took offense to her anger and they fought some more when she got out. The next day on TMZ, there he was—a photo of him having been pulled over later for drinking and driving.

He knew it. His family knew it. His hard-partying days had slowed when the wrestling stopped, but as he struggled to cope with the constant pain and what he realized was a deep sadness that he had missed so much of his children as they were growing up, he couldn't divorce himself from alcohol. He wanted to stop drinking, and now he wouldn't have a choice.

In Los Angeles, the law can come down on celebrities with less mercy than on ordinary people; no judge or police officer wants to be accused of sucking up to an athlete or a movie star. The DUI Roddy got that night was added to a prior from Oregon, which put him in a bad spot. Roddy's lawyer, Sam Perlmutter, reached out through his contacts with the city attorney's office and they struck a deal. Roddy got lucky. The LA attorney's office would settle for Roddy going to rehab.

Early in October 2009, cancer re-entered Roddy's life. Soon everyone knew it—except him.

He hadn't been seen in weeks when a wrestling fan site reported a rumour that he had suffered a relapse. *Bleacher Report*'s coverage typified the media reaction. "Beating cancer twice would be great to see from Piper, but it doesn't look likely this time around," the sports website reported on October 7. "It is being reported from a very good source that WWE Chairman Vince McMahon has told the WWE creative team to be prepared to cut a few segments on *Raw* next week, as he would like to do a video tribute in Piper's honor if Piper were to pass away this week."

The WWE did issue a press release saying that *if* it was true that Roddy was ill, as reported, they would pay him tribute on *Monday Night Raw*, the WWE's flagship program on USA Network. Everyone in Roddy's life had something to say about the news, but nobody could reach Roddy to confirm it.

Noelle Kim called Ariel, flustered. Did she know if the rumours were true? When Roddy had departed Los Angeles a few weeks earlier, he had instructed his manager to cancel his contractual obligations for medical reasons; she could expect to see him back in about a month. She did as instructed, not knowing what exactly was going on. Word must have gotten around that he was ailing, someone presumed his cancer was back and the rumour took on a life of its own.

Ariel knew where Roddy was. He was in Florida at rehab, and he didn't want anyone but family to know. He'd explained to them that this was something he needed to do for himself, and he'd left it at that. What worried Ariel was the possibility that he had used rehab as a smokescreen. Saying he was going to rehab when in fact he was wasting away in a cancer hospice was too much like something Roddy might do. He hated anyone seeing him vulnerable. After his near-fatal car wreck in Los Angeles, he had warned us not to visit until he came home over a week later, black, blue and concussed.

Roddy's first two weeks in rehab were rough. He'd quit drinking cold turkey—he'd wanted to do that, and given a little help, his will was stronger than his addiction. But the tightly controlled living conditions of the rehab centre aggravated his lifelong grudge against authority. When he wanted to work out in the evening and the gym was closed, he'd get angry. If he was hungry in the middle of the morning, he'd go looking for food, no matter what the dining schedule demanded. The fact that he was detoxing couldn't have helped his patience.

The centre was geared toward high-profile clients and wouldn't call the police under any circumstances, but the staff didn't dare try to contain Roddy. He wasn't violent, but he was stubborn, irritable and menacing enough to make them nervous. Staff called Kitty at home sometimes to talk him down.

After the first couple of weeks, Roddy settled in and put in the rest of his month at the centre without incident. Word eventually trickled out that he wasn't ill. The relapse rumour never exactly died; people often told him how impressed they were that he'd beaten cancer twice. He smiled and thanked them, and he never corrected them. Before leaving the centre, a therapist told him only a very small percentage of patients would succeed in never drinking again. She'd put it to him exactly as he needed to hear it. Challenge accepted.

As if to show everyone for themselves that their former star wasn't dead, WWE brought Roddy in for a *Monday Night Raw* appearance in November. The storyline had him challenging Vince McMahon to a street fight at Madison Square Garden.

An aggrieved Randy Orton showed up instead. He'd just lost his title and was supposed to be seething about it. Much like Roddy when Rick Martel came back for that final match, Orton didn't need his reputation rebuilt so much as shored up.

He confronted Roddy in the ring and beat him up, though Roddy got a few licks in and ended the confrontation on his feet. The scenario was a familiar one. The older generation had just borrowed from its deep well of audience affection and credibility to help a younger guy maintain his reputation. For the son of his old friend "Cowboy" Bob, Roddy was happy to oblige.

Back in 1985 "The Living Legend" Bruno Sammartino had done something very much like that for Roddy during a "Piper's Pit." Roddy had great respect for the retired superstar, but he didn't show any that night.

Roddy recalled their encounter in the ring: "I said, 'You know what, Bruno? I drove here and I got a flat tire, and all the way here the car went, wop, wop, wop.' That comb-over stood straight up, those eyes . . . !" Sammartino slugged him for the comment but most of what followed was Roddy hitting him with a chair.

Roddy hadn't had to show respect in the ring. That was the deal between the old guys and the young guys then, and it was in 2009, too.

After the show at Madison Square Garden, Roddy ran into Sammartino again, with Colt alongside. "Mr. Sammartino," said Roddy, "I'd like to introduce you to my son, Colt."

Without hesitating Sammartino said, "Last time I saw your father, he called me a wop." The indignation ran long, but it didn't run deep. Sammartino spent a couple hours that evening talking with Colt about wrestling, our father and whatever else he thought worth sharing. Roddy always called Sammartino one of the cleanest wrestlers—not a drinker, didn't medicate that he knew of—and also one of the strongest. Even in his fifties, Roddy could appreciate a role model when he needed one.

Later that night, Roddy and Colt attended a gathering of Roddy's old wrestling buddies. As soon as they sat down, one of the other wrestlers put a shot in front of each of them. This wasn't good. Colt wanted to get the drink away from Roddy. He had stayed sober since getting out of rehab, but this was one circumstance that could test his willpower.

Colt threw back his shot, looked at his dad, then grabbed Roddy's drink and knocked it back, too.

"You *are* your father's son," said the wrestler who'd bought the drinks. He left them alone.

A few hours later, shots began appearing again in front of Roddy. As he sat at the table full of his friends, gripping his Diet Coke while he eyed the shot glasses in front of him, he appreciated the position Colt was in. His son wanted to help protect him from temptation and peer pressure without embarrassing him. There's a time and place to stand up for a proud man. Roddy looked at him, as if to say thank you. The permission was in his eyes. Colt reached out and picked up the glass.

The drinks kept coming. Colt had a hard morning ahead.

Comedian Steve Simeone spent Christmas 2009 on the USS *Nimitz*, entertaining American troops in the Middle East. Email was hard to access as he moved from that ship to the next, so he didn't know about the Christmas present waiting for him back in Los Angeles. When he was finally able to check in at the airport in Dubai, he found an email titled "Rowdy Comedy." It asked if he'd like to appear in a stand-up show at the Improv in Hollywood with Roddy Piper on the bill. Astonished, he said yes.

Comedians tend to like wrestling, but Simeone was the only one on the bill with actual wrestling material, stories about staying up late to watch wrestling with his brother, calling his friend about Roddy Piper's mid-80s antics: "Somebody's gotta stop this Piper guy, 'cause this is getting ridiculous!" Excited as he was about the show, Simeone didn't know if he'd even be permitted to meet his wrestling hero backstage that night. He needn't have worried. He not only met Roddy, he got a big hug from him after his set. Roddy liked his material and went to see him soon after at the Comedy Store in LA. The family-friendly nature of Simeone's comedy appealed to the tough guy who called *The Sound of Music* his favourite movie, and Noelle Kim called the comedian a few days later to ask if he'd help develop Roddy's stage show.

"I was his training wheels in that world," said Simeone. In the beginning, Simeone warmed up the audience then turned over the last ten minutes of his fifteen-minute set to Roddy. Soon they were each doing fifteen minutes, back to back, and before long Roddy was telling stories for his own fifteen minutes with no warm up, training wheels off. "That's a difficult environment. He mastered that," said Simeone. "Then we did the podcast together."

Many retired wrestlers found a life after wrestling on the air—the digital era's version of it, anyway. Roddy had wrestled his final match in 2009, a handicap elimination match against Winnipeg-raised Chris Jericho in which Roddy teamed with Ricky Steamboat and Jimmy Snuka. Roddy started the bout and was eliminated when tossed out of the ring. He was fond of Jericho, but not the match. It was mostly a PR exercise for the film *The Wrestler* (after eliminating each of the three legends in turn, Jericho was punched out in the ring by Mickey Rourke, the film's star). It wasn't how Roddy had imagined himself going out. But he was already thinking ahead to a venue where he could put his mic skills to work without having to take his clothes off in a ring surrounded by twenty thousand people.

The Rod Pod was a simple operation. He set up audio equipment in various cities and chatted with old friends for the better part of an hour. As his producer, Simeone offered prompts, much like how they'd approached Roddy's stage routine in the beginning, when Simeone would sit on the edge of the stage and suggest topics for Roddy to riff on. After about thirty episodes, Roddy's constant travel away from LA made it too difficult to continue and they set *The Rod Pod* aside. The idea of a podcast, however, was one that stuck.

Randy Savage hadn't been feeling well. At fifty-eight, the "Macho Man" suffered the same sort of chronic pain as other retired wrestlers. On May 20, 2011, he collapsed at the wheel of his Jeep Wrangler while driving down a four-lane street in Seminole, Florida. The vehicle hopped across the median and his wife, Lynn, had to steer it out of the way of oncoming traffic before it stopped against a tree. Somewhere between his passing out and arriving at the hospital, Randy Mario Poffo died of cardiac arrhythmia.

Life after rehab was treating Roddy well—and his family, too. Whatever cravings remained, he didn't drink again. "That is something that I know he was very proud of and I was very proud of for him," said Falon. She had grown up with our father around home quite a lot and knew how much he'd needed to stop. "It almost seemed like he found a peace in himself after rehab. He was able to change the way he looked at life, change his attitude, and wanted to spend more time with the family, wanted to help us more. He was just happier."

Some of that time with family was spent back in North Carolina, where our big sister, Anastasia, was settling in to married life. Roddy's appearance schedule often pulled him back across the continent to the east coast, and when he was close enough that meant dropping in on some new relatives.

"He would always make time to come see his grandkids and me," Anastasia said. "He was a totally different person, too, with the grandkids. It wasn't Dad, it was Grandpa. They got all the goodies. No lectures."

Roddy hadn't been a strict parent. That had been Kitty's lot—necessarily so, with Roddy away so much. Besides, he disliked rules too much to enforce them. "I could really relate to him with regards to being a free spirit," Anastasia said. "My dad always made it very clear, as long as you have your heart on the right side of life, period, then that's all he cared about. So, I may have gotten in trouble—skip school or something and Dad finds out. But at the end of the conversation with Dad, it would always be, 'I love you, I get it, I understand, just try not to let your teacher find out next time.' He understood. He wouldn't force us to be people we weren't."

If Roddy was finding joy in his family, he still wasn't what he'd call happy. He couldn't settle at night. When he took part in *WWE Legends' House* in 2012, a reality show about retired wrestlers living together for a month, the others wondered why he roamed the halls until so late. He dreaded waking up in the morning, if only because it meant spending the whole day anxious about going to bed the next night, when the old ghosts would close in again. He used to keep them at bay by watching old movies or history documentaries or googling aliens and conspiracy theories with Ariel in LA, anything to distract himself until he nodded off.

He bonded with his roommate, "Hacksaw" Jim Duggan, during that show, a friendship that led to Duggan being one of only two wrestlers ever to visit our Portland home (Sgt. Slaughter—Uncle Bob—was the other). Roddy finished the show, surprised to have made a good friend, and headed to Atlanta, where he reconnected with another new friend, a young Canadian musician named Alan Snoddy.

Snoddy had met him at Toronto's Comedy Bar, where the two had spent an evening talking about music. Snoddy sent him a copy of some original songs, which Roddy liked, and he asked Alan if he could write a song for a documentary Roddy was hoping to make. He did, and Roddy liked it. The song was called "Off the Top Rope," and Roddy flew to Toronto to record it. Then they played the song in Niagara Falls at Light of Day, a Parkinson's disease charity concert. They played with the house band, which included Bruce Springsteen's saxophone player, and made a video out of footage from the performance. Roddy used to build trust with people through sharing extreme experiences—like his binge with Bruce Prichard in Connecticut. Clean now, he developed trust through creative endeavour, and he trusted Snoddy enough to ask him to come on the road with the one-man stage show he'd developed with Simeone and Barry Kolin—*The Tour to Settle the Score: An Audience with Rowdy Roddy Piper*. Through Ireland and the UK, Snoddy sold merchandise and kept track of ticket receipts. He also joined Roddy on stage at the end of each night. In the film *They Live*, Roddy plays "La Brea Tar Pit Blues" on harmonica. He played it at the end of each show accompanied by Snoddy's quiet, bluesy shuffle on guitar.

Mostly he brought Snoddy along as someone to have dinner with and talk to. Roddy wasn't comfortable in the company of strangers; he was never sure which version of himself to be for people. He'd offer Snoddy a drink, but abstained himself. "I've abused my privileges," he said.

The tour was a return to the UK for Roddy. In 2012 he'd done a few "Piper's Pit" sessions on the Legends tour, organized by wrestling Hall of Famer Kevin Nash. Roddy's star had been set with his own Hall of Fame induction, but in 2012 it was gilded by a more recent declaration of his role in wrestling history. The WWE released its ranking of the top fifty villains in wrestling history. Roddy was number one.

When the Legends tour went to Scotland, he and Colt took off after the Edinburgh show to do some sightseeing. Roddy still had his gear on—Hot Rod shirt, kilt, leather jacket and wrestling boots—so he asked a photographer to follow along. They got to Edinburgh Castle and figured it was too perfect a moment not to take some pictures. Colt sat on a stone lion, figuring that would be better yet. Immediately security guards started yelling at him to get down. Not one to bend under pressure, Roddy told everyone to stay put and made the nervous photographer take the picture. The greatest villain still knew how to misbehave.

In Hollywood, Roddy gathered talent around him as quickly as he'd done in wrestling. He just drew people; they wanted to work with him, and for him. They wanted to find him that perfect post-wrestling project that would help him rally his talents to a lucrative future. One of those people was television agent Adam Opitz. "He had told me once that if he wasn't doing what he was doing, he thought he would have made a great psychiatrist or psychologist. He just had this ability to bring things out in people, and you *could* really open up to the guy. Such a sense of showmanship as well. It was just born in him. He knew what to say, how to set people off, when to take it to the right level, when to drop it." In describing Roddy, Opitz described the perfect talk show host.

Opitz had a number of show ideas for Roddy. One was a *Bar Rescue* approach to small-time wrestling promotions; Roddy would help refine the contenders' characters and storylines, and generally advise them on putting forward more complete and successful events. Another was a *Curb Your Enthusiasm*–style scripted comedy in which he played himself as a motivational speaker and actors played the family and his work associates (he'd already done a pilot for a reality TV show with us, his actual family). He liked the scripted show a lot, but the pilot was too low-key for the tastes of USA Network, and Opitz had to take it back to the drawing board. A third idea seemed perfect for Roddy, hosting a talk show in the vein of the chat-show champ he'd once knocked off the throne with a fire extinguisher: Morton Downey Jr. Opitz sat Roddy down to watch a documentary about the late controversy-courting talk-show host, called *Évocateur.* "It couldn't be a right-wing or very political show, but we could just take real topics that resonate with middle America, and he could totally be that guy," Opitz said. Roddy knew how to incite an audience, whatever the subject, and he didn't mind doing it. "He loved the idea."

They brainstormed segments for a pilot, and Roddy mentioned how much he hated seeing bullying online, things like the "knock-out game," in which teenagers were filming themselves punching elderly people in public. They planned a segment on bullying in which they were going to use real grown-up victims of childhood bullying and a couple of teen bullies from a nearby school. The kids backed out an hour before the show.

Opitz hesitated to hire actors—which was always possible in LA, even on short notice—because Roddy wanted to use real testimonials from real people.

The solution came in the form of a pair of magician's assistants. The North Hollywood studio where they were shooting was also home to a magic act, and the assistants and the magician happened to be there that day. The magician assured Opitz that the kids, in their late teens, could act. One was medium height and skinny, the other was tall, and built perfectly to play a bully.

"The segment goes off like you can't believe," said Opitz. "Roddy gets so pissed off at the one guy who's pretending to be the bully, he grabs him by the collar, just shaking him on the stage. And the audience is really kind of feeling this energy. He doesn't even know this kid is acting."

On break after the segment, Roddy approached Opitz. "There's something going on in that bully's head," he insisted. "Something happened with his dad or something like that. I can see it in his eyes. Go find me that boy."

Opitz had a problem. If Roddy saw the kid, he'd know he was an actor. He'd be furious. They shot the next segment on a different subject and afterward Roddy asked if Opitz had found the kid yet.

"We're trying to find him."

After the shoot was over, Roddy pressed the matter.

Opitz found the two assistants cleaning up backstage. He said, "Here's twenty bucks. Go get some beer and go hang out in a parking lot somewhere."

He again told Roddy the bully was nowhere to be found and hoped he'd forget about it. Roddy didn't. Opitz woke up the next morning to his phone ringing. Roddy wanted to see that kid.

Opitz and his producer partner had been working on the show for the better part of a year. It was too much of an investment in the project to screw it up over a white lie, but he couldn't shake the sense that he needed to come clean with their star.

"I had this overwhelming sense of guilt," said Opitz. "It's like George Washington cutting down the cherry tree. It's like I felt like I had to tell the truth to Dad." Opitz took a deep breath and told Roddy the whole story. For fifteen seconds the line stayed silent. "Roddy?" he said.

When Roddy finally spoke, he thanked Opitz for telling him the truth. But even as he finally let the matter drop, Roddy couldn't shake the feeling. "There's still something going on with that kid!"

"There was this sense that he had," said Opitz, still moved by the story. "He just brought out the truth in everybody."

If one of those truths could be bullies understanding the hurt they really cause and turning themselves around, Roddy realized he could be a powerful influence in the lives of many children.

The talk show didn't proceed. Between Jerry Springer, Maury Povich and Steve Wilkos, that corner of the television dial was full to bursting. But bullying segment had lit a fire under Roddy, and in 2015 he appeared as a spokesperson for the Stand for the Silent anti-bullying campaign, which had begun after an eleven-year-old boy named Ty Smalley took his own life. Roddy discovered that his passion—helping people—might be his next calling.

He'd always done charity work, with a soft spot for children's causes. For decades, Roddy visited the cancer unit at Doernbecher Children's Hospital in Portland to cheer up the kids. He promoted annual Christmas toy drives in Portland and involved Ariel in a blood drive at the Children's Hospital in LA. Maybe if people knew more about who he was and what he'd overcome, his story could be a way to expand the good he could do.

In February 2015, Roddy decided to write a new book. "I want it to tell the truth," he said. The problem was, he didn't always know what the truth was anymore. So he flew to Vancouver to begin a week-long journey to re-discover his own past. As he walked into the parking garage at the airport to collect his rental car, he paused.

"Last time I drove anywhere in a Jetta the driver amost killed me."

He ferried to Vancouver Island and drove up and down its lone highway, visiting his sister Cheryl, and his mother. On his second morning, he woke up feeling terrible, struggling to breathe. He'd been dealing with a blood clot in his lung, and it was sucking the breath and energy out of him.

Roddy went to a walk-in clinic in Nanaimo, BC. He was given penicillin and an inhaler, a treatment to open his lungs. The doctor stopped before administering a needle. "This is a steroid. Will that be a problem?"

Roddy smiled. "Got anything in a harpoon?"

Just a week before, he'd been on a flight to LA from an appearance in Tennessee when the lady sitting beside him on the plane asked to get past him. He stood in the aisle to let her out and decided to stay up and stretch his legs. He passed out, fell and hit his head on the way down. When he came to, he got back in his chair and refused to let them land the plane early. When they disembarked, his manager, Bill Philputt, found him on a paramedics' gurney. Worried a particular paparazzo was lurking, he got Roddy out of the airport and into a cab. Just another day, another bump in the business of being Roddy Piper.

On June 11, 2015, days before Roddy set out for Canada, Dusty Rhodes died, aged sixty-nine. As Roddy travelled through BC he was reading tweets from old peers attending the funeral in Orlando. "I should be there," he said quietly.

Feeling well enough after visiting the doctor in Nanaimo, Roddy continued on to Edmonton, where he saw Cam Connor. The reunion was sweet, and agonizing. Connor knew more about Roddy's old ghosts than pretty much anyone, having been there when some of them entered his life. Roddy knew his story could help people who'd been through some of the same things but hadn't been as fortunate to find direction in life. But how much to tell? He leaned on his old friend for guidance. Cam's wife, Sherilyn Connor, was a psychologist who dealt with victims of childhood trauma. After an hour in her office, he and she both realized just how raw so many of his old wounds still were.

From Edmonton he headed south to Calgary, for no reason other than it had better flights to Los Angeles. Then it dawned on him. He put up the batlight and texted Bret Hart, wondered if they'd be able to meet when Roddy pulled into town. Maybe they could watch the WrestleMania VIII match together and break it down beat-by-beat for the book. Hart loved the idea, but he was flying to the UK that day. The near miss seemed to be Roddy's loss, but Bret was sincerely disappointed. He'd been thinking about putting up the batlight himself of late.

When Roddy returned to Los Angeles, all hell broke loose. The old villain had played a joke that wasn't well received when it finally saw the light of day.

By 2014 Roddy had been in a better place to commit to a weekly podcast. He was still flying frequently for appearances around the country, but they were almost always on the weekends. The carrier PodcastOne seemed a perfect venue for his hour-long *Piper's Pit* talks with wrestlers new and old, and other personalities his fans might want to hear from. He relived the behind-the-scenes drama of *They Live* with director John Carpenter and got fatherly with the most famous fighter in America, and now his namesake, UFC star "Rowdy" Ronda Rousey, who'd lost her father when she was young. She had phoned Roddy at Gene LeBell's suggestion to ask if he'd mind her using "Rowdy" herself, as people had started to call her by Roddy's old nickname. Impressed, he'd invited her on the *Piper's Pit* podcast and was even more impressed when she showed up at the studio without an entourage. Permission was granted, gladly.

In 2015 Roddy also picked up a podcast sidekick in comedian "Inappropriate Earl" Skakel. They'd met at the Comedy Store when Roddy was working out the kinks in his stage show. Like Steve Simeone, Skakel was a wrestling fan, but one with an inexhaustible knowledge of the history of the business.

"The comics at the Comedy Store were all wrestling fans. So when he would pull up in his Mercedes, it was like a superhero was coming in," said Skakel. "He'd get on stage and do mostly stories and a couple of jokes, then he would open the floor to questions. Which was probably a big mistake. 'Cause late night at the Comedy Store, it's like the bar in *Star Wars*. Every unsavoury character in LA is there. A lot of the comics were in awe of him. 'Cause it really was like watching Batman do comedy. They'd be shy in asking him questions, so I would lead the way . . . I would start off with a wacky question: 'Hey, Roddy, was Abdullah the Butcher really from the Sudan?' He would tell a half-hour Abdullah the Butcher story about how he would do a tag-team match with him and he wasn't in the ring, so he would run out to the van and Abdullah the Butcher was eating doughnuts."

Roddy recorded more than sixty podcasts in that studio, with Skakel by his side for the later ones. But it was an interview recorded before Skakel's tenure that ultimately buried the show. Canadian comic Will Sasso does a mean impersonation of wrestler "Stone Cold" Steve Austin. Roddy had him do it on *Piper's Pit* and they maintained the ruse that he *was* the wrestler for much of the episode. The real Austin wasn't impressed. Austin had a podcast on the same network, and Roddy had credited him with recommending Roddy to the network as a host in the first place. Austin complained to PodcastOne about the Sasso gag, though he claims he didn't insist they kick Roddy off the air. They did anyway, then quickly reversed their position, worried about a backlash from Roddy's fans. Roddy couldn't accept working for someone who didn't have his back. He'd done that for decades and bore too many scars to show for it.

Roddy moved the show to another podcast network, SoundCloud, but could only produce a couple of shows before he was served by PodcastOne with a cease-and-desist order, citing his still-active contract with them.

The sources of stress were mounting, as was Roddy's need to take better care of himself. His steady diet of Coke and energy drinks was not doing him any favours.

Falon had stayed close to home for her first year of college at Portland State University. She enrolled in communications and one of her professors had an inspired idea for a guest lecturer. "*Not* how you want to start college," recalled Falon, recounting the day her father walked into class. She'd asked him a few days earlier what he was going to talk about. "I haven't even thought about it," he replied.

"He comes into the class and gives this great lecture about public speaking and what you should do and not do, breathing exercises, how to capture the audience. He even tortured people and made them come up and say a sentence or two off the top of their heads to practice things. He was very exuberant about everything. You know how you think about a crazy professor? That's what he was!"

The class of forty freshmen thought they just had a cool celebrity come to class. They had no idea she was his daughter—until he told them.

The next year, Falon had moved schools and was living in Corvallis, an hour and a half south of Portland. On Wednesday, July 22, 2015, Roddy and Kitty were passing through on a drive to LA and stopped in town to have breakfast with their youngest daughter. Roddy was visibly ailing.

"He was definitely not himself," said Falon. "He was having a hard time focussing. He seemed really sick to me at that point." He promised he'd see his doctor when they got to LA. He'd been excited about his shoulder surgery. A surgeon had recently removed a number of bone splinters that inhibited his doing anything much with his right arm. He could throw a jab for the first time in years. He'd always taken Falon to the gym when she lived at home and instilled a strong fitness ethic in all of us kids, and now he could get excited about spending time in the gym himself. "He kept saying, 'I haven't done my best work yet.'"

Almost immediately upon arriving in Los Angeles, with the Austin fiasco still very much in the air and his podcast still suspended, Roddy witnessed an old friend's lifetime of work being struck from the record. A recording of Hulk Hogan unleashing an angry tirade filled with racial epithets had surfaced. The WWE terminated his contract and removed all mentions of him from its website and stores.

Hogan responded to the uproar with a single tweet: "In the storm I release control, God and his Universe will sail me where he wants me to be, one love, HH."

Roddy knew Hogan's comments were indefensible, but the backlash struck him as unbalanced. Hogan had inspired many people and suffered many of the same ailments as Roddy after years of abusing himself for the delight of wrestling fans (Roddy was two inches shorter than in his prime, and Hogan was visibly reduced as well). That all of that should be swept away by a few words—horrible as they were—spoken privately in anger eight years earlier seemed to Roddy to be just too cruel.

One of the reasons Roddy and Kitty had driven back to LA that week was so he could make a Friday appearance on *The Rich Eisen Show.* His segment went off the rails quickly. He seemed short of breath. Roddy was always given to lengthy tangents in his speech, but where he usually found his way back to the original subject, with Eisen he struggled. When Eisen asked him about Hogan's troubles, Roddy tried to give a thoughtful answer, but he lost track of what he was saying.

The television appearance reminded us at first of what it was like talking to him in the early morning, when his thoughts wandered loosely and his stories led themselves astray. The crucial difference here was his inability to pull himself together in front of the camera, something we'd never seen before. The show released the interview, and rumours abounded that he had been drunk or high. He wasn't either. He was dying.

Outside the studio, Roddy taped an interview for TMZ about Hogan's comments. The gossip site sent a very young man who didn't seem to understand the situation well enough to properly interview Roddy.

"We talked about doing it," said Sam Perlmutter, Roddy's lawyer and one of his most trusted confidantes. Getting involved in the Hogan controversy could be dangerous for an older white man in the current political climate. "He did it on his own. He said, 'Look, he was my friend and I'm standing up for him.'" They had to send the videographer to Roddy's apartment to re-shoot it because he hadn't gotten any useful quotes.

"His son was going through a really tough time. He's trying to take care of his daughter. He's trying to keep his family together," said Roddy to the camera, on the sidewalk outside his LA home. "Do I condone it? No. But I think Hulk Hogan has done a whole lot more for society than he has done negative to our society."

Bill Philputt was pacing worriedly in the background. After the shoot, he walked Roddy inside to the elevator and said goodbye, expecting that they'd catch up soon.

Mitch Ackerman sat waiting in a restaurant in Ventura where he and Roddy often met to discuss business, Ackerman's so-called "managerial duties."

He still helped Roddy find screen work, and had accompanied him to a meeting not that long ago about a *They Live* TV series. Ackerman had asked two young writers to come up with an outline for a pilot and direction for the series. Roddy loved the idea, as did John Carpenter and Sandy King. As it turned out, film producer John Davis was considering a remake of the movie anyway, so his team put some effort into further conceiving a direction for the series.

"What it was going to be was, at the end of *They Live*, you don't know whether Roddy lives or not," said Ackerman, "so it was going to be Roddy does live, but he becomes a recluse. This group of younger people are taking on the aliens and go to find Nada, and he becomes their mentor in fighting the aliens."

Ackerman, Roddy, Carpenter and some of Davis's people and their agent had gone to Syfy network for a meeting about putting the show together. Ackerman thought the meeting was going well. Roddy was excited. The writer was pitching their story ideas and responses and concepts were flying back and forth.

"All of a sudden," said Ackerman, "John Carpenter gets up and says, 'Okay, hope this thing goes. Nice to meet you all,' and he walks out."

No one else in the room had thought the meeting was over.

"We get up and we say our proper goodbyes. Roddy and I go out and Roddy says to me, 'I guarantee you, he had to go out and have a cigarette.' And sure enough, we go down the elevator into the garage and there's John smoking a cigarette." In the end, unfortunately, four different entities claimed ownership of the rights to the show concept. The momentum from the meeting slowly dissolved amidst the bickering, and Syfy let it drop.

Roddy and Ackerman hadn't seen each other in a few weeks so they arranged to have dinner. Roddy always walked slowly because of his hip, but when he finally came into the restaurant he seemed to be dragging himself to the table.

"Are you okay?" said Ackerman.

"I'm just beat," said Roddy.

"Well, Rod, you gotta go see somebody about it," said Ackerman.

"Yeah, I know, I haven't had the time."

"Rod, you're best friends with doctors . . ."

Roddy had doctor friends he texted regularly at three o'clock in the morning. He didn't want to see doctors any more than he could help it, but there were so many signs that his body was collapsing, it was tough to avoid.

Roddy ordered soup, which was a few thousand calories short of what he usually considered a meal. He was having a hard time breathing and swallowing.

"Rod, this is serious," Ackerman insisted.

"No," said Roddy. "Let's talk business." He wanted Ackerman to approach an old manager named Barry Bloom. He had managed Jesse Ventura, Chris Jericho, Mick Foley and a few other wrestlers, including Roddy himself, briefly. Ackerman got to know Bloom well when Ventura had been part of the *Tag Team* pilot and series planning. Roddy wanted to make sure there was no bad blood from his having moved on to another manager after Bloom, and wondered if Bloom could help him find some more work. Ackerman promised to make the call.

The dinner was hard for Ackerman. He wasn't comfortable seeing his old friend like this. They were not old men. As they left the restaurant and approached an escalator, Roddy stopped to rest. The escalator wasn't working.

"Do you want to take the elevator instead of walking down?"

"Yeah," said Roddy, a concession Ackerman would never expect to hear from him.

Concerned, Ackerman walked him to his car. He wasn't crazy about the thought of Roddy driving, but he wasn't going to stop him.

"Did you listen to my last podcast?" Roddy asked as they crossed the parking lot.

"No, I didn't."

"I had Lanny Poffo on." Poffo—aka The Genius—was Randy Savage's brother. Their father, Angelo Poffo, had been a famous wrestler also. He died only a year before his most famous son.

"He told some really interesting stories," said Roddy. "Did you know that their father paid for Gorgeous George's funeral?"

"No."

"Listen to the podcast."

"Okay." Then Ackerman ran an idea past Roddy that he'd had for a while. "Speaking of podcasts, Roddy, you've told me I'm your best friend, right?"

"Yeah."

"How about one time when you can't find a guest, have your best friend on the podcast, 'cause I've got a million stories to tell about you."

"That's a great idea," said Roddy. He smiled. "We're going to do that."

Roddy got in the car and drove away. Ackerman made the call to Bloom. The manager said there was no bad blood; he still had great respect for Roddy. The next day, numbers were exchanged and Roddy said he'd contact Bloom soon.

Roddy looked at his phone. He opened a text to find a picture of himself, shaking hands with an enormous toy rabbit.

"Oh, you finally got to tend to those rabbits, champ," wrote Snoddy beside the picture. They'd watched *Of Mice and Men* together, and Snoddy knew the ending always got to him.

"Asshole," Roddy texted back. He was hoping to be back to Toronto before too long, he added, to continue work on the book, maybe go see his other sister, who lived in Ontario. They'd meet again soon.

Roddy had been reaching out to a number of friends lately. Even Virgil, Ted DiBiase's former "bodyguard" (who'd also menaced Roddy as a member of NWO) heard from him, just to say he loved him and he hoped everything was alright.

On the evening of Thursday, July 30, Colt received a text from Roddy:

"Hey son, I miss you. I love you. Can't wait to see you later." Colt replied a half hour later, "I love you too, Dad, have a good night's sleep. Get some rest. Can't wait to talk to you tomorrow."

On Friday morning, Bruce Prichard had a message, too. His phone hadn't rung and he'd been having some trouble with the device. It didn't show who'd called, and when he checked his voicemail the message wouldn't play. Annoyed he set it aside. A little later the phone rang again.

Earl Skakel was looking forward to the afternoon of Friday, July 31. Since Roddy was exiled from his own podcast, Skakel asked him over to his house to do one with him—maybe they'd reverse roles for a while until the situation worked itself out. Skakel sent him a reminder late in the morning: "I got your water. I'll see you at two."

Someone replied, texting, "He's not coming over."

Prichard answered his phone.

"Hey man, that's something about Roddy, huh?" a friend said to him on the other end of the line.

Prichard thought, *What'd Roddy do now*? thought Prichard. They'd just spoken a few days earlier.

"Wow, you don't know, do you?"

His friend explained.

"Fuck you," Prichard said and hung up. He called Roddy but the phone went to voicemail.

"Motherfucker, you better fucking call me back, 'cause I just heard some fucked up news."

Bill Philputt was at home. "A number I didn't recognize kept calling me," he remembered. He wouldn't normally answer unknown calls, but the phone kept ringing. When he answered it was someone from TMZ asking for a statement. Philputt was puzzled. What did the caller mean? "I'm so sorry for your loss," the caller continued. Philputt's ears began to buzz, blocking out any other sound, like his body had figured out what his mind couldn't yet admit.

"I put him on speaker and went to their site. There it was. I don't know what I said to him, but my ears were ringing. I sent him a text: 'Rod?' From then on, the phone blew up. Stupid TMZ."

Prichard sat tinkering with his phone, desperate to hear the message.

"I'm just crying, fucking with my phone . . . and the message plays. And it was just him. Calling to tell me he loved me," said Prichard. "But it—the uncharacteristic part—was this: 'Man,' he goes, 'I'm not feeling real well. I'm really fucking tired, man, but I just wanted to call and tell you I love you and talk to you because I'm going to bed. And I'll talk to you tomorrow.'"

There wouldn't be a tomorrow. Sometime over night, Roddy's blood clot—a condition known to be aggravated by stress and air travel—did what knives, bullets and so many other things had failed to accomplish. He had a heart attack in his sleep. Kitty went into his room late in the morning and found him. He always had Hot Rod shirts around and he'd worn one to bed.

Kitty tried to reach all the kids as quickly as she could. At a gym in Corvallis, Falon was the first to answer. Over the phone, she heard the paramedics arriving in the background.

"No one knows yet, you need to wait," Kitty told her. "You need to let me break it to them."

"I felt so bad because when she first called me she was so distraught I couldn't understand what she was saying. For a good ten minutes, I thought she meant someone else had died. I was just trying to calm her down."

Eventually, Kitty made it clear:

"No, Falon, *your* dad died."

Ariel was the last to learn. It didn't sink in immediately that Roddy was dead. Colt had reached her with the news: "Ariel, you know I love you, right? Everything's going to be okay. I love you . . . Dad's dead. Mom's at the apartment with the paramedics." In shock, she thought for a moment that their presence meant there was still a chance Roddy could pull through. She drove from her house in Van Nuys to Roddy's Hollywood apartment—her apartment, once upon a time. Ariel knew Roddy hated for his family to see him in a weakened state; she couldn't bring herself to see him now. When her husband, Phil arrived, the brave face she'd been putting on for Kitty gave way and the reality of the moment hit her full force. Phil went to the bedroom and removed the T-shirt and Roddy's jewellry so Ariel or Kitty didn't have to see him. The thought of the shirt ending up in an auction was too morbid to contemplate so we destroyed it. Knowing Roddy was supposed to be on Earl's show at three o'clock that afternoon, we all set that as a deadline to reach family, because word would surely get out by then.

The LAPD sent the chief and several officers to make sure the coroner's collection was handled properly. A celebrity death was sure to draw unwanted attention. They stayed a long time to help Ariel and Kitty figure out what to do next, for which they were grateful. Even as they were making arrangements with the coroner, Ariel's phone was ringing already with people wondering if the rumours were true. Secrets didn't keep in Hollywood.

Falon stayed in Oregon, refusing to miss work Friday or Saturday. Roddy had told her once how he'd learned of his own father's death just before going into the ring. He'd taken a moment to collect himself, then gone out and done his job. Only after that had he gone home to make preparations. Falon didn't want to let him down.

After work on Saturday she drove to Portland, picked up Colt and his wife and drove them all to Los Angeles. As soon as they got there they packed up the apartment and returned with Kitty to Oregon.

Portland Wrestling fans were busy putting together a memorial service, but with the funeral to arrange, Roddy's family wasn't able to attend. The funeral was private, for family and close friends only. They'd do their public grieving later, in Los Angeles, at a memorial at the place that felt most like home now that the apartment was vacated: the Comedy Store.

Bret Hart had been one of the first friends to get a call from Kitty. Or maybe he is family; we don't suppose that will ever get sorted out. It doesn't matter. He's family in one way or the other. He had been planning to call Roddy that weekend. After Roddy's trip through BC and Alberta, Bret had had a biopsy that later confirmed he had prostate cancer. He'd learned the result about a week before Roddy's death, but hadn't told him about it.

"There's only one person I can talk to," he'd thought, "and that's Roddy. Then I remember thinking, 'I don't want to bum him out. I feel kinda lousy about it myself.' I wasn't quite ready to talk to him yet. So I put it off."

When we spoke with him, the regret was clear. "The only guy I felt comfortable talking to. I say that with all honesty. . . . It was Roddy. I couldn't believe it when I got the news. He was always my . . . when you got a real problem you call Roddy. I was shining the batlight that day, and he wasn't there anymore to take it."

Ronda Rousey was finishing her weigh-in Friday afternoon for a Saturday UFC bout when she got the news about Roddy. The next night, she dedicated her match to him and her late father. She had promised Roddy she'd do him proud when he'd given his blessing to use "Rowdy." She won that match in thirty-four seconds.

There was a rumour that former WWE star Chyna had "crashed" the funeral in Portland. She hadn't, of course. She and Roddy shared a lawyer in Sam Perlmutter, and Roddy had been very supportive as she got her troubled life and career back on track. She was sober, a process he knew very well. They'd had several intense conversations as she struggled her way back to a good place. She missed him greatly. (Sadly, Chyna died in 2016.)

Friends worried about what finally killed Roddy. Was it stress, work, worry, lingering health problems from so many years of abusing "his privileges"? Had they been themselves responsible, in some small way? Had they pushed him too hard when he needed a rest? Had they not defended him when someone else had pressed him? In a life as complicated as our father's, it would be impossible to say for certain what pushed his health to the breaking point. But that visit with his mother during the Canada trip probably identified the most likely candidate.

While cleaning dishes after dinner, mother and son got to talking about food. A mention of bacon grease prompted Roddy to ask, "Coronaries? For your brothers?"

"Yes, three of them," she replied. Three of Roddy's uncles had died of heart disease.

He looked pensive for a moment, staring at nothing in the middle distance before speaking. "I think a heart attack would be a good way to go."

Roddy had declared in his Hall of Fame speech what Falon had always heard him say: we hadn't seen his best. Several people we spoke to echoed that sentiment. The simple fact was, Roddy never stopped trying. Maybe there would have been film roles that would eclipse anything he'd done before. His role in planning to get the nascent Classic Wrestling Revolution in Las

Vegas off the ground might have led to a vibrant and successful wrestling promotion. He was recording more music, something he'd long wanted to do. His best probably was left unfinished, not because his potential was unfulfilled but because he always raised the bar for himself.

He'd survived his years in the madhouse of the wrestling territories by learning from his mistakes and the mistakes of others who went before him. But he didn't try to improve just so he could survive, he did it because, to him, doing less than breaking new ground for yourself was a waste of the gift of being alive. "He was the first wrestler to do a podcast," said Steve Simeone. "He was the first wrestler to do a storytelling show in person."

Ever forward. Ever better.

Roddy was always trying to be someone he wished he'd had in his own life. He was a gatherer of lost sheep. Chyna was one, but there were others whose stories we won't tell to protect their privacy. He wanted to throw a protective blanket over everyone he knew and loved, and by the time he'd reached the age of sixty-one that was a lot of people. He'd broken the cycle of abuse he'd grown up with, something that he seemed to know probably wouldn't have happened—odd as it seems to say—if he hadn't found a life in professional wrestling.

"The WWE, they allowed me this, the greatest thing that's happened in my life," he said during his Hall of Fame acceptance speech, naming our mother and each of his children, one by one as we looked on. "They're all my family, and it's all because of this family here." He gestured around the stage at his peers. Violence had been his problem growing up. He crashed headlong into a life of it—real and pantomimed—and somehow by mastering it, he released its grip on his bloodline. No amount of stress, no substance he'd abused, no choices from the past that nagged at him as he tried to fall asleep could make him betray himself by betraying us. The fact that we laughed when he broke a kitchen table says a lot about how little reason he'd given us to fear him the way he'd feared his own father. The fact he'd honoured his father by passing on his name and visiting him at his deathbed says equally as much about Roddy's ability to forgive and see past the failings of others. We started this journey wondering what made Roddy rowdy, but it was in keeping his demons at bay that our father scored the most impressive victory in his life.

We did many interviews in writing this book, and often, at the end, Ariel asked Roddy's friends what they would want his fans to know about him that perhaps viewers never would have realized from watching him on television. We asked them because it's not fame that fills the hole Roddy talked about with his sister Cheryl on that trip through western Canada. It's the self-respect that comes with being loved, a gift he gave to us in endless amounts. A few of their answers bear repeating.

Mitch Ackerman: "He was what made life interesting for me. There were so many things that I did in my life that were because of him that I never would have done, nor anybody else in the world would have ever done. Whenever you were with him you never knew what was going to happen."

Earl Skakel: "Just the most kind-hearted man I've ever met. Not just celebrities, but in life. I cried more when I got that phone call confirming that he'd passed than I think I did at my parents' funerals."

"Judo" Gene LeBell: "The world was a better place when he was here. How many people in your life can you really trust? That aren't fair-weather friends? When I was no longer wrestling, no longer able to do things for him—'You gotta be on my program. Only for about five or ten minutes.' I think we were there for about an hour and a half, teasing back and forth."

Marilyn Robertson: "He was so bad, but he was so good, and I loved him to death."

Noelle Kim: "His earnestness. He was always trying his best all the time. Even at the times he was down he was trying his best to not be. He was always trying."

Steve Simeone: "I don't think I've ever met a better person. I've never met anybody that cared that much about other people. Your dad went through so much and I think that's what made him so compassionate. There were times that I wish he would have shown that compassion to himself. There were times he was hard on himself, and I'm like, 'Dude, you're the best person I've ever met.' Honestly, I don't know if the general public knows that, but I think they felt that. I think that's part of the reason why he was so. . . I don't know if mesmerizing's the right word. There was something about him. There's a reason why people connected to him."

So where do we end the story of a man who relished new beginnings? Where do we disconnect and how many stories can we leave untold? Some, we just want to brag about (our dad body slammed Big John Studd!). How many names can we leave unmentioned? Lonnie Mayne, killed in a car crash while champion when Roddy was in Los Angeles in 1978? Eddie Guerrero, Chavo's youngest and ultimately most famous brother, who died the year Roddy entered the Hall of Fame? Art Barr and Rick McGraw, whose deaths haunted him? Our father worked almost every day for forty-two years, from those first matches in Winnipeg in 1973 to the week he died in 2015. We could write another book and not tell the same stories twice. The beauty of all those open-ended wrestling finishes was that you never knew when to look away; every ending was already a beginning of something else. Of course, like any professional wrestler, our father was always baiting the hook for next week's show. He did it in the movies, too: did Nada die?

We shouldn't worry about the ending. As usual, Dad already had it figured out. The end of his book was one of the few parts of this story written before he died. It was something that anyone who knew him had heard him say many times. It was all he thought the world really needed if it were to become a better place. So we end with a few simple words of Roddy's advice.

Hug your kids. Tell them you love them. Tell them to do their homework and to come in on time. Don't get mad at them. Talk it out. And listen to them. Listen close.

They might be trying to tell you something.

Acknowledgements

This book was originally intended to be written by our father and his editor, with a handful of interviews and conversations to help them fill in the blanks. When Roddy passed and we took up the job of finishing his story, many people stepped into the breach to help us complete *Rowdy*. We are grateful to them all.

First and foremost, our mother, Kitty Toombs, and our sisters, Anastasia and Falon, agreed that we could carry the Toombs Clan flag in the effort to complete our father's legacy in print, and they supported our effort throughout with their time, memories and love. As did our spouses, Sarah Toombs and Phil Brock.

While researching the original version of this book, Dad visited with his sister Cheryl Grant and mother, Eileen Toombs, in British Columbia. He also spent two days with Cam Connor in Edmonton, including time with Sherilyn Connor and their son, actor Kristofer Connor. Their memories and insights further helped us put together the story of Roddy's early years. We spoke by phone with Dad's sister Marilyn Robertson, in Ontario. Our thanks to all of them.

Many more of Dad's oldest friends gave generously of their time and memories. Mitch Ackerman was one of the very first people we sat down with, in Los Angeles, and his recollections were crucial to understanding what it was like for Roddy when fame broke, when he stepped back from wrestling and pursued his screen career, and during the final weeks of his life. "Judo" Gene LeBell, also in LA, spends two hours a week at the Hayastan MMA Academy in North Hollywood. The week we visited, he gave us an hour and forty minutes. Everyone wondered who was so important that Gene would dedicate nearly his whole work week to us. That's Uncle Gene for you, and we are hugely grateful for his time and memories. Kellie Cunningham, who helps manage his office work, was generous and helpful as well.

Throughout Dad's wrestling career, he bonded with many of his peers, and even if they hadn't worked with him since the 1970s, their memories were often as sharp as if it had been only last year. Several members of this wonderful fraternity spoke to us at length and we thank them all for helping keep our father's story alive: Big Show, "Edge" Adam Copeland (and Daniel Abrams), Len Denton, Chavo Guerrero Sr., Stan Hansen, Bret Hart, Rick Martel, Bruce Prichard, and Tom Prichard. Manager/trainer Merv Unger took us back to Winnipeg for Roddy's earliest matches, and referee Jimmy Korderas shared his memories with us of Roddy at WrestleMania VI and Maple Leaf Wrestling.

Roddy loved to laugh, and after he'd retired from wrestling he wanted to make a career out of laughter. To that end, he got to know a number of LA's finest comedians, some of whom became dear friends. Steve Simeone, Earl Skakel and Cousin Sal Kimmel spoke to us, as did Barry Kolin, owner of Harvey's Comedy Club in Portland, Oregon. Roddy also never gave up the dream of making music, and we're grateful to Toronto singer/songwriter Alan Snoddy for sharing memories of his friendship with our father.

Being a creature of the old wrestling territories, Dad never got with the idea of having a single person to manage his business. He worked with many managers, producers and assistants over the years, and they often remained good friends even after parting company professionally. Our thanks to Julian Dagnino, Noelle Kim, Freya Miller (aka "Buttons"), Adam Opitz and Bill Philputt, as well as Roddy's lawyer and friend Sam Perlmutter.

At Random House Canada, Associate Publisher Scott Sellers first reached out to Roddy about writing a new book, one that would tell the story of his whole life and not shy away from his Canadian roots. Publisher Anne Collins and Senior Editor Craig Pyette turned that conversation into a reality. Angelika Glover and Gil Adamson ironed out the kinks in the manuscript in record time. Publicist Ruta Liormonas helped announce the book to the world.

And thanks to you, Roddy's fans and our readers, without whom there could be no legends to recall, no icons to remember.

A Note on Sources

Much of *Rowdy* was written from our family's own recollections, as well as those of our more than thirty interview subjects. We've done our best to be clear who told us what throughout the book, and unless we point to a source for those quotes in the notes below, you can presume we were told those things directly by the person speaking. In many cases, quotes from people we did not interview come from Roddy's *Piper's Pit* podcasts (which are, as of this writing, still available on Soundcloud.com), on which he interviewed many of his friends and wrestling peers during more than sixty episodes, or his earlier *Rod Pod* podcasts, (excerpts from which remain scattered across YouTube). Further, Roddy's editor watched hundreds of hours of old match footage and "Piper's Pit" episodes to help us flesh out the blow-by-blow accounts that appear throughout the book.

Introduction

This Isn't Supposed to Happen

Observations of WrestleMania—the original and number two—and Roddy's dealings with Mr. T came from Roddy himself, during interviews on his 2015 road trip with his editor. These two matches and many more that we discuss throughout the book can be viewed on WWE's DVD *Born to Controversy: The Roddy Piper Story*, also a source of some of Roddy's quotes.

1

A Very Active Child

Aside from the attributed quotes, this chapter was informed by interviews with Roddy's mother and two sisters, as well as his own recollections.

2

Concede or Get Up

Cam Connor provided much of the information in this chapter, attributed and otherwise. Roddy supplemented that information in conversation with his old friend. Merv Unger added background. Jesse Ventura is quoted from *Piper's Pit* podcast #30, as are Roddy's recollections of his first match with "Superstar" Billy Graham. The most complete record of Roddy's wrestling matches is here: www.infinitecore.ca/superstar/index.php?threadid=67512. Where possible, we have cross referenced dates and opponents with media reports and www.cagematch.net/?id=2&nr=51&page=4&s=1100

3

The Jesus Years

Roddy's recollection of his first wrestling forays into the US come from his first book (*In the Pit with Piper: Roddy Gets Rowdy*, Berkley Boulevard: New York, 2002) and his one-man stage show, recordings of which were provided to the authors by staff who travelled with Roddy on the 2014 UK tour. There are discrepancies between the accounts (who took him to the diner in 1973, for instance—was it Mad Dog Vachon or Ivan the Terrible?). We have used our best judgment and understanding of the cast of characters in Roddy's life at the time to portray these scenes as accurately as possible. The story of his match with Larry Hennig came from these sources, as well as Roddy's recollections to his editor and the memories of Cam Connor, who was not present at the Hennig match but provided helpful context. Roddy's early harassment at the hands of older wrestlers came from his direct recollections as well as those he shared with Kayfabe Commentaries for its *Timeline: The History of WWE* DVD series, *1984 as Told by Roddy Piper*. Roddy's recollections of Johnny Valentine came from *Piper's Pit* podcast #60. Roddy's Texas run was informed by the memories of Bruce Prichard and Tom Prichard, as well as this fine biographical piece about Red Bastien: http://empirewrestlingfederation.com/2012/08/red-bastien-king-of-men/. We benefitted from the excellent collection of fliers and newspaper reports that included many mentions of "Rod" Piper's Maritimes run at http://mapleleafwrestling.yuku.com/topic/58/Forty-years-ago-this-week-1975#.V4T-rNIrKHs. Background on Eileen Eaton and Roddy's run in Los Angeles came from Gene LeBell and his self-published book, *The Godfather of Grappling* (Gene LeBell Enterprises, LLC: Santa Monica, 2003), as well as our interview with Chavo Guerrero Sr. The late Leo Garibaldi is quoted from http://www.prowrestlingdigest.com/2012/08/12/lano-red-bastien-king-of-men/. Roddy also discusses Los Angeles with Chavo Guerrero Jr. on a pilot episode of *The*

Chavo Show, available online from geeknation.com. The story of Victor the Bear receives an overdue telling on *Deadspin*: http://deadspin.com/the-amazing-true-story-of-victor-the-wrestling-bear-1531930655.

4
Thanks for the Blood and Guts, Kid

Stan Hansen assisted greatly in our understanding of Roddy's first tour to Japan and in helping us understand the Japanese wrestling culture when Roddy was there. Roddy interviewed at length for the book about his experiences in Japan. We cross referenced dates and details of his matches there with the following list: http://www.puroresu.com/forum/threads/5182-Roddy-Piper-in-Japan. Ned York's mistakenly being arrested as the Hillside Strangler comes from Roddy; background about victim Jane King came from https://familysearch.org/photos/artifacts/2164686. We determined Jane King was the victim who knew Ned York by surveying bios online of the victims and the dates when Roddy was in Los Angeles between Japan runs—she was the only actress murdered while he was home from overseas. Roddy told the story of Tiger Nelson to Colt and his editor. A lengthier account is available in Roddy's first book.

5
Don't Call Us, We'll Call You

Rick Martel provided us with much of the insight about his and Roddy's friendship in Portland. Background on Roddy's Hawaii trip was aided by http://www.50thstatebigtimewrestling.com/history5.html. Further stories and insights come from two podcast interviews with Luke Williams on *Piper's Pit* 44 and 45, and our mother, Kitty Toombs. We learned more about the strange life of Chris Colt from this article, originally published in *Betty Paginated* #31: http://docriot.blogspot.ca/2011/07/down-and-out-with-chris-colt.html.

6
Flair and the Family Man

Len Denton and Tom Prichard provided valuable insights into Roddy's Charlotte/Atlanta years, as did Kitty Toombs and Luke Williams' podcast interview. Background on George Scott came from http://www.tampabay.com/news/obituaries/wwf-mastermind-and-promoter-george-scott-dies-at-84/2162810. Ric Flair's story came from episode 14 of his podcast, *WOOOOO! Nation with Ric Flair*. Greg Valentine is quoted from *Piper's Pit* podcast #60. We learned some useful context about the first Starrcade from David Ungar at the blog *Attitude of Aggression* (http://www.attitudeofaggression.com/1983-starrcade-and-the-emergence-of-the-supercard-2/) and also at https://anokasflawless.wordpress.com/2016/01/11/and-im-like-goin-old-school-in-nwa-starrcade-1983-a-flair-for-the-gold/.

7
A Despicable, Disgraceful Display

Bret Hart and Mitch Ackerman gave us wonderful interviews about Roddy's rise to national prominence after he joined the WWF. Roddy's stories about Bob Orton Jr. came from *Piper's Pit* podcast #32. Roddy's comments about Brutus "The Barber" Beefcake at WrestleMania 3 came from his appearance on Steve Austin's podcast, *The Steve Austin Show* episode 81.

8
All Outta Bubble Gum

Background on *Hell Comes to Frogtown* came from the last

known interview with the film's creator, Donald G. Jackson, available at http://www.scottshaw.com/dgjinterview.html. Roddy's comments about that film and *They Live* were mostly made to his editor. Additional sources include a panel discussion with co-stars Keith David and Meg Foster at the Days of the Dead horror convention in Atlanta in February 2013 (https://www.youtube.com/watch?v=B5PfgVgdgZI), Roddy's interview with director John Carpenter on *Piper's Pit* podcast #37, and the audio commentary by Roddy and John Carpenter and a "Making of They Live" from the Collector's Edition DVD of *They Live*. Our account of Roddy's return to the WWF was aided greatly by our interview with Bruce Prichard. The story of *Tag Team* came from Mitch Ackerman. Roddy's comments on WrestleMania 6 were made to his editor and on the July 12, 2012, episode of his *Rod Pod* podcast. Background on Shepard Fairey and the cultural influence of *They Live* was supported by http://www.lataco.com/they-live-tribute-art/.

9
Frats

We discussed Roddy's non-wrestling commercial activities with his former UK manager, Freya Miller, and his US pursuits with manager Noelle Kim. Accounts of the Zahorian steroid trial come from *Sex, Lies and Headlocks: The Real Story of Vince McMahon and World Wrestling Entertainment* by Shaun Assael and Mike Mooneyham (Three Rivers Press: New York, 2002) and Roddy's first book. Additional comments from "Superstar" Billy Graham and Ivan "Polish Power" Putski are quoted from the *LA Times*, March 12, 1992, in an article by John Cherwa and Houston Mitchell, "Wrestling's Star Takes a Tumble." Vince McMahon's admission that he used steroids has been widely reported, including at http://www.canoe.ca/Slam/Wrestling/Bios/mcmahon

-vince.html. The sexual abuse scandal is discussed in many places, including Mike Mooneyham's own site: http://www.mikemooneyham.com/2002/10/20/past-still-haunts-former-wwf-ring-boy/; as well as http://wrestlingperspective.com/issue/78/cole1.html. Roddy's story about the ninja was one of his favourites, and he told this iteration to his editor. Big Show told us his story about Roddy himself. The Los Angeles car crash and the circumstances surrounding it were told by Roddy to his editor. Snippets of HBO's *Real Sports* interviews with Roddy and Vince McMahon are available on YouTube.

10
Finish

The stories of Roddy's induction into the WWE Hall of Fame come in part from his friend and "Coach," Barry Kolin. Roddy's fateful run as tag-team champion to the UK was informed by our very helpful interview with "Edge" Adam Copeland, as well as an account of the Glasgow event written for WrestleView.com by Adam Martin (http://www.wrestleview.com/news2006/1163041553.shtml). The story of Roddy's forgotten black belt came from Noelle Kim and Gene LeBell. Details of the death of Buddy Rose originated here: http://www.onlineworldofwrestling.com/buddy-rose-found-dead/; details of Randy Savage, here: http://bleacherreport.com/articles/1643969-the-final-days-of-randy-macho-man-savage. Besides Ariel's own recollection of the Kress nightclub incident, Roddy told the story to his editor. The *Bleacher Report* article about Roddy's supposed second bout with cancer is here: http://bleacherreport.com/articles/267986-sad-sad-day-wwe-hall-of-famer-rowdy-roddy-piper-may-be-gone-soon. Details of Roddy's final TMZ interview came from our interview with Roddy's manager, Bill Philputt.

Image Credits

Unless otherwise stated below, all images appearing in *Rowdy* are from the personal collections of the authors or Kitty Toombs.

"Wrestling hurts . . ." Photo courtesy of Tom Prichard.

"Setting the stage . . ." Walter Iooss Jr. (Photo by Walter Iooss Jr./Sports Illustrated/Getty Images).

"Bruce Prichard as . . ." Photo courtesy of Bruce Prichard.

"Mitch Ackerman . . ." Photo by Mike Lano, courtesy of Mitch Ackerman.

"Right where 'Uncle Gene' . . ." Photo courtesy of Gene Lebell.

"Ariel and Roddy . . ." Maury Phillips / Contributor, via Getty Images.

"Bruce Prichard on . . ." Photo courtesy of Bruce Prichard.

"*Piper's Pit* podcast . . ." Photo courtesy of Earl Skakel.

"Making music again . . ." Photo courtesy of Alan Snoddy.

"The last word . . ." Photo courtesy of Bill Philputt.

Index

A

Abdullah the Butcher (Larry Shreve), 289, 352
Ackerman, Mitch, 213–14, 249, 258–59, 270–72
  as friend, 235, 314, 356–59, 366
Adonis, Adrian. *See* Franke, Keith
Albano, "Captain Lou," 143, 206, 216–17
Ali, Muhammad, 87, 92–93, 196, 224–25, 226
All Japan Pro Wrestling, 109, 116, 190, 193
American Wrestling Association, 46, 65–75
Anderson family, 3–4, 10, 22–24, 31–32. *See also* Toombs, Eileen Anderson
  Barbara (aunt), 3, 7, 21
  Charlotte (grandmother), 3, 6, 331
  Doris (aunt), 22, 24
  Ernie (grandfather), 3–4, 22
  Glen (uncle), 22, 23
Anderson, Ole, 168, 169, 170, 176
Andre the Giant (André Roussimoff), 100, 119, 143–44, 196, 227, 231, 238
  as friend, 208–10, 275, 290, 292, 315
  as opponent, 93–94, 208–10, 290

as tag-team partner, 153, 184
Armstrong, Brad, 185–86
The A-Team (TV series), 232
Atlanta, GA, 182–86
Austin, "Stone Cold" Steve, 352–53

B

Baba, Shohei "Giant," 109, 116
Backlund, Bob, 171, 211
Barnett, Jim, 176
Barr, Art, 315, 367
Bastien, Red, 77, 81, 128–29, 138, 182
The Beast. *See* Cormier, Yvon
Beefcake, Brutus "The Barber" (Edward Leslie), 241
Benítez (Puerto Rican wrestler), 187
Bergman, Sandahl, 246, 247–48
Big Boss Man (Ray Traylor Jr.), 78, 324
Biggs, Tyrell, 232
Big Show (Paul Wight Jr.), 304–5
Big Time Wrestling, 77
Big Trouble in Little China (movie), 252, 253
Bischoff, Eric, 302. *See also* New World Order
Blassie, Freddie, 143, 144
Bleacher Report, 338
Bloom, Barry, 357, 358
Bockwinkel, Nick, 61
Body Slam (movie), 246
Boesch, Paul, 79
Bollea, Terry. *See* Hogan, Hulk
Borne, Matt, 155
Boyd, Jonathan, 165
Brandon, MB, 58
Bravo, Dino (Adolfo Bresciano), 315
Braxton, Dwight (Muhammad Qawi), 232
Brisco, Jack, 171, 172, 174, 218
Brisco, Jerry, 171, 172
Brock, Phil, 362
Brody, Bruiser (Frank Goodish), 242, 315
Brooks, Tim "Killer," 136, 137, 139, 142–43, 146, 153
Brown, "Bulldog" Bob, 83
Brown, D'Lo (Accie Connor), 319–20
Bundy, King Kong (Christopher Pallies), 205, 219, 227, 231
Burke, Leo (Leonce Cormier), 84–85
Burns Lake, BC, 22–24, 31–32
Bushwackers. *See* Sheepherders

C

Caber Feidh (pipe band), 30–31, 66
California, 81–82, 86–94, 103–8, 220. *See also specific cities*
Campbell, John, 57
Carpenter, John, 248–59, 356–57
Cauliflower Alley Club, 310
Celebrity Wrestling (ITV), 319–21

Charlotte, NC, 167–82, 218
Chiba, Sonny (Shin'ichi), 293
Chicago, 230–34
Chivichyan, Gokor, 89
Choshu, Riki, 109
Chubbuck, Ivana, 293
Chyna (Joanie Laurer), 363, 365
Cincinnati, 229–30, 328
Clay, Cassius. *See* Ali, Muhammad
Coage, Allen ("Bad News Brown"), 273–75
Colt, Chris (Charles Harris), 158–59
Columbus, OH, 328
Condello, Tony, 49, 57
Connor, Cam, 35–37, 234–35, 326–27
  as friend, 38, 39, 49–57, 59, 80–81, 350–51
  hockey career, 36, 44, 234
Connor, Sherilyn, 351
Cormier family, 84–85, 149
Cormier, Yvon "The Beast," 85, 149, 155
Cortez, Fidel, 165
Costas, Bob, 220
Crockett, Jimmy, 167, 176, 188–89, 197, 200, 303. *See also* Mid-Atlantic Wrestling; Starrcade
Crystal Billy, 234

D

Dano, Sal, 251
Dauphin, MB, 20–21, 25–26
David, Keith, 248, 252, 253–54, 258
Daytona Beach (TV movie), 297
Decatur, GA, 182
Denton, Len "The Grappler," 168–69, 171, 172, 228, 267–70
  as friend/business partner, 269–70, 319–21, 325–27
DeVito, Danny, 220
Diamond, Sweet Ebony (Rocky Johnson), 188
DiBiase, Ted "Million Dollar Man," 276–78, 280
Downey, Morton, Jr., 260–61, 347
Dreamer, Tommy (Thomas Laughlin), 330
Duggan, "Hacksaw" Jim, 345
Duke Nukem 3D (video game), 258
Duncum, Bobby, 188
Duprée, Emile, 84
Duva, Lou, 232–33

E

Eaton, Aileen, 87–88
Eaton, Cal, 87
Edge (Adam Copeland), 328, 329–30
"Eight O'Clock in the Morning" (Nelson), 249–50
England, 292, 329–30

Entertainment Tonight (CBS), 254
Eugene, OR, 137, 152, 165
Évocateur: The Morton Downey Jr. Movie, 347

F

Fabulous Moolah (Mary Ellison), 217
Fairey, Shepard, 258
"Fighting Fit" (fitness video), 280
Flair, Ric (Richard Fliehr), 171, 187, 197, 200, 203, 290, 330
  as friend/tag-team partner, 173–74, 325, 328
  as opponent, 59, 167–69, 188–89
Florida, 188
Foley, Mick, 357
Foxx, Redd, 130
Franke, Bea, 242
Franke, Keith ("Adrian Adonis"), 94, 119, 139, 154, 236–38
  as friend, 229, 239, 240, 241–42, 315
Freeman, Ian, 319
Fresno, CA, 99–102, 184
Fuji, Mr. (Harry Fujiwara), 271
Fujinami, Tatsumi "The Dragon," 192, 268

G

Gagne, Verne, 46, 47, 65, 72, 76–77, 81
Garibaldi, Leo, 92, 108, 116–18, 121, 124
  as mentor, 81, 86, 88, 133, 134
Geigel, Bob, 73, 74
The Genius (Lanny Poffo), 358
Georgia, 182–86, 194–96
The Giant. *See* Big Show
Gilbert, Eddie, 207
"Girls Just Wanna Have Fun" (Lauper), 216
Goldust (Dustin Rhodes), 297–98
Gordienko, George, 47–49
Gordman, Black (Victor Barajas), 115
Gorgeous George (George Wagner), 88, 358
Gotch, Karl, 90
Goulet, Rene, 177–82, 196
Graham, "Superstar" Billy (Eldridge Coleman), 61, 143–44, 281
Grand Olympic Auditorium, 86–89, 92–94, 115, 126–27, 129–30, 132, 213–14. *See also* Garibaldi, Leo; LeBell, Mike
  Hispanic audience, 92, 143, 274
Grand Prix Wrestling, 85
Grant, Cheryl, 4, 13-14, 27, 29, 44-45, 350
Greensboro, NC, 189, 197–99
Greenville, SC, 173
Guerrero, Chavo, 91–92, 95–98, 108, 153–54, 196

as friend, 95–96, 103–5, 133, 190–92
as opponent, 96–98, 116, 118, 121–24, 126–29, 274
Guerrero family, 89, 92, 96, 126–29
Chavo Jr., 92, 94
Eddie, 92, 128, 367
Gory, 92, 94, 96, 126–27
Hector, 92, 116, 127–28, 137, 139
Mando, 92, 94, 108, 116, 126, 127–29

H

The Haiti Kid (Raymond Kessler), 233
Halifax, NS, 85
Hamilton, Rick, 82–83
The Hangman (Bruce Pobanz), 128
Hansen, Bobby, 29
Hansen, Stan, 109–12, 196
Hanson, Robert "Swede," 171
Hart, Bret, 203–5, 227, 280–81, 284–90. *See also* Hart Foundation
as friend, 223, 229, 292, 311–12, 351, 362–63
Hart Foundation (tag team), 230, 231, 239, 280, 284–85. *See also* Hart, Bret; Neidhart, Jim
Hart, Jimmy, 237, 324
Hart, Owen, 315
Hart, Stu, 48, 77, 203, 204
Hawaii, 148–50
Hayes, "Lord" Alfred, 73–74, 83
Haynes, Billy Jack, 283
Hell Comes to Frogtown (movie), 246–48
Hennig, Curt "Mr. Perfect," 66, 78, 189, 324
Hennig, Larry "The Axe," 66–67, 76
Highlanders (tag team), 328–29
Highlander: The Series, 294–95
Hillside Strangler, 113–14
Hoffman, Horst, 76
Hogan, Hulk (Terry Bollea), 172, 196, 205, 301–4, 324
as friend, 301–2, 325, 354, 355
as opponent, 217, 219, 222, 225–27, 229–30, 306
Wrestlemania appearances, ix, x, xiii, 315–16
Hollywood, 245–46, 335–36, 346–49. *See also* Los Angeles
Holyfield, Evander, 232
Hope, Bob, 130

I

Iger, Bob, 272
Imada, Jeff, 253
Immortal Combat (movie, a.k.a. *Resort to Kill*), 293
"I'm Your Man" (Piper), 280, 292
Indonesia, 299–300
Inoki, Antonio, 92–93, 109, 196

International Wrestling, 85
In the Pit with Piper (book), 314
Ireland, 292
Iron Sheik (Hossein Khosrow Vaziri), 89, 177–82, 229, 239, 324
ITV (British network), 319–21
Ivan the Terrible (Juan Kachmanian), 70–72

J

Jackson, Donald G., 247
Japan, 108–12, 116, 189–93, 268
Jericho, Chris (Christopher Irvine), 342, 357
Jerry Lewis Telethon, 249
Jerry Springer Show, 230
Johnson, Dwayne "The Rock," 148, 324
Johnson, Jack, 131
Johnson, Rocky, 206
Jonathan, Don Leo, 84
Jones, Bobby, 69
Jones, Tom, 94
Junkyard Dog (Sylvester Ritter), 228, 315

K

Kaufman, Andy, 132–33
Kay, Rudy (Jean-Louis Cormier), 85
Kelly, Mike (William Arko), 242
Kelly, Pat (Victor Arko), 242
Kim, Noelle, 332, 336–37, 338, 342, 367
King, Jane, 114
King, Sandy, 252, 258, 356
King, Steve (Juan Rivera), 144
Kizer, R.J., 247
Kolin, Barry, 324–25

L

Las Vegas, 335–36
Lauper, Cyndi, 216–17, 220–21, 228, 230
LeBell, "Judo" Gene, 88, 93, 103–8, 290–92, 332, 351, 366
  as trainer, xix, 101, 134, 169, 317
LeBell, Mike, 88, 126, 133, 142
  as promoter, 108, 119–21, 123, 124, 128
Legend, Joe E. (Joseph Hitchen), 319–20
Legends of Wrestling, 346
Lennon, Jimmy, 119, 123, 125
Lewis, Joe, 93
Liberace, 225
Los Angeles, 86–89, 99, 103–34, 231, 274, 337, 355. *See also* Hollywood
The Love Boat (ABC), 265
Luck, Tom, 52–53

M

Madison Square Garden, 142–44, 205, 209–11, 214–15, 217, 219–21, 339–40. *See also* Wrestlemania 1

Maivia, Peter, 148, 150
Mandela, Nelson, 276
Maple Leaf Gardens (Toronto), 176, 203–4
Maple Leaf Wrestling, 176
Maritimes (Canada), 82–85
Marked Man (movie), 295
Martel, "Mad Dog" Michel (Michel Vigneault), 85
Martel, Rick (Richard Vigneault), 148–49, 150, 239, 279–80
  as friend, 85, 154–55, 157–62
  as tag-team partner, 151, 153, 156, 161–62
Martin, Billy, 225
Martin, Tommy (Leonce Cormier), 84–85
Mayne, Lonnie "Moondog," 242, 367
McDaniel, Edward "Wahoo," 171–72, 173, 200, 315
McGraw, Rick, 315, 367
McKigney, Dave, 242
McMahon, Vince, Sr., 124, 142–43, 144, 196–97, 200, 205–6
McMahon, Vince, Jr., 221–23, 267, 271. *See also* Wrestlemania; WWE; WWF
  and Roddy, 212, 263, 269, 279–80, 298, 301
  as wrestler, 73, 315–16, 339
Mexico, 96–98
Mid-Atlantic Wrestling, 167–74, 175, 176, 188, 200, 303
Miller, Freya, 292–93, 294
Miller, Robert "Butch," 151–52, 156, 170. *See also* Sheepherders
Minneapolis, 59, 60–61, 69–70
Monsoon, Gorilla (Robert Marella), 221, 296
Morales, Pedro, 196
The Morton Downey Jr. Show, 260
The Mountie (Jacques Rougeau), 284
Mount St. Helens, 159–60
MTV, 217
Muir, Dave, 58, 69
Mulligan, Robert "Blackjack," 109, 110–12, 188–89
The Mummy Returns (movie), 324
Muraco, "Magnificent" Don, 206, 229, 237
Myer, Jason, 57–58

N

Nash, Kevin, 346
Nassau Coliseum (Uniondale, NY), x, xi–xiii, 233–34
National Wrestling Alliance (NWA), 197, 267
  titles in, 91, 94, 108, 116, 156, 189
Needles, CA, 128–29
Neidhart, Jim "The Anvil," 229, 230, 280. *See also* Hart Foundation

Nelson, Ray, 249–50
Nelson, Rosie, 130–31
Nelson, "Tiger," 129–31
New Japan Pro Wrestling, 108, 109
New World Order (tag team), 301–3, 304, 359
New York City, 142–45, 196–97, 205–11, 215–16. *See also* Madison Square Garden

O

"Off the Top Rope" (Snoddy), 345
Okerlund, "Mean Gene," 211, 219–21, 278, 287
Oliver, Lawrence "Rip," 165
Olympic Auditorium (Los Angeles). *See* Grand Olympic Auditorium
O'Malley, Father (wrestling coach), 42
The One and Only (movie), 105–8
Opaskwayak Cree Nation (The Pas, MB), 11, 19–20
Opitz, Adam, 346–49
Orient Express (tag team), 271
Orndorff, Paul "Mr. Wonderful," x, 205, 206, 211, 220, 225–26, 324
Orton, Bob, Sr., 88, 228
Orton, "Cowboy" Bob ("Ace"), 171, 217, 220, 228–29, 324
  and Mr. T, xi, 225–26, 231
  on "Piper's Pit," 215–16, 237
Orton, Randy, 328, 329–30, 340
Osborne, Helen Betty, 21
Owen, Barry, 267–68
Owen, Don, 133, 137–38, 163, 267–69
Owen, Elton, 135–37, 151–53, 154, 163

P

Pacific Northwest Wrestling, 267–69. *See also* Owen, Don
Page, Diamond Dallas (Page Falkinburg), 306–7
Parsons, "Iceman" King, 155
Patrick, Nick, 185–86
Patterson, Pat, 61, 115, 222, 225–26, 273
Paul, Adrian, 294–95
Payne, Lynn, 343
Pelloquin, Fred, 49
Perlmutter, Sam, 337, 355, 363
Perry, William "Refrigerator," 231
Perschmann, Tammy, 335
Philputt, Bill, 350, 356, 360–61, 362
Pillman, Brian, 315
Piper, Dave, 63
Piper, Rowdy Roddy (Roderick George Toombs). *See also* Toombs family; *specific places*
  acting career, xiv, xv, 245, 250–51, 333 (*see also specific productions*)
  as boxer, xi, 9–10, 32–33, 36, 89, 231–34

car misadventures, 27–29, 218, 307–8, 313, 333–35
childhood and youth, 5–20, 25, 37–46
as comic/storyteller, xiv, 324–25, 341–42, 343, 345–46, 352
emotional issues, 29, 56, 140–42, 156, 323–24, 337, 350–51
final illness and death, xvi, 350, 354, 355, 357–64
health problems, 21, 295–96, 331, 344–45
injuries, 7–8, 62, 235–36, 297, 307–8, 313–14, 329–31, 350
mentors, 68–69, 75, 83, 182
as musician, 25, 28, 30–31, 34, 44, 51, 52, 66, 79
origin story, 61–63
promos, 14, 58–59, 91–92, 118, 121–22, 194–96, 297–99
rehab and after, 338–39, 341, 343–44
as singer, 13–14, 280, 292, 345
and substance abuse, 34, 178–82, 184–86, 190, 192, 228, 264, 314–15, 336–37
wrestling training, 41, 46–49, 51, 89–91
as writer, xiv–xv, 314, 349–51
"Piper's Pit," 207–9, 211–13, 216–17, 238, 250, 346, 351–52. *See also* Orton, "Cowboy" Bob
and Wrestlemania, 162, 263, 276–77
Piper's Pit Stop (Portland), 269, 270, 325–26
Piscopo, Joe, 220
PodcastOne, 351–53
Poffo, Angelo, 358
Pontiac, MI, 239, 240–41
Popovich, Mike, 165
Port Arthur, ON, 26–30
Portland, OR, 135–42, 145–47, 150–65, 182–83, 240, 267–69
Portland Wrestling, 362
Prichard, Bruce, 79, 260–65, 315–16, 359, 360, 361
Prichard, Tom, 79, 184–86, 201
Puerto Rico, 187
Putski, Ivan, 283

Q

The Quiet Man (movie), 252

R

Race, Harley, 119, 197, 267
Ramey, Ken, 73
Ramon, Razor (Scott Hall), 297, 299
Rated-RKO (tag team), 329–30
Real Sports (HBO), 315, 316–17
Reiner, Carl, 106–7
Resort to Kill (movie, a.k.a. *Immortal Combat*), 293
Rhodes, Dusty (Virgil Runnels Jr.), 169, 242–43, 328, 350

The Rich Eisen Show, 355
Richmond, VA, 168
Richter, Wendi, 217, 228
Rich, Tommy, 185–86
Rickard, Steve, 148, 151
Ritchie, Ron, 200
Rivers, Joan, 141
Roberts, Jake "The Snake" (Aurelian Smith Jr.), 299–300
Robertson, Marilyn (née Toombs), 5, 10, 26–28, 33, 367
childhood memories, 7, 9, 11, 18–19, 21
Robinson, Billy, 76
Rocco, Tony, 88
Rock 'n' Wrestling Connection, 216–17, 219
Rocky III (movie), 220, 231–32
Roddy's Rowdies (tag team), 264
The Rod Pod (podcast), 342–43, 351–53, 358, 360
Rodz, Johnny (Johnny Rodriguez), 116–19, 197, 220
Rogers, Buddy "Nature Boy," 206–7
Roseberg, OR, 137, 153
Rose, "Playboy" Buddy (Paul Perschmann), 137–39, 148, 153, 162–65, 183, 228, 335
Rourke, Mickey, 342
Rousey, "Rowdy" Ronda, xv, 351–52, 363
Rude, "Ravishing" Rick (Richard Rood), 264–65, 315
Ruuk, Java. *See* Rodz, Johnny

S

St. Louis, MO, 73
Salem, OR, 136, 137, 151, 152, 165
Sammartino, Bruno "The Living Legend," 196, 219, 340–41
San Bernardino, CA, 90–91
San Francisco, CA, 142
Santana, Tito, 228
Saskatoon, SK, 5–10, 21
Sasso, Will, 352–53
Sato, Akio, 271
Savage, Dutch (Frank Stewart), 160
Savage, Randy "Macho Man" (Randy Poffo), 239, 280, 290, 299, 306, 343
Sawyer, Buzz "Mad Dog" (Bruce Woyan), 194–96
Schultz, David, 206, 209, 211
Scotland, 328–29, 346
Scott, Byron, 218
Scott, George, 163, 189, 200, 218–19
Serrano, Don, 79
Sheepherders (tag team), 150–53, 156, 161, 170, 265
Shire, Roy, 81, 99, 142
Simeone, Steve, 341–43, 364, 367
Skaaland, Arnie, 275
Skakel, "Inappropriate Earl," 352, 360, 366
Slater, Dick, 171, 190

Slaughter, Sergeant (Robert Remus), 171, 206, 326, 345
Smalley, Ty, 349
Smith, "Davey Boy," 292
Snoddy, Alan, 345–46, 359
Snuka, Jimmy "Superfly," 205, 206, 209, 211–13, 220, 225
as tag-team partner, 265, 342
Solie, Gordon, 189, 199, 323
South Park (cartoon series), 258
Spelling, Aaron, 266
Spinks, Leon, 232
Spirit Squad (tag team), 328–29
Springer, Jerry, 230
Stampede Wrestling, 48, 85, 203–4
Stand for the Silent campaign, 349
Starrcade, 197–99, 303–4. *See also* Crockett, Jimmy
Starr, Ron, 139
Steamboat, Ricky "The Dragon" (Richard Blood), 169, 171, 189, 227, 239, 342
Steele, George "The Animal," 219
Steinem, Gloria, 220
Sting (Steve Borden), 81
Strongbow, Chief Jay (Luke Scarpa), 289
Studd, Big John (John Minton), 205, 219
Sydney, NS, 82–83
Syfy (network), 356–57

T

Tacoma, WA, 159–60
Tag Team (proposed TV series), 271–72, 357
Tanaka, Pat, 271
The Terminator (movie), 254
Texas, 77, 78–80, 81
The Pas, MB, 11–20
Thesz, Lou, 85, 89
They Live
movie, 248–59, 284, 345, 351
proposed TV series, 356–57
T, Mr. (Laurence Tureaud), ix–xiii, 220, 221, 223–26, 231–32
TMZ, 337, 355–56, 360–61
Tomko, Al, 46–49, 59–60, 65, 67–69, 76
Toombs family
children's births, 188, 228, 266–67, 295
family life, xv–xvii, 239–40, 343–44
Roddy as father, xviii–xix, 259–60, 300–303, 308–11
Toombs, Anastasia, 188, 259–60, 344
Toombs, Ariel Teal, xvii, xix, 309–10, 331, 338, 361–62, 365
Roddy and, 335–36, 337
Toombs, Charles Tupper (great-uncle), 8
Toombs, Cheryl (sister). *See* Grant, Cheryl

childhood memories, 5–6, 8–9, 10–11, 23–24, 26
Toombs, Colton Baird ("Colt"), 266, 331, 333–35, 340–41, 362
martial arts career, xvii, 317, 318–19
Roddy and, xviii–xix, 298, 300–302, 308–9, 314, 346, 359
Toombs, Eileen Anderson (mother), 1, 4, 5, 10, 183, 350, 364
in Roddy's childhood, 6–7, 9, 15, 20, 22–28, 30, 32
Toombs, Euphemia Baird (grandmother), 1–2
Toombs, Falon, 295, 302–3, 307–8, 343, 353–54, 361, 362
Toombs, George (grandfather), 1, 2
Toombs, Jack (uncle), 2
Toombs, Kitty (wife), 182–83, 196, 206, 247, 311, 339, 361
courtship and engagement, 145–47, 148, 150, 165, 174–76
as parent, 303, 307, 308, 309, 344
Toombs, Marilyn (sister). *See* Robertson, Marilyn
Toombs, Stanley Baird, 1, 4–6, 306
as father, 8, 12–13, 18–19, 31–33, 45
personality, 9, 10, 16–17, 18, 30
relationship with Roddy, 10, 34, 38, 141–42, 182–83, 267
Toronto, 30–34, 44, 53–55, 176, 203–4, 272–75, 326
The Tour to Settle the Score: An Audience with Rowdy Roddy Piper (stage show), 345–46
Truesdell, Tuffy, 99–100, 101
Tunney, Frank, 176
Tunney, Jack, 176

U

Ultimate Warrior (James Hellwig), 81
The Undertaker (Mark Calaway), 282
Unger, Merv, 46, 49, 58–59, 60–61, 63, 65, 79
United Kingdom, 319–21, 328–30, 346

V

Vachon, Maurice "Mad Dog," 61, 68
Valentine, Greg "The Hammer," 80, 171, 188–89, 214–15
as opponent, 193–94, 197–200, 203, 227–28
Valentine, Johnny, 80
Vancouver, BC, 156, 161–62
Van Dyke, Dick, 132
Ventura, Jesse, 61, 153, 236, 238, 271, 357

Verdu, Oscar "Crusher," 128
Victor (fighting bear), 99–102
Virgil (Michael Jones), 276–78, 359
Volkoff, Nikolai, 177–82, 239, 324
Von Erich family, 78, 242
  Chris, 315
  David, 242, 315
  Fritz (Jack Adkisson), 77
  Kerry, 77–78, 315
  Mike, 242, 315

W

Wawa, ON, 52
Wells, George, 139
West Four Matchmakers, 58
White Men Can't Jump (movie), 112–13
Williams, Frankie, 207–8
Williams, Luke, 154, 162. *See also* Sheepherders
Williams, Pat, 101
Williams, Vicki, 140–42
Wilmington, NC, 193–94
Winkler, Henry, 105–7
Winnipeg, MB, 37–44, 45–51, 56–61, 63, 80–82, 333–35
  Winnipeg Arena, 65–69, 76
Wiskoski, Ed, 137, 139
Wolff, Dave, 217, 221, 246
World Championship Wrestling (WCW), 301–4, 306–7
World Wide Wrestling Federation, 197, 205. *See also* McMahon, Vince, Sr.
WWE (World Wrestling Entertainment), 317, 328. *See also* McMahon, Vince, Jr.
  Hall of Fame, 324, 325, 365
  Monday Night Raw, 338, 339–40
  WWE Legends' House, 344–45
WWF (World Wrestling Federation), 205–6, 222–24, 239, 260–61, 289–90, 316. *See also* McMahon, Vince, Jr.; "Piper's Pit"; Wrestlemania
  Battle Royal (1986), 231–34
  "The Body Shop" (Jesse Ventura), 236
  Brawl to End It All (1984), 217
  "The Brother Love Show," (Bruce Prichard), 260–63, 264–65
  "Buddy Rogers' Corner," 206–7
  "The Flower Shop" (Adrian Adonis), 236, 237–38
  Hollywood Backlot Brawl (1996), 297–99
  Showdown at Shea (1980), 196–97, 221
  steroid scandal, 281–84, 317
  SummerSlam (1992), 292
  Survivor Series, 264
  "Tuesday Night Titans," 220
  War to Settle the Score (1985), 219–21

Wrestlemania
1 (New York, 1985), ix–x, 222–28
2 (New York/Chicago/Los Angeles, 1986), x–xiii, 230–34
3 (Pontiac, 1987), 236, 238–39, 240–41, 243
V (Atlantic City, 1989), 263
VI (Toronto, 1990), 272–75, 276
VII (Los Angeles, 1991), 276, 278, 280
VIII (Indianapolis, 1992), 285–91
XII (Anaheim, 1996), 297, 298–99
XIX (Seattle, 2003), 315–16
The Wrestler (movie), 342

Y

York, Jay "The Alaskan," 100, 101, 113–15, 315
York, Ned, 114–15
Youngblood, Jay (Steven Romero), 171

Z

Zahorian, George, 281–83
Zorro (TV series), 280